International Taxat[illegible] Extractive Industries

The taxation of extractive industries exploiting oil, gas or minerals is usually treated as a sovereign, national policy and administration issue. This book offers a uniquely comprehensive overview of the theory and practice involved in designing policies on the international aspects of fiscal regimes for these industries, with a particular focus on developing and emerging economies.

International Taxation and the Extractive Industries addresses key topics that are not frequently covered in the literature, such as the geo-political implications of cross-border pipelines and the legal implications of mining contracts and regional financial obligations. The contributors, all of whom are leading researchers with experience of working with governments and companies on these issues, present an authoritative collection of chapters. The volume reviews international tax rules, covering both developments in the G20-OECD (Organisation for Economic Co-operation and Development) project on base erosion and profit shifting and more radical proposals, identifying core challenges in the extractives sector.

This book should become a core resource for both scholars and practitioners. It will also appeal to those interested in international tax issues more widely and those who study environmental economics, macroeconomics and development economics.

Philip Daniel is Honorary Professor at the Centre for Energy, Petroleum and Minerals Law and Policy at the University of Dundee, UK, and Senior Fellow, Natural Resource Governance Institute. He served in the Fiscal Affairs Department of the IMF from 2006 to 2015.

Michael Keen is Deputy Director of the Fiscal Affairs Department of the International Monetary Fund. Before joining the Fund, he was Professor of Economics at the University of Essex, UK.

Artur Świstak is an economist in the Fiscal Affairs Department of the International Monetary Fund, where he works on tax policy issues. Prior to joining the IMF in 2011, he worked for the Polish Ministry of Finance as a chief of tax policy analysis division.

Victor Thuronyi is a graduate of Cambridge University and Harvard Law School. He has practiced tax law, served in the U.S. Treasury Department and taught tax law before joining the International Monetary Fund (1991–2014).

Routledge Studies in Development Economics

For a full list of titles in this series, please visit www.routledge.com/series/SE0266.

124 **Trade, Investment and Economic Development in Asia**
Empirical and policy issues
Edited by Debashis Chakraborty and Jaydeep Mukherjee

125 **The Financialisation of Power**
How financiers rule Africa
Sarah Bracking

126 **Primary Commodities and Economic Development**
Stephan Pfaffenzeller

127 **Structural Transformation and Agrarian Change in India**
Göran Djurfeldt with Srilata Sircar

128 **Development Management**
Theory and practice
Edited by Justice Nyigmah Bawole, Farhad Hossain, Asad K. Ghalib, Christopher J. Rees and Aminu Mamman

129 **Structural Transformation and Economic Development**
Cross regional analysis of industrialization and urbanization
Banji Oyelaran-Oyeyinka and Kaushalesh Lal

130 **The Theory and Practice of Microcredit**
Wahiduddin Mahmud and S. R. Osmani

131 **The Economics of Child Labour in an Era of Globalization**
Policy issues
Sarbajit Chaudhuri and Jayanta Kumar Dwibedi

132 **International Taxation and the Extractive Industries**
Edited by Philip Daniel, Michael Keen, Artur Świstak and Victor Thuronyi

International Taxation and the Extractive Industries

Edited by Philip Daniel, Michael Keen, Artur Świstak and Victor Thuronyi

Routledge
Taylor & Francis Group
LONDON AND NEW YORK

INTERNATIONAL MONETARY FUND

MNRW
TRUST FUND

First published 2017
by Routledge
2 Park Square, Milton Park, Abingdon, Oxon OX14 4RN

and by Routledge
711 Third Avenue, New York, NY 10017

Routledge is an imprint of the Taylor & Francis Group, an informa business

British Library Cataloguing in Publication Data
A catalogue record for this book is available from the British Library

Library of Congress Cataloging-in-Publication Data
Names: Daniel, Philip, editor.
Title: International taxation and the extractive industries : resources without borders / edited by Philip Daniel, Michael Keen, Artur Swistak and Victor Thuronyi.
Description: Abingdon, Oxon ; New York, NY : Routledge, 2017.
Identifiers: LCCN 2016018657 | ISBN 9781138999626 (hardback) | ISBN 9781138240612 (paperback) | ISBN 9781315658131 (ebook)
Subjects: LCSH: Mineral industries. | Natural resources—Taxation. | Taxation—International cooperation.
Classification: LCC HD9506.A2 I636 2017 | DDC 336.2/783382—dc23
LC record available at https://lccn.loc.gov/2016018657

ISBN: 978-1-138-99962-6 (hbk)
ISBN: 978-1-138-24061-2 (pbk)
ISBN: 978-1-315-65813-1 (ebk)

Typeset in Bembo
by Apex CoVantage, LLC

MIX
Paper from responsible sources
FSC www.fsc.org FSC® C014174

Printed and bound in the United States of America by Sheridan

Contents

Figures

Tables

Boxes

Contributors

Joseph C. Bell is Of Counsel at Hogan Lovells in Washington, DC. His current practice is principally devoted to resource management and fiscal issues in developing countries in Africa, Asia and the Middle East and the negotiation and re-negotiation on behalf of governments of long-term concession and investment agreements in the agricultural and mining sectors. He is Chair of the Board of the International Senior Lawyers Project, www.islp.org, co-chair of the Advisory Board of the Natural Resource Governance Institute, http://www.resourcegovernance.org and a member of the Council on Foreign Relations.

Lee Burns is Honorary Professor, Graduate School of Government, University of Sydney. Lee specialises in international and comparative tax law. Lee has authored many papers and articles on international tax and has advised the Australian Treasury and the Board of Taxation on the reform of Australia's controlled foreign company and foreign trust regimes. Since 1991, Lee has provided assistance on the design and drafting of tax laws under the technical assistance program of IMF to more than 30 countries. In recent years, Lee's technical assistance work has focused particularly on the design of tax law regimes for extractive industries.

Jack Calder, now retired, had a long career in the UK Inland Revenue, in the course of which he occupied various senior positions, including latterly that of Deputy Director of the Oil Taxation Office. He then worked for a number of years as a consultant for the IMF and other organizations, advising governments in a wide range of developing countries on the administration of their natural resource revenues. He is author of *Administering Fiscal Regimes for Extractive Industries: A Handbook.*

Peter Cameron is Director of the Centre for Energy, Petroleum and Mineral Law and Policy at the University of Dundee and Professor of International Energy Law and Policy. He is Co-Director of the International Centre for Energy Arbitration, Professorial Fellow of the Law School at the University of Edinburgh, Fellow of the Chartered Institute of Arbitrators and member of the London Court of International Arbitration. He is the author or editor of more than a dozen book-length publications, mostly on international investment and energy. He has given oral and written testimony in a number of international arbitrations.

Jasmina B. Chauvin is a Research Fellow at the Center for International Development at Harvard University and a doctoral candidate in Strategy at Harvard Business School. Her research seeks to understand the drivers of firm location and firm productivity, with a particular focus on the role of trade and of transportation barriers. Prior to starting her doctoral studies, Jasmina was policy advisor to the government of Liberian President Ellen Johnson Sirleaf. Previously she worked in infrastructure and energy finance at Citigroup and as a freelance consultant to the World Bank, the National Resource Governance Institute and various national governments.

Philip Daniel is Honorary Professor at the Centre for Energy, Petroleum and Minerals Law and Policy, University of Dundee, and Senior Fellow, Natural Resource Governance Institute. He Chairs the Advisory Board of the Oxford Centre for the Analysis of Resource Rich Economies in the Department of Economics, University of Oxford. Philip Daniel previously worked for nine years at the Fiscal Affairs Department (FAD) of the IMF, part as Deputy Head, Tax Policy Division and part as Advisor in FAD's Front Office. He is co-editor of *The Taxation of Petroleum and Minerals: Principles, Problems and Practice*.

Janine Juggins is EVP Global Tax Unilever. Before joining Unilever, she was the Global Head of Tax at Rio Tinto. Janine has more than 25 years of international tax experience gained with companies in the engineering, energy, mining and FMCG sectors working in both the U.S. and the UK. She has a special interest in tax and development issues. She graduated in French with German from Manchester University, UK, and subsequently trained as a Chartered Accountant with KPMG in London. She is also a Chartered Tax Advisor, UK, and Associate Corporate Treasurer, UK.

Michael Keen is Deputy Director of the Fiscal Affairs Department of the International Monetary Fund. Before joining the Fund, he was Professor of Economics at the University of Essex and Visiting Professor at Kyoto University. He was awarded the CESifo-IIPF Musgrave Prize in 2010, and is an Honorary President of the International Institute of Public Finance. He has led technical assistance missions to more than 30 countries and is co-author of books on *The Modern VAT,* the *Taxation of Petroleum and Minerals* and *Changing Customs*.

Honoré Le Leuch has more than 40 years' professional experience in international oil and gas activities and is an acknowledged consultant on petroleum legislation, taxation and contracts, institutional and regulatory regimes, economics and negotiation. He was formerly with IFPEN and its affiliate Beicip-Franlab. H. Le Leuch is an Honorary Lecturer at the Centre for Energy, Petroleum and Mineral Law and Policy (CEPMLP) of the University of Dundee. He is a co-author of the reference book on *International Petroleum Exploration and Exploitation Agreements: Legal, Economic, and Policy Aspects.*

Mario Mansour is Deputy Chief, Tax Policy Division, IMF Fiscal Affairs Department. Before joining the IMF in 2004, he managed tax policy projects in the Middle East and Eastern Caribbean islands for a consultancy (2000–03), and was a tax policy analyst for the Canadian Federal Department of Finance (1992–2000), where he started his career, specializing in business and international taxation and micro-simulation modeling. Mario has advised on tax policy issues in more than 30 countries. His recent publications cover taxation issues in the Middle East and Africa, tax coordination in West Africa and fiscal stabilization in the oil and gas sector.

Jack M. Mintz is the President's Fellow at the University of Calgary after stepping down as the founding Director of the School of Public Policy, July 1, 2015. He is also the National Policy Advisor for EY as well as serving on several private and public boards. He has served as the Clifford Clark Visiting Economist at the Department of Finance 1996–1997, when he chaired a panel whose report became the basis for business tax reform in Canada.

Peter Mullins is a Deputy Division Chief with the Tax Policy Division of the Fiscal Affairs Department of the International Monetary Fund in Washington, DC. Peter has extensive experience in tax policy and tax law, having been involved in the area for more than 25 years. Peter has provided advice to more than 40 countries on a range of tax policy issues including corporate tax, personal tax, VAT, international tax issues, natural resources taxation and property taxes. Prior to joining the IMF in 2005, Peter was the General Manager of the Business Tax Division in the Australian Treasury. He has worked in both the private and public sectors, including many years as a senior official in the Australian Tax Office.

Stephen E. Shay is a Senior Lecturer on Law at Harvard Law School. Before joining the Harvard Law School faculty as a Professor of Practice in 2011, Mr. Shay was Deputy Assistant Secretary for International Tax Affairs in the United States Department of the Treasury. Prior to joining the Treasury in 2009, Mr. Shay was a tax partner for 22 years with Ropes & Gray, LLP. Mr. Shay has published scholarly and practice articles relating to international taxation and testified for law reform before Congressional tax-writing committees. He has had extensive practice experience in international taxation, including in transfer pricing counseling and controversies. Mr. Shay is a 1972 graduate of Wesleyan University, and he earned his J.D. and his M.B.A. from Columbia University in 1976.

Emil M. Sunley served at the IMF as an Assistant Director in the Fiscal Affairs Department, specializing in tax policy advice to transition countries, post-conflict countries and countries with petroleum extraction or mining. Prior to that, he was a tax director at Deloitte and Touche, Deputy Assistant Secretary for Tax Policy at the U.S. Treasury and a senior fellow at the Brookings

Institution. He is a graduate of Amherst College and earned his Ph.D. in economics at the University of Michigan.

Artur Świstak is an economist in the Fiscal Affairs Department of the International Monetary Fund, where he works on tax policy issues. He has advised more than 15 countries on their tax reforms, including on natural resources taxation. Prior to joining the IMF in 2011, he worked for the Polish Ministry of Finance as a chief of tax policy analysis division. Mr. Świstak holds M.A. and M.P.S. degrees. Currently he is pursuing his Ph.D. in economics.

Victor Thuronyi is a graduate of Cambridge University and Harvard Law School. He has practiced tax law, served in the U.S. Treasury Department and taught tax law before joining the International Monetary Fund in 1991. He has worked on tax reform in numerous countries. He is the author of *Comparative Tax Law* (2003) and other writings on tax law and policy. He retired in 2014 as lead counsel (taxation), IMF.

Chandara Veung was formerly a research assistant in the Tax Policy Division of the Fiscal Affairs Department. He managed databases of fiscal regimes for extractive industries, regularly analyzed them using the FARI modeling framework as part of the IMF's missions and conducted modeling trainings. He is currently pursuing an MBA at Harvard Business School.

Alistair Watson was formerly a technical assistance advisor in the Tax Policy Division of the Fiscal Affairs Department and is now a freelance consultant. He specializes in extractive industry fiscal regime design and analysis and helped develop the modeling framework FAD uses in this work. After FAD, Alistair worked as a commercial director with Baker Hughes, a major oil field services company, and since returning to freelance he works with the IMF, World Bank and a number of consulting firms.

Foreword

The topic of this book may sound esoteric. It is not. What is at stake are the economic prospects not only of one of the world's important economic sectors, the extractive industries, but the prospects for many of the world's poorest people.

The reason is simple. Revenues from the extractive industries make a critical contribution to the fiscal position of resource-rich countries, including many lower-income countries struggling to find the means to strengthen their infrastructure and protect their vulnerable; much of those revenues come from multinationals; and multinationals are hard to tax in ways that secure reasonable revenue without discouraging investment.

So for many countries a central part of their development agenda involves the international dimension of the tax treatment of multinational enterprises active in the extractive industries. For some, too, the regional and cross-border dimension of projects or policies adds further tax issues. Managing these complex challenges is, for them, key to achieving the robust revenue base and effective institutions needed for sustained growth.

These issues lie at the intersection of two broader topics to which the Fund has devoted considerable attention. The first is the design and implementation of fiscal regimes for the extractive industries. In this, the present book complements two earlier Fund publications, Daniel and others (2010) and Calder (2014). The second is the taxation of multinationals more widely. This has been the focus of much attention in recent years, notably with the G20-OECD project on base erosion and profit shifting (BEPS), now entering its implementation phase. The Fund itself has long been active in supporting our members in this area, as described in IMF (2013), including through analytical work (such as IMF, 2014). Despite significant progress, however, considerable challenges clearly remain.

In drawing together these two themes, this book draws deeply on the Fund's extensive technical assistance work with our members. Much of this has been made possible by the generosity of donors contributing to a dedicated trust fund to support our work in the extractive industries – including the preparation of this book. It is a pleasure to thank, for this, the governments of Australia, the European Union, Kuwait, the Netherlands, Norway, Oman and Switzerland.

Addressing the highly technical difficulties raised in the various chapters will require a mix of legal, economic and administrative skills, as well as a detailed understanding of how the extractive industries operate. This book does not provide any simple or single route to success. But it will, I hope, help those seeking to navigate these always difficult, sometimes murky and often stormy waters.

Christine Lagarde
Managing Director, IMF

References

Calder, Jack. (2014), *Administering Fiscal Regimes for Extractive Industries: A Handbook* (Washington, DC: International Monetary Fund).

Daniel, Philp, Michael Keen and Charles McPherson, eds. (2010), *The Taxation of Petroleum and Minerals: Principles, Practices and Problems* (London, New York: Routledge).

International Monetary Fund. (2013), *Issues in International Taxation and the Role of the IMF* (Washington: International Monetary Fund). Available at http://www.imf.org/external/np/pp/eng/2013/062813.pdf

International Monetary Fund. (2014), *Spillovers in International Corporate Taxation*. Available at www.imf.org/external/np/pp/eng/2014/050914.pdf

1 Introduction and overview

Philip Daniel, Michael Keen, Artur Świstak and Victor Thuronyi

Issues and context

The mismatch between where natural resources are found and where they, or their derivatives, are needed means that the business of finding, developing and selling them has for centuries been inherently international. The modern manifestation of this is the importance within the sector of large multinational enterprises – and their dominance where the state does not own all assets above the ground, as well as the resources below. Several state-owned enterprises have now themselves become important multinationals in the resource sector. Among resource-rich countries, for instance, multinationals account for the vast bulk of fiscal receipts from private business activity in the sector, especially in petroleum: in Ghana, Liberia, Peru and Trinidad and Tobago, they account for all such receipts (see Figure 1.1). In designing fiscal regimes for the extractive industries, international aspects – including the opportunities for tax planning by multinationals to avoid their liabilities – thus need to be center stage. This book aims to provide a comprehensive (and comprehensible) account of these sometimes difficult issues.

The importance for resource-rich countries of managing these difficulties needs little emphasis. Receipts from the extractive sector are a – often – the major source of revenue in many countries (Figure 1.2), especially, though not only, in Africa and the Middle East (where state-owned enterprises have a central and even dominant role). The central task for policy makers is to design fiscal regimes for the extractive industries that raise sufficient revenue, provide adequate incentives to invest and are implementable at reasonable cost to both the government and taxpayers. These challenges receive considerable attention when resource prices and the potential revenue are high. But those are precisely the circumstances in which achieving these objectives is easiest. It is when resource prices seem set for a lengthy subdued spell, as at the time of writing, that the trade-offs can be most brutal, the resilience of regimes most tested, coherence in the design and implementation of taxation in the extractive industries most needed – and the importance of ensuring effective taxation of multinationals is most pronounced.

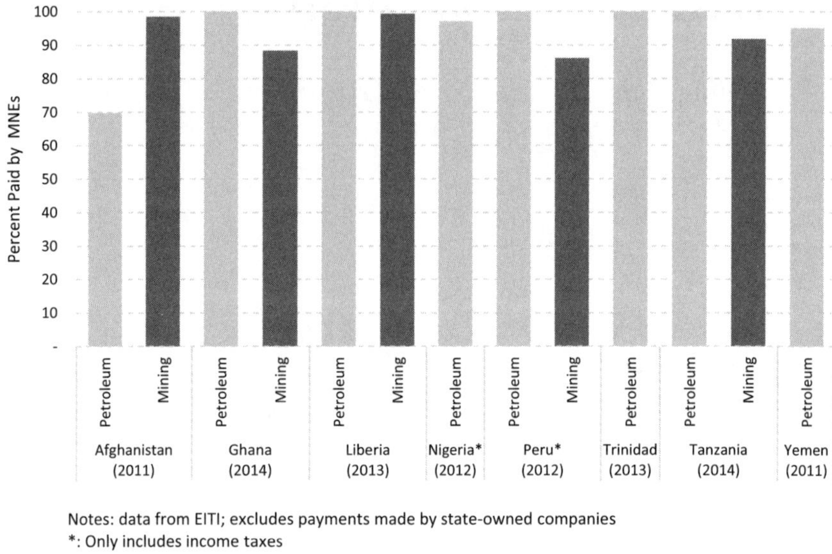

Figure 1.1 Proportion of natural resource taxes paid by multinational enterprises

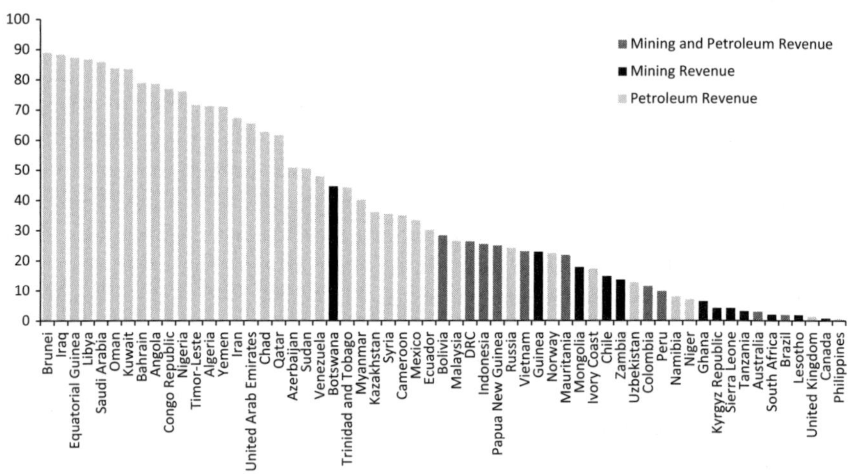

Figure 1.2 Government receipts from natural resources, averages 2000–2013 (Selected countries, in percentage of total revenue excluding grants.)

The difficulty of taxing multinationals – not only or even especially in the extractives, has attracted considerable concern and attention in recent years. Discontent is apparent not only in public disquiet at the success of aggressive tax planning by many multinationals but also in the discourse and actions of many emerging and developing countries that have perceived themselves as being placed at a disadvantage by current arrangements. This discontent has been especially apparent in the extractive industries. Mongolia's renunciation of its tax treaty with the Netherlands, for instance, was prompted by dissatisfaction at the consequent treatment of a large copper mining project;[1] and one of the more controversial responses to the difficulties of transfer pricing – the 'sixth method' – is used specifically in relation to natural resources and other broadly homogeneous commodities for which some benchmark market price can be found. Substantial discontent is perhaps not surprising, as the basic structure of the current international framework was set out at the time of the League of Nations, when the extent of transactions within firms and importance of hard-to-value intangibles were much less and political power relations very different. It has led to an ambitious attempt to strengthen that system, in the G20-OECD project on base erosion and profit shifting (BEPS).[2] While the implications remain to be seen (and are considered in various chapters of this book), it seems clear that while they may mitigate they will not eliminate many of the challenges that arise – including not least in the extractive industries. What is increasingly clear is that the revenue at stake is substantial and quite possibly greater (relative to GDP) in non-OECD economies: Crivelli, de Mooij and Keen (2016) put it, for them, at around 1 percent of GDP, which, given that tax revenues are commonly in the order of 15 percent of GDP in low-income countries, is a sizable amount. And there is increasing evidence too that the sums at issue can be especially large in the extractive sector.

Many of the international tax issues that arise in the extractive industries are, of course, far from unique to the sector. Profit shifting through intra-firm lending, for instance, is a generic difficulty with multinationals. But, as in other areas, common problems often loom especially large by virtue of the sheer scale of their operations and the unusually high nominal tax rates that are commonly applied, since these amplify the gains from shifting profits to lower tax jurisdictions. Moreover, the location of resource deposits often does not respect national boundaries or requires cross-border co-operation for development and export of products. These features present special cases of the wider international fiscal challenges.

This book does not address all aspects of international taxation but focuses on two sets of issues: those that have proved especially important, problematic and recurrent in the extractive industries and those that arise from specific aspects of the operations of extractive enterprises, such as those that arise from cross-border infrastructure or joint developments in disputed maritime zones.

In focusing on these issues, this book complements both Daniel, Keen and McPherson (2010), which focuses mainly on domestic aspects of fiscal regime design, and Calder (2014), which focuses on administrative issues. As there, the present book mainly takes the perspective of resource-producing emerging-market and developing countries. That is where the international tax challenges for the extractive sector arise in most pronounced form and, within the wider fiscal scheme of things, are most significant for both revenue and wider economic performance. Their significance in Africa, for instance, is highlighted and explored in Africa Progress Panel (2013). These are also the cases in which the IMF, through its technical assistance and other activities, tends to become most closely involved[3] with many of the authors of this book playing leading roles. An appendix later in the chapter lists some of the international tax issues that are most frequently encountered in this advisory work and that guided the selection of topics for this book.

This book

The book can be thought of as falling into four parts. The first sets the scene for the discussion of international tax issues in the extractive industries. The second part takes up generic issues in international taxation with an eye to the specifics of the application to the extractives, focusing on transfer pricing issues, tax treaty strategies and design and the taxation of capital gains associated with natural resources. Cross-border issues, including those related to international pipelines and joint development zones, are taken up in the third part of the book. The fourth part takes up some core policy issues: the interactions between components of fiscal regimes and inter-governmental tax competition and coordination in the extractive sector.

Setting the scene for the chapters that follow, Michael Keen and Peter Mullins provide in Chapter 2 an overview, with an eye to the extractive industries, of the current international tax framework, common tax planning devices and recent initiatives to address them. They also review the emerging evidence pointing to the considerable scale of profit shifting both in general and, perhaps especially, in the extractives and in non-OECD countries. This chapter also highlights three specific issues that later chapters examine in more depth: the difficulties of the arm's length principle and transfer pricing, treaty abuse and the taxation of capital gains on asset transfers.

On the first of these issues, transfer pricing, Stephen Shay provides in Chapter 3 an overview of major rules that apply in the context of extractive industries in resource-rich developing countries. He considers a number of examples and discusses steps that developing countries can take to mitigate transfer pricing tax avoidance by multinationals. Jack Calder complements this analysis in Chapter 4 by focusing on complications added by ring-fencing, special methods for valuing extractive industry sales and special rules for costs. In addition, he considers a number of tax administration issues, particularly special benchmarking and 'physical audit' procedures.

Chapter 5 by Philip Daniel and Victor Thuronyi outlines the principal international tax and fiscal regime issues faced by developing countries engaged in natural resource extraction or exploration. The focus of the chapter rests on corporate tax issues for extractive industries. It considers the principal elements in tax treaty strategy that form an integral part of tax policy making. The chapter concludes with a brief discussion of defensive steps that developing countries can take unilaterally.

The role of tax treaties in the extractives sector is further taken up in Chapter 6 by Janine Juggins, who – writing from the investor's point of view – provides an overview of the different types of taxes that arise over the life cycle of a mine, followed by a discussion of the relevance of tax treaties to investment financing decisions, the role that tax treaties play in relation to capital gains and in supplementing gaps in domestic tax law. Further to that, she considers the importance of tax treaties as a component of foreign investment tax policy development and choices.

In Chapter 7 Lee Burns, Honoré Le Leuch and Emil M. Sunley focus on the tax treatment of gains arising on a transfer of a mining or petroleum right under both domestic tax law and tax treaties – which has proved a controversial issue in many countries. They investigate the complexities concerning the characterization, valuation, timing and geographic sourcing of the gain both made directly by the holder of the right or indirectly by a person disposing of an interest in the entity holding the right.

Joseph C. Bell and Jasmina B. Chauvin in Chapter 8 set the scene for discussion of cross-border projects. They focus on potential arrangements for allocating the taxable income from a project crossing national boundaries among different national entities, using as an example a hypothetical mining project with the mine and infrastructure in two different countries.

In Chapter 9 Honoré Le Leuch focuses specifically on the key role of cross-border pipelines in the global oil and gas industry and their commercial structure and taxation. He highlights the striking differences and challenges between the two main categories of transnational pipelines and provides a brief review of the international law applicable to landlocked countries and transit countries. The chapter also highlights the special issues pertinent to the design of the tax regime applicable by each state to the segment of a transnational pipeline under its jurisdiction, as well as possible interactions between the regime and international taxation and double tax treaties.

Joint development zones are discussed in Chapter 10 by Peter Cameron and Chapter 11 by Philip Daniel, Chandara Veung and Alistair Watson. Chapter 10 discusses design of joint development zones (JDZs) treaties and international unitization agreements. This outlines the conceptual framework for both arrangements and the differences between them, focusing largely on legal aspects and international obligations. It compares JDZ and unitization structures, providing examples of actual operations and challenges therein. Chapter 11 then examines the fiscal structure of JDZs and sets out examples from around the world, drawing lessons for the future use of this important institutional structure.

Interactions between different tax regimes and instruments are the topic of Chapter 12, by Jack M. Mintz. He shows how to assess the impact of oil tax and royalty regimes on investment decisions by calculating an effective tax and royalty rate for marginal projects. The analysis highlights several cross-border fiscal issues that affect the incentive to invest and the resource revenues derived by governments. This chapter also looks at the impact of various financial strategies of multinational companies when investing abroad such as transfer pricing, conduit financing and the discount rate for carrying forward unused deductions under rent-based royalties.

The book concludes with an analysis by Mario Mansour and Artur Świstak of the issues of tax competition and coordination in the extractive industries. In Chapter 13 they attempt to answer the key questions of whether tax competition is a reality in relation to the extractives and if so, why (which is far less obvious than it may seem), which taxes it affects – and, critically, to what extent and in what ways governments should consider coordinating their tax treatment of the extractive industries.

Appendix

International tax issues in some IMF FAD advisory work on resource-rich countries

Coverage

This appendix draws upon advisory work between 2010 and 2014 in about 20 countries and upon regional workshops. Advice or analysis specific to individual countries remains confidential.

Scope

The international or BEPS issues arising included: source and residence taxation, double tax treaties (including border withholding taxes), transfer pricing, thin capitalization limitations, taxation of gains on transfers of interest in immoveable property and mineral rights and the treatment of financial instruments. Recent activity reflected an upsurge of interest from the authorities in the content and desirability of double taxation treaties and in the taxation of gains on transfers of interest.

Source and residence taxation

A few countries inherited territorial systems at independence that had already been substantially amended in the jurisdictions formerly governing. In some cases, technical assistance (TA) recommended an explicit switch to worldwide taxation of resident individuals and corporations. In other cases, recommendations to widen the definition of permanent establishment (especially for provision of services) and to strengthen or clarify definitions of domestic source income were made.

Double tax treaties

TA consistently recommended that governments refrain from concluding new tax treaties, at least until a uniform and consistent national policy on treaties has been formulated. The policy should ensure full taxing rights with respect to extractive industries, border withholding on dividend, interest and royalty payments abroad and also payments for services. Where the existing treaty network was limited, the recommendation sometimes included maintenance of full legislated rates of border withholding.

As an alternative to treaties, TA sometimes recommended tax information exchange agreements (TIEAs) or joining the Convention on Mutual Administrative Assistance in Tax Matters. Full integration of treaty policy with domestic tax policy was advised, making the point that many things done in treaties could be done in domestic law in a non-discriminatory way. One example concerns introduction of a rule that a cost is not deductible unless the counterpart receipt is also taxable and perhaps taxable at some minimum rate.

Some of the TA reports gave a detailed analysis of existing treaties and the treaty-shopping opportunities the treaty network might present. More recent TA has recommended introduction of a provision in domestic legislation that would protect against treaty-shopping practices. The same suggestion (together with a possible 'principal purpose' rule) came from the BEPS reports: should a multilateral treaty instrument eventually become effective, the appropriate national action might, of course, change.

TA has not called for repudiation of ratified treaties, but recommendations were made to clarify the validity or operation of very old treaties. In some cases, treaties that were signed but not ratified had serious inadequacies, and the authorities were advised to review them before ratification. In one case (Mongolia) the authorities independently decided to seek treaty renegotiations.

Transfer pricing

The detail of treatment of transfer pricing policy issues deepened in more recent advice. The standard position has called for adherence to the arm's length principle and implementation, by various means, of the OECD guidelines on transfer pricing. In many cases, the introduction of advance pricing arrangements (APAs) was proposed. In more recent cases, TA suggested stronger powers for the authorities to make regulations on transfer pricing. Some TA called for consistent transfer pricing rules for transactions among residents as well as with non-residents.

Some TA (especially where oil and gas is involved) has suggested use for tax purposes of transfer pricing rules devised for transactions among private parties (such as the 'transfer at cost' rules among affiliates for services under joint operating agreements) or devised for production-sharing contracts.

For the pricing of extractive industry outputs, reference prices (sometimes with adjustments) have been put forward where these are available.

Thin capitalization limitations

The recommendation has usually been to strengthen overall limitations on the deductibility of interest rather than to propose something specific for extractive industries. In some cases, however, it was necessary to recommend removal of provisions in production sharing contracts that permitted recovery of interest as a cost. TA has offered both a debt-equity ratio test and a test of the ratio of interest expense to income in different circumstances. In a few cases, both were suggested in combination.

In one case legal advice called for reclassification of finance leases as loans and also for use of rules analogous to those for thin capitalization for other types of base-eroding payments.

TA usually advised against using a distinction between interest payments nominally between third parties and those between affiliates.

Taxation of gains on transfers of interest in immoveable property and mineral rights

Recent TA has recommended that such gains be taxed as income within the corporate tax system rather than through a separate capital gains tax or segregated stream of capital transactions within the corporate income tax. The recommendation to tax follows political preference rather than a specific economic analysis or consideration of alternatives. In earlier TA, the point was made that (as, for example, in Norway) transactions within the petroleum tax ring-fence could be considered post-tax – in the sense that no tax would be due on any gain and no deduction available for any outlay – provided that the overall taxation of resource rents was appropriate.

Recommendations have differed on whether to follow the course of segregating capital transactions (the U.S. model) so that payment of premiums for acquisition can only be offset against future capital transactions of a similar nature or to follow the more widespread treatment of the cost of acquisition of mineral rights under which the cost is amortized (usually over the life of the right). Both courses have justification, and the choice between has depended on local circumstances.

In either case, a frequent issue has been whether to define mineral rights as immovable property (or to make transactions in them taxable in their own right as assets) and then to ensure that both domestic law and treaties permit the taxation of transactions in such property by non-residents.

TA has adopted more than one approach to the problem of taxing indirect transfers of interest through disposal of shares in companies holding mineral rights or non-resident companies holding such companies. Recommendations were usually made to tighten rules on 'change of control'. Obligatory notification of transfers and change of control can be required in sector legislation or in tax law or both, with stiff penalties for failure to notify (financial or forfeiture of the license). There are differences among legal advisers on the merits (and treaty implications) of using a 'deemed disposal' mechanism to tax the local entity, obliging a local entity to withhold tax due from a non-resident or attempting directly to tax the transaction by the non-resident as domestic source income. Withholding pending final assessment is in any case an option.

In some cases, TA has dealt with farm-in/out, with work obligations as consideration, as the method of transfer of interest and also with the creation of an over-riding royalty.

Financial instruments

For extractive industries the issue is usually the use of instruments for hedging, not only of commodity prices but also foreign exchange and the cost of debt. The common approach has been to attempt to exclude transactions in financial instruments (or forward sales) from the regime of resource taxation (royalty, rent taxes or production sharing) and thus to get as close as possible, for calculating the tax base, to the intrinsic costs and proceeds of resource production. For income tax purposes, the recent recommendation for extractive industries is to quarantine losses on financial instruments so that they can only be set against losses on financial instruments. More work on the taxation of hedging is warranted.

Notes

1 See more details in IMF (2012b).
2 OECD (2015) summarizes the outcome; a brief account is in Keen and Mullins (2016), Chapter 2 in this volume.
3 More detail on these activities is in Appendix 2 of IMF (2012a).

References

Africa Progress Panel. (2013), *Equity in Extractives: Stewarding Africa's Natural Resources for All*. Available at http://app-cdn.acwupload.co.uk/wp-content/uploads/2013/08/2013_APR_Equity_in_Extractives_25062013_ENG_HR.pdf

Calder, Jack. (2014), *Administering Fiscal Regimes for Extractive Industries: A Handbook* (Washington: International Monetary Fund).

Crivelli, Ernesto, Ruud de Mooij and Michael Keen. (2016), "Base Erosion, Profit Shifting and Developing Countries," forthcoming in *Finanzarchive*.

Daniel, Philp, Michael Keen and Charles McPherson, eds. (2010), *The Taxation of Petroleum and Minerals: Principles, Practices and Problems* (London and New York: Routledge).

International Monetary Fund (IMF). (2012a), *Fiscal Regimes for the Extractive Industries: Design and Implementation*. Available at https://www.imf.org/external/np/pp/eng/2012/081512.pdf

International Monetary Fund (IMF). (2012b), *Mongolia: Technical Assistance Report – Safeguarding Domestic Revenue – A Mongolian DTA Model*, IMF Country Report No. 12/306. Available at https://www.imf.org/external/pubs/ft/scr/2012/cr12306.pdf

Organization for Economic Cooperation and Development. (2015), *OECD/G20 Base Erosion and Profit Shifting Project: Executive Summaries 2015 Final Reports* (Paris: OECD Publishing). Available at http://www.oecd.org/ctp/beps-reports-2015-executive-summaries.pdf

2 International corporate taxation and the extractive industries

Principles, practice, problems

*Michael Keen and Peter Mullins**

1 Introduction

International aspects of the corporate taxation of the extractive industries (EIs) arise, of course, within the context of a wider international tax framework. That framework is contentious, complex, and changing. Contentiousness is doubtless to some degree inevitable, given the scope for countries to disagree on how to share tax base between them, but has risen to new heights in recent years: the unprecedented cancelation of tax treaties, a warning of risks to the established framework, signals an increasing discontent that has been amplified by growing public concern at the apparently small amounts of tax that many multinational enterprises (MNEs) manage to pay – including, not least, in the extractive industries.[1] Complexities, which create the scope for such tax planning, are themselves to some degree inherent in dealing with the intersections between national tax systems but also arise from the attempts of policy makers to shape those rules to their own advantage. And these tensions have generated pressures for change that have led to major initiatives, most notably the G20-OECD project on base erosion and profit shifting (BEPS) which produced, in late 2015, proposals that are now in the course of implementation – but which remain contentious, as some observers continue to press for still more radical reform of the international tax framework, and may even add to complexity.

This chapter aims to set the scene for those that follow by providing an overview of these controversies, complexities, and reforms, all with a particular eye to the EIs. Some international tax issues tend to arise more often in the EIs than in other sectors, and we shall touch on these. But what is often most striking about tax issues in the EIs is less their qualitative nature than their sheer scale. Particularly high nominal tax rates associated with distinct taxes on upstream operations, for instance, can imply particularly large incentives to use transfer pricing and other devices to shift profits to where they face lower rates. And the huge capital gains that can be associated with resource discoveries lend special urgency to the question of where (and whether) those gains should be taxed. Experience in the EIs thus provides wider insights into the challenges that MNEs face in coping with, and that policy makers face, in designing international tax rules more generally.

This overview begins, in Section 2, with an account of the main features of the current international tax framework (though that term itself risks overstating its coherence and the degree of conscious design underlying it). Section 3 reviews some of the main tax planning devices open to MNEs and the evidence on their quantitative significance. Section 4 discusses three specific problems of particular relevance to the EIs, which are further explored in later chapters: transfer pricing (Chapter 3 [Shay] and Chapter 4 [Calder]), treaty issues (Chapter 6 [Juggins]), and indirect transfers of interest (Chapter 7, [Burns, Le Leuch and Sunley]). The nature and likely implications of the BEPS project and other recent initiatives are taken up in Section 5. Section 6 concludes.

2 The international tax framework

The present international corporate tax framework arises from the interplay of domestic laws and tax treaty obligations, primary concerns being the allocation of taxing rights between countries – that is, which country or countries tax a particular item of income. The framework provides opportunities for MNEs to use planning devices to avoid tax and reflects governments' attempts to limit them. These arrangements have evolved over the last century or more with little explicit coordination (other than through bilateral treaties that touch only a subset of relevant matters)[2] – until, that is, the BEPS project discussed in Section 5.

2.1 Principles and concepts

2.1.1 Allocating taxing rights: source and residence

It is generally accepted that the country in which profits are derived (the *source country*) has the first right to tax that income, directly or through withholding taxes on payments made abroad. *Source* refers – very loosely – to where investment is made and production takes place and is traditionally determined largely by the physical presence in a country of labor and/or capital. A source country may forgo its right to tax for its own policy purposes or under a double tax treaty, although this is rare for rents from natural resources.

A foreign company (i.e. one that is not legally resident – as discussed later) is usually taken to have enough presence in a country to be liable to its income tax when it meets conditions laid down (in domestic law or treaties) deemed to create what is known as a *permanent establishment* (PE). The country in which it operates then has the right to tax such of the profits of that business as are associated with that presence. Importantly, the location of 'sales' (in the sense of the country into which the goods or services produced are sold) is not, under this long-standing consensus, in itself taken to give rise to a place of 'source,' and so does not trigger any liability for income taxation.

In the case of the EIs, it is usual for countries to make certain that a foreign company undertaking any EI activities in the country is treated as a PE. This is commonly achieved by ensuring that the definition of a PE, in domestic law and tax treaties, covers activities at a mine, gas or oil well, quarry, or any other place of extraction of natural resources, and any activities for the exploration and exploitation of natural resources.

Countries in which the taxpayer resides (the *residence country*) may also tax the same income as that taxed by a source country. The right to tax profits is, under the traditional architecture, retained by the *residence* country unless it chooses to give it up through domestic law or treaty rules (which establish, for instance, what will be considered to constitute a PE). In the case of companies, residence can depend on factors such as place of incorporation (applicable for example in the U.S.) or place of management and control (in most countries). A PE in a source country is usually taxed like a resident.

These notions of source and residence are, however, proving increasingly inadequate as concepts upon which to build the international tax framework. Identifying the country that is the 'source' of income is increasingly problematic, having been made more difficult, conceptually and practically, by the increased importance of intra-firm transactions, including in financial and managerial services. For example, in 2002, 24 percent of U.S. oil and gas imports were related party transactions; and that had increased to almost 43 percent in 2013.[3] These intra-firm transactions increasingly relate to intangible assets of various kinds – patents, trademarks, and other intellectual property (IP) – which can be much more easily relocated than can the bricks-and-mortar facilities of the world for which the current framework was initially built. Though perhaps less central than in other sectors, such transactions relating to intangible assets can play an important role in the EIs, for example, as payments for IP relating to new ways of extraction or the design of new machinery for extraction.

The notion of residence is also becoming increasingly outmoded. The rationale for residence-based corporate taxation was, in large part, to provide a backstop for the personal income tax levied on shareholders; but with the increasing disconnect between a company's country of residence and that of its shareholders this argument is becoming ever more flimsy. Moreover, the ability of companies to change their residence (by *inversion*) opens scope for tax planning. So too do cross-country mismatches in tests of residence, which have been exploited by some companies to claim that they are not resident for tax purposes in any country: by, for instance, incorporating in a country that relies on a management and control test and placing management in a country that relies on the incorporation test.

2.1.2 Allocating profits: arm's length pricing

The standard rule, in the current international tax framework, for allocating the income of a multinational across its constituent entities, so as to capture the contribution of each as a source of that income, is by the *arm's length principle* (ALP) – which means valuing transactions within MNEs at the prices that would have been agreed by unrelated parties.

The underlying rationale for the ALP is to allocate income across members of a corporate group, and hence countries, in such a way as to preserve neutrality between MNEs and independent operations while also defining the tax base on which countries can exercise their primary taxing rights. Close comparability with independent transactions between unrelated parties is crucial for establishing that prices satisfy the arm's length principle. The challenge for tax administrators is in verifying these prices, which requires reviewing the functions performed, assets used, and risks genuinely assumed by the entities within an MNE. Their difficulty in doing so is that such comparable prices may simply not exist – even for some traded minerals – so that arriving at a valuation will depend very heavily on the facts and circumstances of each case and require some degree of judgment, with the MNE potentially enjoying advantages of having better information than the tax authorities, for instance on the potential value of an intangible it has developed or a resource deposit it has found.

2.1.3 Residence country taxation of foreign source income

Residence countries have two broad choices for taxing profits or other income earned by their residents from another geographic source (*foreign source income*): the worldwide and territorial tax systems. Under *worldwide* (or *residence*) *taxation*, a country asserts under its domestic law the right to tax its domestic resident companies on their foreign source income, while a *foreign tax credit*[4] may be given for income and withholding taxes levied in the source country in order to avoid *double taxation*[5] – full taxation, that is, by both source and residence countries.[6] This can be provided for in domestic law and/or in bilateral treaties. The result is that the residence tax is usually limited to the excess, if any, of the residence country's effective tax rate over that in the source country. Worldwide taxation is broadly based on the concept of *capital export neutrality* – the notion, that is, that a country's residents should pay the same amount of tax irrespective of the geographic source of their income. This would mean that there is no tax distortion between foreign and domestic investment, so that capital will simply be invested wherever it generates the highest return, without regard for tax considerations.

Under *territorial taxation* – based on the source principle of taxation and often referred to in Europe as the *exemption method* – certain foreign source income is exempt from tax in the taxpayer's country of residence and, therefore, is taxed only in the source country. Territorial taxation is broadly based on the concept of *capital import neutrality* – that is, all investors in a country face the same tax rate irrespective of the tax rate in their home country.[7] The rationale for this is that foreign and local investors then compete in each country on the same footing in terms of their tax treatment basis.

In practice, neither worldwide nor territorial taxation is found in pure form.[8] Countries with a notionally worldwide tax system often have considerable elements of a territorial system. In particular, the deferral of tax on certain foreign source income of a subsidiary – such as *active business income* (by which is meant, broadly, income arising directly from some commercial activity entered into directly or controlled by the company in question) – until it is repatriated to the country of residence effectively brings the system closer to source taxation for such income. And countries with a notionally territorial system often impose limitations on access to the exemption for foreign source income, bringing income outside those limitations into tax. For example, such countries usually only allow an exemption if the resident company holds a significant (non-portfolio) interest in the foreign company, and they may not exempt 100 percent of the foreign income. Also, to prevent tax avoidance, the exemption usually does not apply to *passive income* (the complement of active income) such as interest, rent, royalties, and portfolio dividends and to income from countries that have very low rates of tax.

Countries of both broad types in many cases also employ *controlled foreign corporation* (CFC) rules that seek to immediately tax passive income arising abroad that has not been subject to at least some minimum amount of tax in the foreign country. For worldwide countries, CFC rules in principle provide some protection against tax avoidance through deferral; for territorial countries, they typically ensure that only active – not passive – income is exempt in the residence country. CFC rules make the distinction between passive and active income arguably the most critical one for modern tax planning, since they normally apply only to the former. In the case of the extractives sector, the operation of a mining or petroleum project is clearly active business income.

There is thus a spectrum between worldwide and territorial systems, so that it is best to speak of countries having predominantly worldwide or predominantly territorial tax systems – as in Table 2.1. The trend in recent years has been towards the territorial end of the spectrum, with Australia, Japan, and the UK, all having moved in this direction.

Table 2.1 Tax treatment of foreign sourced dividends received by corporate taxpayers, 2015

Worldwide Taxation Countries

Country	*Minimum ownership level for full foreign tax credit (FTC)*[1/] *(in percent)*	*Comments*
United States	10	No tax sparing.
Ireland	5	
South Korea	10	Allows tax sparing in some double tax treaties.

Territorial Taxation Countries

Country	*Level of exemption*[2/]	*Minimum ownership level*[3/]	*Other conditions*
Australia	Full	10%	
Austria	Full	10%	
Belgium	95%	10% (or €2.5 million)	Holding must not be in a tax haven or country with a substantially lower tax rate.
Canada	Full	10%	Dividend must be paid out of active business income from a treaty country.
France	95%	5%	

(*Continued*)

Table 2.1 Continued

Territorial Taxation Countries			
Germany	95%	10%	
Luxembourg	Full	10% (or €1.2 million)	Comparable tax rate in the source country (i.e. at least 10.5%).
Netherlands	Full	5%	Profits subject to at least 10% tax in source country.
Norway	97%	10%	
Switzerland	95%	10% (or CHF1 million)	
United Kingdom	Full	None	

Source: European Commission and IBFD.

Notes:

1/ Full FTCs includes credit for withholding taxes and underlying corporate income tax. If the minimum level of ownership is not met, the taxpayer would usually only be entitled to a credit for withholding taxes.

2/ A number of countries only allow 95 percent exemption as a proxy for disallowing expenses relating to exempt income.

3/ The EU Parent-Subsidiary Directive (which seeks to eliminate tax obstacles in profit distributions within groups of companies in the EU) requires a holding of at least 10 percent.

2.2 Some implications for the extractive industries

It is of course usual for resource companies to be taxed in the producing (source) country, with the necessary PE rules in place to ensure this. Beyond that, MNEs resident in countries with worldwide taxation (notably the U.S.) will be taxed in their home country on repatriated profits and so may be subject to additional tax payments there and may even be subject to double taxation unless foreign tax credits are available for taxes paid in the source country. The creditability of source taxes can thus be critical to the attractiveness of investing in the source country for investors from countries with a worldwide system, though it is unlikely to be an issue for MNEs with headquarters located in a country with a territorial tax system.

Whether or not a tax is creditable depends on the tax law in the residence country and on any bilateral tax treaties in place. However, a tax paid in the producing country that in nature resembles a home country income tax (for example, is on net income rather than – like a royalty – gross income) is most likely to qualify for a tax credit. Specialized mineral taxes, such as a resource rent tax and in particular payments under a production sharing agreement, may be deemed to differ in nature from a standard corporate income tax (CIT) and, therefore, could face difficulties in qualifying for a tax credit. Some countries try to overcome this limitation by treating a portion of the government's share under a production sharing agreement (PSA) as CIT; this is sometimes referred to as CIT *paid-on-behalf* of the company.[9] Countries such as Australia, Canada, the United Kingdom, and the United States offer credit for some of these types of taxes, but often with restrictions and sometimes only under a bilateral tax treaty.[10] Box 2.1 sets out the

Box 2.1 Crediting of resource taxes in the United States

Section 901 of the Internal Revenue Code allows a credit against U.S. income tax for the amount of any income, war profits, or excess profits tax paid to a foreign country. The regulations (see Regs. 1.901–2 and 1.901–2A) provide that a foreign levy is a creditable income tax if (i) it is a tax and (ii) the 'predominant character' of that foreign levy is that of an income tax in the United States. A foreign levy is considered to be a tax if it is a compulsory payment pursuant to the authority of a foreign country to levy taxes. There are three requirements that a foreign levy must satisfy to qualify as an income tax:

- Realization: the tax is imposed on or after an event that would result in the realization of income under the Internal Revenue Code.
- Gross receipts: the tax is imposed on gross receipts that are not greater than fair market value.
- Net income: the base of the tax is computed by reducing gross receipts by the recovery of significant costs and expenses reasonably attributable to the gross receipts.

However, a foreign levy is not a tax if the payer receives, directly or indirectly, a specific economic benefit from the foreign country – an economic benefit includes a right to use, acquire, or extract resources (such as government-owned petroleum). In such cases, the regulations set out a safe harbor formula that limits the credit available to the amount of tax that would have been paid in the foreign country by a taxpayer not receiving the economic benefit. Any excess tax is deductible rather than creditable (similar to the tax treatment of royalties).

A foreign tax credit is also limited to the extent that income tax is imposed by a foreign country as a 'soak-up tax' – that is, a tax in which the liability for it depends on the availability of a credit in another country.

There are further special crediting rules (under section 907) specifically for the EIs. These apply to combined foreign oil and gas income – that is, two types of foreign income from natural resources: foreign oil–related income (FORI), which is income from processing, transporting, distributing, or selling oil and gas (and/or its primary products) and income from disposal of assets used in those activities; and foreign oil and gas extraction income (FOGEI), which is income from the extraction of oil and gas and from the disposal of assets used in the extraction activities. The foreign tax credit for combined foreign oil and gas income is limited to the U.S. CIT rate, with any excess able to be carried over to other years but used only against oil and gas income. These provisions could apply where, for example, a resource-rich country imposes a differentially higher CIT rate on oil or gas activities.

basics of the law in the United States. The treatment of these taxes can be clarified by making it clear in a bilateral tax treaty that such taxes are covered by the treaty; for example, the UK treaties often refer to its petroleum revenue tax.

The crediting of taxes on foreign source income also has implications if the source country offers a tax incentive (such as a tax holiday) to resource companies. That incentive may be undone in the residence country (albeit to an extent that may be muted if repatriation of profit is deferred) if it has worldwide taxation, unless the two countries have a bilateral tax treaty that allows for *tax sparing* – that is, a form of double tax relief under which the effect of a tax incentive provided by the source country is preserved in the residence country. (South Korea allows tax sparing in some treaties, while the United States does not – see Table 2.1.) In contrast, if the investor is from a country with a territorial system, then generally no further tax will be paid in the residence country irrespective of the tax rate (or tax incentives) provided by the source country. Exceptions to this arise if the residence country imposes conditions on the exemption along lines mentioned, requiring for example that the profits not be derived in a low-tax country or exempt in the source country.

One other aspect of crediting is important for source country tax design. This is the possibility of maximizing the foreign tax credit in the residence country (and so increasing the investor's after-tax earnings at no cost to the source country itself) by ensuring that any offsetting of one domestic tax against another is done in such a way that this does not reduce whichever of those domestic taxes is creditable in the residence country. For example, it will generally not matter for the source country's own revenue if a resource rent tax is creditable against a CIT or vice versa. For a foreign investor, however, the CIT is more likely to be creditable in the residence country, giving them a distinct preference for the CIT being creditable against the resource rent tax in the source country rather than vice versa.

3 Tax avoidance and tax planning

Once a country has established its legal framework for taxing international transactions, it will be faced with the use of tax planning devices by many MNEs to reduce their tax liabilities. These planning devices exploit weaknesses in the source and residence rules, often through the use of related party transactions: Box 2.2 sets out some of the main tools of the tax planning trade, and Section 5 will set out some of the recent initiatives to address them.

All these tools are commonly available to EI companies, which are often involved in multiple countries with vertically integrated operations covering various stages of the EI value chain. For example, an oil and gas group could extract oil and gas in one country using technology owned and developed at

Box 2.2 International tax planning – tools of the trade

The central aim of cross-border tax planning schemes is to shift taxable income to low-tax jurisdictions (or into more lightly taxed forms) and away from higher-tax jurisdictions (or out of more highly taxed forms). Precisely how this is done is driven by specific features of national tax systems and treaty networks,[1] but common strategies include:

- **Abusive transfer pricing** (stretching, violating, or exploiting weaknesses in the arm's length principle), ranging from potential mispricing of natural resources to the transfer of IP rights to low-tax jurisdictions early in their development, when they are hard to value verifiably – this is discussed in what follows.
- **Taking deductions in high-tax countries** by, for example, borrowing from affiliates in lower-tax jurisdictions or leasing high-cost EI assets from related entities in a low-tax country.
- **. . . and as many times as possible –** passing on funds raised by loans through *conduit companies* (ones, that is, serving solely as intermediaries within a corporate group) may enable *double dipping* – taking interest deductions twice (or more) without offsetting tax on receipts – leading to *thin capitalization* (high debt-to-equity ratios).
- **Risk transfer –** conducting operations in high-tax jurisdictions on a contractual basis, so limiting the profits that arise there.
- **Exploiting mismatches –** tax arbitrage opportunities can arise if different countries classify the same entity, transaction, or financial instrument differently (the U.S.'check the box' rules[11] being a prime example).
- **Treaty shopping –** treaty networks can be exploited to route income so as to reduce withholding taxes and narrow the definition of a permanent establishment – also taken up in what follows.
- **Locating asset sales in low jurisdictions –** to avoid capital gains taxes (a particular concern in the context of recent resource discoveries in some low-income countries) – explored in what follows.
- **Deferral –** companies resident in countries operating worldwide systems can defer home taxation of business income earned abroad by delaying paying it to the parent.
- **Inversion –** companies may be able to escape repatriation charges or CFC rules by changing their country of residence.

Schemes often combine several of these devices, turn on quite fine legal distinctions, and span several countries and tax systems. They can be extraordinarily complex.

1 Excellent accounts are in OECD (2013) and Mintz and Weichenreider (2010).

an R&D center in a second country; the product could be shipped by a vessel owned by the group; while administrative services could be provided by an affiliate in a third country and financial services by an affiliate financing company in a fourth country.

There is strong evidence of extensive profit shifting by MNEs. For example, more than 42 percent of the net income earned by U.S. majority-owned affiliates is earned in 'tax havens,'[12] while less than 15 percent of their value added is created there;[13] and the presence of an additional 'tax haven' subsidiary reduces the consolidated tax liability of a corporate group by 7.4 percent of total assets.[14] More granular evidence – Box 2.3 provides an

Box 2.3 International tax planning by multinational enterprises – evidence[1]

There is a large and growing literature, often exploiting firm-level data (available in usable quantities only for advanced economies) tending to confirm that the planning opportunities outlined in Box 2.2 do indeed have significant effects on corporate behavior:

- **Transfer pricing abuse.** Direct empirical evidence is scarce and does not unequivocally point to large effects. Clausing (2003) finds signs of significant tax-motivated transfer pricing abuse of intracompany trades by U.S. multinationals; and Heckemeyer and Overesch (2013) attribute about two thirds of their consensus spillover effect to transfer pricing abuse. Swenson (2001), on the other hand, reports responses of transfer prices with respect to cross-country differences in tax rates that are very small. It seems likely that the potential for abusive transfer pricing in advanced countries occurs not so much for trade in tangible goods – as it may for developing countries, which often lack appropriate information on comparable prices even for these transactions – as for transactions for which even advanced countries may lack comparables, such as intangibles, risk premia, or management services.
- **Location of intangible assets.** Higher CIT rates appear to have large negative effects on the number of patents filed by a subsidiary (Karkinsky and Riedel, 2012) and on the magnitude of intangible assets reported on a company's balance sheet (Dischinger and Riedel, 2011). This is consistent with profit shifting, and indeed there is evidence that profit shifting activities are larger in MNEs with high IP holdings and R&D intensities (Grubert, 2003).
- **Intra-company debt shifting.** There is substantial evidence that taxation induces intracompany borrowing to reduce tax payments

in high-tax locations (De Mooij, 2011). Effects are larger for affiliates located in developing economies than for those in developed economies (Fuest, Hebous and Riedel, 2011) and are found to be important also for multinational banks (Gu, de Mooij and Poghosyan, 2015).

- **Mismatches and other devices.** For the U.S., Altshuler and Gruber (2008) find that the 'check-the-box' rules generated a revenue loss for the U.S. Treasury of $7 billion between 1997 and 2002.
- **Treaty shopping**. Using firm-level data, Mintz and Weichenrieder (2010) find strong effects for German MNEs, while Weyzig (2014) documents a significant impact of Dutch Special Purpose entities on the routing of FDI.
- **Inversion.** Between 1997 and 2007 about 6 percent of all MNEs relocated their headquarters. Voget (2011) finds that a 10-percentage-point higher tax on repatriations increases the probability of such relocation by more than one third. Huizinga and Voget (2009), moreover, estimate that if the U.S. were to eliminate worldwide taxation, the number of parent companies that would choose residence in the U.S. after a cross-border merger would increase by 5 percentage points.
- **Deferral.** When the U.S. tax rate on repatriated dividends was reduced from 35 percent to 5.25 percent for one year in 2005, corporations repatriated $312 billion (less than 2 percent related to EI sector companies), much of which was distributed as dividends to U.S. shareholders (Dharmapala and others, 2011; Marples and Gravelle, 2011; Redmiles, 2008). Studies by the Joint Committee on Taxation and the U.S. Treasury estimate that eliminating deferral would yield an annual revenue gain in the U.S. of between $11 and $14 billion (Gravelle, 2013), allowing a revenue-neutral reduction of the CIT rate to around 28 percent (Altshuler and Grubert, 2008).

1 Based on Box 2 of IMF (2014).

overview – also increasingly confirms the long-standing but largely anecdotal impression that the opportunities for profit shifting indicated earlier are indeed used extensively.

It is very difficult to estimate the overall amount of tax revenue that is lost through such avoidance by MNEs. Doing so requires, for instance, assessing the counterfactual of what their behavior would have been in the absence of such opportunism and recognizing that while profit shifting reduces revenue in the jurisdiction out of which profits are shifted, it may well increase revenue where it is shifted to. For developing countries, analysis is severely constrained by the paucity of firm-level data. Some attempts have nonetheless been made. Gravelle (2013) puts the loss to the U.S. at around 25 percent of corporate tax revenue, while OECD (2015d), using entity-level panel data for MNEs headquartered in 46 advanced and emerging economies, puts it at an average of 4 to 10 percent of CIT revenue. Figure 2.1 illustrates results from Crivelli, de Mooij and Keen (2016), who use a cruder approach based on country-level panel data but for a wider set of 173 countries. These show, as one might expect, that the absolute amounts at stake are substantially larger for OECD than for non–OECD countries. Relative to GDP, however, they seem noticeably larger in developing countries and, at around 1 percent of GDP, are quite substantial relative to overall levels of tax revenue. It may thus be that avoidance issues are actually a greater concern outside the OECD, where, moreover – with the VAT often under stress, the personal income tax still relatively weak, and an aspiration to move away from trade taxes – alternative sources of revenue to the CIT are harder to find.

The estimates in Figure 2.1 exclude resource-rich countries.[15] Anecdotal evidence touched on later suggests that avoidance can on occasion be an even greater concern for them. More systematically, Beer and Loeprick (2015), using entity-level panel data for MNEs in oil and gas over 2004–12, conclude that in countries with sector-specific add-ons to the regular CIT, profit shifting reduced taxable profits by the order of one third. And they too find that developing countries seem to be more vulnerable than advanced.

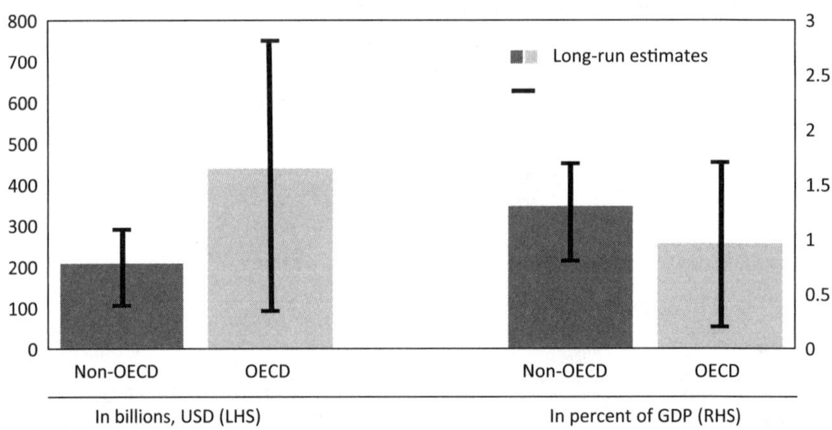

Short-run estimates

	USD, billions	Percent of GDP
Non-OECD	28 (15, 40)	0.2 (0.1, 0.3)
OECD	95 (170, 20)	0.2 (0.1, 0.4)

Figure 2.1 Estimating the revenue loss from BEPS

4 Some problem areas

There are, it is clear, many problem areas in dealing with avoidance by MNEs. Which are to the fore will vary, of course, across countries and specific sectors of the economy. This section (which draws on parts of IMF, 2014) considers three that are particularly prominent in the EIs.

4.1 Arm's length pricing

The ALP is seen by many as having become too complex and permissive, enabling a concentration of corporate profits in a few low-tax jurisdictions. The empirical evidence on profit shifting through transfer pricing, discussed earlier, reaches no consensus on precise magnitudes, but few doubt that the sums at stake are very considerable. Reflecting this, the arm's length principle has come under increasing pressure – and criticism – both conceptually and in application.

The most common theoretical objection to the ALP is that MNEs exist precisely as a more efficient alternative to market transactions, so that market prices cannot provide an appropriate benchmark (see Coase, 1937). A counter to this is that, on this view, MNEs will expand up to the point at which they are no more efficient than the market – in which case market prices are, at the margin, just as relevant for them as for independent parties. There may though be cases in which MNEs undertake, for non-tax reasons, operations that are hard to imagine unrelated parties entering into; or they may enter transactions for which there is no unique price at which one would expect unrelated parties to arrive. Examples in the extractives sector include situations in which an MNE undertakes, through separate entities, mining activities and transport to and from the mine, production and sales activities,[16] or extraction and pipeline activities in oil and gas; or in which intra-group transactions take place in rare minerals for which there is no established world market. Intra-group transactions that may plausibly occur only because of MNEs' ability to exploit cross-border tax differentials are still more problematic. One example is the transfer of intangible assets within a corporate group at an early stage in their development to low-tax jurisdictions (where the subsequent return will then accrue), which raises valuation problems at the time of transfer given the inherent absence of comparables, with significant issues of asymmetric information. Another is risk transfer among affiliates, standard practice in MNEs, by contractual arrangements that, in effect, provide some (potentially quite complex) degree of insurance between affiliates; the allocation of risk within a group may be driven by commercial considerations, but the question for transfer pricing purposes is how to value the transactions by which such risk transfers are achieved.

The current methodological framework is inadequate for dealing with such schemes because it asks what independent parties would do in such a situation – but with no comparables to use, as none could exist. Application of the ALP under such circumstances allows re-characterizing transactions so as to ignore for tax purposes those deemed artificial; but this potentially introduces discretion, uncertainty, and complexity.[17]

The practical difficulties in applying the ALP are also substantial. The burden on companies of justifying and on the authorities of verifying that transfer prices used correspond to the ALP is widely recognized to be substantial. And they will continue to increase as businesses become ever more knowledge intensive and technology driven, management becomes more geographically diffuse, and intra-group operations become easier to undertake and more difficult to price. This does not necessarily mean that other arrangements would be any simpler – though alternatives have been suggested, as touched on in Section 5 – but is cause for legitimate concern. It is especially difficult for developing countries, where applying the ALP is challenging given weak administrative capacity. Strengthening that capacity – including by improving access to necessary information[18] – is key to progress, though even the most sophisticated administrations struggle with these issues.

The minimum in addressing the challenges in applying the arm's length principle is to have appropriate transfer pricing rules in place, with most countries applying the OECD's transfer pricing guidelines (OECD, 2010). It is also important to make the best use of the existing tools based on the ALP: much tax planning by MNEs in developing countries is perceived by at least some observers as not just stretching the ALP but flouting it.[19] Countering this aggressiveness would be greatly facilitated by developing concrete guidance where it is lacking and repudiating perverse interpretations of the ALP (commonplace and often tacitly accepted), such as condoning risk stripping and other arrangements that provide no documented productivity gain for the MNE. Carefully designed safe harbors that apply a fixed mark up to certain costs can play a greater role than has often been recognized – though subject to the caveats already mentioned.[20] The use of joint ventures, common in the oil and gas industry, can also limit transfer price abuse on the cost side – purchases for the project from an entity related to one of the partners – as the partners have conflicting interests and hence an incentive to keep an eye on each other. So too can paid-on-behalf arrangements, to the extent that profit shifting actions which reduce CIT payable do not affect the profit oil calculation under the PSA.

While transfer pricing rules usually focus on cross-border transactions, they should also apply to related party domestic transactions.[21] Domestic transfer pricing can be a particular concern for the EI sector, which may be subject to a higher statutory tax rate on profits than other sectors, or in which a single company may be subject to different tax rates between upstream and downstream activities. Beer and Loeprick (2015) find that such domestic profit shifting accounts for about one third of the total shifted.

Countries with weak tax administrations may have to rely on simpler anti-avoidance measures to protect the tax base.[22] These might include, for instance, imposing withholding taxes on payments for services or restricting allowable deductions for some types of expense, such as those related to services provided by the parent company headquarters, and limitations on interest deductions, perhaps particularly targeting operations with low-tax jurisdictions, as well as simplified transfer pricing techniques. Some countries, in particular in Latin America, have adopted what is known as the sixth transfer pricing mechanism to deal with commodity transactions. This method, which may be seen as another form of the comparable uncontrolled price method, assumes a transaction takes place at the quoted commodity price on the date the goods are shipped. This is discussed further in Chapter 4 (Calder, this volume).

4.2 Tax treaties

Bilateral tax treaties (BTTs) make more certain and set limits to the taxation of cross-border investments. They set out the allocation of taxing rights between source and residence countries, including by specifying maximum rates of withholding tax (WHT) on interest, dividends, royalties, and other payments from source countries – generally below those otherwise applicable by domestic law. As with the CIT itself, rates of WHT have been trending down in both treaties and domestic law but remain a significant concern for investors. BTTs also generally provide agreed PE definitions; specification of taxes for which foreign tax credits will be provided (of particular importance in relation to the special resource rent taxes applied by many countries, as mentioned), non-discrimination rules, and dispute resolution procedures.[23] BTTs may also include provisions for exchange of taxpayer information (EOI), though this may be provided for in stand-alone *tax information exchange agreements* (TIEAs) or by acceding to the 1988 Council of Europe/OECD Convention of Mutual Administrative Assistance in Tax Matters. Treaties differ, but – building on a framework first established by the League of Nations – are strongly guided by models developed by the OECD and UN, along with associated commentaries.

As Figure 2.2. shows, there has been a proliferation of BTTs over the last 20 years, driven by an increasing number that involve developing countries. Initially, almost all BTTs were between advanced economies. The tripling of the number of treaties since the early 1990s, however, almost entirely reflects an increase in the number to which at least one party is a non–OECD country – many of which, of course, will have few capital exports. Overall, there are now around 3,000 BTTs: a large number, but only a small fraction of the number of potential bilateral relationships.

The experience of resource-rich countries in entering into double tax treaties varies. For example, of resource-rich countries in the OECD, Canada and Norway each have more than 80 treaties, while Australia has fewer than 50. This suggests that, while investors in the resource sector may pursue governments to

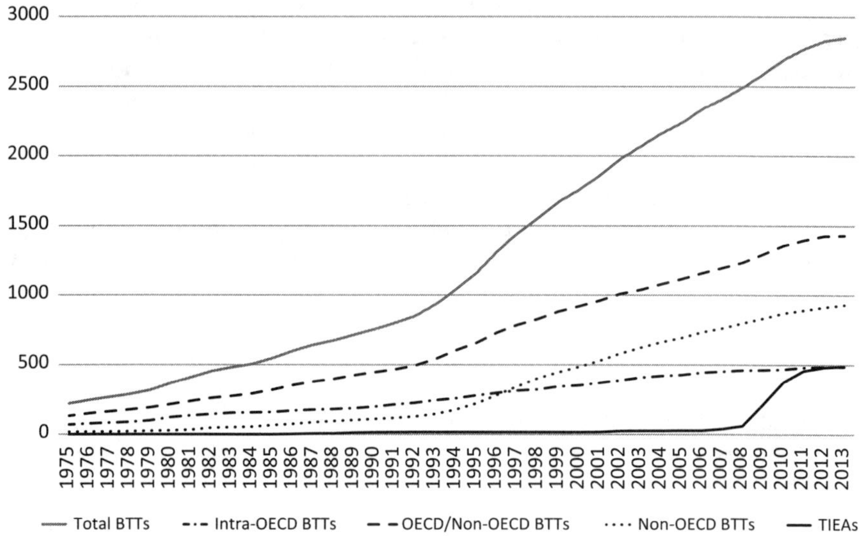

Figure 2.2 Numbers of BTTs and TIEAs, 1975–2013

enter into BTTs in order to provide tax stability and to ensure creditability of taxes, other factors may be more important in driving the negotiation of BTTs, such as political pressures and negotiating capacity.

The primary benefit for a capital-importing country from signing a BTT is supposedly increased inward foreign direct investment (FDI) – an important policy consideration for many countries, given the perception of significant associated external benefits – as a result of both increased certainty and lighter taxation (further discussed in Chapter 6; Juggins, this volume). The main potential disadvantages are the revenue foregone from reduced WHT rates and the costs of treaty negotiation and administration.[24] The net benefits of a BTT then depend on whether it realizes sufficient gains from increased FDI to offset any revenue loss.

The empirical evidence on the investment effects of treaties is mixed.[25] Identifying causality is inherently problematic, since treaties may precede investment not because they spur the latter but because they may be concluded only when there is a strong expectation of such investment. This can be a deliberate feature of treaty policy, as it traditionally has been in the United States. Studies using macro-level data indeed find a wide range of effects, though perhaps with some signs that a positive effect on FDI is most likely for middle-income countries. Work using firm-level data suggests a significant impact on firms' entry into a particular country, though not on the level of their investment once they are present.

Box 2.4 Treaty shopping

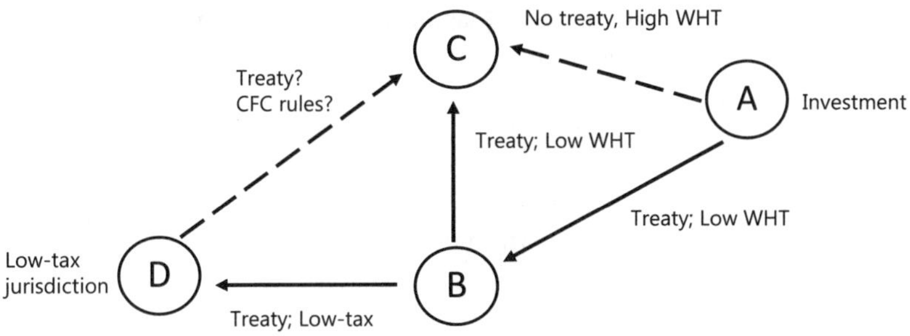

Country A has a treaty with B but not with C, so that residents of C investing directly in A face the relatively high WHT rates specified in A's domestic law. If C has a treaty with B, however, investors there may be able to benefit from A's treaty-reduced WHT rates by investing through an affiliate in B. which acts as a *conduit*. It may, moreover, be that B has a treaty with some country D that taxes such income at a low rate; receipts can then be further passed there, without (unless C applies CFC rules) attracting any further immediate liability in C.

The potential revenue loss, especially to developing countries, has caused increasing concern. With a treaty in place, the MNE's incentive is to extract income in forms that attract a low or zero WHT rate, which may be ones – management fees, for instance, or royalties – that the host authorities find particularly difficult to value. The opportunities for this are amplified by the possibility of *treaty shopping*: constructing advantageous routing by linking bilateral tax treaties, typically through low-tax conduit countries[26] (as illustrated in Box 2.4). In effect, a treaty with one country can become a treaty with the rest of the world. These effects can be very sizable. One estimate, for instance, is that treaties with the Netherlands led to foregone revenue for developing countries of at least €770 million in 2011;[27] similar, very rough calculations suggest that U.S. tax treaties cost their non–OECD country counterparts perhaps $1.6 billion in 2010.[28] Treaties are rarely cancelled, so it is indicative of the level of current concerns – and the wider pressures on the international tax system – that both Mongolia and Argentina have done so since 2011.

These concerns have been addressed in part by the inclusion in BTTs of *limitation of benefit* (LOB) or *principal purpose test* (PPT) provisions. These provide, respectively, that reduced WHT rates and other treaty provisions apply only to companies that meet specific tests of having some genuine presence in the treaty country (such as a minimum share of ownership by its residents or a minimum level of income from conducting an active trade or business there) or when the transaction is assessed to be not primarily tax motivated. Such provisions have not been commonplace, though the U.S., which has routinely included LOB provisions, is a notable exception. But anti-abuse provisions have been spreading: India and Japan have been moving in this direction, and the Netherlands has taken the very positive step of indicating an intention to approach all developing countries with which it has (or is negotiating) a tax treaty with a view to strengthening anti-abuse provisions. The BEPS project has also addressed this issue, as described later. LOB and PPT provisions are, however, often complex and are not self-executing: where capacity is weak and access to information limited, verifying that the pre-requisites for treaty benefits are met can be difficult.

Given the concerns with BTTs, a key decision for any primarily capital-importing country is whether it can achieve more by signing a treaty than it can simply through its own domestic law.[29] The reciprocal benefits that a treaty could provide to such a country may actually be of relatively little value, except perhaps for the EOI aspects – but those can in principle instead be achieved through a TIEA or by signing the Convention on Mutual Administrative Assistance. And key provisions regarding, for instance, WHT rates and the PE definition, can be provided in domestic law. Treaties are, moreover, inherently discriminatory as between partners and others. The main or even only advantage that a BTT can offer may then be one of signaling, acting as a strong commitment device for the tax assurances given to foreign investors. But that in turn may become less needed as countries build up credibility in tax policy making, which they may not have had some years back. It is clear that countries should not enter BTTs lightly – all too often this has been done largely as a political gesture – but with close and well-advised attention to the risks that may be created.[30] It is worth noting that there are important instances of large MNEs investing in countries without BTTs (as with, for instance, Chevron's investments in Angola, Nigeria, and Kuwait).

In those resource-rich countries relying on BTTs, the detailed provisions of the BTTs are of course critical for both EI companies and the government. A more detailed discussion of these issues is provided in Chapter 5 (Daniel and Thuronyi) and Chapter 6 (Juggins).

4.3 Transfers of interest

The issue here is the possibility that the owners of some asset with respect to which a capital gain arises can avoid tax in the country to which that asset – often involving an EI asset such as a mineral license – inherently relates by holding it through a chain of companies and then selling the asset in a low-tax jurisdiction (as set out in Box 2.5). Such transactions can involve the host country receiving little or no revenue when substantial gains are indirectly realized on assets located there. Over the last few years, including in the context

Box 2.5 Indirect transfers of interest

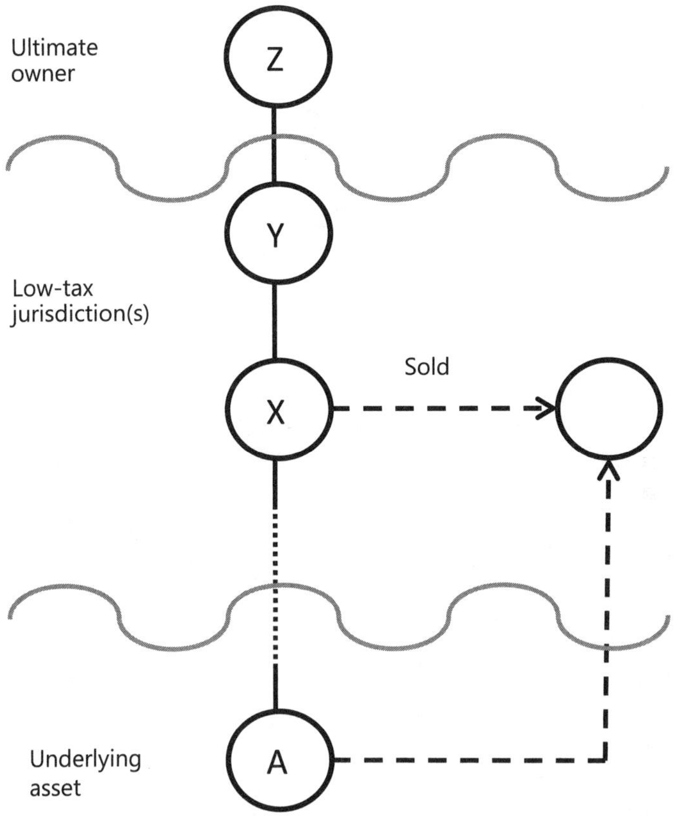

Company A holds an asset (e.g. a mining right) located in a relatively high-tax source country that increases in value. The ultimate owner of A, Company Z, realizes this gain by selling X, an intermediate entity holding A, in a low-tax jurisdiction. The result may be that little or no tax is payable anywhere.

of resource discoveries, this has emerged as a macro-relevant concern in several low-income countries: IMF (2014), for instance, cites a gain on a gold project in Mauritania of around $4 billion – about 90 percent of GDP – that escaped tax by being transacted in the Bahamas.

This is a controversial and difficult topic. Conceptually, there are arguments as to whether or not it is appropriate to tax such gains at all: they presumably reflect retained past and expected future earnings, so it may not be necessary or appropriate to tax them if those earnings have been or will be adequately taxed in other ways.[31] Nonetheless, many countries do wish to tax such capital gains, and the non-taxation of indirect transfers can raise serious equity and political concerns. Domestic tax laws need to provide an adequate basis if indirect transfers are to be brought into tax, and BTTs can play a role in protecting and clarifying the source country's rights. The challenge is in implementing these rules, especially in discovering the transactions and collecting the tax due. These issues are discussed in detail in Chapter 7 (Burns, Le Leuch and Sunley), including potential rules and procedures that can be used to bring indirect transfers into tax.

5 BEPS and all that: a changing landscape?

The last few years have seen growing concern at the extent of international tax planning. In many countries, there has been widespread public dismay at the small amounts of tax paid by many multinationals – at a time when many countries face a post-crisis austerity and need to strengthen their medium-term fiscal positions. And within the system itself, strains have become increasingly evident, notably with the termination in a number of countries of tax treaties that had come to be seen as harmful to national well-being (often, as in Mongolia, in relation to EI investments). The most prominent coordinated policy response has been the G20-OECD BEPS project. Building on the central role that the OECD has played in developing and maintaining standards and guidance in international tax matters, this project does not seek to change the broad features of the international tax framework but is an ambitious effort to make it less vulnerable to many of the avoidance devices set out earlier.

Final reports and recommendations, touching 15 Action areas, were approved by the G20 leaders in November 2015. These outcomes, summarized in OECD (2015a) and more briefly in an Appendix that follows, take a variety of forms: in four areas there are minimum standards; for the rest there is amendment of the guidance in core OECD documents or simply agreement on a common approach. The project has now moved to implementation, to which initially (only) the 44 OECD and G20 members are committed but with a strong intention to encourage and facilitate global participation.

It is too early, of course, to know how governments and MNEs will react to these developments. The necessary domestic legislation and, especially, treaty revision may take some time, but it may also be that increased reputational risk from highly aggressive tax planning is already having some effect on MNEs' tax behavior. It is natural, nonetheless, to speculate on what the BEPS outcomes might mean for developing countries in general and those rich in resources in particular.

Of the three specific issues raised in the previous section, two received attention in the BEPS project – the exception being indirect transfers of interest, which was not considered. This though is to be the subject of a report from the OECD and IMF with the World Bank and UN, due in 2016.

Notable in relation to implementation of the ALP is the adoption of minimum standards in respect of transfer pricing documentation and of a form of country-by-country reporting (CbCR).[32] Under the former, the resident country of the parent will share information (subject to treaty obligations and confidentiality assurances) on high-level operations of the MNE, and detailed transactional information will be provided to the source country. Under CbCR, MNEs (with global turnover of more than €750 million) will report their pre-tax income and tax paid and accrued, in all jurisdictions in which they operate, to each of those jurisdictions. The impact of CbCR – which can help auditors better grasp the precise tax strategies that an MNE is pursuing – may be less in the EIs than in other sectors, since EI companies already have disclosure obligations as a result of transparency initiatives such as the Extractive Industry Transparency Initiative (EITI), Dodd-Frank Act and EU directives. The EITI was established to improve transparency of transactions between governments and resource companies, by providing stakeholders and interested parties with credible information on company payments made to government and on payments received by government.[33] This initiative has gained worldwide recognition as an indicator of a country's commitment to transparency in the resource sectors, with close to 40 countries now participating (as fully compliant members or candidates). The Dodd-Frank Act requires the Securities and Exchange Commission (SEC) to issue rules requiring companies involved in the commercial development of oil, gas, or minerals to disclose annually the amount of payments by type, project, and government; this though has prompted legal wrangling, the latest step being the SEC's announcement of proposed rules in December 2015. The EU's Transparency and Accounting Directives were amended in June 2013 to include disclosure rules similar to those envisaged in the Dodd-Frank Act, with each member state to adopt the provisions into law no later than July 2015. All these initiatives in an important respect go beyond the BEPS CbCR standard in that the information is made public.[34] And indeed some MNEs have taken their own initiatives to provide more disclosure: BHP Billiton and Rio Tinto, for instance, publish the taxes they pay by country).[35]

The challenges that developing countries face in finding transfer pricing comparables, including in relation to minerals, were recognized in the BEPS discussions but left for future work. A report on this to the G20 Development Working Group, led by the OECD and World Bank with the IMF and UN, is due in December 2016, with work on minerals pricing underway at the OECD.

Action is also proposed – as a minimum standard – to address treaty abuse. This has the potential to substantially reduce the scope for treaty shopping described earlier but is of course contingent on treaty revision. Work on the development of a multilateral instrument (due for end 2016) is intended to allow such revision without the need to reopen – and potentially renegotiate – several thousand bilateral treaties.

Other BEPS actions will of course also have an effect on the EIs (though some arguably signal no real change: it is, for instance, already open to countries – indeed commonly recommended – to adopt limitations on interest deductions). Some of these effects may be unintended. For example, the proposed changes to the definition of PE include rules to prevent the artificial fragmentation of business activities to avoid the PE rules.[36] These changes could pose difficulties for oil and gas companies that often split contracts for a variety of reasons, including meeting local content rules. Another example is the proposed rules to address hybrid mismatches – different tax treatment of an entity or instrument – which may impact oil and gas companies that, for sound commercial reasons, often operate as joint ventures by treating them as a single entity. And in some cases the direct impact on source countries may be limited, but indirect effects might be significant: the adoption of tighter CFC rules by residence countries, for instance, reduces the incentive to shift profits to low-tax jurisdictions. Restrictions on the use of hybrid mismatches might come to have similar effect; and even if such devices are not widely used in relation to developing countries, they might otherwise have become more heavily used as a reaction to tighter limits on the use of other profit shifting devices.

In addition to but consistent with the OECD-G20 BEPS project, the European Commission (EC) has also been increasingly active in addressing a range of international tax issues in the context of the single market, recognizing the distinct constraints and obligations that EU law imposes, notably in terms of non-discrimination between residents of member states (which affects, for instance, CFC rules). It has a long-standing Code of Conduct on harmful tax practices and has recently issued recommendations on aggressive tax planning.[37] The EC has also been conducting investigations into beneficial tax rulings that allow for cross-border tax planning to determine if the tax rulings are in breach of the EU State Aid rules.[38]

These initiatives amount to an unprecedented attempt to fix an international tax system that was, by common consent, broken. They do not address all avoidance routes and potential counter-measures: perhaps most notably, the BEPS project has not addressed the indirect transfers of interest issue noted earlier, which is a major concern for many lower-income countries in dealing with the EIs. And some important aspects of the project remain to be fully specified, including in relation to their application in the particular circumstances of developing countries; on this, the OECD, together with other international organizations, is to produce a series of 'toolkits' in 2016 and 2017. Nonetheless, much more has already been achieved in two years than many would have thought possible. Without detracting from that, however, it is important to recognize some inherent limitations of these efforts.

Implementation – just beginning at the time of writing – is of course critical. Actions need to be adequate and credible if they are to lead to genuine improvement. In the EI context, lingering concerns about the use of transfer pricing to overstate costs, for example, may encourage countries to significantly increase their reliance, despite all the potential inefficiencies they can cause, on royalties rather than taxes on harder-to-measure profits or rents.[39]

The importance of the coverage of actions taken also bears emphasis. This is so in terms of both measures adopted and the set of participating countries. For the former, closing down some avoidance routes but not others – limiting interest deductions without addressing hybrid mismatch, for instance – can simply result in planning changing its nature much more than its extent and even taking forms that are more wasteful of resources. And it is important to recognize too that the effect of a country's adopting anti-avoidance measures may be to increase effective tax rates on inward investment and/or lead to reduced inward profit shifting. Unless others adopt similar measures, a country that takes unilateral action may thus place itself at a competitive disadvantage – likely to be a significant concern for many developing countries, whose tax policies are largely driven by the desire to attract FDI and which are heavily reliant on CIT revenue. Collective action is likely needed to overcome this coordination problem.

More fundamental issues relate to the scope of the exercises in themselves. They aim only at restricting avoidance opportunities within the current architecture. This means, first, that they do not directly address the wider challenges of international tax competition: the strategic use by governments of the tax system to secure a national advantage at the expense of others (discussed, in the specific context of the EIs, in Chapter 13 by Mansour and Świstak). While some such devices are in principle curtailed by the BEPS recommendations – such as offering 'patent boxes' unconditional on underlying activity being undertaken in the jurisdiction concerned – many are not. Most obviously, there is nothing to prevent countries competing by setting low corporate tax rates. Indeed, it may be that the adoption of measures to counter avoidance may spur more aggressive tax competition as countries react to what would otherwise be higher effective tax rates on inward investment. It may not be overly cynical to see some of the avoidance devices currently in operation as means by which governments have selectively lowered effective rates on more mobile elements of the tax base while maintaining relatively higher rates on less mobile ones. Preventing them from doing this can, under some circumstances, make tax competition more rather than less harmful to the collective well-being.[40]

Nor has the BEPS project considered the more radical reforms of the international tax architecture that some have urged – largely on the reasonable grounds that these are not practical possibilities in the short term. Some of these options are reviewed in IMF (2014). Prominent amongst them is the suggestion to move instead to some form of 'formula apportionment' (FA), allocating the worldwide profits of an MNE across the jurisdictions in which it operates by some formula proxying the extent of its activities in each. All current subnational corporate taxes (in Canada, the U.S. and elsewhere) use some sort of formulaic allocation, suggesting that – as activities become as mobile between nations as they now are within them – the eventual application of such an approach across countries cannot be ruled out. And indeed the EC relaunched in 2015[41] a proposal for the adoption within the EU of a common consolidated corporate tax base (CCCTB) that would be of this broad form. The principle appeal of this approach is that it dispenses with the use of prices internal to corporate groups, since these would be taxed on a consolidated 'unitary' basis. But FA brings its own difficulties: it is not neutral with respect to organizational form, and effects operating through the formula by which profits are allocated can lead to its own distortions of behavior (in the form of over-use of high-weight factors in low-tax jurisdictions) and can even cause more intense tax competition. And the specific issue arises in the EIs that the factors conventionally used by FA schemes – destination-based sales (meaning sales in the location of the purchaser), payroll, and assets – may be seen as under-allocating profits to the jurisdiction in which extraction takes place. This can in principle be dealt with by using in the allocation formula origin-based sales (those in the location of production), as the EC proposal allows,[42] or – as Alaska does for oil and gas in its state-level corporate tax – by explicitly including production as one of the weighting factors.[43]

6 Concluding

The design of a fiscal regime for the EIs has to take careful account of international aspects if it is to ensure the government receives an acceptable share of MNEs' earnings while remaining attractive to investors. This includes recognizing the opportunities for tax planning that MNEs will face, addressing which is a matter not only of strengthening administrative capacity – even the most capable administrations struggle with tax avoidance by MNEs, including in the EIs – but of shaping rules and international commitments appropriately. For the host country, it means, for instance, aiming to maximize the creditability in the residence country of taxes levied on profit and guarding against profit shifting by considering, for example, limits on interest deductibility and the judicious use of withholding taxes on other payments, being careful too to ensure that treaty commitments do not lock in exposure to such shifting devices. It may also mean tilting the balance between profit-related taxes and royalties further towards the latter than might otherwise be the case, on the grounds that monitoring deductible costs is harder than monitoring revenues.

The BEPS proposals and other recent initiatives are an unparalleled attempt to bring change, in a reasonably coordinated way, to the international tax framework. But their impact will become clear only after some years, and they leave the fundamentals of that framework unchanged. Complexity (perhaps now even greater) and contentiousness are likely to remain for some time.

Appendix

Summary of BEPS outcomes

In four areas there are minimum standards, the expectation being that domestic law and/or treaties will be amended so as to adopt them:

- To counter ***treaty shopping***, by including in treaties either limitation of benefit or more general-principle purpose test provisions so as to restrict access to benefits.
- On ***transfer pricing documentation and country by country reporting***, MNEs are to make available general information on their activities to all countries in which they are active, more detailed transactions information to each, and – those with group turnover greater than €750 million – also to provide information on pre-tax profit, tax paid and accrued in each jurisdiction (shared by the parent country in line with information exchange agreements).
- In relation to ***harmful tax practices***, a particular focus on 'patent boxes' led to a 'nexus' principle that preferential regimes should only be offered conditional on substantial underlying activity, and rulings that raises BEPS concerns are to be shared automatically.
- For ***dispute resolution***, measures are to ensure timely and good-faith outcomes.

In some areas, guidance is captured by amendments to core OECD reference documents:

- The definition of a ***permanent establishment*** in the OECD Model Tax Convention will be widened so as to include, for instance, commissionaire arrangements (under which an agent undertakes sales without being the owner of the product) and to address avoidance of PE status by fragmentation of activities.
- On ***transfer pricing***, the OECD Guidelines are to be amended, notably to address artificial transfer of risk within groups and difficulties associated with intangibles (clarifying that taxation need not follow legal ownership of an asset, and with some guidance in dealing with hard-to-value transactions).

In others, the outcome is guidance on a common approach, with an aspiration of convergence:

- On ***hybrid mismatch*** – the potential difficulty arising when an entity or instrument is regarded differently in different countries (debt in one, equity in the other, for instance) – rules are to ensure that deductions not be given unless the associated income is taxable to the recipient (possibly, as a matter of policy, at zero rate).

- ***Interest deductions*** to be limited to 10 to 30 percent of earnings before interest, taxes, depreciation and amortization (EBITDA), with carry-forward of unused deductions or allowances, but with the possibility of increasing deductions up to the group-wide ratio of interest to EBITDA.
- Recommendations are given on details of ***controlled foreign corporation*** rules – to ensure, for instance, that credit is given for any foreign taxes actually paid. . .
- . . . and on provisions for ***mandatory disclosure of aggressive tax planning*** to enable the authorities to identify and address emerging risks.

Some recommendations, and the minimum standards in particular, will require treaty changes. To facilitate this:

- Work continues towards agreement, by the end of 2016, of a ***multilateral instrument*** that would simultaneously modify each.

Ongoing work is to flesh out various aspects of these broad outcomes, including use of the transactional profit split method, application of the interest limitation rules for financial institutions, and transfer pricing issues for commodities. During 2016–18, a series of 'toolkits' are to be developed, by the OECD and other international organizations, for application of the BEPS outcomes in the special circumstances of developing countries.

Notes

* Fiscal Affairs Department, International Monetary Fund, Washington DC 20431. Parts of this chapter draw on IMF (2014). We are grateful to Emil Sunley, Artur Świstak, and Victor Thuronyi for helpful comments and suggestions. The views expressed here are those of the authors and should not be attributed to the IMF, its Executive Board, or its management.

1 These are raised forcefully in, for instance, Africa Progress Panel (2012).

2 These bilateral treaties are informed by guidelines produced by the OECD and, with somewhat less impact, the UN. Some regional agreements also have considerable effect; notably in the EU, where directives and decisions of the European Court of Justice reflecting the principle of non-discrimination among member states continue to have a major impact.

3 U.S. Census Bureau (2013).

4 A credit directly reduces tax payable; a deduction, in contrast, reduces the base on which tax is charged.

5 While the rhetoric commonly abhors 'double taxation,' what investors presumably care about (compliance costs aside) is not how many times they are taxed but how much.

6 Worldwide taxation of this form is the usual treatment of income from portfolio investments.

7 These and other notions of efficiency in relation to international taxation – and why their practical usefulness is limited – are discussed in Appendix VII of IMF (2014).

8 Countries may also have a worldwide system in their law, but the practice may be different due to the administrative difficulty of taxing residents on their worldwide incomes, for example owing to a lack of effective information sharing with other countries.
9 Examples include Algeria, Kenya, Oman, Guyana, South Sudan, and Cote d'Ivoire.
10 Now that Australia, Canada, Japan, and the United Kingdom apply territorial tax systems, the crediting of these taxes is less relevant.
11 Issued by the U.S. Treasury in 1996, these essentially allow businesses to elect – for themselves and for each of their foreign and domestic subsidiaries and within certain parameters – whether to be taxed as a corporation or treated as transparent for tax purposes (a 'disregarded entity'). These rules gave rise to major tax planning opportunities, including, among others, the easier avoidance of CFC rules.
12 The ill-defined term 'tax haven' is used only to refer to specific lists of jurisdictions found in the literature cited.
13 Dharmapala (2014).
14 Maffini (2009).
15 This is because it rests on modeling the CIT base, which may behave differently in resource-rich countries and will not capture shifting affecting other profit-based taxes more likely to be found there.
16 For example, BHP Billiton and Rio Tinto have acknowledged transfer pricing disputes with the Australian Tax Office over the use of marketing hubs in low-tax Singapore. In the case of BHP Billiton, the tax in dispute is A$522 million (including interest and penalties).
17 In this respect, the ALP is akin to a General Anti-Avoidance Rule (GAAR), which would apply to the generality of transactions. Indeed, a GAAR can be helpful in addressing international tax issues more broadly, but with the same weaknesses, including often having to rely on judicial interpretation to resolve its scope.
18 Public availability of information is critical, as taxpayers can only apply the arm's length principle with publicly accessible data.
19 See for instance Schatan (2012).
20 Brazil has taken a much-noted and somewhat controversial approach in this regard: "Brazil does not follow the OECD guidelines, rather imposes unique standards for evaluating transfer prices . . . with related parties and [other] companies located in low-tax jurisdictions" (KPMG, 2013). The rules involve minimum gross profit margins, very specific rules based upon indices for commodities transactions, limitations on intracompany export transactions as a total of net export transactions, and strict limitations on interest expense deductions based upon sovereign bond rates. No 'profit-based' methods are allowed, and functional and risk analyses may not be used.
21 India, for example, has specifically included domestic transactions of various sorts within its transfer pricing rules.
22 See for instance Dubut (2015).
23 Countries may also enter into bilateral investment agreements, but these do not reduce tax rates or address possibilities of double taxation.
24 Multilateral treaties can reduce these (Thuronyi, 2001), and several regional treaties have been negotiated (as, for instance, in the Arab Maghreb Union and West African Economic and Monetary Union).
25 For a discussion of the impacts, see Appendix V of IMF (2014).
26 And/or jurisdictions that offer low WHT rates even without a treaty.
27 McGauran (2013). These estimates do not include revenue foregone on royalties.
28 Taking into account dividends and interest only.
29 Easson (2000) remains the classic treatment.
30 As discussed for example in Brooks and Krever (2015) and IMF (2014).
31 On these grounds, Norway, for instance, does not tax such transfers.
32 See OECD (2015b).

33 See https://eiti.org/.
34 Although some EU countries may require the public to pay a fee for accessing the information.
35 See http://www.bhpbilliton.com/investors/news/bhp-billiton-releases-first-economic-contribution-and-payments-to-governments-report and http://www.riotinto.com/our commitment/taxes-paid-in-2012-4757.aspx.
36 See OECD (2015c).
37 European Commission (2012).
38 See European Commission IP/14/1105 of 7 October 2014: "State aid: Commission investigates transfer pricing arrangements on corporate taxation of Amazon in Luxembourg"; IP/14/663 of 11 June 2014: "State aid: Commission investigates transfer pricing arrangements on corporate taxation of Apple (Ireland) Starbucks (Netherlands) and Fiat Finance and Trade (Luxembourg)". On 30 September 2014 the Commission published non-confidential versions of its preliminary findings regarding Ireland (Apple) and Luxembourg (Fiat); C(2014)3606 and C(2014)3627 of 11 June 2014.
39 Boadway and Keen (2010) discuss both these inefficiencies and the use of royalties in response to difficulties in verifying costs. Clausing and Durst (2015) argue on these grounds for a royalty increasing more than proportionally with the resource price.
40 See for instance the discussion in Keen and Konrad (2013).
41 http://ec.europa.eu/taxation_customs/taxation/company_tax/common_tax_base/index_en.htm
42 Article 100 of EC(COM)2011/12/14.
43 The 'extraction factor' in Alaska is production in barrels of oil plus 1/6 Mcf of natural gas. Siu and others (2015) assess experience and possibilities for FA with respect to the EIs.

References

Africa Progress Panel. (2012), *Africa Progress Report 2013: Equity in Extractives: Stewarding Africa's Natural Resources for All.* Available at http://www.africaprogresspanel.org/publications/policy-papers/africa-progress-report-2013/t

Altshuler, Rosanne and Harry Grubert. (2008), "Corporate Taxes in the World Economy," in John W. Diamond and George R. Zodrow (eds), *Fundamental Tax Reform: Issues, Choices, and Implications* (Cambridge: MIT Press), pp. 319–354.

Beer, Sebastian and Jan Loeprick. (2015), "Profit Shifting in the Oil and Gas Industry," mimeo, The World Bank.

Boadway, Robin and Michael Keen. (2010), "Theoretical Perspectives on Resource Tax Design," in Philip Daniel, Michael Keen and Charles McPherson (eds), *The Taxation of Petroleum and Minerals: Principles, Practices and Problems* (London and New York: Routledge), pp. 14–74.

Brooks, Kim and Richard Krever. (2015), "The Troubling Role of Tax Treaties," in Geerten Michielse and Victor Thuronyi (eds), *Tax Design Issues Worldwide* (Wolters Kluwer: Alphen aan den Rijn), pp. 159–178.

Coase, Ronald H. (1937), "The Nature of the Firm," *Economica*, 4(November), 386–405.

De Mooij, Ruud A. (2011), "The Tax Elasticity of Corporate Debt: A Synthesis of Size and Variations," IMF Working Paper 11/95 (Washington: International Monetary Fund). Available at http://www.imf.org/external/pubs/ft/wp/2011/wp1195.pdf

Dubut, Thomas. (2015), "Designing Anti-Base-Erosion Rules for Developing Countries: Challenges and Solutions," in Geerten Michielse and Victor Thuronyi (eds), *Tax Design Issues Worldwide* (Wolters Kluwer: Alphen aan den Rijn), pp. 141–156.

Clausing, Kimberly A. (2003), "Tax-Motivated Transfer Pricing and U.S. Intrafirm Trade Prices," *Journal of Public Economics*, 87(September), 2207–2223.

Clausing, Kimberley A. and Michael Durst. (2015), "A Price-Based Royalty Tax?" International Centre for Tax and Development Working Paper no. 41.

Crivelli, Ernesto, Ruud de Mooij and Michael Keen. (2016), "Base Erosion, Profit Shifting and Developing Countries," forthcoming in *Finanzarchive*.

Dharmapala, Dhammika. (2014), "What Do We Know About Base Erosion and Profit Shifting? A Review of the Empirical Literature," Illinois Public Law and Legal Theory Research Papers Series No. 14–23 (Champaign: University of Illinois College of Law).

Dharmapala, Dhammika, C. Fritz Foley and Kristin J. Forbes. (2011), "Watch What I Do, Not What I Say: The Unintended Consequences of the Homeland Investment Act," *Journal of Finance*, 66(June), 753–787.

Dischinger, Mathias and Nadine Riedel. (2011), "Corporate Taxes and the Location of Intangible Assets within Multinational Firms," *Journal of Public Economics*, 95(August), 691–707.

Easson, Alex. (2000), "Do We Still Need Tax Treaties?" in *Bulletin for International Fiscal Documentation* (Amsterdam: International Bureau of Fiscal Documentation), 54(12), pp. 619–625.

European Commission. (2012), *Commission recommendation of 6.12.2012 on Aggressive Tax Planning* (Luxembourg: Publications Office of the European Union). Available at http://ec.europa.eu/taxation_customs/resources/documents/taxation/tax_fraud_evasion/c_2012_8806_en.pdf.

Fuest, Clemens, Shafik Hebous and Nadine Riedel. (2011), "International Debt Shifting and Multinational Firms in Developing Economies," *Economics Letters*, 113(November), 135–138.

Gravelle, Jane G. (2013), "Tax Havens: International Tax Avoidance and Evasion," Congressional Research Service Report for Congress (Washington: Congressional Research Service).

Grubert, Harry. (2003), "Intangible Income, Intercompany Transactions, Income Shifting, and the Choice of Location," *National Tax Journal*, 56(March), 221–242.

Gu, Grace W., Ruud de Mooij and Tigran Poghosyan. (2015), "Taxation and Leverage in International Banking," *International Tax and Public Finance*, 22(2) (April), 177–200.

Heckemeyer, Jost H. and Michael Overesch. (2013), "Multinationals' Profit Response to Tax Differentials: Effect Size and Shifting Channels," Centre for European Economic Research Discussion Paper No. 13–045 (Mannheim: Zentrum für Europäische Wirtschaftforschung GmbH).

Huizinga, Harry and Johannes Voget. (2009), "International Taxation and the Direction and Volume of Cross-border M&As," *Journal of Finance*, 64(June), 1217–1249.

International Monetary Fund. (2014), *Spillovers in International Corporate Taxation* (Washington: International Monetary Fund). Available at http://www.imf.org/external/np/pp/eng/2014/050914.pdf

Karkinsky, Tom and Nadine Riedel. (2012), "Corporate Taxation and the Choice of Patent Location within Multinational Firms," *Journal of International Economics*, 88(September), 176–185.

Keen, Michael and Kai Konrad. (2013), "The Theory of International Tax Competition and Coordination," in Alan Auerbach, Raj Chetty, Martin Feldstein and Emanuel Saez (eds), *Handbook of Public Economics*, Vol.5 (Amsterdam: North Holland), pp. 257–328.

KPMG International. (2013), *Global Transfer Pricing Review* (KPMG International Cooperative). Available at https://home.kpmg.com/content/dam/kpmg/pdf/2016/02/global-transfer-pricing-review-consolidated.pdf

Maffini, Girogia. (2009), "Tax Haven Activities and the Tax Liabilities of Multinational Groups," Centre for Business Taxation WP 09/25 (Oxford: Oxford University).

Marples, Donald J. and Jane G. Gravelle. (2011), "Tax Cuts on Repatriation Earnings as Economic Stimulus: An Economic Analysis," Congressional Research Service Report for Congress (Washington: Congressional Research Service).

McGauran, Kattrin. (2013), "Should the Netherlands Sign Tax Treaties with Developing Countries?" for *Stichting Onderzoek Multinationale Ondernemingen* (Amsterdam: SOMO).

Mintz, Jack and Alfons Weichenrieder. (2010), *The Indirect Side of Direct Investment* (Cambridge: MIT Press).

OECD. (2010), *OECD Transfer Pricing Guidelines for Multinational Enterprises and tax Administrations 2010* (Paris: OECD Publishing). Available at: http://dx.doi.org/10.1787/tpg-2010-en

Organisation for Economic Co-operation and Development. (2013), *Addressing Base Erosion and Profit Shifting* (Paris: OECD Publishing). Available at http://dx.doi.org/10.1787/978 9264192744-en

Organisation for Economic Co-operation and Development. (2014), *Transfer Pricing Comparability Data and Developing Countries* (Paris: OECD Publishing). Available at http://www.oecd.org/ctp/transfer-pricing/transfer-pricing-comparability-data-developing-countries.htm

Organisation for Economic Co-operation and Development. (2015a), *OECD/G20 Base Erosion and Profit Shifting Project: Executive Summaries 2015 Final Reports* (Paris: OECD Publishing). Available at http://www.oecd.org/ctp/beps-reports-2015-executive-summaries.pdf

Organisation for Economic Co-operation and Development. (2015b), *Action 13: Country by Country Reporting Implementation Package* (Paris: OECD Publishing). Available at http://www.oecd.org/ctp/transfer-pricing/beps-action-13-country-by-country-reporting-implementation-package.pdf

Organisation for Economic Co-operation and Development. (2015c), *Preventing the Artificial Avoidance of Permanent Establishment Status, Action 7–2015 Final Report* (Paris: OECD Publishing). Available at http://www.oecd.org/tax/preventing-the-artificial-avoidance-of-permanent-establishment-status-action-7–2015-final-report-9789264241220-en.htm

Organisation for Economic Co-operation and Development. (2015d), *Monitoring and Measuring BEPS, Action 11–2015 Final Report* (Paris: OECD Publishing). Available at http://www.oecd.org/tax/measuring-and-monitoring-beps-action-11–2015-final-report-9789264241343-en.htm.

Redmiles, Melissa. (2008), *The One-Time Received Dividends Deduction* (Washington, DC: Internal Revenue Service, Statistics of Income Bulletin). Available at http://www.irs.gov/pub/irs-soi/08codivdeductbul.pdf

Schatan, Roberto. (2012), "Tax-Minimizing Strategies and the Arm's Length Principle," *Tax Notes International*, 5(January 9), 121–126.

Siu, Erika Dayle, Sol Picciotto, Jack Mintz and Akilagpa Sawyerr. (2015), "Unitary Taxation in the Extractive Industry Sector," International Centre for Tax and Development Working Paper 35.

Swenson, Deborah L. (2001), "Tax Reforms and Evidence of Transfer Pricing," *National Tax Journal*, 54(March), 7–26.

Thuronyi, Victor. (2001), "International Tax Cooperation and a Multilateral Treaty," *Brooklyn Journal of International Law*, 26(4), 1641.

United States Census Bureau. (2013), "U.S. Census Bureau News: U.S. Goods Trade: Imports & Exports by Related Parties," Available at http://www.census.gov/foreign-trade/Press-Release/2012pr/aip/related_party/rp12.pdf

Voget, Johannes. (2011), "Headquarter Relocations and International Taxation," *Journal of Public Economics*, 95(October), 1067–1081.

Weyzig, Francis. (2014), "Tax Treaty Shopping: Structural Determinants of Foreign Direct Investment Routed through the Netherlands," *International Tax and Public Finance*, 2(December), 910–937.

3 An overview of transfer pricing in extractive industries

Stephen E. Shay[1]

1 Introduction

This chapter provides an introduction to transfer pricing in extractive industries operating in resource-rich developing countries. Managing natural resource wealth is central to efforts to mobilize revenue to achieve sustainable development and prosperity in developing countries (IMF, 2011, p. 57; UN, 2000, 2002). Natural resources (fossil fuels, metals and ores) rose to 22.7% of total global merchandise trade in 2012 and they are the largest sources of government revenue for many developing countries (Boadway and Keen, 2010; WTO, 2014). Developing countries rely substantially on foreign private investment to explore for, develop and extract these resources, and transfer pricing administration and enforcement are an integral part of maintaining host government revenues from resources. Remarkably little attention has been given in leading international transfer pricing guidelines to issues or examples involving extractive industries. Only recently has attention been paid to transfer pricing involving developing countries (IMF et al, 2011; UN, 2013).

This chapter will focus on transfer pricing challenges facing a developing country that is a host for foreign investment in nonrenewable resources, such as petroleum and hard minerals. Generally, the process of exploring for and finding a deposit, developing the well or mine, removing and shipping the resource and closing the depleted site takes long time periods and involves substantial investment early in the project (Boadway and Keen, 2010). Unlike intangibles, the resources are immobile and, because there is limited supply and in some cases the resource has unique attributes, economic "rents" often can be earned from their exploitation (Gruber, 2011, pp. G-9; WTO, 2010, pp. 65–68). Much of the development of natural resources is by private investment under a long-term contractual agreement with the host government that controls the mineral resources.

The private participants in the extractive industries include the world's largest and most sophisticated multinational companies. From a transfer pricing perspective, the extractive industries present a range of challenges; some are distinctly different from and others are quite similar to the challenges presented by intangible-rich industries that are the focus of current attention by the G20,

OECD and United Nations. The final OECD BEPS report on transfer pricing adds five paragraphs to the OECD Transfer Pricing Guidelines on commodities but adds little new (OECD, 2015c, pp. 51–54).

The purpose of this chapter is to provide an overview of transfer pricing issues in a developing country extractive industry context. It identifies difficulties host country governments face in administering transfer pricing rules and considers strategies governments may adopt to constrain tax avoidance within the scope of current international tax law and practice. The primary focus of this chapter is on the legal framework and business context in which transfer pricing issues arise for host countries. This chapter does not address local issues of governance and tax administration.

There is a great deal a host country government can do in the area of transfer pricing to protect its tax base while fostering a climate for investment. The key ingredients for effective transfer pricing enforcement are political will, an effective legal regime, disciplined administration and tough but fair enforcement.

Section 2 describes what "transfer pricing" refers to in the context of taxation and why it is important. Section 3 discusses taxpayer objectives in structuring transfer pricing and host country objectives in administering and enforcing transfer pricing. Section 4 explains why the arm's length principle is used as the international standard for transfer pricing in related party transactions. Section 5 briefly describes characteristics of foreign investment in nonrenewable resources and identifies challenges from a host country taxation perspective of applying the arm's length principle to related party transactions in the extractive industries. Section 6 reviews strategies that governments may employ to combat transfer pricing noncompliance with the arm's length principle. Section 7 concludes.

2 What is transfer pricing and why is it important?

In the context of taxation, transfer pricing refers to the prices that are charged for transfers of goods, services, property or other items of value in transactions between persons that are under common control. "Common control" is a factual concept and can include persons within a family, corporations or businesses that have a common owner or owners and even unrelated persons when one person can direct the action of another person in the context of the transaction in question. The term used internationally for persons subject to transfer pricing rules is "associated persons," and transactions among associated persons that are subject to transfer pricing rules are referred to as "controlled transactions" (OECD, 2010, p. 23; UN, 2013, p. 474). In this chapter, the discussion will focus on associated persons that are companies in a multinational group or enterprise (MNE).

Why is transfer pricing an important taxation issue? In most business contexts involving unrelated persons, the pricing of a transaction is a zero-sum game on a pre-tax basis; what one side wins the other side loses. If the seller receives a higher price, the buyer loses by paying more and *vice versa*. Moreover, in a competitive market, the interplay of supply and demand provides an effective price discovery mechanism that tax systems may reasonably rely on.

Where a transaction is between related persons, or persons that, if not formally related, are under common control, there is little adversity of interest between these persons. If the parties to a transaction view their outcomes in terms of the combined result of both sides, the zero-sum nature of the pre-tax pricing decision is unimportant. If, in addition, associated companies that are parties to a transaction are taxed differently, and a price is charged so that there is a lower overall tax, together the two companies are better off. The related or associated person condition for application of transfer pricing tax rules is a proxy for the absence of adverse interests. Absent adverse interest, it is possible to shift tax burden through transfer pricing and share the benefit of a reduced combined tax.

In the context of transactions occurring solely within one country or, more relevantly, within one tax system, transfer pricing acquires significance where the parties to the transaction will be taxed differently. One company is subject to full income tax and the associated company may be operating under a tax holiday. Transfer pricing also can be important where companies are subject to exactly the same taxing rules, but one has a "tax attribute" that will result in a different tax on the transaction. A common example is when one company has a net operating loss for tax purposes that it may not be able to deduct because it does not have enough income but the other company is profitable. In each of these cases, in the absence of other considerations, there is an incentive to lower the companies' combined taxes by arranging the transfer price so that the companies together pay a lower tax.

One reaction may be despair that transfer pricing concerns must be everywhere since there often are tax disparities among associated companies, both in a purely domestic context involving one tax system as well as in cross-border contexts involving two or more tax systems. There are (at least) three reasons transfer pricing is less frequently a concern in a purely domestic context. First, tax systems tend to be internally coherent, so situations that offer great opportunities for tax advantage are fewer or are intended to provide an incentive to engage in certain behavior. Second, unintended opportunities for advantage tend to be temporary or episodic in nature and do not pose systemic tax risk to the host country. Third, where unintended systemic risks occur, it generally is possible within a single tax system for the host government to take steps to address them.

While the question whether a transfer price is "correct" arises most often with respect to transfers of value across the borders of two or more countries, the resource sector, particularly in developing countries, is an exception to this general observation. Some royalty and most resource rent taxes apply to the value of the mineral at the point of extraction – the mouth of the mine or the wellhead. To calculate the value at extraction, the income must be calculated at the point of extraction and thereby separated from the value added after that point. Another example arises when a company operates several mines in one country through nonconsolidated corporations and uses centralized services charged to each separate corporation (see Chapter 4, this volume, Calder).

The potential for tax advantage, however, is common in cross-border controlled transactions. In even the simplest two-country case it is likely that there are disparities in tax rates, and there may be tax base differences as well. Where two countries impose tax on the same transaction, the countries always have different revenue interests. Even if there is no adversity in interest among commonly controlled companies involved in the transaction, because the effective tax rate is the same in both countries involved in the transaction, the transfer pricing nonetheless is a zero-sum game as between two taxing countries. If one country has more revenue in its tax base as a result of its taxpayer receiving a higher price, the other country's tax base is reduced by the higher cost and therefore smaller taxable income of its taxpayer and *vice versa* (IRS, 2006).

Increasingly transactions and ownership of operations are structured through legal entities that do not bear a meaningful corporate tax because they are located in countries that do not tax income or facilitate very low effective tax rates on the income. These include countries that do not tax income (Bermuda, the British Virgin Islands, the Cayman Islands, the Channel Islands), that purport to tax but do not (Cyprus, Malta), that allow structures that deliberately under-tax (Ireland, Luxembourg, Mauritius, Switzerland) or that do not tax income outside the jurisdiction and either allow holidays from tax or impose low tax on domestic income (Hong Kong, Singapore). In these cases, only one country involved in the transaction may have a genuine tax

Example 1

Assume that Company A in Country X owns all of the stock of Company B in Country X and Company C in Country Y. Assume that Country X taxes income at a 30% rate and Country Y taxes income at a 20% rate. Further assume that Company B mines coal at a cost of 100 and sells the coal to Company C in Country C for 160 for a profit before tax (PBT) of 60 (freight cost is ignored). Company C, in turn, incurs 20 of selling and marketing expense and sells the coal to customers in Country C for 200, for a pre-tax profit of 20. Under this structure, Company B would pay 18 of tax to Country X (60 × 30% = 18) and Company C would pay 4 of tax to Country Y (20 × 20% = 4). See Figure 3.1.

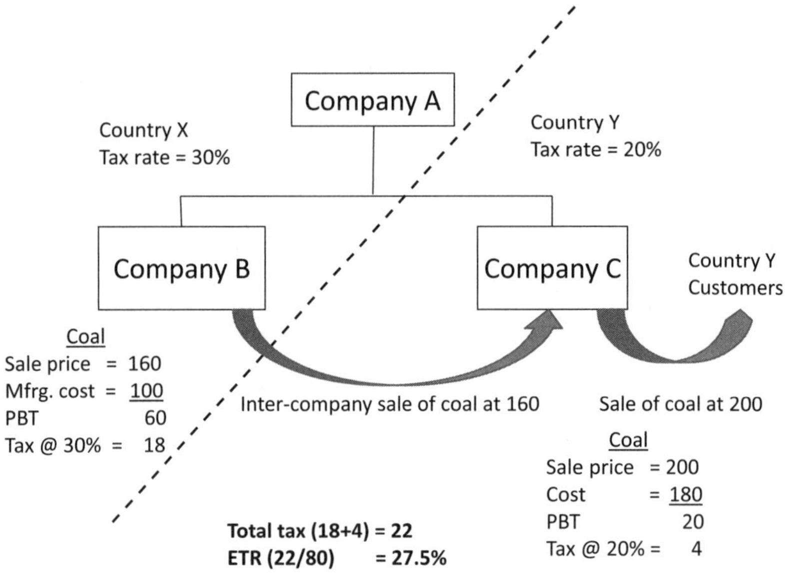

Figure 3.1 Transfer pricing between two countries – example 1

interest, so there is little or no intergovernmental dispute.[2] The benefit from income shifting in those cases goes almost exclusively to the taxpayer. This chapter will focus on contexts in which the taxpayer benefits from income shifting through transfer pricing. The potential stakes may be seen in the following examples.

From the perspective of the Company A controlled group as a whole, the total pre-tax income in Example 1 is 80 (60 earned by Company B and 20

Example 2

Assume the same facts as in Example 1, except that Company B sells coal to Company C for 140 (instead of 160). Company B will have a pre-tax income of 40 (instead of 60) and have a Country X tax of 12 (40 × 30%) instead of 18. If Company C again incurs 20 of marketing costs and sells the coal to Country Y customers for 200, Company C would have pre-tax income of 40 (instead of 20) and the Country Y tax would be 8 (40 × 20%) instead of 4. See Figure 3.2.

earned by Company C), and total taxes are 22 (18 paid by Company B and 4 paid by Company C). The Company A controlled group's overall effective tax rate, determined by dividing the group's total taxes paid (22) by the group's pre-tax income (80), is 27.5% (22/80 = 27.5%).

The disparity in tax rates between Country X (30%) and Country Y (20%) creates the opportunity and the incentive to shift profit from Country Y to Country X through changing the transfer price.

From the perspective of the Company A controlled group as a whole, the total pre-tax income in Example 2 remains 80 (40 earned by Company B and 40 earned by Company C). However, by lowering the transfer price paid by Company C to Company B from 160 to 140, total taxes are reduced to 20 in Example 2 (12 paid by Company B and 8 paid by Company C) from total taxes of 22 (in Example 1). The Company A controlled group's overall effective tax rate, determined by dividing the group's total taxes paid (20) by the group's pre-tax income (80), is 25% (20/80 = 25%) instead of 27.5%.

By decreasing the transfer price, 20 of pre-tax income is shifted from Company B to Company C and taxed at 20% instead of Company B's 30% rate. Because Company B and Company C are members of the same controlled group, they are largely indifferent as to which company earns the income, while the group as a whole pays lower overall tax (20 × 10% = 2). The after-tax return is increased from 52.5 (PBT of 80 – tax of 27.5) to 55 (PBT of 80 – tax of 25), or from 26.25% (52.5/200) to 27.5% (55/200), with a simple and non-transparent change. This example illustrates what may be thought of as "plain vanilla" transfer pricing.

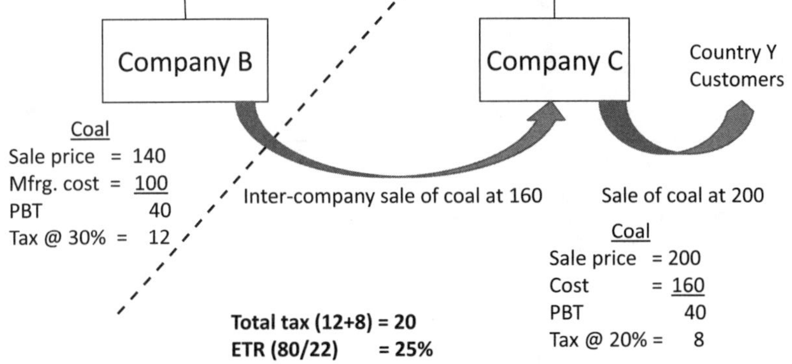

Figure 3.2 Transfer pricing between two countries – example 2

Before turning to the next example, it must be acknowledged that this example is greatly simplified to illustrate the point. Many other tax and non-tax factors can come into play and constrain what taxpayers can charge. Customs duties and covenants in loans from third-party lenders are examples, but experience demonstrates that in almost all cases these constraints can be worked around when the tax savings are material.

As observed, in the international context it is more and more common, if not customary, for a multinational business to structure intercompany transactions using a company in a third country to act as an intermediary and carry out one or more elements of the transaction. An intermediary company often is used to accomplish tax reduction objectives. A multinational can search its global portfolio of companies to find a low-taxed entity to use as an intermediary, or if the amounts involved justify the cost, it can form a new entity for the transaction or structure.

Example 3

Assume the same facts as in Example 1, except that Corporation B establishes Subsidiary D in Country Z. Country Z taxes income at a rate of 5% and has no dividend withholding tax. Assume that Country X has a dividend exemption system so that Corporation B pays no tax on earnings distributed from Subsidiary D. Now assume that Corporation B sells the coal it mines to Corporation D for 120. Corporation D incurs 10 of marketing expense and sells the coal to Corporation C for 170. Company C incurs 10 of selling expense and sells the coal to customers for 200. The same pre-tax income of 80 now is divided, 20 to Company B, 20 to Company C and 40 to Company D. See Figure 3.3. The pre-tax income and taxes paid by Corporations B, C and D and the Company A group's effective tax rate (ETR) are shown in Table 3.1.

Table 3.1 Example 3: EBT and taxes by company

Country	*Country tax rate (percent)*	*Corporation*	*Pre-tax income*	*Tax*
X	30	B	20	6
Y	20	C	20	4
Z	5	D	*40*	*2*
Total			80	12
ETR				15%

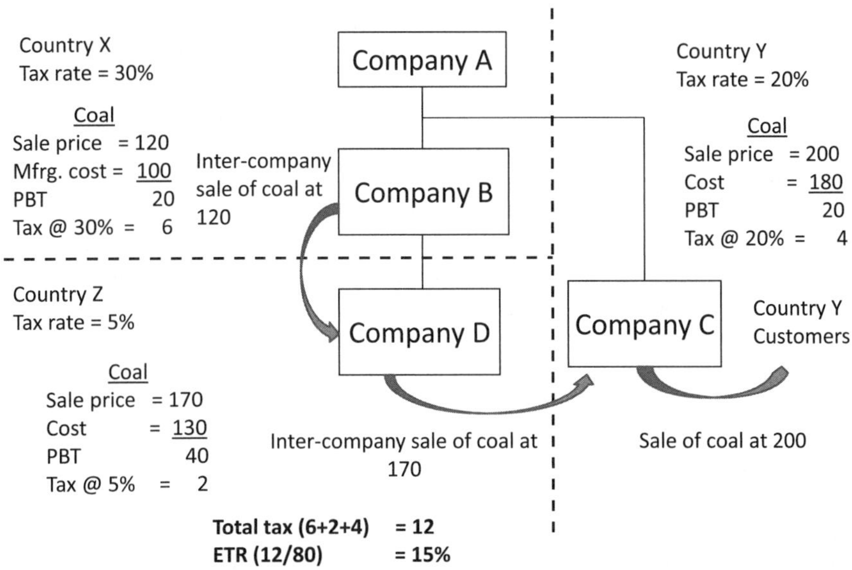

Figure 3.3 Low-tax intermediary – example 3

By adding flexibility to shift income to an even lower-tax country, the intermediary case offers greater opportunities for taxpayers and poses challenges for governments. By shifting 40 of income from Company B (taxed at 30%) to Company D taxed at 5%, 12 in tax is saved. The after-tax return is increased from 52.5 (PBT of 80 – tax of 27.5) to 68 (PBT of 80 – tax of 12), increasing the after-tax return on sales from 26.25% (52.5/200) to 34% (68/200). While not as simple and non-transparent a maneuver as in Example 2, if the Company A Group already had a Company D in Country Z carrying on other activity, the pricing structure would still be reasonably non-transparent.[3]

Starting from the base line of Example 1, these simple transfer pricing steps reduced the effective tax rate from 27.5% to 15% and increased the after-tax return on sales from 26.25% to 34%. It should be evident from these examples that transfer pricing has the potential to significantly affect government revenues. Analyzing the appropriateness of this transfer pricing requires a detailed understanding of the facts surrounding the transactions, making this planning difficult for governments to monitor. Moreover, this planning involves the largest and most sophisticated taxpayers, whose aggregate income is measured not just in millions but in billions of dollars (sometimes exceeding the GDP of the host country). The evidence of tax-motivated income shifting in the context of developed countries is strong (Clausing, 2011; Grubert, 2012). There is less available data from developing countries, but the available data and anecdotal evidence support a strong inference that the same problems arise in a developing-country context (ActionAid, 2012, 2013; Fuest and Reidel, 2010; Schatan, 2012). It is clear that transfer pricing is important to governments as a matter of revenue protection.

Another reason transfer pricing is important is that, if one taxpayer engages in non–arm's length pricing and another does not, the differences in outcomes can result in unfair disparities between taxpayers. If in Example 3 the income shifted to Corporation D is not consistent with arm's length pricing, it allows the Corporation A group to have a higher after-tax return (with an effective tax rate of 15%) that would advantage this group over another business that does not engage in non–arm's length transfer pricing.

The potential for revenue loss and disparate treatment of competing taxpayers are not the only reasons transfer pricing is important. Non–arm's length transfer pricing may distort real investment decisions as well as profit location.[4] Moreover, the cost of planning to maximize tax savings from transfer pricing is not a socially productive use of resources. These costs are reasons in addition to revenue loss that transfer pricing is an important issue. It may not always be clear whether or the extent to which the host country benefits from tax competition, though recent work suggests it may be harmful (IMF, 2014, pp. 20–21).

Permitting tax avoidance through transfer pricing likely is not a desirable way to attract investment, because the tax loss is not related to the scope of the benefit to the host country. From the perspective of the host country, preservation of tax revenue justifies attention to transfer pricing issues (Schatan, 2012).

In summary, transfer pricing is the price charged for transfers of goods, services, property or other items of value in transactions between persons that are under common control. Three reasons transfer pricing is an important issue for any tax system are:

- The potential for substantial revenue loss to governments from shifting income to countries with low or no income taxes
- The potential unfair advantages for taxpayers that engage in non–arm's length transfer pricing
- The potential for distorting the allocation of activity among countries and possible economic welfare loss

In the developing-country context, the primary focus generally is on revenue loss, but that is not the only benefit from well-managed transfer pricing administration and enforcement.

3 What are taxpayers' and governments' transfer pricing objectives?

Taxpayers organize their business operations to achieve efficient delivery of goods and services to customers and at the same time to maximize global after-tax returns. Global businesses take advantage of modern communications to carry out functions either as part of the overall corporate group or through out-sourcing according to whichever approach is most cost-efficient. It is more feasible today than in the past for a company to exercise quality control as a purchaser or customer using contractual rights and remote as well as on-site monitoring. Businesses also use multiple geographies as necessary. The ability of business to separate functions, to carry on functions that earn a higher return and to subcontract other functions, each in multiple geographies, also brings with it the ability to minimize taxes.

Taxes increasingly are viewed by MNEs like any other cost, and tax structuring is layered into and integrated with the functional analysis described in the preceding paragraph. MNEs routinely establish structures that allow them to minimize taxation in the country where activity is performed and shift income to lower-tax countries. Sometimes the tax and non-tax planning go hand in hand. Where it is possible to achieve a favorable tax result without disrupting the needs of the business, MNEs will take steps to accomplish that result. Equity analysts and the business media review an MNE's tax disclosure in its financial statement and take note of the company's effective tax rate (taking into account whether the rate is sustainable).

There are important constraints on MNE tax planning. In relation to an income tax, taxes only come after there are profits from the business. It does not make sense to spend time and resources on tax mitigation unless the potential tax savings will exceed the direct and indirect costs of the planning. The indirect costs can be substantial if tax-related planning adds complexity to business operations (e.g., through frequent pricing adjustments) or uses valuable management time (such as requiring executives to attend board meetings in remote locations to satisfy "substance" requirements).[5] If the tax savings are substantial enough, however, a company will take the actions necessary to support the tax position.

Transfer pricing is an integral part of an MNE's overall tax planning. Many countries require documentation of material transfer pricing positions, and in some there are penalties for failure to produce the documentation (OECD, 2012, p. 20). Transfer pricing is an important item reported in financial statement tax reserves, and financial statement auditors reviewing a company's tax reserve generally will review material transfer pricing exposures (IRS, 2015). An MNE generally seeks to avoid adjustments that increase its tax liability, but a publicly traded MNE also focuses on avoiding a tax adjustment that is not reserved against in financial statements and would result in a reduction in reported earnings. Accordingly, for corporate taxpayers there may be a helpful tension between seeking to reduce taxes through transfer pricing and seeking to avoid adjustments to financial statement earnings. This tension depends in part on a host country having the legal and practical ability to bring a transfer pricing adjustment with some likelihood of success. The capacity to administer transfer pricing rules and litigate, if necessary, adjustments to a successful conclusion is lacking in some, if not many, developing countries (IMF et al., 2011, p. 34).

The objectives of a government in applying transfer pricing rules principally are (i) to promote neutral tax treatment of controlled and uncontrolled transactions, (ii) to collect its fair share of revenue from national economic activity and resources and (iii) by following international transfer pricing standards, reasonably interpreted and applied, to signal to foreign investors a general intent to avoid international double taxation of the same income and to adhere to recognized standards in relation to taxation issues. Each of these objectives bears elaboration.

A fundamental objective of transfer pricing is to promote efficient economic decision making in the context of applying an income tax. Absent special circumstances, neutrality in taxation of domestic and cross-border businesses operating in the same country and industry should be welfare enhancing. It is good tax policy to minimize systemic tax advantages and disadvantages for businesses that compete, whether directly or indirectly, for economic resources within the same economy. As discussed, efficiency concerns may not carry the same policy weight in the context of a developing country's taxation of extractive industries. The resource sector in developing countries generally involves limited competition between inbound foreign direct investment and domestic industry, though important exceptions apply in relation to artisanal mining and similar local industry.

In addition to the more abstract efficiency and fairness reasons to identify a "neutrality" objective, a perhaps more important reason is to preserve public support for the tax system as a whole. Neutral treatment of controlled and uncontrolled transactions is necessary so that multinational business is not perceived to have a tax advantage over domestic business. If multinational business is allowed a systemic advantage as a result of the country's tax treatment of transfer pricing, there are multiple sources of risk to the tax system. One is that public outrage pushes for political solutions that are superficially appealing but are ineffective or counterproductive over the longer term.[6] A second risk is that public cynicism sets in or is increased, such that the public will to comply with the tax law generally is eroded. Every tax system relies on public trust. There is a very high cost from losing the public's confidence in a tax system's fairness, including the cost and difficulty of restoring trust that has been lost.

A second objective is to further the primary purpose of a tax system, which is to collect the revenue authorized by law to fund public goods and services. One risk to tax revenue is the inappropriate allocation by a taxpayer of income to another fully taxing country. In this case, the taxpayer may be indifferent regarding the allocation of the income; the two countries should where possible try to agree on a consistent allocation of the income. This generally requires legal authorization under an international agreement between the two countries, alternatives for which are discussed later in the chapter. Increasingly, though, income is allocated to a low- or untaxed intermediary company in an intermediary country that makes no effective claim to tax the income. In this case, the risk is effective double non-taxation, and the principal beneficiary of the transfer pricing is the taxpayer not the other country. Because these cases typically involve taxpayer planning, they involve the greatest potential risk exposure and come up often in the context of cross-border extractive industry tax planning.

The third objective, to reasonably apply international transfer pricing standards, has as one important purpose signaling to potential foreign investment that reasonable transfer pricing will be respected. This does not imply renouncing responsibility to closely scrutinize controlled transactions under applicable law. It does imply being able to justify adjustments under a reasonable interpretation of international standards and trying to mitigate actual international double taxation (amounts paid to two countries on the same income). As discussed later in the chapter, reliability in taxation is particularly important to investors in the development phase of mineral extraction because of the long-term nature of the investment.

There is a natural tension among the government's objectives between administering the tax law according to its purpose to collect revenue and the important objective for most developing countries of fostering a favorable climate for investment (the latter may be better addressed through tax design and non-tax measures). The tensions between the interests and objectives of governments and investing businesses are clearer in relation to, respectively, obtaining tax revenue and mitigating tax liability. In both cases, the disparate objectives should be reconciled by principled and even-handed application of the law and not with special arrangements or other non-transparent mechanisms that provide opportunity for rent-seeking payments and corrode public trust.

4 Why is the arm's length principle the internationally agreed standard for transfer pricing?

The arm's length principle is described in the OECD Transfer Pricing Guidelines by reference to the operative language of paragraph 1 of Article 9 of the OECD Model Tax Convention, which provides in part as follows:

> [Where] conditions are made or imposed between the two enterprises in their commercial or financial relations that differ from those that would be made between independent enterprises, then any profits that, but for those conditions, would have accrued to one of the enterprises, but by reason of those conditions have not so accrued, may be included in the profits of that enterprise and taxed accordingly.
>
> (OECD, 2010, ¶1.6)

The Guidelines go on to provide:

> By seeking to adjust profits by reference to the conditions which would have obtained between independent enterprises in comparable transactions and comparable circumstances (*i.e.* in "comparable uncontrolled transactions"), the arm's length principle follows the approach of treating the members of an MNE group as operating as separate entities rather than as inseparable parts of a single unified business.
>
> (OECD, 2010, ¶1.6)

The arm's length principle also is known as the separate accounting method or separate transactions method, since it treats commonly controlled entities as separate and evaluates the transactions between the members of the group. The base line reference point for transfer pricing is what an independent enterprise would have charged *in comparable transactions and comparable circumstances*. What does this mean?

If the touchstone of the arm's length method is comparability with an arm's length transaction, how does a tax authority or a taxpayer identify a comparable transaction when for the transaction in question the taxpayer decided to contract with a related instead of an unrelated person? And what is to be done if there is no unique price that would be reached by independent parties (e.g., because of different bilateral negotiating power)? Under what "comparable circumstances" would there be a "comparable transaction' with an unrelated person?

The paradigmatic comparable transaction is found when the same taxpayer is selling the same property to an unrelated person as to the related person in the same market (under the same terms of sale). This is not a frequent circumstance.[7] Sales of commodity-type fungible goods may provide a market yardstick against which to measure a related party sale. However, even in those cases marginal under valuations can have a material impact in large-volume or large-value transactions. The difficulty inherent in the arm's length principle is applying it in practice (Schatan, 2012, p. 126). Determining an arm's length price requires knowing the specific facts of the transaction and understanding the market in which the transaction occurs. The transaction-based and profit-based methods set out in guidelines are described in what follows, but in all but the simplest cases arm's length pricing involves market knowledge and reasoned judgment.

The principal alternative to the separate accounting approach is to take the profit of a business conducted in multiple jurisdictions and allocate it among the jurisdictions in which the business is conducted according to a formula that uses proxy measures intended to identify where the income is earned or which jurisdiction should have the claim to tax profit. Although formulary apportionment methods have not been used at the national jurisdiction level, many states of the United States have employed formula apportionment methods. In addition, formulas are used to apportion income among Canadian provinces and Swiss cantons and the EU Commission has proposed a common corporate consolidated tax base (CCCTB) allowing use of formulary allocation of income to member countries (EU Commission, 2011; Hellerstein, 2012, p. 223). The typical factors are property, payroll and sales, but experience shows that jurisdictions adjust these factors to take account of their own circumstances for their own advantage. There has been a robust debate over many years about the relative advantages and disadvantages of formula apportionment in relation to separate accounting arm's length pricing as a method for allocating international income, but it so far has not been adopted as an international standard.

Why is arm's length the international standard? The answer is found partly in the objective that transfer pricing regulation is trying to achieve and partly in history and path dependency. The more powerful reason is the primary objective of the transfer pricing rules: to achieve broad parity of treatment for associated enterprises and independent parties. In other words, transfer pricing rules should be aimed at achieving tax neutrality in the decision whether to engage in a controlled transaction or an uncontrolled transaction (Grubert, 2005, p. 149; OECD, 2010, ¶1.08). Ideally, the optimal after-tax decision regarding choice of a controlled versus an uncontrolled transaction is the same as the pre-tax decision. Similarly, the choice of how to conduct and where to locate economic activity should be unaffected by considerations of transfer pricing.

There is substantial indirect evidence that this objective is not always met in developed as well as in developing countries. The indirect evidence comes in the form of aggregate data showing foreign margins increasing in inverse relation to the foreign tax rate and disproportionate income in low-tax countries (Clausing, 2011; Grubert, 2012). In public hearings, some prompted by media reports, indirect anecdotal evidence of income shifting by individual companies has been brought into public view (U.S. Senate [PSI], 2012, 2013; UK House of Commons [Public Accounts], 2012). In addition, activist groups and media have highlighted cases of individual companies in developing countries using transfer pricing along with other tax planning techniques to shift income from developing countries to havens or low-taxing countries (ActionAid 2012, 2013; Bergin, 2012a; Schatan, 2012).

In light of this accumulating evidence, why would countries continue to follow the arm's length principle in transfer pricing, particularly if income is lost to havens and low-tax intermediary countries? One question is whether formulary apportionment would be better, particularly for developing countries with natural resources. When the usual apportionment factors of property, payroll and sales are considered, it is not likely that resource-rich developing countries would fare well. Payroll typically is low. Most sales are to foreign buyers, and these sales may or may not be shifted outside of the country. Finally, the extractive industry companies generally do not own the mineral property but operate by concession, so the property factor likely would be modest. Moreover, even if the resource property investment were taken into account, property values do not reflect the discovery value of the minerals. An investment at cost understates the value of a successful find and development. There is substantial reason to think formulary apportionment would not be in the interests of a developing country with an important extractive industry sector.[8]

Another powerful reason not to move to formulary apportionment is simply the fact that the international tax regime has achieved a remarkable consensus around the arm's length principle, and it is extremely unlikely that a comparable level of consistency could be achieved in relation to any form of apportionment in a reasonably near time frame (Fleming, Peroni and S. Shay, 2014, p. 9). Consistency is a key, since inconsistent income allocations can result in double non-taxation, which results in windfall gains for affected taxpayers and revenue loss to governments that has to be made up with higher taxes on other taxpayers and double taxation, which discourages investment (OECD, 2015c).

There are ways in which the stress on transfer pricing can be reduced, and there are opportunities to improve enforcement through constructive engagement with investing companies. A range of potentially effective unilateral as well as multilateral strategies may be employed by governments to respond to transfer pricing challenges that are consistent with the arm's length principle. The starting point is risk assessment, structural responses and thoughtful choice of cases for enforcement. A taxpayer's incentive to engage in income shifting is related to the costs to structure, implement and defend the arrangements, so there has to be enough benefit from aggressive planning to justify the direct and indirect costs. Tax law changes can materially affect taxpayer incentives. Enforcement matters, though governments with scarce enforcement resources must target enforcement where the payoff is highest. Possible host government responses to address transfer pricing are discussed in Section 6.

5 How is the arm's length principle applied?

5.1 The OECD guidelines and UN manual approaches

The OECD Transfer Pricing Guidelines and the United Nations Practical Manual on Transfer Pricing each set out generally accepted methods for determining a transfer price that may be appropriate in circumstances in which relevant comparable uncontrolled pricing information is available to allow the method to be applied in a way that is likely to yield a reliable arm's length price. The UN Manual acknowledges that

> in reality two transactions are seldom completely alike and in this imperfect world, perfect comparables are often not available. . . . To be comparable . . . means that either none of the differences between them could materially affect the arm's length price or profit or, where such material differences exist, that reasonably accurate adjustments can be made to eliminate their effect.
>
> (UN, 2013, ¶5.1.5)

This captures the practical reality and difficulty of transfer pricing.

The UN Manual describes arriving at an arm's length price as involving a process that includes determining the "economically significant characteristics of the industry, taxpayer's business and controlled transactions," identifying comparable transactions and making comparability adjustments as necessary and applying the most appropriate transfer pricing method to determine an arm's length price or profit (or range of prices or profits; UN, 2013, ¶5.2). The following discussion follows the UN Manual terminology and structure, which does not differ in any material respect from that of the OECD Transfer Pricing Guidelines. The five major transfer pricing methods are broken into two groups of methods, three so-called "transaction-based methods" and two profit-based methods."The UN Manual describes the transaction-based methods as follows:

> *Transaction-based methods*
>
> **1.5.4.** *Comparable Uncontrolled Price (CUP)* The CUP Method compares the price charged for a property or service transferred in a controlled transaction to the price charged for a comparable property or service transferred in a comparable uncontrolled transaction in comparable circumstances.
>
> **1.5.5.** *Resale Price Method (RPM)* The Resale Price Method is used to determine the price to be paid by a reseller for a product purchased from an associated enterprise and resold to an independent enterprise. The purchase price is set so that the margin earned by the reseller is sufficient to allow it to cover its selling and operating expenses and make an appropriate profit.
>
> **1.5.6.** *Cost Plus (C + or CP)* The Cost Plus Method is used to determine the appropriate price to be charged by a supplier of property or services to a related purchaser. The price is determined by adding to costs incurred by the supplier an appropriate gross margin so that the supplier will make an appropriate profit in the light of market conditions and functions performed.
>
> (UN, 2013, ¶¶1.5.4–1.5.6)

In these transaction-based methods, a search must be made for a relevant comparable transaction, comparable resale price margin or comparable gross margin on costs, respectively, to reach operating profit. The transaction-based methods may be a reliable indicator of a market price where a comparable transaction may be identified; however, as observed in the UN Manual quote above, a comparable transaction often is unavailable or requires too many adjustments to be considered reliable. If transaction-based methods are not appropriate for the tested transaction or relevant comparable transactions are not available or are not reliable, then another alternative is to use "profit based-methods," which are broken into profit-comparison methods and profit-split methods.

The profit comparison methods are called the "transactional net margin method" (TNMM) in the OECD Guidelines and the UN Manual and, alternatively, in some countries such as the United States, the comparable profits method (CPM). (As a practical matter, these methods are interchangeable.) The profit comparison methods involve finding businesses that are functionally similar to the business whose related party transactions are being tested but whose operating margins are not affected by related party transactions (and may be found in the public record). The comparable businesses' margins are used as the basis to identify a profit-level indicator metric (such as an operating return on invested capital) that is applied to the relevant part of the tested business to determine an arm's length return. The profit split methods similarly look to unrelated businesses for an allocation key that may be used to test the division of profits in the related party case.

The profit-based methods are described in the UN Manual as follows:

> *Profit-based methods*
>
> **1.5.8.** *Profit comparison methods (TNMM/CPM)* These methods seek to determine the level of profits that would have resulted from controlled transactions by reference to the return realised by the comparable independent enterprise. The TNNM determines the net profit margin relative to an appropriate base realised from the controlled transactions by reference to the net profit margin relative to the same appropriate base realised from uncontrolled transactions.
>
> **1.5.9.** *Profit-split methods* Profit-split methods take the combined profits earned by two related parties from one or a series of transactions and then divide those profits using an economically valid defined basis that aims at replicating the division of profits that would have been anticipated in an agreement made at arm's length. Arm's length pricing is therefore derived for both parties by working back from profit to price.
>
> (UN, 2013, ¶¶1.5.8–1.5.9)

The metrics for dividing profits, particularly under the profit split method, places these methods somewhere between transaction-based methods and a formulary apportionment approach. One key distinction is the extent to which an attempt is made to tie back to market-based benchmarks in developing a profit-level indicator or allocation key. The comparable profit benchmarks usually are obtained from searches of databases and yield a range of profits. M. Durst (2010) observes that multinational businesses that distribute products, provide services to affiliates or manufacture in developing countries or some combination of those activities "overwhelmingly use 'profit-based' pricing methods."[9] Another key distinction is that formulary apportionment allocates the net income of an enterprise or line of business, whereas the arm's length methods determine the price for a transaction or grouping of similar transactions.

Modern transfer pricing rules accept that in many if not most cases there is not a single arms' length price for a transaction but that prices within a range of prices may be accepted as arms' length (UN, 2013, Ch. 6). This recognizes the inexact nature of the transfer pricing exercise and forestalls minor adjustments. But even allowance of a range of outcomes does not surmount fundamental difficulties in applying the arms' length standard in the absence of a market comparable (Auerbach, Devereux and Simpson, 2010; Benshalom, 2013). There are numerous circumstances in which an action would be taken between related parties that would not between unrelated parties; the arm's length standard still must be applied, but it cannot be by reference solely to an inapposite comparison with a transaction that occurs between unrelated parties. Instead, it is necessary to ask what rational economic actors would do in the circumstances (OECD, 2015c).

In addition to conceptual difficulties, the fundamental differences between the information available to the taxpayer and that available to the government make enforcement that achieves realistic outcomes extremely difficult (Shay, 2009, pp. 327–330). This provides particular advantage to taxpayers that use a "one-sided method," that is, a method that only looks to the results of one of the related parties to the transaction. (The transfer pricing methods identified other than the profit-split method only analyze one side of a related party transaction.) A one-sided approach can hide outcomes that if made fully transparent would be subject to question. Use of a "two-sided" profit split method, whether as a primary method or as a test of the results of another method, protects against outlier outcomes in the related counterparty. Nonetheless, taxpayers resist disclosing information about the party outside of the jurisdiction and providing information to determine the "see through" profit for a line of business. In the author's experience, this information often is critical to fairly evaluate the allocation of income.

Fee charges for management and other "high-value" services are an ongoing and material risk exposure for developing countries. At the other end of the risk spectrum are charges for sharing of routine or ministerial services. Some countries have cost-based transfer pricing methods for routine services. The OECD observes that there are cases of low-hanging fruit for transfer pricing enforcement: "if a company is paying for goods and services (such as Head Office costs) when it has not received any real value, the cost may be disallowable on first principles" (OECD, 2012, p. 69). Even in relation to cost-based services, when a pool of costs is charged out, it is important to confirm that the costs have actually been incurred and that the allocation key is reasonable and appropriate (Schatan, 2012).

This chapter will not further discuss the specific methods recommended for determining an arm's length price in relation to the various categories of income from sales of tangible goods, performance of services, transfers of intangibles and so on and how to determine comparability of uncontrolled transactions and data for profit based methods. These are extensively, indeed exhaustively, described in the OECD Guidelines and the UN Manual (OECD, 2010, 2015c; UN, 2013).

While familiarity with transfer pricing methods and comparability guidelines published by the OECD and the United Nations provides a framework for consideration of transfer pricing in general terms, these documents are not directed at extractive industry transfer pricing and are of limited help in identifying risk exposures in extractive industries. The OECD Global Forum on Transfer Pricing recently published a draft *Handbook on Transfer Pricing Risk Assessment*. This is a promising tool for risk assessment; however, it also does not address extractive industry issues except in passing. The sole reference to extractive industries is in paragraph 38, which gives this example of a recurring transaction risk exposure: "For example, if a local taxpayer in one of the extraction industries sells all of its local country output to related entities, small pricing discrepancies in each individual sale can add up to large reductions in the local tax base" (OECD, 2013c, p. 38). This provides an appropriate segue to the discussion of extractive industry transfer pricing challenges.

5.2 Extractive industry transfer pricing challenges: determining the sales price

In many cases, a developing country with an important extractive industry will rely on the revenues from the extractive industry for a material portion of its government revenues. In a review of 57 resource-rich countries, oil and gas revenues in 22 petroleum-producing countries surveyed by the IMF rose to a weighted average of 35% of government revenues in 2010. Revenues from mining were more volatile, but in the period 2006 to 2010 ranged from 10% to over 25% of government revenues (IMF, 2012, p. 62).

Oil and gas and mining share some important characteristics and differ in others. Both industries require substantial up-front capital investment that is not easily recoverable until sustainable production is achieved. There is substantial risk of market price variability, and cost recovery extends over long periods. Individual projects will have a finite life. Generally, exploration is riskier in oil and gas, but development of the resource and exploitation is riskier in mining (IMF, 2012, pp. 8–10).

Natural resource exploration and development typically are governed by a concession agreement that governs the obligations of the company or consortium undertaking exploration and development and the host government (CCSI, 2015). Most such agreements include provisions that attempt to freeze the law governing taxation of income from the project for the life of the project (so-called stabilization clauses) and the dispute resolution clause may or may not pre-empt the usual host country process for resolving tax claims. The agreements' royalty and tax provisions normally refer to fair market value for selling prices but typically do not address or otherwise limit application of normal transfer pricing rules in the determination of selling price for income tax or royalty purposes.

It is common under a mining or petroleum concession for a company exploiting mineral resources (particularly after the exploration stage) to be a multinational enterprise with substantial production and marketing skills and a broad geographic footprint (IMF, 2012, p. 8). In many, if not most, such cases, the initial sale of the mineral is to a related party. In cases in which the affiliate buyer is engaged in further processing or other substantive activity in relation to the mineral, as opposed to serving as a conduit selling immediately to an unrelated buyer, these inter-affiliate sales present important transfer pricing risks and challenges.[10]

The following discussion considers what would appear to be a simple question, how to determine the arm's length sales price of a controlled sale of a mineral. For purposes of this discussion, the mineral will be iron ore.

It is customary in a mineral-development arrangement for the host country to charge a royalty on the sale of the mineral at the port of shipment as well as impose income tax on the profit of the producing company (IMF, 2012, pp. 30–33).[11] The sales price will affect, possibly materially, the royalty charged on gross sales of the mineral, which is received by the host country once the mineral is first shipped, as well as the gross income for determining the corporate income tax, which is realized by the host country after the mining company's income exceeds its period costs and, in some countries an additional profit or "resource rent tax."[12] Over the life of a mining project, no single issue is more important for determining the host country revenue from the project than the price at which the mineral is sold.[13]

To the uninitiated, there may be a view that determining the sales price for a mineral is straightforward and does not pose meaningful transfer pricing risk. Are there not published indices? Unfortunately, the issue is not so simple, and the circumstances can differ materially according to the mineral in question. Where the sales price is intended to compensate the producer solely for production and not for manufacturing into ingot, pricing for income tax purposes usually is at the port of shipment for minerals (see Chapter 4 by Calder, this volume). Determining the sales price for minerals, such as iron ore sold "FOB port," can have practical complications, as discussed in what follows.

Each shipment of iron ore has differences in quality. Iron ore has impurities, including silica and alumina, which affect the efficiency of a blast furnace in processing the ore. The silica and alumina content can vary for ore from the same mine, depending on where in the mine the ore is taken, as well as for ore from different mines. In addition to impurities, the moisture content of the ore affects the freight and processing. If the moisture content is too great, the ore simply cannot be shipped by ocean vessel because of the danger of moisture affecting the stability of the ship in certain conditions. Insurers will not insure cargos outside certain parameters for moisture (Chapter 4 by Calder, this volume).

The explosive growth of Chinese steel manufacturing changed the dynamics of the iron ore industry and has affected the pricing mechanism for iron ore. Pricing has moved from changes made once a year to pricing for each shipment, generally at an average of market prices for a recent period such as a month. Since 2010, industry indices, such as Platts IODEX, have provided daily China cost and freight (CFR) prices,[14] which means that FOB port prices used for royalties and income tax payments to a producing country must be net back from the index CFR China prices.[15] The Platts index is constructed from a survey of prices paid by purchasers in the relevant market for ore within its specifications (Platts, 2015). It is common to use the Platts iron ore index price for the iron ore grade closest in iron (Fe) content to what the mine produces and adjust from that price for each shipment. Key variables in arriving at an arm's length FOB port price for an iron ore shipment in a controlled transaction include:

- Which Platts iron ore grade (i.e., 62% Fe, 58% Fe, 52% Fe, etc.) will be used as the base from which to adjust for Fe content? Each grade has prescribed tolerances for silica and alumina, though the actual tolerances accommodated by producers may vary.
- Will the Fe content adjustment be based on straight-line between prices for surrounding grades or take account of the increasing value of higher Fe content?

- What will be the basis for adjusting from the index for impurities that exceed the tolerances for the grade used as the measuring point?
- Will freight be based on actual freight or, if the taxpayer has available a portfolio of ships, be based on an index to avoid risk of adverse ship selection?
- If the taxpayer sells ore shipments to different steel producers, should the CFR priced be reduced for a marketing allowance to the intermediary entity?[16]
- If the mine is a new mine, should a trial allowance discount be allowed to encourage different steel producers to use the ore in their furnaces?

As is evident from the technical nature of the issues described and further taking account of the fact that iron ore pricing methodologies are in a period of flux, a host country should work with an industry expert to establish a method for determining an arm's length FOB port price for iron ore from a major concession. An MNE's knowledge of its industry and its own business poses a challenge for a tax authority in relation to any industry, but this is especially true for extractive industry issues. It is a powerful illustration of the breadth of the so-called "information asymmetry" advantage that MNEs have in transfer pricing generally.[17]

From a transfer pricing perspective, the iron ore case is an example of using a comparable uncontrolled price, based on an index, and making adjustments to reach an "arm's length price" or fair market value. Concerns for the host government's administration of transfer pricing that may be identified to this point are (i) the potential for disparity in technical knowledge of the industry and market between a global multinational in a specialized industry and the host government and (ii) the host government's need for information regarding the multinational's operations relevant to the mining business. Even limiting consideration to the sale price of the property, it would be valuable for the host government to have a "see through" profit analysis of the iron ore business and test a derived comparable price by seeing the resulting profit split from the business with all of the relevant affiliates. This would be using a "two-sided" method to test the results under a one-sided transactional method. Finally, it seems very unlikely, even acknowledging potential weaknesses in using the Platts index as a starting benchmark price, that a host country would be better off on almost any basis applying a formula apportionment regime to this or indeed to most any other mineral extraction case.

While the pricing of the extracted product is the most significant potential transfer pricing issue, even if a host country is successful in achieving an arm's length price for the physical product, there are numerous other ways that an MNE can reduce its effective rate of tax in the host country that also have transfer pricing elements. The next subsection considers other, systemic transfer pricing challenges that a host country for an extractive industry investment must face. These challenges are common across a range of industries engaged in substantial foreign direct investment in host countries, including non-extractive industries such as telecommunications.

5.3 Extractive industry transfer pricing challenges: a host country tax minimization example

Once the sales income of the in-country producing company is determined, the objective of an MNE will be to achieve the lowest practical global tax rate taking account of the transactions cost of engaging in tax planning. Another element in a transfer pricing review should be to assess whether the MNE investment in its plant and equipment includes material controlled purchases that should be assessed. Use of "purchasing company" markups is a common way to shift profits, but it will not be discussed further here (Tuerff et al., 2011). Other standard income shifting techniques that are routinely used to reduce the effective tax rate of a producing company include (i) holding the company through a favorable low-tax country, such as the Netherlands, Mauritius or some other location, (ii) capitalizing the producing company with intercompany debt, (iii) charging management and other service fees to the producing company and, in some cases, (iv) charging the producing company with a royalty for use of technology, know-how, a trademark or trade name, as the case may be.[18]

The offshore holding company or another offshore affiliate often will fund the producing company with material amounts of intercompany debt, which (subject to third-party loan covenants) permits repayments of principal, which are not subject to the restrictions on dividends (such as a requirement that the company have current or retained earnings or surplus). In addition, interest on the intercompany debt generally is deductible, sometimes even when accrued but not paid with cash (but by issuing additional debt or increasing the principal amount of the debt).[19] Often the offshore holding company (or another affiliate) also will charge a producing company a management services fee. While in some cases this is passing through allocated costs of a central or regional headquarters, the fees also may be marked up with a profit margin. As noted, using intangibles to strip profits also is an additional strategy. These strategies are illustrated with respect to interest and management fees in Example 4.

Example 4

Assume that an iron ore producer's parent company is Company A organized in Country W. It wholly owns an offshore holding company, Company B, organized in Country X, a low-tax jurisdiction. Company B owns all of the stock of the iron ore producer, Company C, in Country Y where the mine is located. The mine is the largest source of potential mineral revenues in Country Y. Company C sells most of its output to steel producers in Asia or Europe. On each continent, Company C may sell ore to a local distribution company, Company D in Country Z, wholly owned by Company B, to Company B for on-sale to customers or directly to customers. Company B reduces Company C's Country Y tax through charges for interest on intercompany debt and management fees. See Figure 3.4.

Assume that Company C has 500 of sales income and 100 of income before taxes, interest and fees. If the Country Y tax rate is 30%, Company C will pay 30 in tax to Country Y. If Company B makes an intercompany loan to Company C of 100 at 13% interest and charges Company C a management fee of 20, Company C's Country Y income before tax will be 67 and its Country Y tax will be 20 instead of 30. Assuming no Country Y withholding taxes by reason of treaties or a concession agreement and a Country X tax rate of 10%, the Group's Country X tax will increase by approximately 3 for a net tax reduction of 7. The Group's effective tax rate on the mining income is thereby decreased from 30% to 23%.

Several pricing issues are raised by charging service costs: were the costs actually incurred, do the allocated costs benefit the producing company's business such that they should be allowable as a deduction by the host country, are the costs allocated under a reasonable methodology consistently applied to all similarly situated affiliates over relevant years and is the profit markup (if any) arm's length? With respect to interest, the questions include: Is the amount of debt and the interest charged on the debt arm's length in amount (OECD, 2015d)? Issues similar to those for service fees and royalties also apply to royalties (Schatan, 2012). These issues are susceptible to audit, but it also is possible

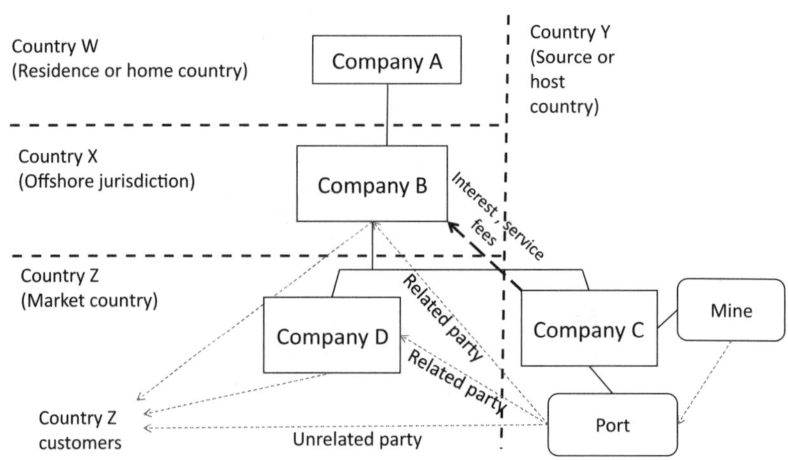

Figure 3.4 Host country tax minimization – example 4

to consider tax law changes that would reduce the potential benefits from this kind of intermediary tax planning. In this respect, tax system design, within a corporate income tax, can affect incentives to engage in transfer pricing as a tax avoidance strategy.

This leads to the question, what strategies are there for governments to follow to address transfer pricing exposures and the base erosion strategies described in Example 4?

6 How government strategies respond to transfer pricing challenges

6.1 Have a strategy

Is the situation with transfer pricing hopeless? Of course it is not. Like any other tax issue, transfer pricing compliance improves when rules are reasonably clear, incentives for aggressive transfer pricing are reduced and enforcement is focused, tough and fair. This section discusses several elements that should be included as part of an overall strategy to achieve the objectives described: protection of the host country's tax base against profit shifting to offshore havens, reasonable application of international standards to avoid double non-taxation and double taxation of income and neutral treatment of controlled and uncontrolled transactions (so transfer pricing does not *advantage* MNEs).

6.2 Limit benefits from transfer pricing

As discussed, the incentives for transfer pricing are related to the extent to which taxes may be reduced. Under current international rules, it is difficult for a host country acting alone to affect the taxation of income earned from sales of minerals to persons outside the jurisdiction. While it is possible in theory to adjust the overall corporate tax rate, because of the revenue cost it is not practically possible to match the zero or very low rates of havens or low-tax countries. A host country can, however, scrutinize the transfer price. It can require the taxpayer to provide see-through profit information and test the price against the reasonableness of the resulting profit split among relevant affiliates in relation to the actual activity carried on by those affiliates. This should be made easier by adoption of country-by-country reporting called for by the OECD's BEPS project (OECD, 2015e).

In the case of deductible payments or payments that may potentially be subject to withholding tax, however, many countries do limit the advantages of income stripping through imposition of a withholding tax on royalties, management and other service fees and/or by limiting deductions in relation to such payments as well as interest. It is important that these protections not be given up in concession agreements or income tax treaty provisions without obtaining equally meaningful economic benefits in exchange. A country should be able to protect its source tax base by measures that may include imposing withholding tax on and/or restricting deductions for deductible payments of income paid to or treated as beneficially owned by related foreign persons in countries that do not "effectively tax" the income. In addition to applying to hybrid mismatch arrangements, such a rule also should apply with respect to income paid to an intermediary entity where the income is subject to a low effective tax rate in relation to the source country's tax on the payor company. The rate of tax on the recipient to apply for this purpose would be determined in relation to the level of tax that otherwise would apply in the source country (Fleming, Peroni and S. Shay, 2015; Lodin, 2013; OECD, 2015a).

In many cases, an intermediary company is not located in a treaty jurisdiction or, as in the case of a nonresident Irish company, is not eligible for treaty benefits. Where the intermediary is resident in a treaty country and is eligible for treaty benefits, however, the issue may arise whether in the particular circumstances the nondiscrimination limitation of Article 24(4) of the OECD and UN Model treaties would apply. In general, it appears that the OECD takes the view that nondiscrimination does not prevent application of properly designed anti-tax arbitrage rules (Fleming et al, 2015, pp. 704–709; OECD, 2015a, pp. 148–149). It is fundamental to a coherent international tax system that the discrimination principle be applied in a way that allows a country reasonably to protect its tax base (Graetz and Warren, 2006).

If the income of an intermediary company is taxed by a third country under a CFC regime, there is a risk that income would be taxed by both the host country and by the ultimate residence country in the same year. The OECD proposes that in a hybrid instrument case where a deductible payment is not included in income (D/NI), the primary response should be for the source country to deny the deduction. If the host country and the ultimate residence country in relation to an intermediary are parties to a bilateral income tax treaty, they could agree on a bilateral approach.

The objective of these changes would be to restrict the incentive to engage in the kind of planning and pricing issues that are raised in Example 4. A host government will need to evaluate the advantage of adopting provisions that protect its tax base in relation to a range of considerations that include investor perceptions. Moreover, even if base erosion provisions are added to a host country's law, depending on how stabilization provisions in mineral concession agreements are drafted, in some cases the base erosion law changes may apply only to new concessions. In any event, the G20 and OECD attention to the base erosion issue is extremely helpful in validating the legitimacy of host country concerns and responses.

6.3 Transfer pricing legislation and regulations

A threshold question for many developing countries is whether they need transfer pricing legislation. In order to address transfer pricing abuses, it is necessary for host country tax authorities to have authority in their domestic law to make adjustments to income or deductions in controlled transactions. Most countries, however, do have provisions that grant substantial authority to the tax authorities to adjust a taxpayer's income and deductions in transactions with associated persons (Tanzania, 2006). The question posed is more often a question whether *in addition* to broad statutory authority it is necessary to have *more detailed* legislation or regulations. Almost by definition, it is not "necessary" unless there is a specific reason to do so.[20] In this regard, it is useful to distinguish between adoption of elaborate transfer pricing regulations and guidance that either address a specific industry context or is important for the tax authority to be able to administer and enforce arm's length transfer pricing (Chapter 4 by Calder, this volume).

Whether to favor elaboration of detailed transfer pricing rules depends on the context. If a tax authority is willing to use broad statutory discretion, perhaps supported by guidance on principles, the courts (or an arbitrator) will support reasonable exercise of that discretion, taxpayers are deterred by the prospect of exercise of the authority and investors do not have reason to lose confidence in the reasonable exercise of the authority, little more may be needed. The United States and the OECD have promulgated mind-numbingly detailed rules hundreds of pages in length in the form of regulations (in the case of the United States) and guidelines in the case of the OECD (OECD, 2010; UN, 2013). The evidence from the United States is that highly detailed regulations have not staunched a virtual flood of profit shifting. More limited data available for other OECD countries is not inconsistent.

A possible reason to elaborate transfer pricing rules is to counter the possible effect of another country's adopting more specific rules (and presumably stronger enforcement), such that there is concern that taxpayers perceive the path of least resistance is to allocate income to the other country (UN, 2013, ¶1.3.8). Effective enforcement of existing rules may be of greater relevance to address this concern, but it can be (and has been) a factor in countries' decisions to adopt regulations.

Another potential reason to elaborate transfer pricing rules is to provide a "climate of certainty" to foreign investors. While it is more likely that a "climate of certainty" is determined by the level of confidence that investors have in the host country's legal system and tax administration, the availability of rules to point to as a reason for a court to *not* make an adjustment also may support taxpayer confidence that a totally unreasonable position will not be sustained. In the particular context of extractive industry concessions, which generally include separate dispute resolution mechanisms (usually arbitration) outside of the host country court systems, it would be expected that taxpayers would have fewer concerns about the need to specify transfer pricing rules.

As mentioned, the OECD has promulgated detailed guidelines, and it is possible to adopt more generalized rules that make reference to those guidelines (without incorporating the OECD rules). A significant concern for tax authorities, especially those relatively inexperienced in transfer pricing, is that taxpayers may use any of the relatively general statements in the OECD Guidelines to the disadvantage of the tax authority in ways that will not advance the search for an arm's length price. The OECD has addressed potential problems of excessively detailed rules with the publication by the Secretariat in 2010 of a paper that presents a simplified approach to drafting what could be either legislation or regulations (OECD, 2011). The draft proposed by the OECD includes rules for taxpayer documentation of their transfer pricing and authorizes correlative adjustments if an adjustment is made. While the paper is very helpful, it is advisable for legislation or regulations following its guidance and that make reference to the OECD Guidelines to make clear that the local law takes precedence over the Guidelines (Uganda, 2011).

6.4 Penalties, return information and documentation

An objective of a transfer pricing legal regime is to encourage compliant behavior from the first filing of the return and obviate the need for enforcement. The other side of "lowering the benefits" of engaging in aggressive transfer pricing is to increase its risks through adoption and enforcement of a transfer pricing penalty regime.[21] The objective of the penalty regime should be to encourage taxpayers to take reasonable transfer pricing positions on their tax return by changing the risk calculus. One approach, which is used in the United States (but which is not well enforced), causes the penalty to increase as the size of the adjustment relative to the original tax return position increases. Thus, if a transfer price used on a tax return is 200% or more (or 50% or less) of the amount finally determined to be the arm's length price, the penalty is 20%, but if the erroneous price is 400% or more (or 25% or less) of the amount finally determined, the penalty increases to 40%. In some countries, transfer pricing documentation serves as a defense against penalties.[22]

In transfer pricing, the critical advantage for taxpayers and problem for governments is the non-transparency of pricing issues generally. Unless specific issues are highlighted in lines or schedules of a tax return, there is little to signal tax authorities that there is a transfer pricing issue or what the issue involves. In some countries, the type and volume of controlled transactions is reported on a schedule to a tax return, which can be a useful screening tool to determine whether a transfer pricing exposure exists. Transfer pricing adjustments typically must be initiated by the government and therefore only are found on audit.

Another tool to help tax administrations assess transfer pricing exposures that has been increasingly adopted since the mid-1990s has been a "contemporaneous" documentation requirement that taxpayers demonstrate that their transfer pricing is arm's length using the best method available and yields an arm's length price.[23] The utility of documentation as well as whether its value exceeds the costs of producing it depends on its design and the uses to which it is put. In some countries, preparation of documentation has become routine to the point that little thought is put into the analysis, and it is little more than a fig leaf to protect against penalties. Nonetheless, to the extent that it collects in one place information relevant to a pricing transaction and forces the taxpayer to take a position on the taxpayer's pricing it has added some discipline to a process where previously there was none. It is a helpful starting point for a tax authority's analysis of the transaction covered, but great caution should be taken in relying on public comparables used in documentation, as an array of techniques may be used to bias the sample of comparables with consequent effect on the soundness of the analysis.

If the taxpayer is unable to satisfactorily support its transfer pricing, then the tax authority may and should make an adjustment to restore the pricing to an arm's length amount or, in the absence of a comparable transaction, a price that is within a range that rational actors would agree to under the actual circumstances of the transaction. It also is appropriate to assert penalties.[24] If the taxpayer does not agree to the adjustment, the next stage is dispute resolution.

6.5 Transfer pricing dispute resolution

The objective of a dispute resolution mechanism is to achieve timely and cost-effective case resolutions. Because of the intensely factual nature of a transfer pricing case, litigation of transfer pricing cases in courts has in almost every case proven extremely time consuming and expensive for both governments and taxpayers. The resource intensity and delay of litigation has led countries to consider alternatives. Alternative dispute resolution mechanisms may be mutually advantageous for an MNE and a host government.

6.5.1 Advance pricing agreements

One alternative is for the government and taxpayer to reach agreement in advance on a method for determining pricing (an "advance pricing agreement" or APA). In a typical APA program, a taxpayer submits an APA request and discloses substantial information about the proposed transaction or business operation with respect to which a pricing agreement is requested. One question for governments is what standards it should apply in agreeing to consider a request. The overwhelming tendency has been to accept all requests, but that in essence cedes the allocation of APA resources to the decision of taxpayers as to whether to ask for advance guidance. It is reasonable to assume that taxpayers do not make requests in cases in which it may be advantageous to take a more aggressive position on a tax return and then defend it if attacked. Before accepting an APA case, the tax authority should have clarity about the objectives it hopes to achieve with the investment of resources in an APA for a single taxpayer.

One advantage of an APA for a government is that it can be more efficient than litigating a case. It may be questioned, however, whether the same taxpayer that voluntarily submits to the APA process would be adopting an aggressive pricing position in the alternative. Another advantage for a government is that it can learn about an industry from processing an APA. A taxpayer's objective in reaching an APA is to achieve certainty. This may be particularly valuable in a large, long-term project such as an investment in mining production or oil and gas development. This taxpayer's objective should not be underestimated as leverage for the government to achieve a favorable outcome in the particular case.

Another issue relates to transparency and disclosure of APAs. The government will benefit if an outcome is made public so that the result of its investment of resources is available to other similarly situated taxpayers. Transparency also reduces the risks of unequal treatment of taxpayers. Taxpayers typically are reluctant to disclose information about APAs, and many countries have restrictions on disclosure of taxpayer information. If there is not meaningful disclosure of the results of an APA, then the government is devoting resources to a single taxpayer with limited collateral benefits. If a government pursues an APA program, it should be thoughtful how to structure it so that it maximizes the use of its scarce resources. While the APA process has been used in a number of countries, the preceding discussion suggests why it is not a panacea for transfer pricing and certainly does not serve as a substitute for a robust enforcement program.

In the extractive industry context, an APA–type agreement might be considered as an integral part of negotiating the concession agreement and be required for all concessions in similar categories. This would enhance the bargaining leverage of the host country and could build in flexibility for changes that might be carved out from an arbitration procedure.[25]

6.5.2 Treaty mutual agreement procedures

As observed earlier, Article 9 of the OECD and UN Model Treaties provide the framework for arm's length pricing. This standard has been incorporated in one form or another into most countries' domestic laws, so arguably the treaty adds little. Perhaps the greater contribution of treaties is to authorize an administrative dispute resolution mechanism that does not require court intervention. The mutual agreement procedure, authorizing the competent authorities of the two countries to resolve tax disputes relating to the treaty, is a major feature in the resolution of international disputes that threaten double taxation. While many countries do not break out their mutual agreement procedure case statistics reported to the OECD by category of case, the most frequent use of the mutual agreement procedure in Mexico and the United States is to resolve transfer pricing differences of the two countries (OECD, 2015f).

For many years, the mutual agreement procedure was not required to achieve a resolution. Increasingly mutual agreement cases under treaties are subject to mandatory arbitration if not otherwise resolved. While experience with arbitration in tax matters remains limited, preliminary indications are that it is working well in the cases arbitrated to date. It is increasingly common to use a form of arbitration in which each party suggests a resolution and the arbitrators have to choose one or the other (known in the U.S. as "baseball arbitration"; IRS, 2010). This is intended to force the countries to moderate extreme positions and limits the scope for arbitrator discretion. The mutual agreement process has become an important part of the international legal landscape in mitigating potential double taxation.

6.5.3 Concession agreement arbitration

As discussed in the preceding paragraph, some countries are starting to adopt mandatory arbitration in bilateral income tax treaties. Resource concession agreements routinely include arbitration clauses that in most cases would apply automatically in the event of a failure to agree on transfer pricing.[26] Concession agreement arbitration clauses, however, routinely utilize procedures for traditional commercial arbitration. If the procedures used under treaties for transfer pricing cases prove to be efficient and fair (by comparison with litigation), countries should consider adapting similar procedures for transfer pricing cases in concession agreement arbitration clauses. Some commentators encourage developing countries to take a cautious approach to arbitration generally (Lennard, 2014).

6.6 Other treaty considerations

> Treaties do little directly to reduce the threat of international double non-taxation. The exchange of information article, however, is a valuable enforcement tool. It authorizes exchange of tax information on an administrative basis, subject to the protections of domestic law, without intervention of a court process. In recent years, a tax information exchange agreement ("TIEA") can accomplish the same objective without having the rest of the provisions of a bilateral income tax treaty.

A host country treaty with a low-tax treaty partner – or a high-tax treaty partner that allows its tax base to be eroded or compromised – can contribute significantly to tax avoidance. Thus, for example, a number of Sub-Saharan countries have treaties with Mauritius, notwithstanding that it is possible to achieve very low rates of tax in Mauritius. For example, if a Mauritius company that does not have a permanent establishment charges a host country affiliate a fee for services, Article 7 of the UN Model Treaty prevents taxation of the "business profit," a deduction normally is allowed for the payment and the income will be taxed at a very low rate in Mauritius. (This has the same result as described in Example 4.) This creates a substantial incentive for the MNE taxpayer to overstate the management services fee that the Mauritius affiliate charges the host country affiliate. One alternative is for the host country to impose and to include a treaty provision that allows a withholding tax on services consumed in the host country. If it is necessary for host country to have a treaty with a country whose tax law or practice offers such scope for tax avoidance, consideration should be given to adopting a robust limitation of benefits provision that would limit its benefits to persons with substantial economic nexus in the treaty partner country and an anti-abuse provision to cover abusive cases not covered by this provision (OECD, 2015b).

There has been increasing question about the utility of treaties for developing countries (Dagan, 2000; Thuronyi, 2001). One proposal might be to limit a host country treaty to the same scope as a tax information exchange agreement (TIEA) plus an Article 9 arm's length pricing commitment and an Article 26 mutual agreement procedure (Thuronyi, 2010). This would achieve most of the benefits of an income tax treaty without sacrificing the source country tax base.

6.7 Transfer pricing enforcement

It is beyond the scope of this chapter to discuss enforcement, but clearly a critical element of an overall response to transfer pricing is to build an enforcement capacity and prioritize use of resources (see Chapter 4 by Calder, this volume). The starting point of a transfer pricing enforcement strategy is an effective risk-based approach to allocating resources, training and capacity building and winning initial cases to build morale and achieve deterrence objectives. As described, for very important specialist issues, it is critical to retain an industry expert. There are useful resources for guidance and technical assistance in this area (OECD, 2013c).

7 Conclusion

Transfer pricing is a challenge for governments in resource-rich developing countries, but it is a challenge that can be addressed and revenue loss mitigated. The amounts at stake in the context of mineral extraction are material. Host countries should draw on strategies that have been shown to work and adapt them to their specific context. It is possible to address transfer pricing challenges and foster a climate for investment with smart tax system design, disciplined administration of transfer pricing rules and tough but fair enforcement.

Notes

1 Mr. Shay thanks Joseph Bell, Jack Calder, Joseph Guttentag, Michael Keen, Leandra Lederman, Michael Lennard, Emil Sunley, Artur Świstak and participants at a Harvard Law School Workshop on Current Research in Taxation for comments on earlier drafts. He also thanks the Harvard Law School and the Harvard Fund for Tax and Fiscal Policy Research for summer research support. Mr. Shay discloses certain activities not connected with his position at Harvard Law School, one or more of which may relate to the subject matter of this article, at https://helios.law.harvard.edu/public/ConflictOfInterest Report.aspx?id = 10794. The views expressed in this article are those of Mr. Shay and do not reflect those of Harvard University, any client of Mr. Shay, or any organization for which he serves as an officer or renders pro bono services.

2 In some intermediary cases, a third country may impose tax under a controlled foreign company (CFC) regime on the income of the intermediary company and thereby also have a tax interest in the transfer pricing. In practice, this issue rarely arises largely because of the ability to plan around or otherwise avoid CFC regimes. If, as suggested in the OECD's BEPS action plan, CFC regimes are strengthened, provision should be made (in treaties or other agreements) for the host country and the ultimate residence country to reach a mutual agreement on how each country is pricing transactions with the intermediary company to avoid double taxation or double non-taxation (OECD, 2013d).

3 Joel Slemrod refers to the ability to use real investment to credibly support profit shifting as an "avoidance-facilitating effect" of real decisions (Slemrod, 2010, p. 856).

4 If the effective tax in a host country is reduced by tax avoidance planning, then investments with a lower pre-tax return may be made that would not otherwise be made.

This result disadvantages the alternative investment with a higher pre-tax return – the alternative investment may not be made if the multinational can earn a higher after-tax return by using non–arm's length transfer pricing. Foregoing the alternative investment may be favorable for the host country if the alternative investment is not in the host country and depending on the other consequences of the unintended erosion in tax base. The non–arm's length outcome may be unfavorable for the host country if the revenue loss over the life of the project does not justify the marginal gain from the project.

5 A response by some countries to objections to treaty shopping and other practices using third-country intermediary structures is to require more "people" functions in the country where the intermediary entity is located (Netherlands, 2013). This is perceived to be in response to pressure from the OECD project on base erosion and profit shifting (BEPS; OECD, 2013a).

6 One could argue as well that actions by taxpayers such as making voluntary tax payments is an ineffective or counterproductive response at least from the perspective of tax policy. Tax laws should not operate based on the marketing objectives of businesses or on the impulses, however well meaning, of taxpayers to pay a larger share of the costs of public goods (Neville and Treanor, 2012).

7 As Professor Isenbergh notes, "An arm's length price has in common with a policeman that as often as not you can't find one when you need one" (Isenbergh, 2010, p. 68).

8 It is possible that formulas could be adjusted, for example to include discovery value of a concession in the property factor, for extractive industries. This would exacerbate the difficulties of implementation. A number of commentators argue that formula apportionment would not improve on arm's length separate accounting (Andrus, Bennett and Silberztein, 2011; Altshuler and Grubert, 2010; Hines, 2010; Morse, 2010; Roin, 2008). Recently prominent commentators favor a sales-only formula (Avi-Yonah, Clausing and Durst, 2009).

9 Durst recommends that countries use safe harbor profit ranges for these activities in order to simplify administration and conserve resources. The OECD recently modified the Transfer Pricing Guidelines' discussion of safe harbors to be open to the possibility that in certain circumstances they may be warranted (OECD, 2013b). If not properly limited, there is a risk that a safe harbor becomes either a floor or a ceiling and operates against the interest of the government.

10 Where the sale to an affiliate is immediately followed by an uncontrolled sale to an unrelated purchaser, it generally is possible to make reference to the uncontrolled sale price. We do not discuss here the problem of accommodation or "straw" uncontrolled buyers who in turn resell to affiliates of the taxpayer or have offsetting purchase arrangements. Such intermediate or arranged sales of course should not be considered uncontrolled sales.

11 In mining, royalty rates generally are a relatively small fraction of typical income tax rates but normally are applied to gross sales at the time of production. Even taking into account the time value of money effect of income tax collections coming later in the life of a project than royalty receipts, in many cases the income tax is expected to yield more revenue than the royalty.

12 Some countries use a production sharing regime instead of a royalty; however, the pricing is equally important.

13 In cases where there is a market for hedging price risk of the mineral in question, there is a further issue of how to address gains and losses. There have been examples that suggest mining producers are consistently on the loss side of hedging transactions raising the concern that there may be offsetting positions held by offshore affiliates. For this reason, some countries "ring-fence" hedging gains and losses so that they do not affect the royalty or income tax base – see Chapter 4 by Calder, this volume, at p. 83.

14 CFR means cost and freight to the named port of destination. The seller pays the costs of moving the goods to destination, however, risk transfers to the buyer once the goods are placed on board the ship for transport so the buyer bears risks of loss or damage. The term generally applies to maritime transport.

15 FOB stands for "free on board." The seller delivers the goods on board the ship. From that point, the buyer bears all costs and risks of loss or damage.

16 A marketing allowance raises a number of issues, including whether it is appropriate; if appropriate, whether it properly is in the sales price or would be separately compensated; and if separately compensated, whether the amount or what amount properly is allowable as a host country deduction. If management fees are charged to the host country affiliate, the fee may take account of the costs of the business's marketing organization. As a general principle, a host country should resist adjustments that are not based on transparent information or third-party information.

17 There may be fewer issues for oil than for minerals. The differences in quality of different crude oils may be more readily accepted by or adapted to by producers and the quality of oil from a reservoir generally is consistent. There are quoted prices for "benchmark" crudes, including liquid forward markets, and standard methods for adjusting for quality differences. The costs between the wellhead and the delivery terminal where oil is most often sold at arm's length are limited and measurable – see Chapter 4 by Calder, this volume, at pp. 90–92.

18 For a major extractive industry MNE, the costs of forming and using entities are spread over multiple projects. It often is possible to use existing entities for "double purpose" as a conduit for income shifting while relying on "substance" of other business activity to support recognition of the intermediary entity.

19 The interest which is paid by issuing additional debt often is referred to as "payment in kind" or PIK debt. PIK debt can preserve cash while maximizing the tax deduction for interest.

20 At first blush, this would seem to be at variance with the position stated in the UN Practical Manual on Transfer Pricing, which states, "For developing countries, transfer pricing rules are essential to provide a climate of certainty and an environment for increased cross-border trade while at the same time ensuring that the country is not losing out on critical tax revenue. Transfer pricing is of paramount importance and hence detailed transfer pricing rules are essential" (UN, 2013, ¶1.2.13). As discussed in the text, it simply is not correct that detailed transfer pricing rules are essential. Potentially affected taxpayers who are seeking certainty and tax authorities who find courts reluctant to support broad discretionary authority may find them useful.

21 The UN Manual's discussion of penalties is confined largely to the use of penalties as an incentive to provide transfer pricing documentation and no discussion of penalties as a disincentive to partake of aggressive transfer pricing. It is unclear why it did not consider penalty regimes that would provide a disincentive to aggressive pricing, though it is possible that it was assumed that tax understatement penalties would apply automatically. This is unlikely if fraud or negligence is a condition for the penalty.

22 The determination whether a penalty threshold is exceeded does not take account of an adjustment if contemporaneous documentation establishes that the method used was reasonable. It is interesting to consider the range of cases in which it would be true that the pricing should be subject to an adjustment but the incorrect price used by the taxpayer was nonetheless reasonable and therefore should not be subject to a penalty. It seems unlikely that the tax authority would acknowledge that the documentation was adequate in a case in which it also makes an adjustment.

23 The UN Manual includes a chapter on documentation (UN, 2013, Ch. 7). Transfer pricing documentation generally should include information about (i) the associated enterprises engaged in controlled transactions, (ii) the nature and terms of the controlled transactions, (iii) business structure and operating results of the enterprises, (iv) potentially comparable uncontrolled transactions, (v) pricing, business strategies and special circumstances relevant to the controlled transactions (including set-offs) and (vi) other information relevant to evaluating the functions performed, assets employed and risks taken by the controlled parties to the transactions (UN, 2013, ¶¶7.2.1.4–5).

24 In the context of extractive industry concessions, it is important that the concession agreements do not foreclose the ability to make adjustments and assert penalties.

25 This chapter does not consider the broader issue of whether stabilization clauses should apply to taxes in the first place. Among other considerations, applying stabilization to taxes places substantial burdens on tax authorities in having to enforce different generations of tax laws depending on when a concession was entered into.

26 It would be a matter of domestic law whether an applicable treaty mutual agreement procedure would take precedence over concession's arbitration clause and be finally binding. The parties clearly could contractually agree to be bound by a treaty procedure.

References

ActionAid. (2010), *Calling Time: Why SABMiller should Stop Dodging Taxes in Africa.* Available at http://www.actionaidusa.org/publications/calling-time-why-sabmiller-should-stop-dodging-taxes-africa [Accessed November 22, 2015].

ActionAid. (2013), *Sweet Nothings: The Human Cost of a British Sugar Giant Avoiding Taxes in Southern Africa.* Available at http://www.actionaidusa.org/publications/sweet-nothings [Accessed November 22, 2015].

Altshuler, R. and H. Grubert. (2010), "Formula Apportionment: Is it Better than the Current System and Are There Better Alternatives?" *National Tax Journal*, 63(1145), pp. 1145–1184.

Andrus, J., M. Bennett and C. Silberztein. (2011), "The Arm's Length Principle and Developing Economies," Transfer Pricing Report (BNA) (October).

Auerbach, A., M.P. Devereux and H. Simpson. (2010), "Taxing Corporate Income," in J. Mirrlees, S. Adam, T. Besley, R. Blundell, S. Bond, R. Chote, M. Gammie, P. Johnson, G. Myles and J. Poterba (eds), *Dimensions of Tax Design: The Mirrlees Review* (Oxford), pp. 837–893.

Avi-Yonah, R., K.A. Clausing and M.C. Durst. (2009), "Allocating Business Profits for Tax Purposes: A Proposal to Adopt a Formulary Profit Split," *Florida Tax Review*, 9(497), 497–553.

Benshalom, I. (2013), "Rethinking the Source of the Arm's Length Transfer Pricing Problem," *Virginia Tax Review*, 32(425), 425–460.

Bergin, T. (2012a), "How Starbucks Avoids UK Taxes," *Reuters* [online] Special Report, Available at http://uk.reuters.com/article/2012/10/15/uk-britain-starbucks-tax-idUKBRE89E0EW20121015 [Accessed November 25, 2015].

Boadway, R. and M. Keen. (2010), "Theoretical Perspectives on Resource Tax Design," in P. Daniel, M. Keen and C. McPherson (eds), *The Taxation of Petroleum and Minerals: Principles, Problems and Practice* (London, New York: Routledge), pp. 13–74.

Clausing, K.A. (2011), "The Revenue Effects of Multinational Firm Income Shifting," *Tax Notes*, 130(1580), 1580–1586.

Columbia Center on Sustainable Investment (CCSI). (2015), *ResourceContracts.Org: A Database of Publicly Available Oil, Gas and Mining Contracts*, Available at http://ccsi.columbia.edu/work/projects/resourcecontracts-org-a-database-of-publicly-available-oil-gas-and-mining-contracts/ [Accessed November 26, 2015].

Dagan, T. (2000), "The Treaties Myth," *New York University Journal of Law and Politics*, 32(939), 939–996.

Durst, M.C. (2010), "Making Transfer Pricing Work for Developing Countries," *Tax Notes International*, 60(851).

European Commission, COM. (2011) 121/3. Proposal for a Council Directive on a Common Consolidated Corporate Tax Base.

Fleming, J., R. Peroni and S. Shay. (2014), "Formulary Apportionment in the U.S. International Income Tax System: Putting Lipstick on a Pig?," *Michigan Journal of International Law*, 36(1), 1–57.

Fleming, J., R. Peroni and S. Shay. (2015), "Getting Serious About Cross-Border Earnings Stripping: Establishing an Analytical Framework," *University of North Carolina Law Journal*, 93(763), 673–742.

Fuest, C. and N. Reidel. (2010), *Tax Evasion and Tax Avoidance in Developing Countries: The Role of International Profit Shifting* (Oxford University Centre for Bus. Tax'n Working Paper 10/12).

Graetz, M. and A. Warren. (2006), "Income Tax Discrimination and the Economic Integration of Europe," *Yale Law Journal*, 115(1186), 1186–1255.

Gruber, J. (2011), *Public Finance and Public Policy*, 3rd edition. Worth Publishers, New York.

Grubert, H. (2005), "Tax Credits, Source Rules, Trade, and Electronic Commerce: Behavioral Margins and the Design of International Tax Systems," *Tax Law Review*, 58(149), 149–190.

Grubert, H. (2012), "Foreign Taxes and the Growing Share of U.S. Multinational Company Income Abroad: Profits, Not Sales, Are Being Globalized," *National Tax Journal*, 65(247), 247–282.

Hellerstein, W. (2012), "Tax Planning under the CCCTB's Formulary Apportionment Provisions: The Good, the Bad and the Ugly," in D. Weber (ed), Kluwer: CCCTB Selected Issues. Page range is 221–252.

Hines, J. (2010), "Income Misattribution Under Formula Apportionment," *European Economic Review*, 54(108), 108–120.

IMF. (2011), *Revenue Mobilization in Developing Countries*, Policy Paper (March 11, 2011).

IMF. (2012), Fiscal Regimes for Extractive Industries: Design and Implementation.

IMF. (2014), *Spillovers in International Corporate Taxation*, Policy Paper (May 9, 2014).

IMF, OECD, UN and World Bank. (2011), "Supporting the Development of More Effective Tax Systems," Report to the G-20 Development Working Group.

IRS. (2006), *IRS Accepts Settlement Offer in Largest Transfer Pricing Dispute (IR-2006–142)*, Available at http://www.irs.gov/uac/IRS-Accepts-Settlement-Offer-in-Largest-Transfer-Pricing-Dispute [Accessed November 22, 2015].

IRS. (2010), *U.S. – Canada Arbitration Board, Operating Guidelines*, Available at http://www.irs.gov/pub/irs-utl/2010_-_arbitration_-_board_operating_guidelines_nov_8–10_final.pdf [Accessed November 22, 2015].

IRS. (2015), *Schedule UTP TY2013 Filing Statistics*, Available at http://www.irs.gov/Businesses/Corporations/UTPFilingStatistics [Accessed November 22, 2015].

Isenbergh, J. (2010), *International Taxation* (New York: Foundation Press).

Lennard, M. (2014), "Transfer Pricing Arbitration as an Option for Developing Countries," *Intertax*, 42(179).

Lodin, S. (2013), "Intragroup Royalties as a Vehicle for International Tax Arbitrage," *Tax Notes International*, 71(1317), 1317–1319.

Morse, S. (2010), "Revisiting Global Formulary Apportionment," *Virginia Tax Review*, 29(594).

Netherlands, Decree of 18 December 2013, Stb. 569, 2013 (December 30, 2013), 593–644.

Neville, S. and Treanor, J. (2012), "Starbucks to Pay £20m in Tax Over Next Two Years After Customer Revolt," *The Guardian* [Online] Available at http://www.guardian.co.uk/business/2012/dec/06/starbucks-to-pay-10m-corporation-tax [Accessed November 22, 2015].

OECD. (2010), Transfer Pricing Guidelines for Multinational Enterprises and Tax Administrations 2010 (Paris: OECD Publishing). Available at: http://dx.doi.org/10.1787/tpg-2010-en

OECD. (2011), Transfer Pricing Legislation – a Suggested Approach. (Paris: OECD Publishing) Available at: http://www.oecd.org/ctp/tax-global/3.%20TP_Legislation_Suggested_Aproach.pdf

OECD. (2012), *Dealing Effectively with the Challenges of Transfer Pricing*, OECD Publishing, Paris.

OECD. (2013a), *Addressing Base Erosion and Profit Shifting*, OECD Publishing, Paris.

OECD. (2013b), *Revised Section E on Safe Harbors in Chapter IV of the Transfer Pricing Guidelines*, OECD Publishing, Paris.

OECD. (2013c), *Draft Handbook on Transfer Pricing Risk Assessment*, OECD Publishing, Paris.

OECD. (2013d), *Action Plan on Base Erosion and Profit Shifting*, OECD Publishing, Paris.

OECD. (2015a), Neutralising the Effects of Hybrid Mismatch Arrangements, Action 2–2015 Final Report, OECD/G20 Base Erosion and Profit Shifting Project, OECD Publishing, Paris.

OECD. (2015b), Preventing the Granting of Treaty Benefits in Inappropriate Circumstances, Action 6–2015 Final Report, OECD/G20 Base Erosion and Profit Shifting Project, OECD Publishing, Paris.

OECD. (2015c), Aligning Transfer Pricing Outcomes with Value Creation,, Actions 8–10, 2015 Final Report, OECD/G20 Base Erosion and Profit Shifting Project, OECD Publishing, Paris.

OECD. (2015d), Limiting Base Erosion Involving Interest Deductions and Other Financial Payments, Action 4–2015 Final Report, OECD/G20 Base Erosion and Profit Shifting Project, OECD Publishing, Paris.

OECD. (2015e), Transfer Pricing Documentation and Country-by-Country Reporting, Action 13–2015 Final Report, OECD/G20 Base Erosion and Profit Shifting Project, OECD Publishing, Paris.

OECD. (2015f), *Mutual Agreement Procedure Statistics 2006–2014*, Available at http://www.oecd.org/ctp/dispute/map-statistics-2006–2014.htm#US [Accessed November 27, 2015].

Platts. (2015), *Methodology and Specifications Guide*, Available at http://www.platts.com/IM.Platts.Content/MethodologyReferences/MethodologySpecs/ironore.pdf [Accessed November 22, 2015].

Roin, J. (2008), "Can the Income Tax Be Saved – The Promise and Pitfalls of Adopting Worldwide Formulary Apportionment," *Tax Law Review*, 61(169), 169–240.

Schatan, Roberto. (2012), "Tax-Minimizing Strategies and the Arm's Length Principle," *Tax Notes International*, 65(121), 121–126.

Shay, S. (2009), "Ownership Neutrality and Practical Complications," *Tax Law Review*, 62(317), 317–332.

Slemrod, J. (2010), "Location, (Real) Location, (Tax) Location: An Essay on Mobility's Place in Optimal Taxation," *National Tax Journal*, 63(843), 843–864.

Tanzania Income Tax Act (Rev. Ed. 2006).

Thuronyi, V. (2001), "International Tax Cooperation and a Multilateral Treaty," *Brooklyn Journal of International Law*, 26(1641), 1641–1681.

Thuronyi, V. (2010), "Tax Treaties and Developing Countries," in M. Lang, P. Pistone, J. Schuch, C. Staringer, A. Storck, & M. Zagler (eds), *Tax Treaties: Building Bridges between Law and Economics* (IBFD: Online books), n.p.

Tuerff, T., Sierra, G., Trump, C. and Narayan, M. (2011), Overview of Outbound Tax Planning for U.S. Multinational Corporations Tax Management International 40 (No. 7).

Uganda. (2011), The Income Tax (Transfer Pricing) Regulations. Author.

UK House of Commons. (2012), Committee of Public Accounts, HM Revenue & Customs: Annual Report and Accounts 2011–12, Nineteenth Report of Session 2012–13, (HC 716), Available at http://www.publications.parliament.uk/pa/cm201213/cmselect/cmpubacc/716/716.pdf [Accessed November 22, 2015].

U.S. Senate. (2012), Permanent Subcommittee on Investigations of the Committee on Homeland Security and Government Affairs, Hearing on Offshore Profit Shifting and the U.S. Tax Code (Part 1 Hewlett Packard and Microsoft), Memorandum from Chairman

Carl Levin and Senator Tom Coburn to Subcommittee Members, Offshore Profit Shifting and the Internal Revenue Code. Available at http://www.hsgac.senate.gov/subcommittees/investigations/hearings/offshore-profit-shifting-and-the-us-tax-code [Accessed May 30, 2013].

U.S. Senate. (2013), Permanent Subcommittee on Investigations of the Committee on Homeland Security and Government Affairs, Hearing on Offshore Profit Shifting and the U.S. Tax Code – Part 2 (Apple Inc.), Memorandum from Chairman Carl Levin and Senator John McCain to Subcommittee Members, Offshore Profit Shifting and the Internal Revenue Code – Part 2 (Apple Inc.) Available at http://www.hsgac.senate.gov/subcom mittees/investigations/hearings/offshore-profit-shifting-and-the-us-tax-code_-part-2 [Accessed May 30, 2013].

UN. (2000), (Millennium Declaration) Resolution 55/2 (September 18, 2000).

UN. (2002), International Conference on Financing for Development, (A/CONF.198/11).

UN. (2013), Practical Manual on Transfer Pricing for Developing Countries.

WTO. (2010), World Trade Report.

WTO. (2014), World Trade Report.

4 Transfer pricing – special extractive industry issues

Jack Calder

1 Introduction

The previous chapter (Shay) presented an overview of transfer pricing. It set out the policy arguments and objectives for valuing controlled transactions on the basis of the arm's length principle for tax purposes, discussed methods of determining arm's length prices and the challenges of applying them in practice, particularly to extractive industries, and outlined general strategies available to governments to respond to those challenges.

This chapter as far as possible avoids repeating the general discussion of the previous chapter and instead focuses, in more detail than was possible there, on transfer pricing issues special to extractive industries, particularly in developing countries.

It starts by discussing extractive industry transfer pricing risks and explains in more detail how the special nature of extractive industry tax regimes affects those risks and how, particularly through ring-fencing, it extends them into domestic as well as cross-border transactions. It then considers transfer pricing methods but looks in more detail than the previous chapter at the use of special methods for valuing commodity[1] transactions. It then discusses separately oil, gas and minerals, bringing out the similarities and differences in the challenges they present for the use of such methods. In the course of this discussion it looks at transfer pricing issues relevant to royalties, not considered in detail in the previous chapter. Next it looks at transfer pricing of costs, again considering in more detail the use of special rules for extractive industries, for example the no-profit rule for payments to associates common in petroleum agreements, and special rules for limiting finance costs. It concludes with a discussion of practical administrative issues, looking in more detail at the administrative consequences of special valuation rules, for example benchmarking and "physical audit" procedures.

A general theme is the scope for reducing transfer pricing uncertainty and risk by developing rules that are specific, objective and predictable while still *broadly* consistent with the arm's length principle.

2 Extractive industry transfer pricing risks

Risks of tax loss from abusive transfer pricing are not peculiar to extractive industries, but a number of special features affect the nature of those risks and of the typical responses to them.

Governments often impose special taxes[2] on "upstream"[3] extractive industries. They can, of course, tax anything they like, and these special taxes are not necessarily based on profits or on the value of commodities sold.[4] Where they are not, transfer pricing is of limited relevance.

The main taxes imposed by governments are, however, usually profit based. These include income tax, but often, particularly with petroleum, this is charged at a special rate and with other special modifications, such as ring-fencing, explained more fully in what follows. Sometimes (again more commonly for petroleum than mining) governments also impose other profit-based taxes such as resource rent tax (RRT), excess profits tax or production sharing. These profit-based taxes are clearly vulnerable to abusive transfer pricing. Particularly in developing countries, governments often take equity participations in extractive industries, and profits from these are vulnerable too.

Governments generally (with limited exceptions, mainly in developed countries) also impose royalties. In a few countries these are profit based, but in developing countries they are normally output based. Royalties can be based simply on the weight or volume of output, in which case transfer prices are irrelevant. Volume-based royalties are rare, however, applying mainly to low-value bulk commodities like sand and gravel. Value-based royalties are a much more common and important fiscal instrument, but there is considerable variation in how output is valued, and the royalty value may not be the same as the sales value. There is no international convention requiring valuation at arm's length prices as there is for income tax. Where royalties are not based on sales value, transfer pricing may again be of limited relevance. Many governments do, however, as a policy choice, base royalties on sales value, in which case they are equally vulnerable to transfer pricing abuse.

The result of these higher or special taxes is that the total tax take from extractive industry profits can be very high, sometimes in excess of 70% (though some high tax rates may have been reduced by recent falls in commodity prices). This provides exceptional incentives for transfer pricing abuse.[5]

There are also exceptional opportunities. In developing countries, large-scale extraction operations are carried out mainly by foreign-owned multi-national enterprises (MNEs); most production is exported; operations are financed with foreign capital; and the highest-value goods and services used are imported. The MNEs are often "vertically integrated", carrying out the full range of operations from exploration through to sale of final products, so that sales to downstream associates are common. Even without vertical integration, sales are often channeled through an associated marketing or trading company. Goods and services are commonly provided to locally based upstream companies by a foreign-based group management and services company. Associates are often based in tax havens, maximizing potential tax savings from non–arm's length pricing.

Transfer pricing risks are normally associated with cross-border transactions, but, where special extractive industry taxes apply, they also arise in transactions with *domestic* associates not subject to those taxes. (Structures involving domestic downstream associates are a common feature of complex extractive projects.) The implications of this are discussed more fully later in this section.

It is often said that withholding taxes (WHTs) are the first line of defense against transfer pricing abuse. There is undoubtedly some truth in this, but WHTs generally apply at standard income tax rates and provide limited protection where extractive industry profits are taxed at higher rates.[6]

Some factors may be considered to *reduce* extractive industry transfer pricing risks compared with other industries. Extractive industries are physical operations. They are tied to their location – they cannot be transferred to a favorable tax jurisdiction overnight like an Internet trading business. Outputs are standard commodities, not branded products. They can be physically weighed and measured. Variations in their type and quality can likewise be physically defined and measured. Standard commercial measurements are used. The most common commodities have prices quoted on international exchanges such as the London Metal Exchange (LME), or published by price-reporting agencies. These features increase price visibility. A barrel of oil is easier to value than a designer handbag, and although its value on any particular date may be subject to dispute, this will usually be within a narrow range. Costs generally relate to physical goods and operations, not nebulous intellectual property; and, in the case of petroleum, the prevalence of unincorporated joint ventures may limit transfer pricing risks, as discussed in more detail in section 5.

None of this means that the risks are negligible. Comparable transactions can be hard to find; for some commodities there are no quoted prices; even when there are, they may need significant, complex and uncertain adjustments to establish a comparable price. MNEs may furthermore be able to exploit the high day-to-day volatility of prices to shift profits, if they can use hindsight in selecting pricing dates for controlled transactions. As the OECD points out,[7] if a taxpayer in an extraction industry sells all its local-country output to associates, small pricing discrepancies in each individual sale can add up to large reductions in the local tax base. Costs paid to associates often relate to services and provision of know-how, where transfer pricing can again be problematic, as discussed in Chapter 3 (Shay, this volume).

MNE representatives often maintain that extractive industry transfer pricing risks are wildly exaggerated. Apart from the risk-reducing factors listed earlier, they point out that transactions with associates are relatively minor in many cases; that such associates are not always tax haven based; that their trading subsidiaries are incentivized to treat associates and non-associates equally; that reputable MNEs make efforts to comply with laws requiring arm's length pricing; that antagonizing governments by aggressive tax planning is not in their interest given the political vulnerability of their massive up-front investments; and that the scope for abuse is often limited by imposition of special valuation rules (discussed in section 3). Despite this, tax authorities should not be complacent about these risks. Chapter 3 (Shay, this volume) presented general evidence of such abuse, and specific examples in the extractive industries can be found.[8] But authorities should understand that abuse is just a *risk*, not a certainty, and may not materialize in every case in practice.

2.1 Upstream, downstream and ring-fencing

The prevalence of special taxes on extractive industries means that transactions with *domestic* associates may be vulnerable to transfer pricing abuse, in which case governments need to ensure they are appropriately valued.

Additional complications arise where a company or its associate is involved in domestic refining or processing. Special extractive industry taxes are generally intended to apply only to upstream operations. This may be because downstream operations do not have the same capacity as upstream operations to generate rents (excess profits), which special taxes are intended to capture; or because, unlike upstream operations, processing can often be carried out abroad, and special taxes might encourage this, reducing rather than increasing tax collection.

Governments in developing countries often see domestic processing of the nation's natural resources as particularly desirable, because they see it (sometimes with scant justification) as a higher value-adding activity than extraction and/or as a stimulus for wider industrial development. Far from imposing special taxes, they often provide special tax *incentives* for it. This further increases domestic transfer pricing risks. Purchases or sales may be routed through downstream domestic associates to exploit their favorable tax status. It is worth noting that governments sometimes inflict transfer pricing losses on themselves by requiring highly taxed upstream companies to supply production for domestic processing and consumption at below market prices.[9]

If special taxes are limited to upstream operations, they must be clearly defined and "ring-fenced" from other operations. Production must be valued fairly at the point where it passes from upstream to downstream (*vertical* ring-fencing). It can sometimes be difficult, particularly for mining, to identify the appropriate point of valuation. There is considerable variation in the approaches governments take to this issue in practice, as will be discussed in more detail in section 4. If upstream and downstream activities are carried on within the same company, there will not be an actual sale at that point, making it necessary to establish and use an *internal* transfer price for tax purposes.

Where special upstream taxes are profit based (more common for petroleum), downstream costs must be defined and excluded from the calculation (*horizontal* ring-fencing) to ensure that costs of lower-taxed activities are not deducted from revenues of higher-taxed activities. Where an MNE carries on both upstream and downstream operations, costs have to be fairly allocated between them, in effect requiring use of internal transfer prices.

Some governments impose different levels of profit taxes on different license areas or even different developments within a license area.[10] To prevent companies setting losses from one area against profits from another or allocating costs disproportionately to more highly taxed areas, these areas are *individually* ring-fenced. Where a company operates in several ring-fenced areas, as is common, its costs must then be fairly apportioned among them, again requiring use of internal transfer prices. Area-based ring-fencing thus hugely increases the volume of controlled transactions. Sometimes MNEs are required to create separate subsidiaries for each project, which formalizes the need for separate cost accounting but does not reduce the incidence of controlled transactions within the group.[11]

The commercial pricing basis used for sales is an important issue for both vertical and horizontal ring-fencing. There are four main commercial pricing bases:

- Free on Board (FOB) – property and risk pass to the buyer at the point of loading, and the buyer is liable for any costs of further transport and insurance.
- Costs, Insurance, Freight (CIF) – although property passes to the buyer, the seller remains responsible for costs and risks till the cargo is unloaded.
- Costs & Freight (CF) – similar to CIF except that the seller is not liable for cargo insurance.
- Delivery – property and risk pass on delivery at the final destination point, and the seller is liable for all costs to that point.

Clear and consistent rules are needed on the basis to be used at the point at which sales are valued for the purposes of upstream taxes. Most commonly this is the FOB price. In that case any costs of the seller beyond that point must be disallowed as downstream costs, since they are already reflected in the FOB price. Where sales are made on terms such as CIF or CF, prices are normally adjusted to FOB for tax purposes. If there is no other way of establishing the FOB price this can be done by netting back the seller's costs beyond the point of loading from the CIF or CF price, but if these are paid to an associate the costs must be charged at arm's length prices. Standard international freight charges could be required to be used for transport by associated companies – for example, awards under the London Tanker Brokers Panel, widely used in the extractive industries to fix shipping rates.

2.2 Hedging

A controversial issue is whether gains and losses from hedging against movements in commodity prices (for example by use of forward contracts) should be recognized in calculating upstream taxes. There is considerable variation on this among countries in practice. This chapter does not aim to set out all the arguments for and against,[12] but it is worth mentioning that hedging contracts sometimes involve associated parties, directly or indirectly, and transfer pricing issues will have to be addressed if such gains and losses are recognized. Sometimes the transactions are so clearly disadvantageous that they can be challenged on simple commonsense grounds, but often the position is less clear-cut and requires some understanding of commercial pricing of hedging instruments.

3 Extractive industry transfer pricing methods

Extractive industry transfer pricing rules vary considerably from country to country. Some allow more transparent and effective administration than others.

3.1 General transfer pricing rules

Income tax legislation normally contains a general rule requiring use of arm's length transfer prices, sometimes backed up by regulations and/or reference to OECD guidelines.[13] Sometimes there are no such rules in royalty legislation – a serious weakness if royalties are based on sales values.

In some countries general transfer pricing rules are deficient:

- Sometimes the definition of non–arm's length transactions is too narrow. Association may be poorly defined.[14] Or the definition may not capture transactions with a non-associate that form part of a wider agreement involving an associate.[15] Chapter 3 (Shay, this volume) explains the definition of controlled transactions in more detail.
- Sometimes the rules do not oblige taxpayers to report transactions with associates at arm's length prices for tax purposes. In Anglophone developing countries, transfer pricing rules are sometimes still based on the UK's pre-1998 legislation, which merely *permitted* the tax authority to substitute arm's length prices if transactions between associates were priced in a way that reduced tax. This leaves taxpayers free to misprice such transactions with impunity and puts the onus on the tax authority to detect such mispricing and determine the arm's length prices to be substituted. This is an inadequate foundation for ensuring appropriate transfer pricing and is incompatible with self-assessment principles.[16]
- Transfer pricing rules may not apply to domestic transactions (a problem if extractive industries are taxed differently from other domestic businesses).

It is essential to eliminate these weaknesses if tax authorities are to have any hope of using general transfer pricing rules effectively. Merely strengthening administrative capacity and training will not suffice. The rules should be amended, or supplemented by regulations, to define non–arm's length transactions comprehensively and to require taxpayers to price them on arm's length terms for tax reporting purposes and maintain records showing how they established arm's length prices. The onus should be clearly on taxpayers to demonstrate that prices equate to arm's length terms. Penalties should apply for non-compliance with these procedural requirements, in addition to penalties for understatements in returns. (Penalties are discussed more fully in Chapter 3; Shay, this volume.) In many developing countries extractive industries benefit from tax stabilization agreements, but in most cases these would not prevent governments from changing procedural rules in this way.

Some transfer pricing methods can only be verified with data from the foreign associate. Tax authorities in developing countries are sometimes fobbed off by claims that this data is unobtainable or confidential. It is often recommended that they enter exchange-of-information or mutual-assistance agreements with other countries. These are fine in principle but can be a slow, cumbersome and ineffective way of resolving audit enquiries. A more effective approach may be to make deductibility of payments to associates conditional on tax authority access to the associate's accounts and records, where reasonably required to verify the pricing basis used. This is particularly important where tax havens are involved.

Even if general transfer pricing rules are strengthened, the question remains how exactly extractive industry transfer prices should be calculated in practice. Chapter 3 (Shay, this volume) explained five standard pricing methods recommended by the OECD and UN, and those explanations are not repeated here. For extractive industry costs, any of the standard methods may be appropriate. Comparable uncontrolled price (CUP) may be difficult to establish, since costs may not involve widely traded goods and services, but alternative methods can have varying and unpredictable results. For sales, CUP is arguably the most suitable method, with resale minus a possible alternative. (For commodities, "netback" pricing is the term generally used to describe the resale minus method, though if the costs netted back include a profit element, it becomes more like a profit-split method.) The case for CUP is based not just on the standard physical properties of commodities but on the fact that other methods might produce values with no relation to normal market prices. For example, since commodity market prices bear no fixed relation to production costs, the cost plus method would be unlikely to produce normal market values. Likewise profit-split methods would be unlikely to produce normal market values, since there is no consistent relationship between the profitability of upstream and downstream operations. Factors producing high rents in the former do not apply to the latter (indeed, overcapacity has often resulted in refining industries struggling to generate any profit at all). To price transactions between upstream and downstream operations on the strength of a comparison of their functions, assets and risks might, therefore, particularly at times of high commodity prices, produce values lower than normal market prices. For these reasons commodity-producing countries normally prefer the CUP method wherever a CUP is available. If differences of timing, quality, location and contract terms make it difficult to find a true CUP, they normally prefer to adjust the price of a known transaction to reflect those differences, modifying the normal CUP method, rather than fall back on alternative pricing methods that are complex and uncertain and may not reflect the economic dynamics of commodities markets. But companies may not follow this approach, and even if they do it may be unclear what type and level of adjustments are appropriate.

General transfer pricing rules may therefore leave companies with considerable latitude to manipulate transfer prices. The risk identified by the OECD that systematic minor discrepancies could have a major impact on the local tax base is clearly present.

Most developed countries struggle to apply general transfer pricing rules effectively. Highly trained specialists are normally employed, but even then transfer pricing audits can require long and complex investigations and negotiations, often with conclusions disputed, outcomes uncertain and limited evidence of any wider impact in stemming profit shifting. Tax authorities in developing countries may have neither the resources nor the capacity to undertake these. They are often recommended to resolve uncertainties by negotiating specific transfer pricing methods with individual taxpayers under advance pricing agreements (APAs) but may lack both information and negotiating skills for this.[17]

Developing countries may in any case prefer, where possible, to base transfer pricing on standard, published, objective methods, for reasons of transparency as well as simplicity. The importance of transparency of extractive industry taxation is widely emphasized, particularly for countries where general standards of governance are poor. Tax law that is clear and predictable and not a matter for departmental discretion or negotiation is an important element of transparency. Individually negotiated agreements on transfer prices are arguably inconsistent with this.

3.2 Special rules for commodity sales

General transfer pricing rules are therefore often supplemented or overridden by special rules, in legislation or contractual agreements, setting out exactly how extractive industry transfer prices are to be calculated. This is particularly common (not just in developing countries) for commodity *sales*. An example of a special rule might be that non–arm's length sales of a commodity must be valued for tax purposes on the basis of a published international benchmark price. Benchmark prices (discussed in more detail in section 4) can produce realistic arm's length values if the benchmark price relates broadly to the same commodity and appropriate adjustments are made for any differences affecting relative values. The government may specify the benchmark to be used and the adjustments to be made to it and may supplement this with further rules prescribing the pricing date or period to be used in applying it. Latin American countries often call this approach the "sixth method", though there are variations in its detailed application. Under the BEPS project, the OECD has issued a discussion draft on commodity transfer pricing[18] proposing additional guidelines, first to clarify that CUP would generally be the appropriate method for pricing commodity transactions between related parties and that quoted prices can be used under this method – but only if appropriately adjusted; second to allow imposition of a deemed pricing date – but only if there is no reliable evidence of the actual pricing date agreed by the parties; and third, in due course, to provide additional guidance on comparability adjustments to quoted prices. In practice the qualifications included in these proposals are not always observed by countries using the "sixth method".[19]

Other types of special rule also depart to some extent from the normal arm's length principle. A fairly common rule is for commodity sales to associates to be valued at the average (or weighted average) arm's length sales price for all sales of that commodity over the period – say the month or quarter – in which the sale occurred. Since there may not be enough arm's length sales in a period to provide reliable data, there is often provision for average benchmark prices to be used as well or instead. An advantage of the use of average prices is that it increases the pool of arm's length sales from which prices can be established, allowing use of a modified version of the CUP method. Use of average prices also simplifies administration – once the average has been established it can be published and applied uniformly to all non–arm's length sales in the period. It makes it harder for companies to benefit from manipulating pricing dates with the benefit of hindsight. It is not strictly in accordance with the arm's length standard, since commodity prices are highly volatile (with particularly wild swings in recent years), so that the average price may differ significantly from the market price on the contractual pricing date. This could lead to double (or non-) taxation, since it is unlikely that the associate's purchase will be valued on the basis of average prices in its home tax jurisdiction. MNEs might therefore in theory be able to seek adjustments under mutual agreement procedures, but often developing countries will not have the necessary double taxation treaties, and MNEs may in any case be prepared to accept an element of rough justice if they assume that these differences will cancel out in the long run.

A risk for governments is that companies may be able to exploit the use of average prices. For example, at the end of the period they may choose whether to sell to an associate or a non-associate depending on whether prices at that stage are higher or lower than the likely average (see Figure 4.1). They may be able to use hindsight to decide which deliveries to treat as sales made to non-associates. The longer the period over which prices are averaged, the greater are the risks of this kind of manipulation. It is necessary to examine the rules in detail to establish how far it is possible (they are often more complex than the description suggests). But often it is, and if it is possible in theory, it will almost certainly happen in practice. In 2006 the UK revised its petroleum valuation rules to curb substantial tax losses resulting from this kind of manipulation.[20] There is often little awareness of this risk.

Although general transfer pricing principles should be set out in primary legislation, it may be sensible to include special transfer pricing rules in secondary regulations to allow flexibility, for example to respond to the emergence of more appropriate benchmarks.

An alternative and more radical approach sometimes adopted is to apply a general valuation rule to *all* sales of a particular commodity, *whether or not an associated party is involved*. An example might be that *all* sales of crude oil in a period must be valued for tax purposes at the average of the arm's length sales prices achieved in the period for sales of that crude rather than on the basis

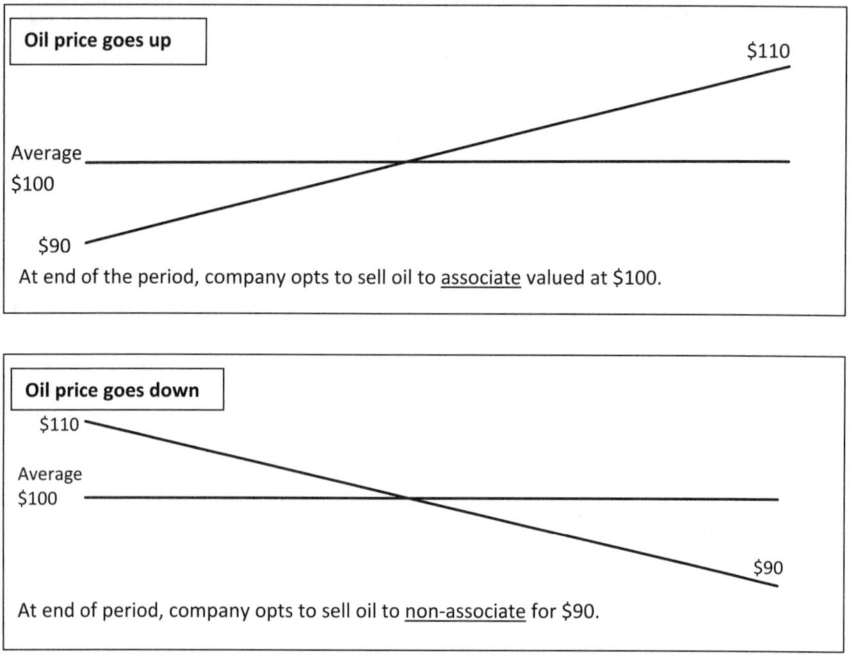

Figure 4.1 Exploiting the use of average prices

of the actual sale price achieved in any particular transaction. (Again possibly benchmark prices or a combination of actual prices and benchmark prices might be used instead.) Another example might be that (say for royalty purposes) all sales of a mineral ore must be valued at the closing LME price for its mineral content on the date of export. Since all sales are valued on the same basis, there is no need for transfer pricing rules (though the main rationale may be to prevent transfer pricing abuse). This approach is sometimes described as reference or norm pricing or, where benchmark prices are used, as benchmark pricing (though there is a risk of confusion since benchmark prices are also a common feature of special transfer pricing rules of the kind described earlier).

The intention of a general valuation rule is normally to produce a reasonable approximation of arm's length sales values where it applies for income tax purposes; but this may not be the intention with royalties, since these are often not based on sales values (as in the second example, where the value of an ore's mineral content would exceed the sales value of the unrefined ore).

General valuation rules may reduce the importance of transfer pricing rules, but they usually remain of *some* importance, because a general valuation rule may not be practicable for all commodity sales and will usually be impracticable for valuing costs.

Valuing all sales on the basis of a common rule has advantages and disadvantages compared with a special transfer pricing rule.

- It further simplifies administration, since sales can be valued by simply measuring physical production and applying the stipulated price. (As with specific transfer pricing rules, average prices are often used, so that all production in the period concerned can be valued by this simple calculation.) In theory this makes it possible to verify taxable revenues entirely on the basis of "physical audit" (though this may not be advisable in practice). Physical audit is discussed more fully in section 6.
- If average prices are used the "rough justice" problem discussed earlier is worse with a general valuation rule, because the average applies to *all* sales, not just non–arm's length sales. This could again raise double taxation issues, as discussed earlier. The problem is reduced, though not eliminated, if the period over which any average is calculated is kept short.
- The scope for companies to exploit average prices by choosing whether to sell to associates or non-associates is eliminated. Where general valuation rules are not based on average prices, there may be scope for avoidance if MNEs can set pricing dates with the benefit of hindsight.
- Where a general valuation rule requires use of benchmark prices, a significant advantage is that it removes the need for tax authorities to identify non–arm's length transactions. These can be hard to identify. Tax authorities may be able to spot suspicious transactions, but while it is one thing to spot them, it is quite another to prove they were non–arm's length in order to impose a transfer pricing adjustment.[21] (Where a general valuation rule requires use of the average price of arm's length sales in a period, it still remains necessary to identify and exclude non–arm's length transactions, since their inclusion might depress the average.)
- General valuation rules based on benchmark prices may also be perceived as having advantages for transparency. These prices can be published and verified, and the public may have more confidence in the government's ability to ensure they are applied than in its ability to identify non–arm's length transactions and ensure they are valued appropriately.

There are many variations both between and within countries in how these different types of rules are used. Special transfer pricing rules may provide greater simplicity, clarity and predictability than general transfer pricing rules, but it is hard to design them to value non–arm's length transactions realistically (with some types of commodity presenting greater difficulties than others). They are generally unpopular with investors because of the administrative burden of substituting government-imposed transfer prices and the risk that the imposed prices will overvalue sales in practice, whether because of averaging or because they use an inappropriate benchmark or pricing date or because they are applied asymmetrically. (The "heads I win, tails you lose" application of special valuation rules is not uncommon – for example, Argentina and Nigeria apply them only where they produce a higher value than the recorded price.) A general valuation rule may have additional advantages for governments but will be even more unpopular with investors, since it applies to all sales and not just controlled transactions.

4 Commodity valuation

Transfer pricing of different extractive industry products involves common broad issues, but there are significant differences of detail among oil, gas and minerals.

4.1 Oil

Crude oil is normally valued, for the purpose of both royalty and profit-based taxes, at the point of sale or delivery, that is, the point at which ownership passes to a buyer in a sale, and at which production is measured for sale purposes. The point of valuation tends to be less of an issue for oil than it is for gas and minerals. Upstream and downstream operations are fairly distinct. Extraction and refining are usually carried out by separate companies. Operations between the point of extraction and point of delivery normally consist of limited initial treatment (removal of water, salt and other impurities), transport and storage, and marketing. There is therefore usually no major difference in value at those two points. The costs, for example pipeline fees and demurrage charges, are normally limited and relatively easy to quantify. In practice they are normally deductible for the purpose of extractive industry profit taxes, subject to transfer pricing issues if paid to an associate. They may or may not be deductible for royalty purposes but in most cases are unlikely to be a major source of dispute either way, so long as the basic rules are made clear. For developing countries exporting most of their production, the point of delivery is most commonly a terminal where oil is loaded onto a tanker. For offshore production the terminal is often at an offshore platform where the oil is brought to the surface, sometimes from a number of different undersea wells. Some production might be delivered to a domestic refinery, in which case the delivery point would be a terminal at the refinery.

There may, however, be exceptional cases in which costs between the point of extraction (the wellhead) and the point of delivery are significant, and in those cases the alternative approach of valuing oil at a point nearer the wellhead may be adopted. One example is where production in a land-locked country is transported by pipeline or less commonly by road or rail transport to a tanker-loading point at a port in another country. The transport costs to the tanker-loading point could be substantial. If the point of valuation is the point of loading into the pipeline, then for purposes of profit taxes the value (or internal transfer price) at that point may be calculated by netting back the pipeline fees from the sale price at the tanker-loading point (assuming this is an arm's length price). If the tanker-loading point is the point of valuation, the sales price at that point would be used, but the pipeline or other transport costs would normally be deductible in calculating profit taxes, effectively producing the same result. (Whether pipeline and transport costs were deductible for the purpose of royalties would depend on whether the government intended them to be based on arm's length sales values.) If deductible pipeline fees are paid to an associate, establishing an arm's length price for them can be a significant and difficult issue, particularly if the pipeline owner has a monopoly, but in these circumstances fees are often government regulated in practice.

Another exceptional case in which substantial costs can arise between wellhead and point of delivery is found in Nigeria, where costs of onshore pipeline transportation are greatly increased by "bunkering" (illegal extraction of oil from pipelines). Oil in Nigeria is valued for tax, royalty and production sharing purposes on the basis of reference pricing, and a controversial issue has been whether, as the authorities have argued, this valuation should be applied to production measured at the wellhead rather than at the point of delivery (where the volume might be substantially lower).

Oil is generally valued for tax and royalty purposes either on the basis of sales prices subject to a specific transfer pricing rule or on the basis of general norm or reference pricing. The latter is less common but is adopted by some major producers such as Norway, Angola and Nigeria. For oil, arm's length sales from the same reservoir can reasonably be regarded as providing a CUP for the purpose of valuing non–arm's length transactions, since the quality is generally fairly consistent, at least over the short to medium term. Oil valuation rules are generally based on this assumption. They commonly allow for use of monthly or quarterly average prices to increase the pool of CUP.

Since there may be insufficient arm's length sales from the reservoir to provide a reasonable range of CUP in the period, some countries require use of benchmark prices. These may be used on their own or in conjunction with actual arm's length sales of the crude to be valued, and combinations of different benchmarks may be used. There are differences in the quality of different crudes – light or intermediate crudes contain a higher proportion of the lighter fractions, such as gasoline, most in demand, and sweet (low-sulfur) crudes can be refined more cheaply than sour crudes – but crude from one reservoir is often physically comparable in quality with crudes from other locations and priced similarly in commercial transactions. FOB prices for a range of widely traded crudes[22] are quoted by price-reporting agencies such as Platts, Argos or ICIS, providing the data required for benchmark or reference pricing. Generally, once a similar-quality benchmark crude has been identified, standard formulae can be applied to adjust its price to reflect measured differences in its physical quality. It may also be necessary to make an adjustment for transport cost differences, in which case, as discussed earlier, standard international freight charges could be used.[23] Benchmark pricing is consistent with commercial practice, since sales between independent parties are often priced on the basis of a benchmark crude with a premium or discount. If arm's length sales of local crude are consistently priced in this way, it may become possible just to use the standard market premium or discount rather than calculate comparability adjustments independently.[24]

Where special valuation rules are not based on average prices, they usually impose a specific pricing date, normally at or around the date of delivery, broadly consistent with normal commercial practice for oil sales (other than forward contracts).

Many developing countries impose royalties and production sharing, with the oil valuation rules for those taxes set out in petroleum law or the production sharing agreement (PSA) itself. These are usually special transfer pricing rules,[25] whereas income tax legislation often contains only a general transfer pricing rule. Such special rules, for example the requirement to use a particular benchmark, could not be inferred from a general transfer pricing rule and might even be inconsistent with it if there is a requirement to use average prices that differ from arm's length prices at the contractual pricing date.

There are clear administrative advantages in valuing oil on the same basis for income tax and production sharing (and also royalties if the policy intention is to base these on sales values).[26] It would be unfortunate, for example, if disputes about oil transfer prices had to be resolved under different rules for different taxes for no good reason. PSA valuation rules might be applied for income tax purposes as a matter of practice, but as a matter of law PSAs cannot normally override general tax legislation. Special legislation is therefore normally required if income tax rules are to be aligned with PSA/Petroleum Act rules.

4.2 Gas

Gas, like oil, is generally subject to a special tax regime, usually either the same as that for oil or a modified version of it. In developing countries some gas may be sold into the domestic market, but usually most is exported. In a few cases it is exported by pipeline, but more often it is exported by tanker as liquefied natural gas (LNG). In that case, unlike with oil, significant local processing costs are necessary, since LNG plants are expensive to develop and need to recover their costs. There are broadly two approaches to the taxation of LNG exports:

- The aggregated approach. Here upstream gas production and downstream (or midstream) operations including LNG processing are taxed as a single project. With this approach, there is a single point of valuation for the purpose of any special taxes on gas extraction, namely the point of sale from the LNG plant. Transfer pricing is relevant only to non–arm's length sales made at that point.
- The (more common) segmented approach. Here upstream production and LNG processing are taxed separately, with a different tax regime for each. Usually the LNG plant is just subject to normal business taxes, though sometimes it enjoys a preferential regime. For the purpose of any special taxes on upstream production, gas has to be valued at the point it passes to the LNG plant. If there is common ownership of the LNG plant and gas fields that supply it, or if the owners of each are associated, a transfer price needs to be established at that point. For various reasons, however,

> governments in developing countries normally regulate the pricing of gas sales to LNG plants. The regulated price might be designed to give the LNG plant a fixed markup on costs or a prescribed after-tax rate of return, and all sales to the LNG plant are calculated on that basis whether they involved associated parties or not. In such cases the government should agree with LNG plant operators what records they must keep and supply on request to show that prices have been charged on the prescribed basis in practice. Auditing these records will require some technical expertise, but the transfer pricing method used should not itself be a source of uncertainty or dispute.[27]

It is more difficult to design specific transfer pricing rules or apply norm pricing for gas than for oil. There are some variations in the quality of gas at the point of extraction, depending on the extent of liquids and impurities, but once processed it is a fairly consistent product. There is nevertheless no standard international spot price that can be used as a proxy for arm's length sales values. Spot prices are quoted in regions like the U.S. and Europe with efficient gas distribution networks and extensive and highly developed infrastructure for domestic gas consumption, but these differ from one region to another. They are of limited relevance to domestic markets in developing countries, whose circumstances are quite different. (Domestic gas prices are, however, often subject to government regulation in developing countries, so that – just as in the case of sales to LNG plants – transfer pricing is not a factor, all sales being priced on the same regulated basis whether or not made to an associate.)

International quoted prices are potentially of more relevance to exports, but, while the huge growth in LNG international trade has led to more standardized spot pricing, for the present there remains considerable regional variation in gas prices based on local supply and demand. It is important that any benchmarks chosen should reflect this. Gas is, furthermore, frequently sold under long-term contracts rather than at spot prices. Prices payable under these contracts are often based on the price at the date of supply of some non-gas comparator in the buyer's location, for example oil or alternative fuels. Sometimes obligations to take a certain amount of supply ("take or pay") are built into the contract. Transport costs may be netted back. Where a gas producer sells gas to an associate, for example a related marketing company, it will often be under a similar long-term contract. There will not usually be a range of arm's length spot price gas sales from the same gas field in the month or quarter that can be used to establish a transfer price; spot prices quoted elsewhere may not be relevant; and in any case use of spot prices is inconsistent with how sales are actually priced in normal arm's length transactions. Although future prices payable under the contract may be based on benchmark prices, *all* the contract terms and other factors such as the buyer's location are relevant in determining whether it equates to arm's length terms. Tax authorities will need to consider whether the comparator used, the length of the contract, any break clauses, take-or-pay obligations, transport cost adjustments, and so on, reflect normal arm's length terms for sales into the same market, and, if not, ensure that any non-standard variations are reflected in the price. This can be a challenging task, especially when gas is first sold. There may well be no local contemporary long-term gas contracts on arm's length terms available to provide a basis for comparison. The fact that international gas markets are evolving rapidly with the growth of LNG and unconventional gas adds to the difficulty. Governments often obtain assistance from external industry experts on valuation of natural resources, and it may be particularly useful for gas.

Since long-term contracts determine prices for years to come, there is a good case for governments to require terms to be approved or agreed in advance if an associate is involved. They should also carry out checks later to ensure that those terms are applied in practice (or modified only with agreement).[28]

4.3 Minerals

4.3.1 Income tax

In many developing countries mining is taxed at the normal income tax rate. Gross revenues are normally based on sales values, usually FOB the export port. In some cases, the vast majority of mining sales are exports to non-associated smelting/refining companies, and transfer pricing issues do not arise.

Even where production is sold to an associate, it is often not because the MNE does its own smelting, but because sales to independent smelters or end users are negotiated by a group marketing company, which collects the proceeds and takes a marketing/administration fee. This company may be based in a tax haven (for example, Singapore for sales to the Asian market). In these cases the resale minus method may be appropriate, with the transfer price based on the sale price achieved by the marketing company. To ensure this method is properly applied the tax authority must be able to verify the resale price from the marketing company's sales records. An arm's length price must then be established for any deductible marketing fee. In the absence of a clear CUP this may involve an analysis of the functions, assets and risks of the marketing associate. This, however, is a much-disputed topic, and in practice developing countries may prefer the simpler approach of setting the fee at a maximum percentage of sales by law (or even, at the extreme, disallowing it as a downstream cost altogether,[29] though MNEs would argue that marketing companies make a real contribution to the value chain, which should be recognized under arm's length principles).

Where production is sold to an associate that is not merely a marketing company, pricing of sales is more difficult. Can special methods or reference pricing reduce this difficulty? Sometimes metals are exported in near-finished form. For example, on-site mining processes may produce copper cathode or gold dore. Quoted prices (for example LME) could be used for the former. The London gold fixing price could be (and often is) used for the latter. This overstates the value of production, but the difference between dore and refined gold values is marginal (and possibly a minor standard adjustment could be applied to allow for it).

Metals are, however, usually exported from developing countries as ore or concentrate, with a value significantly less than refined metal. Unrefined mineral production does not have the same consistency of quality as oil production, so it is more difficult to establish CUP from arm's length sales, even if average prices are used. Where benchmark prices are available only for the refined mineral, much more substantial and varied comparability adjustments are needed to arrive at a price for unrefined product than with crude oil benchmarks. There is some transparency of pricing of more common concentrates such as iron and copper, but it is more difficult to use standard formulae to adjust values for quality differences, as can be done for crude oil. The need for complex and varied adjustments makes it more difficult to design standard, simplified methods that produce a reasonable approximation of arm's length prices.

Norm pricing is generally not a feature of mining income tax, but some countries have attempted to develop special transfer pricing rules based on benchmark prices, reflecting the fact that benchmark prices do play a role in the normal commercial pricing of many common minerals. Usually the terms of an arm's length sale to a smelting/refining company are that it will sell the finished mineral on the mining company's behalf and pay the mining company the price quoted on a recognized exchange such as the LME, less a deduction for treatment and refining costs (TC/RCs) – with credits for valuable mineral by-products and penalties for impurities above a permitted level.

This price – the "net smelter return" (NSR) – is often the basis of valuation used for income tax. It is necessary to ensure that the pricing basis used (FOB, CIF or CF) for the NSR is clear and consistent with rules for deduction of transport costs, as discussed earlier. In controlled transactions it is also necessary to ensure that charges for TC/RCs and other adjustments used in calculating NSR are accurate and reasonable. Full access to the associate's records may be needed for this purpose. There is, however, reasonable pricing transparency on TC/RCs. Market rates for TC/RCs in particular countries are often determined for up to a year in advance, and some commercial organizations publish data on pricing of TC/RCs for certain minerals. It might be possible in those cases to impose a special transfer pricing rule based on benchmark TC/RC rates and include it in regulations (or, if that is not possible, use it as the basis for individual APAs). Some countries instead allow simple percentage deductions for processing costs. Strictly this is inconsistent with the arm's length principle, but where such costs are relatively minor and the percentage used broadly in line with past experience, it may be acceptable in practice and have advantages of simplicity and predictability – though there will inevitably be cases in which either companies or governments lose out from such standardized methods.

For rarer minerals, markets may not be deep enough to allow quoted prices to be developed and used in calculating NSR. The onus must be on companies to demonstrate that sales to associates are priced on an arm's length basis, but it will not be possible to prescribe use of a particular benchmark.

The smelter may pay the miner a provisional amount based on quoted prices at the date of sale or shipment, but it will be noted in the earlier discussion that the final NSR payment reflects the quoted price of the finished mineral when it is sold. If transfer pricing rules required the use of the quoted price at the date of shipment this would differ from the commercial pricing date. There is a very wide range of pricing date conventions for commercial commodity transactions (probably wider for minerals than oil). Many respondents to the aforementioned OECD discussion draft have made this point and argued strongly that imposition of a standard pricing date for tax purposes should be exceptional and limited to cases where reliable documentation of the contractual pricing date is unavailable (though others have pointed out that unscrupulous companies could in that case select with hindsight the transactions in which it benefited them to have reliable documentation). The variety of commercial pricing dates clearly makes it more difficult for a special transfer pricing rule to specify a particular pricing date that will produce results consistent with normal arm's length prices. One option would be to prescribe the most common commercial pricing date in use for the commodity concerned, but – at the cost of some complexity – allow some flexibility to use a different date if approved in advance by the tax authority.

For gemstones, although it is possible to identify characteristics that determine value, there is no standard benchmark, and larger stones may require individual expert valuation. For non–arm's length sales there may be no alternative but to require them to be submitted for physical inspection and valuation by the tax authority before sale, with arrangements for arbitration in case of dispute.[30]

Coal, like oil and gas, is a hydrocarbon. It is also similar in the sense that it generally undergoes less complicated processing than minerals. This may allow the development of similar valuation methods to those described for oil.

4.3.2 *Special mining taxes*

In many developing countries the main special tax on mining is value-based royalty, though there is an increasing interest in imposing special profit-based taxes such as RRT.[31]

One option is to use the same sales value for these taxes as for income tax.[32] This allows for simplified and coordinated administration. The same transfer pricing issues will arise but may be manageable if controlled transactions are limited or satisfactory transfer pricing methods can be established.

A practical difficulty with using NSR for royalties is that they often have to be calculated and paid around the date of sale, perhaps monthly, when the final payment is not yet known. Either they have to be based on the initial payment, or they have to be paid provisionally and adjusted later. This complicates administration, but the solution may be to design better royalty assessment procedures. Most countries successfully administer income tax as an annual tax paid by in-year installments rather than requiring it to be calculated monthly, and there is no obvious reason royalties cannot be administered under a similar regime.

Mining royalties are, however, often *not* based on sales value. There is a huge variety in the methods countries use for valuing mining output for royalty purposes.[33] Royalty policy and administration are often the responsibility of the mining department, with no attempt made to coordinate them with income tax.

Basing royalties on sales value may be considered to have disadvantages. One is that if mining companies process minerals locally, this will be reflected in the sales price: imposing special taxes on that value might discourage local processing, when governments wish to encourage it. This may not be a problem for RRT, since processing should not produce any "rent" or excess profit to which RRT would apply (if it did it would probably be profit shifted from mining).[34] It might not *in practice* be a problem for royalties either, since MNEs might avoid royalties on value added by processing by moving it to non-mining domestic associates.

Some governments prefer, however, to distinguish mining from processing in applying special taxes. But the distinction between upstream extraction and downstream processing is less clear-cut for mining than petroleum. Minerals are found in low concentrations, and the initial extraction is mainly waste earth and rock, which is then subject to a series of further extractive processes. Some of these (e.g., crushing, grinding, leaching) may be carried out at the mine site, others (e.g., smelting and refining) at a separate site (sometimes operated by the mining company). Extraction and processing are thus conceptually similar, and it may therefore be difficult to distinguish them clearly in practice.

A common practical solution is simply to value production at the mine mouth or mine gate. The value at this point excludes any value added by off-site processing, and physical measurement is relatively easy.[35] The main disadvantage is that sales are generally not made at this point, so that all output must be valued at an internal transfer price at a point at which there are no comparable uncontrolled sales and no relevant benchmark prices.

Mine gate market value can in theory be established by taking the value at a later point of sale and netting back costs incurred between the mine gate and that point.[36] But this may not be straightforward. Costs of processing beyond the mine gate may vary significantly and involve several different stages. Ore may contain different minerals with different values and different processing costs. Minerals from different sources may be blended during processing. Varying amounts of transportation may be required, again possibly in several stages. Processing and transport may be carried out by associates, whose charges may not be at arm's length prices. The sale from which costs are netted back may be a sale to an associate, for which a transfer price may in turn have to be established by netting back from a later sale to an independent buyer, with similar difficulties. The farther downstream the point of sale to an independent buyer, the greater the potential complexity of the netback calculation. The netback costs may not be known at the time output is measured at the mine gate, causing difficulty where royalties are payable monthly. Royalties are supposed to be simpler than profit-based taxes, but netback calculation is complex. Ginger Rogers once pointed out that she did all the same dance steps as Fred Astaire, only backwards and in high heels – a netback calculation is rather like doing a profit calculation backwards and in high heels.

Royalties do not, however, have to be based on actual value. Countries can simplify valuation by using benchmark (e.g., LME) prices for finished minerals and restricting netback costs (perhaps to those that are easy to measure). A more extreme option is to disregard *all* costs and simply value output at the benchmark price for its mineral content.[37] This is not entirely straightforward, since it requires expert sampling and assay procedures. But it avoids all the difficulties of quantifying netback costs and identifying the appropriate valuation point (the valuation is the same wherever output is measured and can be done wherever measurement is most convenient). It creates no disincentive for domestic processing; indeed, there is an incentive, since royalties will be a smaller proportion of the value of processed than of unprocessed minerals.

Values calculated by these simplified methods will be higher than the actual value of mining output. Royalty rates can be lowered to compensate for this, but there will be no consistent relation between royalty value and actual value. (Where mineral content is used, 2 tons of 35% concentrate would be valued the same as one ton of 70% concentrate but are worth less because of the higher transport and refining costs required.) Various adjustments are possible to bring the values more closely into line (for example, graduating royalties according to the degree of processing) but often introduce more complication than accuracy.

Does this overvaluation matter? Mining companies see *any* royalty not related to profit as somewhat arbitrary – does this not just make it arbitrary in a slightly different way? Royalties are often a relatively minor tax, so the fiscal impact may be minor and may be balanced by the advantage of a valuation method that is simple and certain.

Countries are, however, increasingly looking to capture a greater share of mining rents, often by introducing graduated royalty rates. Companies do tend to regard royalties as particularly arbitrary and unfair where they bear no consistent relation to sales value, and this could have negative effects on investment and voluntary compliance if royalties assume greater importance.

Governments are furthermore showing increasing interest in the alternative approach of imposing special profit-based taxes on mining. There is a stronger presumption in favor of using arm's length values for taxes such as RRT. Their main rationale is to target economic rent more accurately than royalties, an aim that might be frustrated if profits were based on unrealistic notional values.

Royalty valuation methods based on notional values might make royalty administration simpler, considered on its own, but different valuation methods for royalty and profit-based taxes make the administrative regime more complicated and less coherent overall.

Nevertheless, special taxes do potentially increase the incentive for transfer pricing abuse, as discussed in section 2, and governments may prefer simple valuation methods that eliminate or reduce that risk in relation to royalties. Decisions on how far to impose royalties and what valuation method to use may also reflect wider policy considerations than transfer pricing – valuation based on finished mineral prices may simply have greater political appeal.

5 Extractive industry costs

Extractive industry costs are so variable that a general valuation rule substituting standardized for actual costs is unlikely to be practicable or consistent with the arm's length principle. Developing countries often apply cost recovery limits to profit taxes (limiting costs to a maximum percentage of sales), but generally these merely affect the timing of deductions. Nigeria (which has high costs for many reasons) has considered the idea of benchmarking costs administratively for tax purposes, but there is little clarity about how this would be done in practice. Countries should, of course, seek to compare their costs against costs in other countries and, where they are higher, establish the reasons and, if possible, find ways of reducing them. And cost differences for different projects within a country should feature in audit risk assessment. But such differences are common and often have nothing to do with transfer pricing. They may reflect greater physical and technological challenges, higher costs imposed by regulation[38] or greater perceived risks of providing goods and services to particular countries.

There is, however, some scope for applying specific transfer pricing rules to extractive industry costs. Again practices on this vary significantly from one country to another.

For oil and gas, joint ventures (JVs) are common. An operating company incurs costs on behalf of the JV and bills each participator for its share. The other participators have an adverse interest to the operator in respect of shared costs. If an associate of the operator charges excessive transfer prices, it will reduce the other participators' profits as well as the government's tax. Joint operating agreements, fairly standard throughout the industry, therefore incorporate specific fact-based transfer pricing rules. These are based on the principle that costs charged by an associate should be charged at original cost to the associate. Participators are given powers to audit compliance. This gives governments significant protection against transfer pricing abuse.[39]

Governments cannot necessarily leave it entirely to JV partners to enforce this no-profit rule, but they can and often do build it into PSAs (closely modeled on JV agreements) and/or petroleum tax legislation. The no-profit rule might at first sight seem inconsistent with OECD guidelines, but is arguably the CUP for costs charged between non-associated participators in petroleum JVs the world over.[40]

Where this rule applies, tax authorities need to be able to establish that goods and services were actually provided by associates at cost. General information requirements may be adequate for this purpose, but, if not, specific provisions may be needed. Some PSAs allow the government to require a certificate to this effect from an approved independent auditor of the associate's records.

Alternatively costs charged by associates could be disallowable if for any reason (including claimed confidentiality) the taxpayer could not or would not show they were charged at original cost.

For mining, JVs following the no-profit principle are not common, nor is it standard practice to build this principle into mining legislation and contractual agreements. There may, however, be scope for doing so. Associates often supply mining goods and services that they have in turn brought in from external providers, and it may be reasonable to treat the cost to the group as the relevant CUP for determining the intra-group transfer price. (Again ability to require evidence of the cost to the group would be vital.) An alternative is to allow a small markup under the cost plus basis to reflect any value contributed by the associate, but governments must be aware of the risk that companies will inflate costs by routing them through tax haven-based service companies that add little value in reality.

Alternative specific transfer pricing cost rules are possible. One fairly common approach is to limit management service charges to a maximum percentage of total operating costs or total revenues. The percentages used vary significantly from country to country. This is clearly an inaccurate and somewhat arbitrary method of determining arm's length prices, and the risk of such "safe harbor" rules is that the ceiling quickly becomes a floor. But it does have the important advantages of clarity and objectivity. If it is built into legislation or contractual agreements at the outset, then governments can take the generosity or otherwise of the limit into account in planning their overall natural-resource fiscal regime, and companies can similarly take it into account in planning whether to invest in the country concerned. Within limits, therefore, such rules are often found to be acceptable and workable in practice.

PSAs often contain standard rules for costing previously used equipment.[41] Again these may not strictly meet the arm's length standard but have advantages of simplicity and predictability.

Mining and drilling costs charged by associated companies can be very large and will present significant risks. If it is not possible to "look through" to the original cost, it may be possible to use standard rates, for example, for hire of drilling rigs, but there will often be special factors that make like-for-like comparison difficult, and data may be difficult for tax authorities to obtain. (Countries with natural resources might well benefit from exchange of such data.) It may be impossible to devise specific transfer pricing rules, in which case it is essential to require companies to justify the prices charged.

Payments to associates for intellectual property (special processing technologies, technical research, etc.) are less common than in other industries but are sometimes made. Ownership is often located in tax havens. Pricing is notoriously difficult. Ring-fencing rules may disallow or at least limit such costs if they do not relate specifically to a project in the country concerned, but if not, claims for such costs may have to be considered on their individual merits (which may be questionable).

Ring-fencing adds further difficulties. It may be unclear how shared costs should be apportioned, for example, where machinery is moved from one site to another, or (even more difficult) where costs have to be apportioned between oil and associated gas. The best course may be to prescribe or agree on formulary rules based on measurable outputs or inputs that, while they may not strictly meet the arm's length standard, produce a reasonably fair and even-handed result if applied consistently. Devising, applying and monitoring such rules can, however, be difficult.

Companies may avoid tax by charging excessive finance costs. This puts income tax at risk, because finance costs are generally deductible, whereas costs of equity financing are not.[42] Some governments negotiate generous interest deduction rules as a deliberate tax incentive,[43] but the following discussion assumes the aim is to apply arm's length terms.

Finance costs can be excessive in two ways:

- They may be excessive relative to the amount borrowed (e.g., interest rates or guarantee or facilitation fees at higher-than-normal market rates); and/ or
- They may be excessive because the amount borrowed is itself excessive (generally described as "thin capitalization").

Thin capitalization is a special type of transfer pricing problem. It describes the situation where a taxpayer that is part of a group of companies borrows more than it could or would if it were an independent entity. Thin capitalization risks are not unique to extractive industry taxation, but there are the same special incentives and opportunities as for other transfer pricing abuse. Special features of the extractive industries, such as the high risk of exploration, and their exceptional importance in some cases to government revenues may be seen as justifying special rules.

There is a range of approaches to countering thin capitalization; some lend themselves to more effective and transparent administration than others. Some countries have little protection other than general transfer pricing rules (which, as discussed, are often poorly designed and are particularly hard to apply to this issue). Others impose specific limits. For example:

- A maximum *debt-to-equity ratio*, with interest disallowed on borrowing exceeding that ratio. There is considerable variation, ranging from 1:1 to as much as 4:1. Legislation sometimes leaves it unclear whether this represents a "safe harbor" (with the disadvantages mentioned earlier) or simply a maximum level subject to further possible restriction under general transfer pricing principles. Often there is no special debt-to-equity ratio for extractive industries, so that a generous ratio may apply even to an exploration company operating in a previously unexplored and/or politically unstable area (which could probably borrow nothing at all on arm's length terms if operating independently). Sometimes the restriction applies only to borrowing from abroad and/or borrowing from associates. This may allow excessive borrowing by means of "back-to-back" loans (loans from an associate routed through an independent bank) or parent company guarantee (explicit or implicit). The rules often leave scope for argument on the definition of debt and equity.

- A limit imposed by reference to the *purpose of borrowing*. For example, interest may be deductible only on borrowing to fund development costs or a maximum percentage of such costs. A risk with this approach is that companies may accumulate debt no longer required for the original purpose, so an additional ongoing finance *requirement* test may be needed. An example can be found in Uganda's model production sharing agreement, which allows interest on loans to finance development operations only to the extent it relates to debt (from any source) not exceeding 50% of the total financing requirement, and disallows interest on loans to finance exploration. A restriction of this kind could possibly be supplemented by regulations or guidance to the effect that the financing requirement was to be taken as the cumulative negative cash flow including tax paid but excluding other disallowable costs.
- A limit restricting interest to a maximum *percentage of taxable profits* (sometimes known as an earnings-stripping rule). Again limits vary from country to country. Because disallowed costs are usually carried forward to future years, the effect may be that excessive deductions are merely deferred rather than disallowed altogether.

Deductibility of interest is normally a condition for foreign tax credit, and there is a theoretical risk that it could be prejudiced by such anti-avoidance rules. But there is little evidence of this in practice.

Some countries take simpler approaches than others to limiting interest *rates* paid. General transfer pricing rules may be relied on to limit interest to a normal commercial rate, but this can be difficult to define. Cases have been seen in which, with inadequate thin capitalization rules, companies borrow far more than they could do if operating independently and then argue that the interest rate should be high to reflect the exceptional risk of such high borrowing! An alternative approach is to set the maximum rate at a specific percentage above a quoted benchmark rate, for example, 6-month dollar LIBOR + 2% (assuming that LIBOR is considered a sufficiently reliable measure). This is strictly a departure from the arm's length standard (since companies might be able to negotiate different rates on the open market), but so long as it reflected typical borrowing rates, it might be considered a reasonable approximation and has advantages of clarity and predictability.

Countries sometimes use ministerial or departmental discretion to limit finance costs for large projects. Companies have to seek approval of loans and of the terms applying to them. Sometimes this is the only protection against excessive finance costs; sometimes it is combined with other restrictions.

Clearly it is better than nothing, but it is preferable to have published rules that are administratively transparent and effective.

Some countries re-classify disallowed excessive finance costs as dividends. This adds complexity but, depending on the country's WHT rules, may be necessary to ensure they do not have tax advantages over dividends.

Disguised interest presents a further risk, so restrictions on deductibility need to apply to *all* finance charges, not just those explicitly described as interest. Companies may disguise interest to circumvent restrictions on deductibility of the kind discussed, to circumvent the (normal) disallowance of interest for taxes such as RRT or production sharing or to avoid withholding tax on interest payments. Finance leases are one instrument that may be used for this purpose. A finance lease is in legal form an asset rental but in substance a loan-financed asset purchase (since under the terms of the lease the risks and benefits of ownership are passed to the lessee). International accounting standards recognize the substance and require a proportion of the lease payments to be characterized as interest, but in some countries tax rules do not.[44] Other kinds of payment (e.g., guarantee fees) or financial instruments (e.g., interest rate swaps) may also be used to disguise interest costs.[45]

6 Administrative procedures

Practical and procedural issues need to be addressed if transfer pricing is to be controlled effectively. An essential starting point, already discussed, is that the onus should be on taxpayers to apply transfer pricing rules within a self-assessment framework. This requires that valuation rules should, as far as possible, be clear, predictable and not open to dispute or manipulation. General transfer pricing rules may need to be supplemented by regulations – any special extractive industry rules will clearly need legal or regulatory support. Guidance should be published explaining in detail how the rules will apply in practice if there is any ambiguity about this. Tax authorities should discuss such guidance with industry representatives and seek their agreement. It should be regularly updated in the light of experience.

It then falls to tax auditors to monitor compliance and enforce it if necessary. The key principle of modern tax administration is risk management, and a coherent risk-based approach is needed for transfer pricing. To facilitate this, taxes on extractive industries that are vulnerable to transfer pricing abuse should ideally be audited by a single department, possibly on the basis of a consolidated tax return. Tax returns should be designed to provide data required to assess transfer pricing risks. Taxpayers should be obliged to disclose significant associated party transactions. Cost analyses should be designed to identify categories particularly at risk of transfer pricing abuse, such as management charges.

The tax authority will need to obtain, maintain and analyze data required for transfer pricing risk assessment, develop risk factors, and continually refine them in the light of experience. The data will include not just returns data but also relevant taxpayer data – for example, group structure (especially links with tax haven–based associates) and past compliance history – some of which may need to be gathered from outside sources, such as consolidated group accounts, company websites and foreign tax authorities. It will also include third-party data on production volumes, arm's length sale prices, benchmark sale prices and costs. The industry regulatory department will be a key source of this data, and effective exchange of information is essential (assuming the taxing authority is different from the regulatory authority).

Once a decision has been made to audit transfer pricing, it will be necessary to identify high-risk transactions (including those ostensibly with non-associates), obtain explanations of how they were priced, examine contract documentation and seek further explanations as necessary. If mispricing is established, follow-up action – penalties, education, legislation or whatever – should be planned to reduce the risk of recurrence.

This is demanding work and requires competent, well-trained and qualified staff. Staff employed on this work often do not have the pay, status and authority needed to ensure the required quality, even in countries where only a few key staff are required to administer the tax of a few large companies paying the lion's share of government revenues.

Tax authorities sometimes create specialist transfer pricing teams to assist general audit staff with transfer pricing audits. This may be less appropriate for extractive industries, in which auditors should normally be industry specialists, who will be more familiar with the valuation issues peculiar to the industry and with any special methods applicable. Industry specialists should, however, receive training to increase understanding of transfer pricing risks, issues and procedures.[46]

Where the law imposes a special transfer pricing rule or a general valuation rule for sales, special administrative procedures are required. Key formal procedures become those that establish quantity and price, and audit of revenues becomes largely a question of checking that the quantity-times-price valuation imposed by law is correctly applied in taxpayers' returns. (Where there are no special rules, data on quantity and price should be gathered for risk assessment and audit purposes but will not have the same formal legal status.)

There will usually be documentary evidence of quantity and quality (for example, in sales documents), but real-time monitoring by the authorities of physical production and measurement is advisable to some extent – so-called physical audit. This tends to be more straightforward for oil and gas, which pass through a limited number of delivery points where special metering equipment is installed, than for minerals, which may have a wide range of routes to export, may not have accurate measuring facilities such as weighbridges installed and may need to be assayed by subjecting samples to detailed laboratory analysis. This requires specialist expertise and procedures and gives obvious scope for error and dispute. Physical audit is therefore not foolproof and is best regarded as a supplement to, not a substitute for, financial audit.

Physical audit is often the responsibility of a department other than the tax department – for example, the industry department or, for exports, the customs department. There is considerable variation in countries' approach to physical audit. Some exercise little oversight and rely on the accuracy of company measurements and documentation. At the other extreme, some require direct government measurement of all production.

Companies should be subject to clearly defined obligations to measure and record physical production. The point of measurement for sales valuation should be clearly defined. Companies should be required to implement controls to ensure that all production reaches that point (and to control and measure unsold stock). At the valuation point they should be required to put in place equipment and procedures to accurately measure volume and quality and systems for recording those measurements, which should be reported to the responsible agency under specified rules. The responsible agency should not necessarily have to take all the obligations of measuring volume and quality on itself, particularly in the case of large MNEs – instead it should oversee companies' performance of those obligations and monitor measured output against other data, such as production plans. Large companies are at constant risk of misappropriation of resources by their employees, particularly in the case of precious minerals, and will normally have sophisticated systems and controls of their own in place to prevent it and to ensure proper valuation of sales. The responsible agency should review the adequacy of those systems and controls and can generally build upon them rather than seek to replace them wholesale with its own. It should have unfettered rights to physically inspect the movement of resources up to the point of measurement and to physically monitor and test company measuring equipment and procedures but should adopt a selective risk-based approach reflecting both the amounts at risk and the probability of error (taking company characteristics and history into account among other factors). It should carry out tests (requiring competence in mineralogical analysis and sampling techniques) at unpredictable intervals. It should have a clearly formulated strategy and plan for physical audit and should keep records of its physical audit checks and their outcomes. Where inaccurate measurements or recordings are established, procedures should exist to correct them, including reasonable extrapolation to other periods. There should be penalties for such failures and rights of arbitration where there is disagreement over volume and quality measurement. Procedures should be established for production data to be passed to the department responsible for tax audit.

Where production has to be valued on the basis of specified *benchmark prices* (or on the basis of average prices of actual transactions), there should be clear procedures in place for establishing and publishing those prices. In some countries the tax department is responsible for determining prices; in others it is the industry department or national resource company (but this may create conflict of interest if the company operates commercially); or different agencies may have joint responsibility. In some countries the responsible department takes the lead in identifying suitable benchmarks and calculating the prices to be used; in others resource companies put forward proposals along with supporting evidence, which the department can accept or amend. The latter approach may foster better relations with the industry, enhancing voluntary compliance. Either way, the responsible department needs to have procedures (and funding) in place for identifying, accessing and recording relevant price data.

Normally companies will have rights of appeal against assessments, but where values to be used are prescribed in advance, there is often separate provision for arbitration of valuation disputes, usually involving international experts rather than local courts. In other cases, prices to be used are simply imposed by government. If pricing rules are clear, objective and predictable, rights to arbitration may not be necessary, but often the choice of benchmark, the adjustments made to it, the pricing of actual transactions (where these feature in the calculation), the weighting of different elements of the calculation (where combinations of methods and benchmarks are used) and the calculation of weighted averages are open to dispute, and an arbitration mechanism is appropriate.

In theory, if rules prescribing prices to be used are clear and simple, companies can be left to apply them; in practice, it is often best if they are published by the responsible agency. Pricing can be quite complex for the reasons explained. The data required to calculate prices may not be readily available to all who have a need to report or monitor them. Even if the calculation is simple (e.g., a simple unweighted average mineral price quoted on a particular exchange), it is still best, in the interests of transparency and certainty, if the actual figures to be used are clearly published, for example on an official website. When annual tax returns are received, the correct application of the prescribed prices should be checked as part of the audit or audit risk assessment process. Publication of the figures should leave no room for dispute between companies and tax auditors.

7 Conclusion

MNEs generally favor the arm's length standard for pricing controlled transactions but prefer to be left to make their own choices as to the most appropriate method, including whether to make use of quoted prices, which ones to use if they do, how to adjust them for comparability differences, what contractual terms to use, what pricing date conventions to apply and so on. They see this flexibility as essential to respond to the complexities of commercial commodity markets. They accept the right of tax authorities to challenge transfer prices but want them to do so with a full understanding of all the complex facts and circumstances that may be relevant. They see prescriptive standardized rules as bureaucratic and inconsistent with arm's length principles, since they inevitably fail to reflect the complexity and variety of commercial pricing.

Governments of developing countries, on the other hand, are uncomfortable with some transfer pricing methods that they feel are less favorable to commodity producers than CUP. They are aware too of the risk of sophisticated transfer pricing strategies being used to shift profits. Many have introduced improved transfer pricing legislation consistent with international standards and are seeking help with its application and enforcement. But often their tax authorities lack resources and capacity to establish all the relevant facts and circumstances, let alone identify and challenge abuse effectively; and their standards of governance are ill suited to complex negotiations with a wide range of possible outcomes. "Must try harder" is the advice they often receive, but they may feel that the improvements in capacity and governance needed to counter abuse effectively are, realistically, unlikely to happen any time soon (considering that even developed countries struggle to do so). The arm's length standard may be fine in principle, but if they embody it in law but cannot enforce it, the practical result is likely to be not arm's length pricing but base erosion and profit shifting – which, once their non-renewable resources are gone, they will not have another chance to put right.

It is perhaps unsurprising, therefore, that developing countries have sought to develop more simple, objective and predictable transfer pricing methods for commodities, often based on quoted prices. These can be criticized as not fully consistent with arm's length standards (and sometimes they are themselves vulnerable to abuse). But for oil such methods are now well established, and companies have generally learned to live with them if not to like them. They may not produce entirely realistic arm's length prices, but may be acceptable if they are applied evenhandedly, have some basis in normal commercial practice and achieve a reasonable approximation, taking one transaction with another. For other commodities, the challenges of developing standard, simplified methods that meet those criteria are greater, there is probably more variety in the methods countries have developed in practice and in many cases investors consider them seriously flawed and unacceptable. It must be hoped that the debate initiated by the OECD on this topic and the further research proposed will identify methods that developing countries find appropriate for commodities and within their capacity while producing results acceptable to investors. But there is still a long way to go.

Notes

1 In this chapter "commodities" refers to hydrocarbons and minerals. Special rules often apply to other commodities too, but these are not discussed.
2 In this chapter "tax" is used to mean any payment imposed by government, including, for example, royalties and production sharing.
3 "Upstream" describes exploration and extraction; "downstream" transportation beyond an initial delivery point, refining/processing and distribution, marketing and sales of finished products.
4 Examples of common taxes not based on revenues or profits are signature and production bonuses, volume-based royalties, surface rents, withholding taxes, payroll taxes, dividend taxes, import duties, free and carried equity and infrastructure building obligations. Some "nuisance" taxes for example, education and regional levies, may be based on revenues and vulnerable to transfer pricing abuse, but are not discussed further here.
5 Governments can apply a special *low*-tax regime to extractive industries, and some have done this at times, particularly with mining. In that case transfer pricing can reduce tax by *over*valuing revenues and *under*valuing costs, thus shifting profits *into* the mining tax regime. When commodity prices are high it is more common for extractive industries to be subject to a high-tax regime.

6 For example, say company A paid associated service contractor B $100k when the arm's length rate was $90k, subject to a typical 10% WHT (if one third of a contractor's receipts represents profit, this equates to a 30% tax on that profit). If tax was charged on A's profits at, say, 60%, the excess $10k payment would reduce A's tax by $5k ($10k at 60% less $10k at 10%). B might have to pay foreign tax on the $10k but almost certainly much less than $5k.

7 OECD Global Forum on Transfer Pricing, *Draft Handbook on Transfer Pricing Risk Assessment* ¶38 (OECD 2013).

8 For example, unpublished research by UK tax authorities identified significant tax loss from manipulation of North Sea oil transfer prices (HMRC 2014; http://www.hmrc.gov.uk/manuals/otmanual/ot05012.htm).

9 There are less sophisticated ways of exploiting this than tax planning – for example, smuggling abroad production designated for domestic processing or consumption.

10 The granting of tax holidays for mining operations is fairly common in developing countries. The obvious transfer pricing risks this presents are sometimes exacerbated by lax record keeping and reporting requirements during the tax holiday period.

11 It is beyond the scope of this chapter to consider the policy arguments for and against area-based ring-fencing, but the administrative burdens it imposes and the capacity of companies and tax authorities to meet them are clearly factors to take into account.

12 Appendix 1 to Chapter 11 in *Taxation of Petroleum and Minerals – Principles, Problems and Practice* (Calder 2010) discusses the taxation of hedging instruments in more detail. It outlines the arguments *for* recognizing hedging gains and losses (basically, they affect companies' profits) and *against* (basically, they present risks of tax avoidance, and governments should anyway decide for themselves how far to hedge natural resource revenues and not leave it to the vagaries of whether MNEs choose to do so).

13 Lao PDR's is a rare example of a country without transfer pricing rules in its primary tax legislation, though rules are included in mining contractual agreements.

14 Cases are sometimes seen where a parent company and subsidiary fall within the definition but not sister companies under common control.

15 For example, A could sell production for $X to non-associate B, who as part of a wider agreement undertook to sell it for X + y% to a refinery owned by A's associate. B has no interest in X but only in y, so X is a non–arm's length price. An example of rules to counter this can be found in the UK's legislation; see http://www.hmrc.gov.uk/manuals/otmanual/OT05025.htm.

16 Similarly, section 482 of the U.S. Tax Code ostensibly leaves the onus on the tax authority to identify and adjust non-market prices, but this is supplemented by extensive regulations that in effect require companies to use arm's length prices for tax return purposes and impose penalties for failure to do so.

17 Chapter 3 (Shay, this volume) discussed APAs more fully, and expressed reservations about the limited wider benefits from the resources devoted to them and their lack of transparency. Those reservations are even more relevant in developing countries. Discussions with extractive industry MNEs suggest that they are virtually never used in developing countries in practice. They may nevertheless be an option to consider if other means of producing certainty cannot be found. There may also be cases in which tax auditors and MNEs can reach working agreements without the need for a formal APA.

18 OECD, *BEPS Action 10; Discussion Draft on the Transfer Pricing Aspects of Cross-Border Commodity Transactions* December 2014 (http://www.oecd.org/ctp/transfer-pricing/discussion-draft-action-10-commodity-transactions.pdf).

19 For example, business organizations claim that Argentina's application of the sixth method is unfair because it defines controlled transactions too widely, does not adjust quoted prices appropriately and imposes shipping date price even where other pricing dates are required by normal market conventions, thus – because prices are only adjusted upwards – essentially penalizing companies for market volatility.

20 http://www.hmrc.gov.uk/manuals/otmanual/ot05012.htm

21 Mining and petroleum agreements in some countries apply a specific transfer pricing rule to non–arm's length sales but also have a general rule requiring all sales to be made at international prices or forbidding discount sales, potentially giving the tax authority scope to re-value a sale even if ostensibly negotiated at arm's length.
22 Brent and West Texas Intermediate are among the most commonly quoted.
23 A minor adjustment may also be needed if the volume of the transaction differs significantly from that on which the benchmark price is based.
24 Where oil is not freely tradable on international markets, domestic oil prices may be significantly affected by local supply and demand – for example, where there are legal export barriers (as in the U.S.) or limited export pipeline capacity (as sometimes experienced in Russia). In such circumstances international quoted prices may be of limited relevance, and it can be particularly difficult to establish arm's length prices if the domestic market is dominated by vertically integrated businesses.
25 PSA valuation rules vary but might typically require arm's length sales to be valued at actual sale prices and non–arm's length sales at the weighted average of arm's length sales in the month or quarter but with a provision that if less than half of the oil sold in the period is sold at arm's length, they should instead be valued at the average price of one or more designated benchmark crudes, adjusted as necessary for quality and transport cost differentials.
26 Policy objections to aligning income tax and PSA valuation rules are not obvious, but one might be that meeting international investors' expectations that income tax will be fully consistent with OECD international standards is more important than the administrative advantages of consistency.
27 See Graham Kellas's chapter in *Taxation of Petroleum and Minerals – Principles, Problems and Practice* (2010) for a comprehensive discussion of LNG pricing.
28 Long-term contracts are particularly common for gas but are sometimes used for other commodities, and similar issues will arise.
29 In the UK, for example, marketing fees are deductible for petroleum revenue tax purposes only if the sale is to a non-associate.
30 Many countries require this for *all* sales, not just those to associates. This can be expensive (in Sierra Leone in recent years, valuation fees have amounted to around a third of royalties and export duties on diamond sales). Where the intention is to base taxes on actual values, it is not clear why government valuations should be substituted for arm's length sale prices, particularly where it is clear that the buyer is not an associate.
31 There are often many additional "nuisance taxes", not discussed here.
32 This approach is broadly followed by Zambia for copper, though there is debate about its implications for local smelting.
33 This is comprehensively discussed in Otto et al.: *Mining Royalties* (Washington, DC, World Bank)
34 The greater risk would be that processing was unprofitable, so that its inclusion *reduced* RRT.
35 It includes value added by on-site processing, however. The policy rationale for taxing this but not off-site processing is not clear, and it may encourage companies to reduce royalties by moving processing off site.
36 In broad terms this is the approach adopted in Australia for the purposes of its federal resource rent tax. (Royalties are imposed at state level, and varied methods are used.)
37 This, broadly, is the approach adopted to royalty valuation in Mongolia, for example.
38 Local content obligations, for example, can have an impact on costs and are common in developing countries.
39 It may for this reason be prudent for governments to award petroleum licenses to JVs rather than to single companies.
40 One effect of limiting cost to original cost to the group may be to limit deductions for insurance payments where an MNE self-insures through a captive insurance company that does not re-insure outside the group.

41 For example, used equipment of a defined age and state of repair will be valued at x% of original cost.
42 The application of WHT to dividends may counter some of the tax advantages of excessive borrowing.
43 For example, a London-based mining company investing in a Sierra Leone subsidiary in the aftermath of the civil war persuaded the government that the subsidiary should get interest deductions on loans from its parent company *because* no bank was prepared to lend to it!
44 Another advantage of finance leases for companies is that they may circumvent PSA rules giving the government ownership of assets acquired for petroleum operations if the PSA terms do not treat a finance lease as an acquisition.
45 Interest-hedging instruments may provide scope for other kinds of tax avoidance, especially if there is no requirement to "mark to market", and offset finance costs against finance gains.
46 Auditors in developing countries often see themselves as responsible for controlling industry costs and revenues generally, particularly where they belong to the industry department. This can result in a lack of focus on transfer pricing risks. The author has in several countries met senior audit staff who expressed concerns that companies were undervaluing sales and overvaluing costs but had no real idea of the extent to which they transacted with associates.

References

Calder, Jack. (2010), "Resource Tax Administration: The Implications of Alternative Policy Choices," in Philip Daniel, Michael Keen and Charles McPherson (eds), *The Taxation of Petroleum and Minerals – Principles, Problems and Practice.* (London, New York: Routledge), pp. 331–334.

HMRC (2014), *Oil Tax Manual*, Available at http://www.hmrc.gov.uk/manuals/otmanual

Kellas, Graham. (2010), "Natural Gas: Experience and Issues," in Philip Daniel, Michael Keen and Charles McPherson (eds), *The Taxation of Petroleum and Minerals – Principles, Problems and Practice.* (London, New York: Routledge), pp. 163–183.

OECD. (2013), *Public Consultation: Draft Handbook on Transfer Pricing Risk Assessment.*

OECD. (2014), *BEPS Action 10; Discussion Draft on the Transfer Pricing Aspects of Cross-Border Commodity Transactions.*

Otto, James, Craig Andrews, Fred Cawood, Michael Doggett, Pietro Guj, Frank Stermole, John Stermole and John Tilton. (2006), *Mining Royalties* (Washington, DC: World Bank).

5 International tax and treaty strategy in resource-rich developing countries

Experience and approaches

Philip Daniel and Victor Thuronyi[1]

1 Introduction

Interest in international tax issues has seldom been greater than in the aftermath of the financial crisis that broke out in 2008. In addition to the high-profile cases of tax loss recorded in a number of countries a flurry of initiatives emerged from inter-governmental summits and international organizations. The phenomenon of base erosion and profit shifting (BEPS) and the possibility of initiatives to mitigate damaging effects were the subjects of a joint OECD and G20 project. The IMF (2014) published a major paper on spillovers in international taxation, showing that macroeconomic spillovers from weaknesses in the international tax architecture were significant – especially for developing countries.

The spillovers for countries exporting mining and petroleum commodities appear notably problematic, and developing countries with large extractive industry (EI) sectors have long faced challenges from the commercial organization of these sectors. First, the necessary involvement (in many countries) of multinational mining and energy companies as sources of capital, technology and managerial expertise brings with it the political problem of objection to extraction of host country resources by foreign companies. Second, these companies operate by definition in international capital markets, undertaking myriad cross-border transactions and selling products in international trade; they thus operate squarely within an international system for the taxation of corporate income. Third, fiscal regimes for extractive industries are often complex, involving a mix of contractual and legislated systems and fragmented administration as discussed by Calder (2014).

This chapter addresses issues for EI fiscal regimes from the international corporate tax framework and bilateral taxation treaties (BTTs). The structure and measurement of spillovers for resource-rich countries are discussed by Keen and Mullins in Chapter 2 of this book and in IMF (2014). The chapter outlines the key challenges that have arisen, drawing upon *inter alia* IMF advisory work with member countries. The principal focus is on corporate taxation, though the relevant transfer pricing issues affect other fiscal instruments too (see the chapters by Calder and also by Shay in this book). We illustrate the impact of these issues on potential extractive industry revenues for host countries. Finally, we ask if there are some defensive steps that host countries can take even if overall reform of the international architecture is delayed or fails to materialize.

2 The extent and nature of tax treaties

A number of countries with an important extractive sector already have a fairly extensive tax treaty network, but many do not.[2] Resource-rich countries with an extensive treaty network may have negotiated their treaties on the view that treaties are important in attracting foreign investment, particularly in a sector in which long-term stability is important, and mindful of the important role that multinational companies play in this sector.[3] However, if the question is examined more carefully, it becomes clear that treaties are not necessarily needed to accomplish the goals commonly attributed to treaties. Much of what treaties can accomplish can be done unilaterally, for example, defining permanent establishment in domestic law consistently with treaty models. The appropriate approach therefore is not for countries to rush headlong into signing treaties but rather to weigh the costs and benefits of alternative approaches and to develop a strategy that suits the needs of the country in question.

Tax treaties have proliferated as a part of the international corporate tax framework (Keen and Mullins, this volume). After steady growth in the 1970s and 1980s, the BTT network expanded significantly in the following two decades – partly as a result of the independence of states of the former USSR but also because many developing countries saw expansion of their treaty networks as positive encouragement for inflows of foreign investment. Treaties between OECD countries and non-members multiplied, but not as much as treaties among non–OECD members. Keen and Mullins (this volume) illustrate these points and also the rapid recent spread of more limited tax information exchange agreements (TIEAs).[4]

BTTs aim to avoid double taxation and counter tax evasion. The broad idea stems from the notion that taxing the same income twice in two jurisdictions is inefficient, though the point is not obvious if the sum of two impositions of tax is sometimes less than the amount of single taxation in one place. Similarly, treaties seek to establish the right of at least one treaty partner country to tax income from activities distributed across the two, and thus to prevent "double non-taxation"; treaties also aim to counter evasion of established taxing rights.

The key provisions follow these twin aims. BTTs clarify which party can tax which income and when a taxpayer can obtain a credit in one state for tax paid in the other. For payments from an entity in one state to a recipient in the other, BTTs set out the rights of the state that is the source of the payment to impose withholding tax on it and at what maximum rate. Typically, such payments subject to withholding tax cover dividends, interest, royalties on intellectual property and sometimes management fees or technical service payments. Treaties provide for information exchange between the tax authorities of the parties in certain circumstances. And treaties specifically provide a means for the settlement of tax disputes, both between the parties and with respect to a taxpayer resident in one state and the tax authority of the other. Dispute settlement would cover, for example, the resolution of a transfer pricing issue between related taxpayers.

The pattern of purely bilateral treaties seems inefficient and open to question. Despite the ostensibly bilateral approach, each treaty is in effect a treaty with the world – in the sense that country A, making a treaty with country B, establishes an implied relationship with all of country B's other treaty partners, and *vice versa*. Taking only the 34 OECD countries, full coverage under bilateral treaties (every country has a direct treaty with everyone else) would require 561 separate treaties, and only 33 are needed for all to be indirectly linked – so the separate bilateral treaties probably mean multiple non-equivalent treaty channels.[5] Within the BEPS project, international consideration of a possible multilateral treaty instrument was initiated and due for completion by the end of 2016.

Tax treaties pose important risks for host countries of extractive industries. This is especially true for those developing countries with less diversified economies, unlikely to be the source of investment in EI, of international corporate headquarters, or of technology and services for EI projects. The main areas of concern, discussed in what follows, include (i) base erosion from limitations on withholding taxes on payments to non-residents; (ii) "treaty shopping" – location for tax reasons of providers in source countries with advantageous treaty provisions with the host country; (iii) limitations on the ability of host countries to tax gains on transfers of interest, direct or indirect, in mineral rights; and (iv) exclusions of taxing powers, for example, through narrow definitions of real property or broad definitions of business profits.

Developing a tax treaty strategy implies coming up with an overall plan, based on analysis of the current situation (including existing treaties) and policy aims. The strategy is intended primarily to guide future treaty negotiation. It is particularly important to have a strategy because the treaty area is unforgiving of mistakes. Even a provision found in only one treaty can have an important effect on future negotiations, because it can become a precedent that other negotiating partners will ask for. Moreover, depending on whether the treaty in question has effective anti–treaty-shopping provisions (limitation of benefits), a single treaty with favorable terms can in practice often be used by an investor that is not resident in the treaty partner using a conduit entity that is resident in the treaty partner. Another reason treaties are unforgiving is that, unlike domestic legislation, treaties tend to be difficult and slow to change. To change a treaty, the negotiating partner must agree, and often the partner does not feel a compelling reason to move quickly. While a country can always withdraw from a treaty, countries are reluctant to do so, and instances of this happening are relatively rare.[6] So in the treaty area, changes usually come very slowly. An unfavorable treaty provision can therefore remain on the books (and cause trouble) for years.

Tax treaty policy is (or should be) a subset of tax policy in general. The importance of tax treaty policy compared with tax policy in general depends on the extent of the country's treaty network and the importance of international issues for taxation. But tax policy (including tax treaty policy) also is part of economic policy for the extractive industry sector. The extent of the overlap between these policy areas in a particular country depends on the importance of the natural resource sector and the importance of multinational companies in this sector. In an extreme case in which the EI sector dominates the economy and only multinationals are involved in it, the overlap among tax policy, tax treaty policy and economic policy for natural resources is substantial, so that there are not many tax policy choices unrelated to treaties and the EI sector. This means of course in this case that treaties must be negotiated with the EI sector primarily in mind.

Many of the policy goals of treaties can be achieved by unilateral means.[7] A unilateral approach might involve the following. First, a country can exercise restraint in taxing non-residents, generally doing so only to the extent that typical treaty provisions would allow. This is a flexible approach, because there is no hard-and-fast legal constraint. Thus, for example, withholding tax rates could be limited to rates that would typically be allowed by treaty and could avoid taxing items of income that could not be reached if a treaty were in effect (for example, a withholding tax imposed on "all services", which treaties would not allow in the absence of a permanent establishment). A country could define a permanent establishment using text similar to the UN Model and could tax non-residents only in those situations where treaties would permit. In the transfer pricing area, a country could adopt rules that are consistent with the arm's length principle. A unilateral approach could also involve providing stability to investors through practice or agreements.[8] Finally, a country could assure the creditability[9] of its corporate income tax through careful tax design. In any event, the importance of creditability has been diminished because most countries have now switched to an exemption regime.

The extent to which a country can rely on a unilateral approach depends on how many treaties a country already has. A number of countries with an important EI sector already have a substantial network of treaties. These will presumably continue to expand their treaty network, and can therefore take a unilateral approach only with respect to investors from countries that are not treaty partners. Countries with few or no treaties might consider a unilateral approach. For countries with a substantial number of treaties, gradual expansion, adding or renegotiating two or three treaties a year, may be realistic. A rapid expansion would be difficult or virtually impossible given the limited capacity of treaty negotiators as well as limited negotiating capacity on the part of potential treaty partners. This leaves room for a unilateral approach to some extent.

Stability agreements can be used regardless of overall treaty strategy.[10] They should be designed with care given the pitfalls involved. Stability agreements have a number of advantages. A stability agreement can be concluded more quickly than a treaty. It can cover more taxes than a treaty typically covers. It can cover entities that might reside in different countries. However, there are pitfalls in a complex stability agreement that freeze the entire tax system. It is advisable to draft a stability agreement by focusing it only on the key elements. One reason is the incredible complexity that can be involved in administering frozen law for what can be a long period of time depending on the terms of the agreement.

Preliminary analysis for developing a tax treaty strategy involves the following steps. Types of cross-border transactions that would be affected by treaties, the aggregate volume of which is likely to be significant, should be identified and their quantity estimated. The nature of inbound and outbound investment should be identified and research undertaken to identify whether there are currently any tax barriers to such investment. Similarly identified should be any international tax problems that resident individuals are facing. The operation of any existing treaties should be studied to determine what problems, if any, existing treaties are posing (which might signal the need for renegotiation as well as for negotiating new treaties differently so as to avoid these problems). One can identify some problems on the face of the treaty. Better yet is to quantify the extent of misuse of the treaty or undesired results that the treaty has led to. These should be prioritized for renegotiation. Treaty partners may be interested in renegotiation anyway to reflect the latest updates to the OECD/UN Models (or their own country-specific models).

Using these considerations, negotiating partners can be prioritized. Thus, for example, if existing or potential new investment is coming from a handful of countries, those countries might be at the top of the list, particularly if the existing treaty framework (or absence of treaties) is posing problems for such investment. The overall tax treaty strategy may end up not being driven by EI; this depends on the relative importance of EI in the economy.

Any well-thought-out tax treaty strategy would involve avoiding negotiations that are primarily politically motivated. Priority of potential treaty partners should be based on their importance for the tax system not on political convenience. A country should avoid negotiating a treaty with another country involving no important transactions for which a treaty would be significant.

Each treaty is a treaty with the world. One should generally avoid negotiating a treaty with any country that is a tax haven. This is because such a treaty will likely be used by investors for tax planning in a way that achieves little or no taxation for the investor. In such a situation, the investor will often be stripping profits out of the source jurisdiction into the tax haven. While transfer pricing and other auditing tools can in principle police these transactions, in practice these may not be effective. In short, entering into such a treaty tends to lead to tax administration difficulties down the road and provides an invitation to investors to structure transactions in such a way as to avoid paying significant corporate tax in the source country. Even some OECD countries have some of the features of tax havens, namely that foreign investors will use that country as a country of convenience to make investments into the source country structured to minimize or virtually eliminate corporate tax.

A treaty strategy can be organized around a treaty model. The main orientation of the model should be to protect the source country's right to tax at source and to defend against base erosion of corporate tax. A model should avoid any excessively reduced withholding rates. In developing a model, both UN and OECD Models provide a starting point – the UN Model was specifically designed with the needs of developing countries in mind (UN, 2011).

Several provisions of tax treaties are of particular relevance to extractive industries.

We start with the set of rules that allows a country to defend against base erosion of the corporate tax. Such rules typically provide for taxation (usually through withholding) of payments made abroad, mitigating their use to siphon off profits. The key base erosion threat arises from payments of interest, royalties, technical services payments and management fees. Many older (or even recent) treaties either do not contain provisions on some of these (management and technical services) or provide for exemptions or low or zero rates.

Determining a country's treaty negotiation position could start by identifying what kinds of rules the country might want to include in its domestic law. Then existing treaties could be reviewed to determine whether the country's existing treaties allow the desired rules and, if not, what steps to take. The exercise is not an easy one, because on the one hand one would want to include in treaties sufficiently broad provisions that allow the source country to tax all kinds of payments, but on the other hand an attempt by source country negotiators to stake out their taxing rights too broadly is likely to encounter resistance. Ideally, the source country will not ask for taxing rights that are broader than rights they intend to include under domestic law. But these cannot be delimited exactly, given that the country may change its rules for taxing base-eroding payments as problems arise and as tax planning techniques used by multinationals change.

In respect of interest and royalties, it may be relatively easy to negotiate treaties that are consistent with anti–base-erosion rules. Payments for items like management fees or technical services present more challenges. This is because traditionally tax treaties have allowed the source country to tax such payments only where the payee has a permanent establishment in the source country (on grounds of avoidance of double taxation), which will generally not be the case for base-erosion payments. Expansion of the source country's taxing rights to these types of payments requires defining precisely what is meant by "management fee" or "technical service", and this is not an easy task.[11] A possible approach would be to use a broad definition but then to limit the situations in which the source country may tax to payments made (directly or indirectly) to related parties. Because base erosion typically involves siphoning off profits to a related company (often one residing in a tax haven), this approach meets the need of protecting against base erosion while not expanding taxation to payments for services more broadly. The difficulty of identifying a transaction that occurs between related parties rather than parties at arm's length may work against this approach.

A treaty strategy should be designed bearing administrative capacity in mind. If the treaty network is to be expanded, a tax authority needs to make sure it has in place a unit that can administer the treaties well. This typically raises a need for training. Also needed are procedural rules[12] for how to apply treaties and to make sure they are being applied properly. Greater consistency among the terms of a country's different treaties will reduce the demands upon administrative capacity.

Treaties have an article concerning exchange of information. This might be helpful to obtain information needed in auditing multinationals in the EI sector if the tax authorities have difficulty obtaining information from the taxpayer directly or need a way to verify the information that the taxpayer provides. If the source country has a treaty with the residence country of an investor, then it can ask for information concerning the corporate group from the tax authorities of the investor's residence country. An alternative, or supplement, to an exchange of information clause in a double tax treaty, would be to enter into the Convention on Mutual Administrative Assistance in Tax Matters.[13] Many countries are party to this convention, and it would therefore provide a wider opportunity to obtain information needed.[14]

A treaty strategy should allow treaties to be coordinated with income tax reform. A number of countries with an incipient EI sector have been reviewing their domestic law and making sure that it reflects an appropriate policy. It would be appropriate to coordinate treaty policy with such a review. For example, where a country introduces tax by withholding on payments to nonresidents for technical services, with extractive industry services in mind, a treaty should clearly permit such taxation. Similarly, a treaty should not override any domestic provisions on taxation of gains from transfers of interest in mineral rights, direct or indirect.

Extractive industry investments involve long lead times and high sunk costs. In those circumstances, providers of loans or equity capital may view tax treaties between the host country and source countries as further assurance against the effects of unilateral changes of terms by the host – the time inconsistency problem. While important, this advantage of tax treaties should provide a rationale for allowing anti–base-eroding measures, relative to domestic legislation, to be included in these treaties.

In conclusion, any country with a significant extractive industry sector should develop a strategy for how it will use tax treaties as part of policy relating to that sector. Treaty strategy is needed by all countries but may be of particular salience for countries with extractive industries given the importance of multinational companies for that sector.

3 Base erosion: border withholding

Income tax legislation usually provides for withholding taxes (WHT) on payments to non-residents of dividends, interest, royalties and, less frequently, of management fees and technical service payments. The aim is to ensure that income with a domestic source, when remitted abroad, is subject to domestic tax. In most cases, though not for dividends, the payment from which tax is withheld is deductible for income tax purposes in the source country. The traditional target for dividend withholding taxes was portfolio investment, but where a direct investment originated from a country with a worldwide (residence) tax system the dividend tax would usually be creditable against home country obligations.

For developing countries, in particular, ease of assessment and collection of border withholding taxes can make them an important element in overall income tax. Withholding tax on interest remittances is a first line of defense against "earnings stripping" through use of excessive debt in the capital structure of a foreign-owned enterprise – especially where domestic thin capitalization rules are either inadequate or feebly enforced. Withholding taxes on payments for headquarters services (management fees and the like), technical or professional services or royalties for the use of intellectual property ensure collection of tax if these have a local source and also deter the removal of profits through inflation of these payments. Not all such payments are liable to withholding, notably when, for example, a service is performed overseas with no domestic presence and perhaps paid for by an overseas affiliate or parent of the domestic firm. Source rules on these matters are often complex, have evolved over time and yet frequently present difficulty in keeping up with developments in technology, intellectual property rights or commercial structures.

Treaties conventionally place limitations on withholding tax rates and may modify domestic source rules. For developing countries with extractive industries the potential tax base erosion is significant as illustrated by the IMF (2014). The argument for relief through treaties was originally that it would stimulate two-way flows of investment. In the case of EI, however, the argument seldom holds since the direction of investment is determined by the location of likely resources. Nevertheless, companies exploring for or developing natural resources will seek treaty relief on the grounds that it will reduce the cost of investment. This case is made most vigorously in respect of interest and technical services, where the practice of grossing up by banks or service providers is widespread.[15] Thus countries sometimes use treaties with long-term effects to secure an individual EI investment.

Reduction or elimination of withholding potentially discriminates among sources of investment or services and encourages "treaty shopping". Relief of withholding on payments to one foreign destination rather than another sets up an incentive to source from that destination, or to incorporate an affiliate in that destination through which capital or services are then channeled. From the host government viewpoint, this amounts to another means of unilaterally granting tax relief rather than being a tool for advancing international trade or capital flows. When the host country has a significant network of treaties (and sometimes even where the network is quite limited) companies will consider adjusting commercial arrangements to take advantage of them.

3.1 Treaty shopping

Treaty shopping arises because the most favorable provision in any treaty may be available to the whole world. Keen and Mullins in this volume provide a diagram illustrating the phenomenon, also explained in IMF (2014). The residence country of an investor may, however, apply controlled foreign corporation (CFC) rules – meaning rules for taxing residents on their share of low-taxed foreign income derived by nonresident companies controlled by residents (Arnold, 1986; Vann, 1998). The host country for the activity – the source country – also has tools available to curtail treaty shopping and its effects.

A "limitation of benefits" (LOB) provision in a treaty between the host country and a third country would aim to address this. It would deny the benefits of such a treaty to an investor from elsewhere unless the beneficiary in the relevant third country undertakes some substantial activity. These LOB provisions were originally applied comprehensively only in the United States, but their use has spread. In Kenya, for example, the Income Tax Act now provides that a resident of a country with which Kenya has a tax treaty may not claim the benefits of the treaty when 50 percent or more of its underlying ownership is held by individuals not resident in that treaty partner state unless the resident of the partner state is listed on a stock exchange in the partner state.[16] A "principal purpose test" offers a companion or alternative to a provision on LOB. Under this test, treaty benefits would be denied when it is reasonable to conclude that one of the principal purposes of an arrangement or transaction is to secure a benefit under a tax treaty – unless it is established that obtaining such benefit in these circumstances would be in accordance with the object and purpose of the relevant provisions of the tax treaty. The OECD report on Action 6 under the BEPS Action Plan recommends the use of one or other of these measures, though not that both should be mandatory and offering the opinion that in some circumstance neither may be appropriate.[17]

3.2 An example of treaty-shopping opportunities in source countries: Namibia

Namibia had 11 ratified and effective double taxation agreements (DTAs) in 2011. Key terms of these DTAs are set out in Table 5.1.[18] The limitations on withholding taxes on dividends, interest and royalties differ significantly from country to country. Withholding on technical service payments is mentioned in only three DTAs, and the limit is at a different rate in each case. The treatment of capital transactions in immovable property is broadly consistent, except in the case of France – where business assets are substantially exempted from tax on gains or transactions. Treatment of independent personal services (lawyers' fees, etc.) is substantially similar but varies slightly.

In three cases (France, Sweden and Mauritius) interest paid to a non-resident on a bank loan is exempt from withholding tax. For France and Sweden, moreover, interest paid on export credit financing is also exempt,[19] while for France

Table 5.1 Namibia: double taxation agreements and provisions

Country	*Date*	*Dividends*	*Interest*	*Royalties*	*Technical services*[1/]	*Capital gains, Immovable property*
France	1998	15	10	10	Not mentioned	Taxable, but exempt if part of
		5 with minimum 10% holding	Exempt if export credit, enterprise to enterprise services or bank loan.		Independent personal services exempt[2/]	business assets of a company
Germany	1998	15	Nil – taxable only in recipient state	10	Not mentioned	Taxable[4/]
		10 with minimum 10% holding	Excess over arm's length terms taxable [3/]		Independent personal services exempt unless 183 days in country	
India	1998	10	10	10	10 Independent personal services exempt unless 183 days in country	Taxable
Mauritius	1998	10	10	5	Not mentioned	Not mentioned
		5 with minimum 25% holding	Nil if bank loan		Independent personal services exempt unless 183 days in country	
Romania	1998	15	10	5	Not mentioned Independent personal services exempt unless fixed base in country	Taxable
Russian Federation	1998	10	10	5	Not mentioned	Not mentioned
		5 with minimum 25% holding and min. US$100,000 investment			Independent personal services exempt unless 183 days or fixed base in country	

South Africa	1998	15 5 with minimum 25% holding	10	10	Not mentioned Independent personal services exempt unless 183 days or fixed base in country	Taxable
Sweden	1998	15 5 if 10% minimum holding	10 Nil if export credit or bank loan MFN terms for other OECD treaties[5/]	15 5 for patents and certain other items	15 Independent personal services exempt unless 183 days or fixed base in country	Taxable
United Kingdom	1967	15 5 if 50% minimum voting power Appears to exempt additional tax on branches	20	5, or ½ prevailing rate if less Nil – copyrights	Not mentioned Independent personal services exempt unless "fixed base" in country	Not mentioned
Malaysia	2004	10 5 with minimum 25% holding	10	5	5 Independent personal services exempt unless 183 days or US$10,000/year	Not mentioned

1/ "Technical services" usually means services of a technical, managerial or consulting nature.

2/ "Independent personal services" usually means independent professional services of accountants, lawyers, physicians etc.

3/ This arm's length proviso applies in most of the treaties.

4/ In most treaties, gains on transfers of shares in companies holding immovable property are also taxable.

5/ Provision unique to the Swedish treaty; provides for equal treatment with better terms granted in any arrangement with an OECD country. All treaties have provision for avoidance of double taxation, usually by a mutual tax credit procedure.

Source: Texts of Double Taxation Agreements provided by Ministry of Finance of Namibia, November 2010.

interest on loans that finance "enterprise-to-enterprise services" is exempt. Interest paid by government entities or to government entities is also usually exempt. The exclusion of bank loans may make sense where a third-party lender is entitled to gross up interest charges for any tax withheld (as is commonly the case in international loan agreements) and the host country seeks to reduce the cost of third-party loans, though even when grossed up and fully borne by the borrower withholding at least secures some revenue for the government to offset the tax deduction for interest cost. The blanket provision, however, opens up the possibility of back-to-back transactions in which the ultimate origin of the loan is not a bank at all, but the loan is channeled through one. Namibia also had generous thin capitalization provisions on deduction of interest.

Limits on dividend taxation especially affect direct foreign investment. Most of the treaties have "substantial holdings provisions" under which withholding tax on dividends is reduced to 5 percent (compared with standard non-resident shareholder's tax [NRST] of 10 percent); for some countries 10 percent applies, and the "substantial holdings" criterion varies among 10, 25 and 50 percent as a minimum. In some cases, this would mean not only that portfolio investors bear higher withholding tax but also that minority direct investors who do not cross the relevant threshold will incur a higher rate of NRST than their fellow shareholders in the same business.

Limits on withholding on technical service fees are selective and inconsistent. This type of withholding taxation on payments to nonresidents, whether final or creditable against tax by assessment, can be especially important in a country with developing mining and petroleum industries, such as Namibia (Table 5.2).

Table 5.2 Southern Africa: withholding tax on payments for services to subcontractors

Country	*Resident Contractor*	*Non-resident Contractor*
	Withholding Tax Rate in percent	
Angola[1/]	5.25	5.25
Botswana	3.00	3.00
Lesotho[2/]	10.00	10.00
Malawi[3/]	4.00	15.00
Mauritius[4/]	3.00	3.00
Swaziland		15.00
Tanzania		15.00
Zambia		15.00
Zimbabwe		10.00
Unweighted average	5.05	11.13

Source: Deloitte, *Guide to Key Fiscal information, Southern Africa: 2010–2011*

1/ Construction services attract a 3.5 percent withholding tax.
2/ Management charges: for non-residents it is a final withholding tax unless a return is filed.
3/ Contractors and sub-contractors in the construction industry.
4/ Contractors in the construction industry attract 0.75 percent.

Although in most treaties there is no limitation, in one case, Malaysia, the limit is set at 5 percent – quite likely below a reasonable level for such taxation if it were to be introduced.

The treaties imply discrimination among sources of capital imports, know-how and technical skills. There was no strong reason for this deviation from capital-import neutrality. The DTAs provide extensive opportunities for tax planning by foreign investors in Namibia. For example, investors concerned to minimize tax on dividends (and with no other considerations) could channel investment through subsidiaries in France or Sweden.[20] The same locations would work for the origin of loan capital flows. On the other hand, companies licensing technology, know-how or patents, could channel license payments through Mauritius, Romania, Russia, Malaysia or Sweden. Using a subsidiary in France would minimize possible capital gains tax liabilities. Technical services would be best supplied from Malaysia or India. In summary, the optimal combination might be: capital from France, services and know-how from Malaysia. These possibilities, of course, assume that treaties between these potential conduit countries and the ultimate country of residence of the investor do not stand in the way. Beyond tax planning, however, these options have little logic.

3.3 An example of border withholding and treaties: Kenya

Kenya levies final withholding taxes on payments to non-residents to ensure that tax is paid on Kenyan source income. Standard and treaty rates are shown in Table 5.3.

Dividend withholding tax rates are usefully standardized at 10 percent. With the branch profits tax rate set at 37.5 percent and the standard corporate rate at 30 percent, then the rate of income tax on remitted profits is effectively the same (within half a percentage point) whatever the country of origin of the investment or the legal form of operations in Kenya. Dividend withholding tax, however, does not bear currently upon petroleum companies – for them, any withholding on dividends remitted is met from the government's share of profit oil.

Withholding on interest should reduce the incentive for excessive debt finance. Nevertheless, withholding on interest paid to non-residents may result in higher interest rates being charged on the debt. The reason for this is that (1) many countries have eliminated withholding on interest paid to nonresidents in an effort to attract savings from abroad and (2) suppliers of savings, often in a tax haven or low-tax jurisdiction, set their lending rates taking into account any taxes that are going to be withheld and paid to the source country. Kenya's interest withholding rate is consistent across sectors at 15 percent for interest paid to nonresidents.

Withholding on management and professional fees covers technical service fees except in the case of petroleum. In DTAs "technical fees" are usually defined more broadly to include technical services, managerial services and consultancy services.[21] In Kenya these are taxed at varying rates according to treaty, except

Table 5.3 Withholding rates and the capital gains article in double taxation agreements with Kenya

Country	*Year Signed*	*Dividends (In percent)*	*Interest (In percent)*	*Royalties (In percent)*	*Management/ Professional Fees*	*Capital Gains, Immoveable Property*
Treaties in Force						
Canada	1983	10	15	15	15	Taxable including gains on shares[2/]
Denmark	1973	10	15	20	20	Taxable, but not gains on shares
Germany	1980	10	15	15	15	Taxable including gains on shares
India	1989	10	15	20	17.5	Taxable including gains on shares
Norway	1972	10	15	20	20	Taxable, but not gains on shares
Sweden	1973	10	15	20	20	Taxable, but not gains on shares
United Kingdom	1976	10	15	15	12.5	Taxable, but not gains on shares
Zambia	1964	10	15	20	20	Taxable, but not gains on shares
Memorandum items						
EAC[5/]	2010	5	10	10	15	
Resident withholding rates		10	10	5	3 (5)[2/]	
Nonresident rates		10	15[3/]	20	20	
Petroleum companies		Payable from government profit oil			12.5[4/] 5.625[1/]	

1/ For petroleum service subcontracts, By application of 37.5 percent tax rate (nonresident companies operating through a permanent establishment) to an assumed 15 percent profit margin on the service component of fees to petroleum service subcontractors.
2/ 5 percent when below KES 24,000 per month.
3/ Bank interest – 25 percent appears to apply to "bearer instruments".
4/ For deductible management and professional fees paid outside Kenya.
5/ As currently provided in ITA 3rd Schedule.

Source: Treaty documents and IBFD, situation in 2014

in the case of petroleum, where concessional rates apply both to the main category (12.5 percent) and a special category defined in the 9th Schedule of payments to petroleum service subcontractors (effectively 5.625 percent). These arrangements for petroleum conformed to relatively common practice in the international petroleum industry, but there was a case for reconsidering them and not extending this treatment to other sectors such as mining in order to maintain the integrity of taxation by assessment and provide an incentive to incorporate (or at least register) in Kenya. Subcontractors with permanent establishments should be taxed by assessment not withholding. Where the payment is made offshore for a service performed outside Kenya it should not be deductible for Kenyan tax purposes by the payor.

On the other hand, if the payment is deductible in Kenya it should not matter whether the service is performed in Kenya or abroad. In general, when a good is manufactured abroad or a service is performed abroad, the income earned is considered foreign source income and should not be taxable in Kenya. Some countries (for example, Chile and Uruguay) impose their withholding tax on technical fees whether the service was performed locally or from abroad, because payments of technical fees, particularly management fees, to related parties are often used by companies to shift income abroad, and the tax authority has difficulty making transfer price adjustments.

3.4 Taxation of transfers of interest

One topic relevant to treaties that has assumed importance in the past several years is the taxation of gains resulting from the indirect transfer of a mineral interest.[22] This kind of gain can be particularly challenging from a technical point of view because gains can be realized far outside the jurisdiction. A strategic decision should be made to either pursue taxation of gains seriously or to drop it. If a country determines to tax gains and also plans to have in place a network of treaties, those treaties must be designed so as to allow the taxation that is planned under domestic law. Why tax capital gains in the first place? Profit tax may not capture economic income in practice. One option would be to tax gain but allow a basis step-up. A threshold question is defining what kind of property it is intended to subject to a capital gains regime (real property, any interest in a mining concession?). If capital gains are to be taxed, it is necessary to define indirect interests subject to tax and to specify procedural rules, including withholding requirements. In this respect, it is critical to make sure that procedural mechanisms are in place to secure payment.

A country wishing to tax gains on the transfers of mineral interests first of all needs to examine the domestic law framework and work out appropriate rules. A second step (which might in practice be done in parallel with the first) is to examine the entire network of the country's tax treaties to see what constraints they impose. The exercise needs to be undertaken, as there are several interacting provisions involved, and the language used in specific treaties may differ from the OECD or UN Model, thus requiring an individualized assessment of the effect of each treaty. As a result of such a review, existing treaties may need to be renegotiated and new ones negotiated with particular attention to this issue. This is a fairly technical area, and even a small difference in wording of a treaty might defeat an attempt to impose a tax in the domestic law. Some of the issues involved are as follows:[23]

- Whether article 13 of treaties covers all gains from the disposition of property, including mineral rights.
- Do treaties exclude taxation of overriding royalties? This use of "royalties" refers to continuing payments made to the seller of an interest in a mineral right as part consideration for the sale, usually in the form of a percentage of gross revenues generated.[24]
- Are all interests in mining rights defined as immovable property in domestic law, so that this definition carries over to treaties? Does the definition of immovable property in article 13 incorporate the definition in article 6?
- Does the treaty specify what indirect dispositions of immovable property may be taxed by the source country in a manner that is sufficiently broad to prevent taxpayers from structuring transactions in ways that avoid taxation?

The taxation of direct or indirect transfers of interest in mineral rights (and in other grants of public rights) became a major issue after a number of high-profile cases. The issue is reviewed from an international tax perspective by Keen and Mullins (this volume) and in full detail by Burns, Le Leuch and Sunley (this volume). In this chapter, we set out the key challenges faced by developing countries bearing upon the content of treaties. The most prominent issue arises from trading, directly or indirectly, in exploration rights when there are significant discoveries or the possibility of making discoveries. In countries with diverse portfolios of resource projects and strong systems of rent taxation (take, for example, Norway, the UK, Canadian provinces or Australia) the issue is usually not major, but in low-income countries with few projects it attracts strong public and political attention. At its core is the suspicion that if large gains can be made on transfers, rents were not properly anticipated when the original fiscal regimes were put in place, so that the host country is in a sense "cheated" of the expected value of its resource.

3.4.1 Direct transfers of interest

"Direct transfers" refer to transactions in mineral rights not mediated through a legal entity holding these rights (in the sense also explained in Burns, Le Leuch and Sunley, Chapter 7 of this volume). Transfers within the continental shelf regime for petroleum rights are understood to be exempt from tax in Norway, subject to conditions – but they became a big issue in developing countries during the commodity boom. Uganda, Ghana, Mozambique – and telecoms in India – all provided important examples.

Taxation of such gains through the corporate tax system requires inclusion of EI rights and information in domestic law as a category of property, or indeed as "immovable property", making gains taxable under CIT for companies. The domestic provision then needs not to be overridden by treaties. The amount included in the income of a transferor should be the consideration received, reduced by the undeducted cost of the transferred right. The transferee will be entitled somehow to deduct the consideration paid for the right (there is a step up in cost), but rules differ on treatment of deduction: some jurisdictions permit deduction against the proceeds of future capital transactions of a similar nature, while others permit amortization of these costs in the same way as the initial acquisition costs of a mineral or petroleum right. Some countries retain non-final withholding on the total transaction value as a prepayment of the tax payable on the gain.

A "farm-out" occurs when the holder of a mineral right transfers an interest in that right (either immediately or upon some defined event) to another company that undertakes to fulfill some or all of the initial holder's obligations to explore or develop. Farm-outs create significant complication for the taxation of transfers but form a significant part of commercial and financing operations for EI exploration, so that the provisions must accommodate these in a way that does not obstruct commercially warranted transactions. Income tax law can provide that any initial amount paid under a deferred interest farm-out is income when the amount is received. If the right is transferred, only the additional consideration, if any, is included in income at the time of the transfer. The rules on farm-outs can apply to both mining and petroleum operations.

3.4.2 Indirect transfers of interest

The income tax provisions will deal separately with direct transfers of interest in the manner just outlined. Similarly, the income tax legislation requires specific reference to indirect transfers of interest in mining and petroleum rights and information, so that these EI rights and information are included in the definition of immovable property for ITA purposes. Again, treaty provisions may obstruct taxing rights if the treaties have not been negotiated to protect domestic taxing rights. For a diagrammatic representation of the indirect transfer process, see IMF (2014) and Keen and Mullins in this book.

The most important matter is to set rules for what constitutes an indirect transfer, or a whole or partial change of control, for the purpose of taxing gains on transfers. One possibility is to link the sector (mining or petroleum) legislation to the tax legislation and require notification by the license holder as a condition of rights, then include a reporting mechanism under which the relevant ministry informs the revenue authority of any substantial change in ownership of contractors or rights holders.

Enforcement of payment requires a specific mechanism if the liability effectively lies with a non-resident. Some countries deem the local entity to be the agent of the non-resident for payment of tax due in respect of an indirect transfer of interest. Others operate a scheme in which a transaction in the domestic mineral right is deemed to have occurred and the local entity is liable.

4 Other risk areas

Transfer pricing risks in EI sectors are important but not necessarily greater than in other major sectors. Calder and Shay in this book deals in detail with the risks to taxation of EI, and the principal issues are addressed in Keen and Mullins (this volume). Both special incentives and special opportunities for transfer mis-pricing exist in EI. The special incentive consists mainly in the special tax regimes (usually with higher taxes) in the upstream segment of natural resource extraction: evidently, the risk here arises both in cross-border and in domestic transactions. The special opportunity arises principally from the commercial character of EI investments: investors are international, and their multinational enterprises are often vertically integrated (combining extraction of raw materials, transportation and processing activities).[25] The international character of transactions means low-tax jurisdictions are easily and commonly used as conduits for sales, for purchases of inputs and services and for financing transactions. Other factors, however, reduce transfer pricing risks to the tax base by comparison with other sectors: the physical and measurable character of operations; the availability of standard physical outputs, measures and reference prices; the use of unincorporated joint venture structures (especially in petroleum) that set private parties up with adverse interests from which governments benefit in determining transfer prices.

Other risks are the subject of extensive treatment in the BEPS project (see Keen and Mullins, 2016, in this book). These include: intra-company debt shifting; thin capitalization (excess ratio of debt) usually with debt provided by affiliated parties; "inversions" or removal of headquarters and nominal sources of sales to tax-efficient locations – combining, often, with issues in the location of intangible assets and thus the payments accruing to ownership of them; finally, narrow definitions of source of income, or of business profits, thus eroding the domestic tax base.

Excessive deduction of interest charges, especially those paid to affiliates, poses a threat of "earnings stripping" in extractive industries as in other sectors. "Thin capitalization" refers to a capital structure for a company or project that contains less equity (and thus more debt) than would be commercially warranted in order to maximize deductible interest for tax purposes. It is, in effect, a special case of abusive transfer pricing. The solution probably lies in strengthening overall limitations on the deductibility of interest rather than in proposing something specific for extractive industries. The issue extends beyond corporate taxation when, for example, provisions in production sharing contracts permit recovery of interest as a cost. Traditionally, restrictions on the tax effects of thin capitalization took the form either of a debt–equity ratio test or a test of the ratio of interest expense to income in different circumstances.[26] In a few cases, both have been used in combination. A debt–equity test was until recently more usual, with the recommended ratio tightening from 3:1 or 4:1 to 2:1 or 1.5:1, but BEPS recommendations (report on Action 4) and recent initiatives in some OECD countries (Germany, for example) have restored the potential importance of the income test. Rules usually allow the carry-forward of all or part of disallowed interest for deduction, within annual permitted limits, in future years.

The BEPS recommendations address three main issues concerning debt and debt interest: (i) corporate groups placing higher levels of third-party debt in high-tax countries; (ii) groups using intragroup loans to generate interest deductions in excess of the group's actual third-party interest expense; and (iii) groups using third-party or intragroup financing to fund the generation of tax-exempt income. Not all of these become an issue for tax treaties, but it will be important in treaty strategy to ensure that treaty provisions do not override protective measures on these established in domestic law.

Leasing transactions offer another channel for maximizing deductions in respect of debt. An operating lease leaves legal and economic ownership of the asset in the hands of the lessor, making the payment by the lessee analogous to a payment of rent – and thus clearly an operating expense. Under a finance lease, by contrast, the lessor effectively transfers the benefits and risks of ownership to the lessee while retaining legal title to the asset – at least until all payments are complete. The finance lease thus, in substance, resembles a debt transaction, with interest and principal amounts included in the lease payment. Tax rules, however, sometimes permit the whole payment to be deducted as an operating expense, as for an operating lease. One solution is reclassification of finance leases as loans, accompanied by use of rules analogous to those for thin capitalization for other types of base-eroding payments.

5 What can be done?

International initiatives to relieve these problems have recently centered on the OECD BEPS project. The project had by 2016 produced a significant quantity of reports and proposals. The participating countries have sought reform, in part, through a new multilateral instrument (due for completion at the end of 2016), though implementation (at the time of writing) remains a long-term prospect. Many governments have taken unilateral actions to reduce the extent of base erosion and profit shifting: the UK, for example, introduced in 2015 what is called a "diverted profits tax" – effectively a minimum tax on profits of foreign enterprises operating in the UK.

In the case of low- and lower-middle-income countries with significant extractive industries or exploration activity, a number of useful principles can apply. These are reflected in recommendations of recent IMF advisory work in many relevant member countries (see Appendix to the Introduction for this volume).

Treaty making needs to be integrated with tax policy making. It is preferable to avoid negotiating a treaty simply because another country asks to do so and integrate treaty making with tax policy making. A national strategy will limit new treaties with potential intermediary countries or countries with special holding company regimes. Domestic law could, in addition, provide stronger powers for tax authorities to review and adjust prices used in transactions between the host country and known low-tax jurisdictions.

At the same time, review of unfavorable treaties, especially where created by inheritance from very old treaties, has become a serious option which a number of OECD countries have become willing to entertain. The Netherlands, for example, made a specific offer to review and renegotiate for a selection of its treaty partners among developing countries.

Within reviewed or new treaties, governments can ensure that the treaties enshrine the broad right to levy withholding tax on payments to non-residents and, where relevant, ensure that these are creditable in the partner country. The same applies to permitting consistency with domestic legislation on a broad definition of real property, to include mineral and petroleum rights, and the right to tax gains on transactions in companies that directly or indirectly hold real property in the host country. Certain categories of payments such as royalties on intellectual property, management fees or technical service payments should be open to taxation by withholding and not necessarily be subsumed under "business profits". A sufficiently wide definition of business income will include both gains from continuing commercial activities and gains from disposal of assets (Burns and Krever, 1998).

Domestic law can include a "limitation of benefits" provision in domestic tax law preventing "treaty shopping" or the alternative of a "principal purpose test" for access to treaty benefits. The LOB provision would usually require a business seeking to take advantage of a treaty with the host country to demonstrate a substantial presence in the treaty partner country. The problem of treaty shopping will, in any case, be much reduced if the host government can ensure consistency in the withholding tax provisions of treaties. Where this has proved impossible, alternatives exist in the possibility of taxing underlying profits at higher rates (a practice common for EI in any case) or by imposing some form of minimum taxation.

Notes

1 The authors acknowledge helpful comments on earlier drafts from Michael Keen.
2 See Drevet and Thuronyi (2009). Among countries with a fairly extensive network are Kazakhstan, Indonesia, Mongolia, Turkmenistan, Vietnam and Zambia. A number of resource-rich developing countries lack an extensive network, including Angola, Cameroon, Chad, Democratic Republic of Congo, Republic of Congo, Equatorial Guinea, Iraq, Laos, Liberia, Niger, Timor-Leste and Papua New Guinea (as of 2009 each of these countries had 8 or fewer treaties, some of them no treaties; as of early 2016, this remained the case, counting income tax treaties in force, except for Laos with 9 treaties and Papua New Guinea with 10).
3 For a general discussion of advantages and disadvantages of tax treaties, see Lang et al. (2010).
4 For further discussion of these data and of the impact of treaties, see IMF (2014).
5 Observation from a presentation made originally by Michael Keen.

6 A recent example of a resource-rich country doing so is Mongolia, which recently terminated four tax treaties (with Kuwait, the United Arab Emirates, Luxembourg and the Netherlands). See the website of the General Department of Taxation, Mongolia.
7 This is explored in greater depth in Thuronyi (1998, 2010).
8 For example, through a stability clause in a production sharing agreement.
9 The United States is now one of the few major economies that provides a foreign tax credit for income tax paid abroad on business income. In order to qualify for the foreign tax credit, the foreign tax must be considered an "income tax", and there are various technical rules attached to this requirement. Most other major capital-exporting countries have switched to an exemption system. Under an exemption system, the nature of the tax imposed in the foreign country is not relevant.
10 See generally Daniel and Sunley (2010) and Mansour and Nakhle (2015).
11 In defining "interest" a country can rely on its domestic law so that if a payment is not interest under domestic law (i.e., it is a dividend) it will not be deductible and hence not pose a base erosion problem. "Management fee" or "technical service" payments, by contrast, rely upon more slippery concepts and the payments form deductible costs.
12 For example, rules concerning the procedure for benefitting from the treaty in case of various payments. Some countries require advance permission from the tax authorities based on a certificate of residence in the treaty partner, while other countries extend relief more automatically.
13 The convention can be found at www.oecd.org. It commenced in 1988 and was amended by a protocol of 2010. At end-November 2015 more than 92 countries had signed it, and 78 competent authorities from those countries had signed agreements under Article 6 providing for automatic exchange of information (OECD, 2014).
14 Country-by-country reporting should also assist, especially under guidelines now part of the BEPS Action Plan reports.
15 "Grossing up" describes, for example, the practice of lenders in requiring borrowers to remit to the lender interest and fees at full face value net of any withholding taxes or charges levied in the borrower's home jurisdiction (the source country); for technical services the service fee might similarly be "grossed up" to relieve the provider of the effect of any withholding tax.
16 Republic of Kenya, Income Tax Act (as amended 2013) section 41, subsections (5) and (6).
17 http://www.oecd-ilibrary.org/taxation/preventing-the-granting-of-treaty-benefits-in-inappropriate-circumstances_9789264219120-en;jsessionid=4tps9re0pq57h.x-oecd-live-01
18 The text of the treaty with Portugal was not available at the time of review.
19 Strictly, in the French case, the terms cover the sale on credit of any industrial, commercial or scientific equipment or any merchandise.
20 Subject of course to the tax treatment of the flows in those countries and beyond.
21 Services are of a technical nature when special skills or knowledge related to a technical field are required for the provision of such services. Services of a managerial nature are services rendered in performing the functions of management. Consultancy services refer to services such as the provision of advice by experts or professionals who have special skills and qualifications allowing them to offer such services.
22 This issue is dealt with in Chapter 7 by Burns, Le Leuch and Sunley (this volume) and also highlighted in Chapter 2 by Keen and Mullins (this volume) and therefore is only briefly discussed here.
23 See Chapter 7 by Burns, Le Leuch and Sunley (this volume) for further details.
24 For avoidance of confusion, recent amendments to the Income Tax Act in Kenya refer to these as "natural resource payments" rather than "royalties".
25 Or upstream, midstream and downstream in industry parlance.
26 Income defined, for example, as earnings before interest, taxation depreciation and amortization (EBITDA).

References

Arnold, B.J. (1986), *The Taxation of Controlled Foreign Corporations: An International Comparison* (Toronto: Canadian Tax Foundation).

Burns, Lee and Rick Krever. (1998), International Aspects of Income Tax," in Victor Thuronyi (ed.), Tax Law Design and Drafting, Vol. II (Washington, DC: International Monetary Fund), pp. 587–681.

Calder, Jack. (2014), *Administering Fiscal Regimes for Extractive Industries: A Handbook* (Washington, DC: IMF).

Drevet, Sebastien and Victor Thuronyi. (2009), "The Tax Treaty Network of the U.N. Member States," 54 *Tax Notes International*, 783(June).

IMF. (2014), Spillovers in International Corporate Taxation, *IMF Policy Paper* [online], Available at https://www.imf.org/external/np/pp/eng/2014/050914.pdf.

Lang, Michael Pasquale Pistone, Josef Schuch, Claus Staringer and Alfred Storck, eds (2010), *Tax Treaties: Building Bridges Between Law and Economics.* International Bureau of Fiscal Documentation (IBFD), Amsterdam. Available at: http://www.ibfd.org/IBFD-Products/Tax-Treaties-Building-Bridges-between-Law-and-Economics-Contributors

OECD. (1988, 2010), *Convention on Mutual Administrative Assistance in Tax Matters.*

OECD. (2014), *OECD Model Tax Convention on Income and on Capital*, 2014 and previous versions. Available at http://www.oecd.org/ctp/treaties/oecd-model-tax-convention-available-products.htm.

OECD. (2015), BEPS 2015 Final Reports. Available at http://www.oecd.org/ctp/beps-2015-final-reports.htm.

Thuronyi, Victor. (1998), *Tax Law Design and Drafting (Volumes 1 and 2)* (Washington, DC: IMF).

Thuronyi, Victor. (2010), "Tax Treaties and Developing Countries," in Lang et al. (eds).

UN. (2011), *Model Double Taxation Convention between Developed and Developing Countries*, Available at http://www.un.org/esa/ffd/documents/UN_Model_2011_Update.pdf

Vann, Richard. (1998), "International Aspects of Income Tax," in Victor Thuronyi (ed.), *Tax Law Design and Drafting, Vol. II* (Washington, DC: International Monetary Fund), pp. 718–810.

6 Extractive investments and tax treaties

Issues for investors

Janine Juggins[1]

1 Introduction

It is difficult to know when significant history is being made. Our professional experience accumulates in layers, some of which do not make much sense without an appreciation of the context, some of which assume greater significance because of what immediately precedes or follows, and some that may not seem important at all until viewed with the benefit of hindsight. The international tax system comes under stress when there is a perception that it no longer delivers a fair result for developed and less developed countries alike, taking into account the evolution of business practices. At such times we may be at the cusp of a fundamental once-in-a-lifetime change, or we may be dealing with a natural yet transient response to a weak global economy in the aftermath of the global financial crisis of 2008 onward.

The current focus on the effectiveness of the international tax system assumes a zero-sum game in two senses. First, a redistribution of the cross-border corporate income tax cake – in which there is the potential for winning and losing countries. Second, under the assumption that the corporate tax burden is increased while the overall taxes raised remain constant, an initial redistribution of the direct tax burden from individuals to companies. It is an initial redistribution because ultimately all taxes paid by corporations will be borne by individuals whether in the form of an increased cost of goods or services, reduced investment income, or reduced employment opportunities. However, if instead the focus is on efficient and sustainable global economic growth, the cake is larger, and, all things being equal, everyone's slice of cake is also correspondingly larger. This is as true for the extractives sector as it is for every other business sector. More than ever we need an international tax framework that will support efficient and sustainable global economic growth. Ultimately loss of productivity resulting from double taxation placing barriers in the path of sound investments hurts us all.

The OECD base erosion and profit shifting (BEPS) work aims to reform the international tax framework so that in simple terms tax is paid where value is created. Let's put to one side for a moment the potential for increased double taxation that will undoubtedly arise from different country points of view on where value is created. The real legacy of BEPS could well rest in driving forward the continuing improvements in the tax governance and transparency of the world's largest companies. A further significant achievement for many countries will be access to additional information that will help focus tax compliance efforts and make best use of scarce tax administration resources. The world faces enormous economic and social challenges from a growing population and greater pressure on all natural resources, whether extracted or grown. There are greater mismatches than in the past between where mineral resources are found and where they are consumed, with the scale of those basic physical mismatches compounded by differences in the stage of development and levels of institutional and human capacity among countries in the value chain. Given these mismatches, global economic growth is efficient where the mineral resources (wherever they are located) are delivered to the end consumer (wherever they are located) at the lowest all-in cost. This all-in cost includes the costs of exploration, development, financing,[2] extraction, processing, manufacture, and distribution, including the correct pricing of externalities arising from these activities and including the taxes borne in the value chain from start to finish. In this analysis the taxes paid represent both a contribution to the current budget and also funding for capital investments to meet the development agenda of a particular country and therefore need to be sufficient to meet both. Mechanisms (whether through tax policy, alternative tax systems, or other approaches) that support sustainable consumption in a world where natural resources are under stress must also be part of this equation. Slow to acknowledge the benefits conferred upon us by the contributions of those who have gone before, so too perhaps we have taken for granted the significance of tax treaties in supporting efficient economic development. For investors, tax treaties are an essential part of the international tax framework supporting the foreign direct investments vital for global economic growth.

It is worth pausing to reflect on why tax treaties came about. Remarkably, the first draft of the OECD Model Tax Convention was 52 years old on 8 September 2015, but it built upon the older conventions drafted by the League of Nations.[3] The objectives were to deal with the obstacle to the development of trade and investment posed by double taxation, to cut the length of time needed to negotiate a network of bilateral tax treaties, to achieve common definitions and principles where possible, to minimise distortions in trade, and also to provide the tools to tackle tax evasion. The system of bilateral tax treaties was implemented in the context of one country agreeing to cede taxing rights over income to another country in the furtherance of trade and investment between the two countries. One of the main reasons differences between tax treaties can arise is that certain bilateral trade and investment relationships are considered to be more important than others, and the existence of these differences may give rise to opportunities to optimise investment flows. Put simply the multinational investor has multilateral investment options as it is by definition established in more than one country, whereas tax treaties have their origin in a bilateral relationship, an important consideration for tax treaty policy.[4] Since the first model tax convention was developed, technological advances have changed both the way in which most businesses are conducted and spawned entirely new forms of business, but the fundamental objectives of addressing double taxation and tax evasion remain just as valid today as they were 50 years ago. On the other hand tax avoidance, by which is meant the legal minimisation of taxes by using available tax laws and reliefs, was not one of the objectives. Although clearly since a tax treaty affords reliefs it becomes one of the tax planning tools available to reduce the overall tax burden on an investment, and therefore tax treaty policy should take this aspect into account.

Potential investors in the EI come in all shapes and sizes. They have differing business strategies, core competencies, risk appetites, and ability to bear risk but share a common goal of maximising the return on the capital they have placed at risk, taking into account the need for an extractive investment to be sustainable over the long term whilst complying with all environmental obligations.

When we think about what a tax treaty means for an investor in EI we have to think about the full spectrum of potential EI investors. These include:

- The junior exploration company – which has the technical expertise and the appetite to risk equity capital on the more speculative exploration activity. These investments are highly risky and characterised by many failures and a few outstanding successes.
- The large multinational – which draws on a strong balance sheet to provide equity and debt capital, technology and know-how, project management expertise, communities, environmental and remediation expertise, and is capable of developing and operating a natural resource for the benefit of many stakeholders.
- The buyer of natural resources – who may be willing to provide equity or debt capital to finance the development of a natural resource in exchange for a right to acquire a share of production. This could include a state-owned company whose objective is to secure a supply of raw materials or a trader of minerals whose objective is to secure a position against which to execute or hedge other trading transactions.
- The providers of project finance – generally a group of international financial institutions that may include supranational lenders like the IFC and EBRD.
- The government – either acting directly or through a national champion, which participates through equity and debt funding, typically as a joint venture partner in a mining company.
- The provider of specialist services or capital equipment – for example the sub-contractor or EPCM (engineering, procurement, and construction management) contractor, who may manage all or a significant part of the mine design and construction, sometimes on a fixed-price turnkey basis.

In order to place the relevance of tax treaties for the EI investor in context, we will first review the typical life cycle of an extractive investment. We will then move on to consider how that investment is financed, recognising that the financing requirements will change over the life cycle, and the underlying commercial reasons a change in capital structure or ownership may be required. The one thing that is certain about an extractive investment is its uncertainty. Having then understood the relevance of tax treaties to these investment decisions, we will review how tax treaties may also assist in practice where there may be gaps in domestic law. Finally, it will be time to step back and consider the role of tax treaties in overall tax policy for EI in the round.

2 The life cycle of an extractive investment

Figure 6.1 shows the typical life cycle of a mine. Each phase of the life cycle can last for many years, and once in operation there is the potential for mine life to be extended – or curtailed – through phased expansions, the implementation of new technologies, and significant and sustained changes in relative economic competitiveness. For example, the relative economic competitiveness of a mine can be affected by changes in the commodity price cycle, exchange rate shifts, and changes in restrictive practices, the regulatory environment, or the tax system.

However, most potential investments do not proceed through the full cycle because of various commercial issues – the geology is not as prospective as thought, poor project economics due to changes in key assumptions, lack of

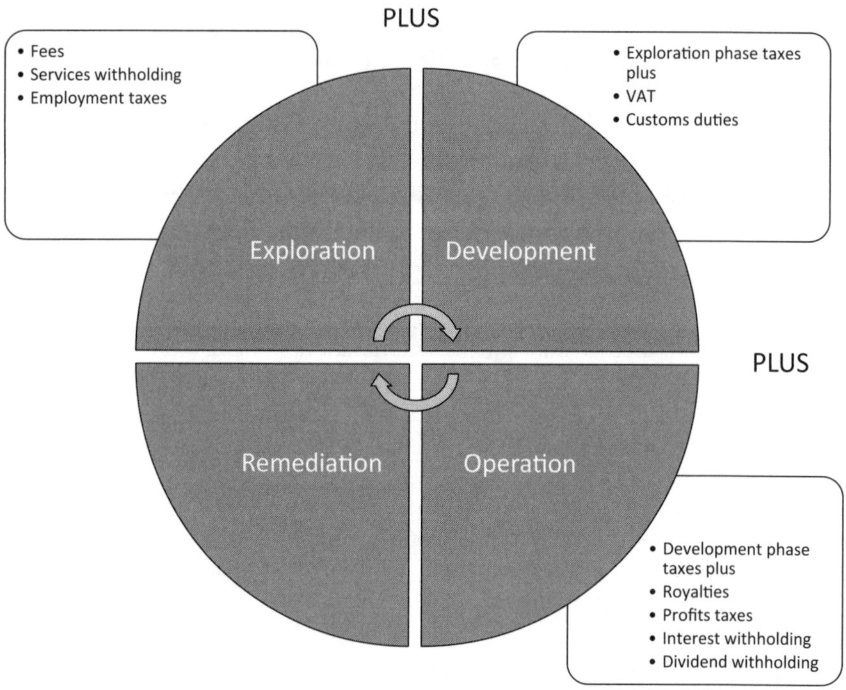

Figure 6.1 Typical life cycle of a mine

political support, lack of access to sufficient capital, inadequate infrastructure, or environmental or local community concerns. Reflective of these risks and the fact that as capital is invested more information for decision making becomes available, an investor's internal capital authorisation processes typically take the form of a series of stage gates. At each such stage gate, a decision can be made to continue, defer, or abort investment programmes, to make changes in scope, or to impose qualitative or quantitative investment hurdles. As the investments are made, the capital at risk becomes greater, since the money is largely spent up front but the payback and profits accrue only over many years into the future. In this most uncertain of investment environments it is not really surprising that EI investors seek to mitigate as many risks as possible.

Different taxes arise over the life cycle of a mine by virtue of the different activities taking place. The exploration phase may require only a small number of employees and fixed assets to support the exploration activities, and some of the exploration services may be sub-contracted. Once the mineral resource has been determined to be economically viable, which is generally only after an extended feasibility analysis, the decision may be taken to develop the mine. The development phase will typically require a much larger number of employees and sub-contractors and significant imports of materials and capital equipment. Some or all of the construction may be sub-contracted under an EPCM contract, and the EPCM contractor will in turn sub-contract elements of the construction and development work. When the mine comes into commercial production in the operating phase the numbers of employees will increase.

During the mine's operating life there will be a certain level of sustaining capital expenditure required. One of the biggest differences between oil and mining is that in general the up-front capital expenditure for an oil project is much larger, but conversely the ongoing sustainable capital expenditure is much greater for a mine. There may also be additional near-mine exploration and development activity. The mine may be expanded in phases for which significant new capital investments are needed, for example moving from an open-pit mine to an underground mine, the investment in additional processing equipment or infrastructure to allow increases in production, a significant expansion of the mine's footprint where new geological information is obtained or the economic environment or mining technologies change such that additional resources become capable of economic recovery. Therefore, although there is a mine plan and a projected outcome based on a mine model, this is based on a significant number of assumptions which may change over time. Although mineral price remains the key variable, all of these factors will influence the actual performance of the mine, the production volumes, and level of profits generated.

Once the mine is no longer economically viable, it enters the remediation and closure phase. This may require only a small number of employees and sub-contractors but may extend for many years after the mine has ceased to operate.

Licence and surface fees may be payable during the exploration phase and throughout the lifecycle of the extractive investment. Employer taxes in respect of employees and the personal income taxes paid by employees will arise throughout the lifecycle but peak during the operating phase when the greatest number of employees will be needed.

Unless there is an agreement to exempt these in the period prior to commercial production, VAT and customs duties on imported equipment and materials will be greatest during the initial development phase and in the course of additional mine expansions when most capital expenditure is incurred. During the operating phase, assuming that the mine's output is exported, under most VAT systems no VAT should be due, and therefore all VAT on purchases should be refunded. Where VAT is not refunded promptly it imposes a significant cash-flow disadvantage. Where no VAT refund is made at all this effectively becomes an additional capital investment to be financed (e.g., assuming a VAT rate of 15 percent, a project with capital purchases of $100m now costs $115m). Irrecoverable VAT is borne by the project and therefore impacts the project economics.

Throughout the lifecycle suppliers of goods and services to the project may be liable for profits-based taxes on the profits they make. This liability may be collected through the project withholding tax on the payments made to suppliers. In some cases the supplier may have negotiated that the project bears the cost of any withholding taxes (through a gross-up clause), and in this case the economic burden of the tax will fall back onto the project. This is a particularly relevant consideration where there is a large EPCM contract.

Profits-based taxes will arise in the operating phase, but only once the capital investments have been amortised in accordance with the applicable tax laws. As the capital investments are large this can mean that taxable profits are not realised for the first years of commercial production, and profits-based taxes will be low at first before increasing in later years. Where the extractive investment is significant for a country's economy this can be a significant budgetary management issue. More immediately, however, this can be a significant expectation-management issue, since the distinction between gross revenues and net profits after taking into account all relevant deductions is not clear to many in less developed countries and indeed in many developed countries also. Occasionally profits based taxes may arise where residual stockpiles are processed, or where provisions that have previously received tax relief and are now no longer required are released to income (although the latter is rare, as in most cases a tax deduction is not allowed until the expense has actually been incurred). There may be the potential for refunds of profits-based taxes if the expenses of remediation are allowed to be carried back for relief against the profits of the prior operating periods.

Royalties can be production or profit based (with some wide variations in the scope and scale of deductible expenses) but in both cases will arise only when the mine is in the operating phase or in remediation where a residual stockpile is processed. As they are independent of profit, production-based royalties will generate a more steady stream of tax revenue and may therefore be an important base component for the country's budget. Profit-based royalties that vary based on the commodity price or level of operating profits can be used to raise additional tax revenue during periods of high prices. However, this means that the project risk profile is changed for the investor – the upside is removed but the downside risk of low profits during periods of low prices remains – and this will be factored into the evaluation of the project economics and the cost of finance.

Withholding tax on interest is likely to be greatest during the first years of the operating phase and immediately after any further mine expansions, as it will take some time to generate the mine revenues to pay down debt finance.

As discussed later in the section dealing with financing, withholding taxes on dividends will generally be greatest once the mine has been operating for a number of years.

Capital gains (or losses) can arise at any stage in the life cycle where there is a disposal event, but would be most common in the exploration and development phases, when a junior company needs to bring in a more experienced partner with skills and capital, or in the operation phase where there is a need to source new capital from a joint venture partner to finance mine expansion. Occasionally an indirect disposal can arise because of mergers and acquisitions at the level of the parent company, or because the investment no longer meets the investment criteria of the provider of equity capital.

Taxes due during the life cycle of the mine may be reduced or more clearly specified by tax treaty provisions relating to:

- Reduced rates of withholding taxes on cross-border payments of interest, dividends, royalties, service fees, technical fees, or management fees
- Specified circumstances in which personal income tax liability will arise, for example, in the case of foreign or seconded employees or contractors
- Circumstances in which corporate income tax liability will arise, for example in the case of non-resident providers of services and technology when those services take place in the country where the extractive investment is being made
- The method by which business profits will be allocated to a tax presence created by a non-resident
- The approach taken to the pricing of related-party transactions
- The process for giving relief from foreign taxes
- The process for resolving double taxation disputes
- Circumstances in which capital gains derived from extractive investments or immoveable property, whether realised directly or indirectly by a non-resident, will be subject to tax by the country in which the extractive investment is located.[5]

3 Tax treaties and financing of investment

Extractive investments are capital intensive with significant initial investment required and the returns – which are inherently uncertain – only earned over a long period of time. Access to capital and its price will have a dramatic impact on whether a resource is economic to mine and therefore whether the investment proceeds at all. The cost of capital will also reflect the fact that interest expense on debt funding is generally tax deductible for corporate income taxes within certain defined parameters, whereas the cost of equity in the form of a dividend payment is not generally deductible for corporate income tax. To understand where tax treaties have a role to play in this process, we examine here how the capital structure for each phase of the investment life cycle will reflect its different financing profile and the requirements of the providers of capital.

Planning for the investment ownership structure will usually be undertaken right at the start of the exploration activity. In some countries it may not be possible for the legal entity holding the exploration licence to transfer the right to convert an exploration licence into a permit or agreement to mine to another legal entity; therefore ideally the optimal investment structure will be decided up front. In addition there is often such a long lead time between an exploration prospect and a decision to mine that the risk of law changes means that it is prudent to work through this at the start including consideration of the possibility of tax relief for any exploration expenditures. Initial decisions also have the potential to create complications later on where there is a change in ownership, and the new investor may have different requirements if it is tax resident in a different country to the original investor and therefore subject to another country's international tax regime. It may be preferable for the investor to have separate legal entities within a country to hold different exploration licences (rather than holding them in a single legal entity) to provide flexibility for different decisions in the future as to whether to proceed to development, sell, establish a joint venture, or relinquish the various interests.

The choice of parent entity for the exploration company in the host country will take into account the tax treaty provisions governing equity investments, in particular those for dividend withholding tax and capital gains. The investor will assess the comparative advantages of the different tax treaties in force with the host country. For a multinational company that has subsidiaries in many different countries the benefits available under a particular tax treaty will depend on whether there is business substance in the relevant treaty partner country. Tax treaties may also contain additional requirements that have the effect of limiting access to the tax treaty only to those who have a real business connection to the country of the tax treaty investor. The choice will also be significantly influenced by the international tax provisions of the country in which the ultimate holding company is tax resident. Finally consideration will also be given to the existence of a bilateral investment treaty network, which may provide some protection in the extreme and unlikely event that the investment is nationalised or expropriated. All of these factors will be taken into account in coming to a decision on the investment ownership structure. As an example, if the investor is tax resident in a country that does not tax dividend income from an active business investment in another country (various forms of territorial tax systems may have reliefs of this kind), any reduction in dividend withholding taxes through a tax treaty delivers an immediate benefit to the investor. Similarly, a beneficial capital gains tax article in a tax treaty may benefit the investor who does not hold its investment in the mine through to depletion. If a country has decided to offer these reliefs in its tax treaties in order to attract foreign investment, it seems unreasonable to criticise a foreign investor for responding. This does highlight though the importance of a thorough understanding of the role played by tax treaties for a country's overall tax and investment policy.

The exploration phase is likely to be funded by equity since, in most cases, the project will not earn any income to allow it to service debt. Equity funding is also more practical because, more often than not, the project does not proceed and therefore the investments made are unlikely to be recovered in full. Similarly, additional funding required during the remediation phase will most likely be made by the shareholders in the form of equity because the investment will no longer produce income at this point.

When the project moves into the development phase there is likely to be a combination of equity and debt finance. At this point the decision to develop a mine has been made – so the project is proceeding on the assumption that cash will be generated in excess of the capital invested. It is therefore appropriate not to over-capitalise the investment and move towards the capital structure that is best suited for the investment in the longer term. During development any debt finance is most likely to be from a related group company initially because at this stage the project will not have any income of its own to service third-party debt funding. The tax treaty withholding tax provisions that apply to related party interest will be most relevant at this point, and these may distinguish between interest on debt from the parent and that from a related party and also distinguish between types of debt that are subject to reduced withholding taxes on interest. The group company debt finance may be refinanced (repaid and replaced) in full or in part with third-party finance once the mine begins commercial production.

Additional finance may also be provided in the form of an earn-in[6] arrangement during the exploration or development phases or to fund expansions during the operating phase. Under an earn-in arrangement the investor may earn a specified equity stake in the project through funding future investments up to an agreed amount. This type of arrangement is not a disposal; rather it is an expansion of or addition to the existing pool of capital.[7] It has the same economic effect as, and indeed may sometimes take the form of, a new issue of share capital the proceeds of which are spent by the company on acquiring or constructing new assets. A new issue of share capital would not usually be treated as a taxable disposal event. Tax treaty provisions that deal with capital gains, interest, and dividends may help provide certainty over the tax treatment of the earn-in structure for a non-resident investor.

A further alternative is for finance to be provided by an EI investor who does not wish to be a full-risk equity investor but who wishes to secure a share of the mine's future production. This could be structured as a loan at commercial interest secured against future production, the purchase of an entitlement to a fixed percentage of future production at a fixed price, or the purchase of an entitlement to a fixed volume of minerals at a price that is indexed to an independent reference price. There are of course many variants on these themes that may be constructed to meet the respective commercial, accounting, and tax requirements of the contracting parties. Tax treaty provisions that deal with capital gains and finance income may help provide certainty over the tax treatment of the arrangement for a non-resident investor.

During commercial production the mine may be refinanced to fund further expansions or to accommodate changes in the joint venture parties. Again the tax treaty provisions relating to withholding tax on interest and dividends and the treatment of capital gains will likely be most relevant for such refinancing during the operating phase.

Any tax treaty benefits that an investor expects to realise will be reflected in the post-tax project cash flows that are used for analysis in support of the investment decision. Therefore, if the tax treaty benefits did not exist, the investor would use different figures in their analysis, and their investment decision may be different. In respect of equity capital, tax treaties may provide for a reduced rate of withholding tax on dividends compared with the usual domestic rate, and this tax treaty rate may vary depending on the percentage shareholding. For debt capital, tax treaties may provide for a reduced rate of withholding tax on interest compared with the usual domestic rate, and the rate may differ depending on whether the lender is a group company, a financial institution, or a government institution.

However, typically, providers of finance (and services) push back the risk of withholding taxes to the project through tax gross-up clauses. Particularly in the area of debt finance, international market practice is that lenders expect to receive their interest without any deduction on account of withholding tax or other costs, as they determine the price of the finance they offer on a cost-of-funds-plus basis.[8] Therefore in addition to a tax gross up by the borrower for withholding taxes there may be a tax indemnity. Typically, the change of tax law risk is also for the account of the borrower. Since the lender has required the price of the debt finance to be increased, the cost of any additional payment in the form of a gross-up is generally treated as an additional payment of interest by the borrower and is therefore a potential deduction for corporate income tax purposes. Therefore, to the extent that tax treaty relief is unavailable, or does not completely eliminate the withholding tax, increased costs imposed on lenders will ultimately be borne by the project. This will reduce the project returns flowing back to the investor. It will also reduce the corporate income taxes paid by the project where the additional cost of the finance is deductible for corporate income tax purposes.

This issue is explicitly recognised in the approach taken for funding provided through the IFC, which is specifically exempt from interest withholding taxes.[9] Some EI investments are significant in terms of a country's GDP and financial institutions associated with the World Bank Group may participate in the financing of such projects. The interest paid on such funding will generally be exempt from withholding taxes regardless of the tax treaty position and regardless of the country's domestic rules.

We have now reviewed some of the financing considerations that apply at different stages of an extractive investment's life cycle. However, there are a number of other practical factors that an investor will bear in mind when considering the right capital structure for an extractive investment. Some of these are tax related, but many are commercial.

- i Extractive investments differ from some other investments, as they will ultimately be worth nothing once fully depleted. Therefore there will be a requirement at some point in the future to extract any residual cash from the company.
- ii In some countries it can be very difficult to redeem or reduce share capital. Where there is a high level of political risk, an investor would most likely wish to maintain a higher proportion of the financing in the form of debt so that it can be repatriated quickly if needed.
- iii Trapped cash can arise where cash accumulates in excess of accounting profits, and there may be a company law requirement for distributable reserves in order to declare a dividend. This is a common problem for capital-intensive investments, as depreciation deductions will depress accounting profits in the earlier years of operation. Trapped cash may also arise where there are restrictions on foreign exchange. Where interest is tax deductible (and subject to any thin capitalisation limits) it generally makes sense to push borrowings taken out to finance extractive investments down to the project itself. This is because under a territorial tax system the parent company will most likely not be allowed to take an interest deduction for borrowings incurred to make equity investments, and in any case the debt has been economically incurred to finance the project and for no other reason.
- iv Debt can be pushed down to the project through group company loans or by the project borrowing directly from a third party. However, as a practical matter third-party debt financing may not be available until the point of commercial production. In general any short-term construction finance raised by the project would need some form of credit support from the extractive investor.
- v Non-recourse third-party finance may be attractive to reduce project risk for the equity investor, but the cost of the third-party finance will reflect the risk profile of the investment. The third-party finance may also contain restrictions on the use of project cash flows until such time as the third-party finance has been repaid.
- vi Domestic law or tax treaties may have different rates of withholding tax that apply to dividends, related party interest, and interest paid to third parties. Taking into account the commercial factors, the net post-tax cost of all of these cash flows would be analysed to determine the most efficient capital structure from a tax perspective.

vii A bilateral investment treaty will generally provide additional certainty to an EI investor in the form of greater legal protections and guarantees than those that may be available under domestic law. It could be considered as a kind of insurance policy for the EI investor, since invoking a bilateral investment treaty would come only after all other avenues for dispute resolution had been exhausted. In the case of a very risky investment, a structure that permits access to a bilateral investment treaty may be a key factor.

How does one weigh up the relative importance of tax treaty benefits to the investment decision compared with the other considerations that are taken into account?

Typically an extractive investment would be evaluated using discounted cash flows and supplemented by other investment appraisal analysis such as the time taken to pay back the initial capital. This requires a project cash flow model to be constructed and the project cash flows discounted back at the chosen discount rate to give a project value in today's terms (this is the net present value). All cash flows that arise in moving the funds from the investment to the hands of the ultimate investor will be modelled, and these will include dividend withholding taxes. The chosen discount rate will be based upon the investor's risk adjusted cost of capital, which, if it assumes a tax deduction for debt, will be applied to cash flows expressed in real terms, based on 100 percent equity finance.

The relative attractiveness of the project can be compared with other projects in the portfolio in terms of the ratio of net present value generated per dollar of capital invested. Where relevant, the overall impact of the investment on the value of the investment portfolio in aggregate can be compared by valuing the portfolio on a "with new investment" and "without new investment basis". For example, a material increase in production of a certain commodity may have a significant impact on the global balance of supply and demand, including causing some higher-cost mines to become uneconomic as a result.

Thinking then in terms of discounted cash flows and the typical life cycle of an extractive investment, it follows that costs that arise earlier in the life of the project are more damaging to the investment economics than costs that arise later in the life of the project. It is the very reason tax exemptions during construction (such as VAT and customs duties on capital equipment and materials) are often critical to supporting the development of a mine. It is also the reason changing the profile of tax payments so that they arise more evenly over the life of the mine – perhaps to address the fiscal needs of the country or province where the investment is being made – can be very expensive for the project economics relative to alternative investments in the portfolio.

Since withholding taxes generally only arise on actual payment of the dividend or interest, in the context of discounted cash flow evaluation, their relative importance for an extractive investment depends upon when they are likely to be paid. Figure 6.2 shows a typical cash waterfall that illustrates the priority use of project cash flows and therefore the impact this has on timing.

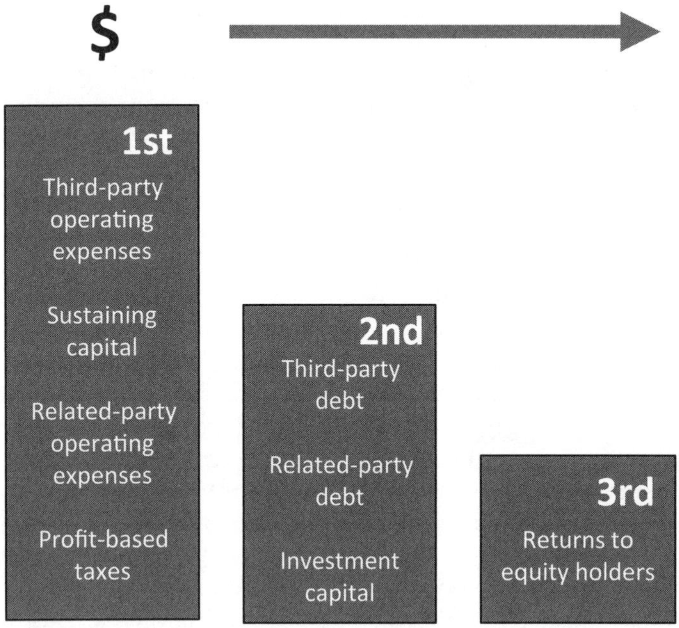

Figure 6.2 Typical cash waterfall

Cash generated by the project will first be used to pay operating expenses, to make capital investments that are needed to keep the mine in operation (sustaining capital), and to pay tax liabilities. The third-party financing arrangements may impose a restriction on the payment of related-party operating expenses if the cash flow generated by the project does not meet certain financial criteria.

Next the cash will generally be used to pay some third-party finance in priority to related-party debt and further capital investments (e.g. project expansion). The remaining cash is available for distribution to equity holders subject to any foreign exchange, corporate law, or accounting restrictions. The depreciation of the up-front capital investments can result in limited accounting reserves available for distribution, even where there is cash on the balance sheet. In practice this lack of distributable reserves, together with the higher-priority claims of debt providers, may mean that dividends will not be paid for many years.

Due to the protections required by third-party lenders, third-party finance will almost always need to be repaid in priority to related-party debt. In turn, generally related-party debt will be repaid in priority to equity. The pricing of the debt in each case will reflect this priority ranking. The principal exception to this usual order is where initial related-party construction finance is repaid in conjunction with a third-party project finance raising as part of a project refinancing.

Therefore tax treaty considerations will certainly be taken into account in determining the optimal capital structure for the investment and to optimise the project economics, but depending on the particular circumstances they may not be the most important factors. In the case of a particularly risky investment it may be the case that access to bilateral investment treaty protection provisions (which may mean forgoing access to the best tax treaty) or the ability to extract cash quickly will be more important considerations.

4 Tax treaties and capital gains

Under their domestic law some countries choose to tax direct and indirect transfers of shares in companies that derive most of their value from immoveable property. Other countries choose only to tax such gains when made by their own tax residents or may choose not to tax certain gains at all. For example, long-term capital gains may enjoy a preferential tax treatment compared with short-term capital gains to encourage investment and to discourage speculation. The Australian TARP (taxable Australian real property) rules, the Canadian TCP (taxable Canadian property) rules and the U.S. FIRPTA (foreign investment in real property tax act) rules are examples of some domestic-law approaches to taxing real property capital gains realised by non-residents.

The reason for the wide variance in domestic-law approaches in different countries reflects the fact that these choices are essentially driven by tax policy decisions. The at times competing requirements to attract foreign direct investment and to maintain a cohesive and sustainable tax base will be important considerations.

There is a broad range of extractive investments to consider. Where the extractive investment is more intangible than tangible or where it is only a part of what is being disposed of, valuation issues can become quite tricky – for example, the sale of the rights to the proceeds from or the sale of the actual production of an operating mine's mineral by-product[10] for a fixed period of time. The extractive sector is also very cyclical and it is not unusual to see sudden changes in forward prices that have a dramatic impact on the fair value of an extractive investment (upwards or downwards) within a relatively short time period. Recent accounting impairments[11] of acquisitions made by a number of large mining companies are practical evidence of these dramatic swings.

The disposal of extractive investments can also be made in different forms. All of the following could be ways in which an interest in an extractive investment is disposed of directly by the holder or indirectly through a disposal higher up the ownership chain:

- The disposal of an existing retained royalty or the granting of a newly carved out royalty;[12]
- The disposal of a percentage of shares in a company that holds an extractive investment – where the extractive investment could range from a mining exploration licence to a fully fledged operating mine;

- The disposal of an unincorporated joint venture or partnership interest in an extractive investment;
- The disposal of a share of or the rights to a percentage of a mine's existing or future production;
- The disposal of capacity or access rights in mining-related infrastructure, for example roads, rail, ports;
- The disposal of an interest in mining technology.

Recognising that there may be practical or policy reasons to limit taxing rights in certain situations calls for some sensible exemptions. For example, in the case of a publicly traded mining company with investments in a number of countries it would be impractical to subject each and every trade of shares on the stock exchange (or, by extension, any over-the-counter derivative trade referenced to the actual share) to a special country-specific extractive investment capital gains tax regime. A further example may be where as part of a group reorganisation there is a transfer of the underlying extractive investment within the group. Stepping back and looking at the position as a whole, the ultimate parent has not changed, and no disposal proceeds have been received into the group. Imposing a tax in this situation would effectively place a barrier in the way of tidying up the group corporate structure[13] or a group's ability to react to regulatory or market changes. Further exemptions may apply in the case of a public bid or where no cash changes hands as in a share-for-share transaction, a demerger or an earn-in arrangement. As discussed earlier, an earn-in arrangement is where a party agrees to fund a certain amount of future expenditure in exchange for a percentage interest and is economically equivalent to (and indeed may be in the form of) a subscription for new shares.

The price paid for an extractive investment will generally be based on the value today of the future post-tax cash flows that the buyer expects to receive in the future. These are project cash flows that will be subject to tax in the country as they are earned. Therefore the taxation of the capital gain in the country where the extractive investment is located may result in the country collecting tax twice on the same income, once on the capital gain and again in the future as the profits are realised and taxed.

To better illustrate this point, consider Investor A which acquires an exploration licence for $10m, invests a further $500m on mine exploration, development, and sustaining capital, and operates a mine for the whole of its life cycle through to remediation and closure. As the mine is a depleting asset, it is worth nothing once it has come to the end of its economic life. The tax contribution made by Investor A consists of all the taxes paid by the mine on its profits, royalties, fees, and any withholding taxes on payments made to non-resident providers of services and debt and equity capital. Now let's assume that the facts remain exactly the same but instead Investor B purchased the exploration licence from Investor A for $100m and Investor B went on to invest the further $500m in the mine and to operate it through to remediation and closure. If the $90m gain made by Investor A on the sale of the exploration licence to Investor

B is taxed in the country where the mine is located without any corresponding increase in the tax basis of the mining assets being given to Investor B, the total tax contribution made by the mine is higher but only because it happened to change ownership during its life cycle. Levying a tax in these circumstances is therefore a deterrent to transfers of ownership that may be essential to ensure the most efficient development of a mining asset.

For completeness, since the capital gain is based on future projections, there can be scenarios in which this is not the case, such as a capital gain on an exploration project that never proceeds to production, an operating project where the future profits generated are either less or more than expected, or because a reduced amount of tax is paid due to tax incentives granted to a subsequent mine operator or changes in the tax law are made.

If the seller's country of tax residence also taxes the capital gain, it may be possible to obtain a tax credit for the capital gains tax paid in the investment country, although this will not generally be the case under a territorial tax system with a participation exemption regime.

To address the issue of potential double taxation, some countries have symmetrical tax rules so that if the seller pays tax on the sale, the buyer benefits by being able to uplift the tax-depreciable basis of the assets to reflect the price paid to the seller. There is still some disadvantage for the investor and a corresponding advantage to the country due to the timing of the tax payment (see the earlier discussion about discounted cash flow investment appraisal), but this at least reduces the disincentive to transfers of ownership that are helpful for the efficient development of mineral assets. Where a capital gains tax will apply and where it is feasible in terms of title transfer and other regulatory constraints, it may make sense to structure the transaction as a domestic sale of assets in country in order to achieve a more symmetrical tax outcome. The purchase price of the assets should provide a higher depreciable tax base for the purchaser. Otherwise for a purchaser based in a country with a territorial tax system and participation exemption regime there may be little benefit from obtaining a high tax basis in the shares for capital gains tax purposes if the purchaser intends to hold what is after all a depleting asset.

A potential buyer of an investment that will be subject to capital gains tax should reflect the potential for a future tax liability on disposal in the price they are willing to pay for the investment and the impact of this on the relative attractiveness of the investment compared with other investment options. Clearly a buyer will not always have a predefined view on how long they will hold the investment, as an extractive investment can be held until it is fully depleted. However, a prudent investor needs to factor this into the asset's valuation, as the future is inherently uncertain, and they may be required to reorganise or divest unexpectedly.

Some business models also deliberately anticipate a disposal at some point in the future. For example, it is relatively common for junior exploration companies to transfer or sell interests in an extractive project to a larger company with greater technical capability to bring the project into production or to gain access to financing. Significant capital gains taxes may deter this beneficial activity and slow down the development of projects.

Most would acknowledge that the prices at which some extractive investments have changed hands in the past decade can appear large particularly when compared to the budget for public services of a lower-income resource-rich country. As the benefits of the natural resources[14] can only be obtained once by the country of extraction, such high prices may result in political pressure to have a greater share of the rent allocated to the country. There is nothing wrong in principle with such a decision, but as with all good legislation it needs to be properly designed and administered. As stated earlier many countries such as Australia, Canada, and the United States tax real-property capital gains realised by non-residents in certain circumstances. However, such legislation needs to be prospective in its application, as retrospective taxation changes are inequitable when applied to investments already made and which cannot be withdrawn or when assessed on those who have not actually realised the gains, as in the case of a purchaser retrospectively assessed for the capital gains of the seller. Retrospective legislation also creates an unstable investment environment that may put off future potential investors. In the context of discounted cash flow evaluation, retrospective tax changes increase the rates of return required to make future investments economic in comparison with alternative investment opportunities (given the higher risk involved and its reflection in the discount rate).

Therefore there is a policy choice to be made, a need to balance the relative importance of attracting foreign investment and the timing and incidence of tax revenues. Key policy decisions include whether to differentiate between short-term and long-term capital gains and whether to differentiate between direct disposals in country and indirect disposals outside of the country. This will impact the overall attractiveness of the investment environment.

Readers who are paying attention will notice that I have not yet mentioned tax treaties in connection with capital gains. This is deliberate. A country must first decide what its capital gains tax policy is with respect to foreign investment in the extractive sector before it can consider how the tax treaty provisions relating to capital gains should operate in support of that policy.

How important are the capital gains provisions of a tax treaty to an extractive investor? For a depleting asset, in practice the capital gains tax provisions are most likely to be relevant in the peaks and troughs of the commodity cycle. The peak may encourage the sale of assets before the commodity cycle turns, especially for those investors whose strategy is based on an exit well before the end of a mine's life. The trough may force sales of assets to repay debts or to reshape the investment portfolio. It may seem counter-intuitive, but even sales of assets at the trough can generate capital gains depending on when the original investments were made and in what currency the capital gains are calculated.

For an investor from a country with a territorial tax system and a participation exemption regime any capital gains tax paid will be an additional cost. An extractive investor in this position should therefore have factored the benefit of any capital gains tax treaty provision into their original investment decision and will also factor it into their disposal analysis. Since the disposal effectively accelerates and crystallises all of the future value of the investment (as the disposal value should be equivalent to the discounted sum of its future post-tax cash flows) it is likely to be a significant figure, and therefore the value of any beneficial tax treaty provisions to this type of extractive investor is likely to be correspondingly significant.

Clearly in the situation in which a resource-rich country decides to change its tax policy on capital gains on extractive investments, there will be a period of time over which tax treaties will need to be renegotiated (or in extreme cases terminated) in order to bring the domestic and the international tax policies into alignment.

Where capital gains are taxed, investors want to have clarity over the process so that they properly understand their liabilities and responsibilities. This includes for example what the withholding and reporting requirements are, whether there are any exemptions, and how they apply in practice. Where there is tax treaty protection an investor would prefer a treaty clearance up front rather than having to pay the tax and make a tax treaty refund claim. A common issue that arises is when the seller is responsible for withholding capital gains tax from the purchase price but the amount of tax to be withheld is greater than the likely tax liability. In some countries it can be difficult to obtain a refund of overpaid tax, and this may become a contentious issue as between seller and purchaser. Some form of tax clearance mechanism would assist in this case. Another common issue is that of purchase price allocation and valuation disputes when the asset subject to the capital gains tax is just one part of a bundle of assets that is being sold. Disputes may also arise over the tax basis of the asset subject to the capital gains tax, particularly if there have been group reorganisations or other changes to the capital structure since the original acquisition.

For these and similar reasons both sellers and buyers have to deal with the risk of a capital gains tax liability in the legal agreement covering the sale, including the application of any relevant tax treaty provisions.

5 Domestic tax law and tax treaties

Investments in the extractive sector have certain characteristics that need to be considered in the context of a country's tax policy and legislation. These issues will assume more importance the larger the share of the economy that is represented by the extractive sector. This is because a large extractives sector relative to the economy as a whole will create more volatility in terms of changes in the fiscal revenues from year to year as the commodity cycle fluctuates. It may also have an impact on the local exchange rate and inflation and therefore indirectly impact the tax base represented by other sectors of the economy as well as impacting the price of basic essentials consumed by the local population.

This can make forecasting tax revenues and budgeting for public expenditure very challenging even for the most sophisticated of countries. But for lower-income resource-rich countries this can seem insurmountable where there is a reduced buffer (such as flexible access to sovereign debt markets or accumulated state reserves) upon which to draw. Such scenarios may create an expectation management issue between the government and the EI sector at a minimum and, at the extreme, foster a sense of mistrust. Paradoxically, extractive companies face a similar dilemma in terms of ensuring that their own capital structure is sufficient to meet future capital expenditure commitments in the face of volatile income streams and in managing the expectations of their various stakeholders.

It is against this background that gaps in the domestic tax law and regulations of resource-rich countries can assume greater significance. The domestic tax law may be unclear or simply not contemplate the particular issue under review, for example how to obtain tax relief for the large remediation and closure costs that are incurred at the end of the lifecycle. Obtaining this further certainty is one of the reasons large extractive investments may benefit from a negotiated fiscal regime, along with any tax concessions needed to make the investment economic. However, where there is weak capacity in the host country tax administration dealing with the combined effects of uncertainty in the domestic law, the impact of a negotiated fiscal regime, and the relevant tax treaty provisions is challenging. So what are the areas in which a tax treaty may help plug these gaps?

At its simplest a tax treaty can help to clarify what host country income earned by the non-resident EI is to be subject to tax in the host country and how the amount of income is to be calculated. A permanent establishment is not always well defined in domestic law, or the domestic law may have been drafted at a time when the type of business conducted or the way in which the business was conducted was very different. Similarly, a country that has not had many foreign citizens working in its country may not have well-defined laws that set out when the foreign citizen becomes subject to domestic taxation, how the taxable income should be determined, and the interaction with another country's tax system.

In practice for large extractive investments withholding taxes are often the earliest matter for potential discussion and dispute with the host country tax authority. This is due to the fact that payments to foreign suppliers and contractors for goods, services, and interest arise much earlier in the life cycle of an extractive investment than do profits taxes. Large extractive investments (relative to the size of the country's economy as a whole) may be expected to generate large withholding tax receipts. A failure to appreciate where these forecasted withholding tax receipts will be impacted by a tax treaty that has lower withholding tax rates than those that apply domestically will cause problems for the budget.

Practical problems can also arise where the impact of tax treaty provisions are not well understood. For example, a tax authority may see a tax treaty withholding tax rate that is higher than the actual domestic withholding tax rate simply as an opportunity to levy the higher tax treaty rate. This results from a lack of understanding of the main purposes of a tax treaty, which are to protect the taxpayer from double taxation (and thereby promote cross-border trade) and to combat tax evasion. Another practical example is when there is insufficient clarity in domestic law over when and how the domestic withholding tax will be applied – perhaps there is no clear concept of source. This can give rise to confusion as to when the withholding tax will be applied to payments made to non-residents, with the default position often being that the withholding tax is applied to all payments whether in respect of host-country source income or not and without any distinction being drawn between payments for services and cost reimbursements.

To the extent that host-country transfer pricing legislation has gaps, the tax treaty provisions that deal with related party transactions can be helpful.

Similarly, in the case when the host country tax legislation is unclear a capital gains tax provision in a tax treaty can clarify if and how a capital gain that derives from an extractive investment is to be taxed.

Clearly, in situations where there are both gaps in the host-country tax law and tax authority capacity is weak, and the extractive investment is significant for the country, it is easy to see that the potential for disputes and misunderstandings may be large. This may be further compounded by other practical considerations. For example, much of the documentation may be in a foreign language and currency or exist in an unfamiliar format, such as purchase orders against a large umbrella contract rather than separate invoices for each item or fixed assets accounted for piecemeal as assets under construction.

Where there is a dispute about a tax issue, a common problem is the lack of a clear process to try and resolve the dispute without by default proceeding to litigation. This is by no means an issue unique to lower-income resource-rich countries. Many countries have struggled to put in place an effective disputes resolution process that provides a fair balance between the rights of the taxpayer to pay only the tax that is due and the goal of the tax authority to collect the right amount of tax and to do so in a way that is transparent as well as being efficient. The governance around this process is critical and can be hard to achieve in a country where the tax authority has weak capacity or there are concerns about minimising the opportunities for corruption. This can lead to a reluctance to delegate or to take decisions, resulting in more tax matters proceeding to court. Tax authority performance management also plays an important supporting role here. Tax authorities that set revenue collection or tax assessment goals for their tax auditors without taking into account the likelihood that the tax demanded will actually be sustained will place increased pressure on the tax courts.

However, where the tax matter under review is a tax treaty issue, the tax treaty can help by providing for a resolution process when one may not exist under domestic law, other than by litigation. Providing that the competent authority of the tax treaty partner is willing to provide support, the mutual agreement procedure (MAP)[15] can be invoked. Unfortunately, most tax treaties require only that the competent authorities use best endeavours to reach agreement unless the tax treaty contains a binding arbitration clause. In countries where there are limited alternative dispute resolution options, it is generally advisable for the affected company to begin the MAP process as soon as a tax adjustment appears probable. This is because in such circumstances the next step may well be tax assessments and commencement of the formal domestic litigation procedures, which may require the payment of the tax in dispute. However, engagement in the MAP process may not be sufficient to prevent the tax in dispute having to be paid into tax court, which will increase the burden on the taxpayer whilst the dispute is resolved, and the tax paid may in practice be difficult to recover should the issue be resolved in the taxpayer's favour. It would be desirable for domestic law or the treaty to provide that any domestic tax litigation should be held in abeyance pending the conclusion of the MAP discussions, because the two processes should not be operating simultaneously.

Clearly tax treaties can play an important role in making up for deficiencies or gaps in the host country legislation, but the practical impact will depend in large part on the host-country tax authority having sufficient capacity and resources to administer the tax treaties.

6 Role of tax treaties in overall tax policy for EI

Tax treaties are sometimes adopted as a badge of statehood, but like any contractual agreement, tax treaties impose responsibilities as well as confer benefits. Whilst tax treaties can be amended by mutually agreed protocols, these take time to negotiate and occur infrequently. As such, a tax treaty is an agreement that is expected at the outset to have a long life, and therefore the provisions of the tax treaty should be ones that each country is willing to live with over the long term. Given this it is clear that governments need access to expert advice so that no party is placed at an undue disadvantage at the negotiating table. This applies both to tax treaty negotiation and to foreign investment tax policy more broadly.

However, when faced with changed circumstances agreements that are negotiated by others can become problematic for their successors. This is particularly so where the issues at stake are significant for the country as a whole and thus assume greater political and economic importance. So a tax treaty negotiated in an earlier time may in an altered environment no longer appear to be a reasonable and equitable agreement.

Ironically there are parallels here with the negotiated investment agreements that may be put in place to support a significant extractive investment. Such a negotiated investment agreement may contain fiscal stability provisions amongst other things and may draw from or cross-refer to the existing tax treaty network. A common criticism is that such agreements are too inflexible and should provide formal opportunities for amendment. But in the context of EI investments, both the tax treaty and the fiscal stability provisions of an investment agreement are serving a critical function, which is to provide greater certainty to investors when significant money needs to be invested up front for a return that will be realised over a long period of time. The major differences are in scope and in the degree of the incentive to respect the agreement. The tax certainty in an investment agreement is tailored to the specific requirements of extractive investment, whereas the tax treaty provisions apply uniformly across all business sectors. There will be sovereign state-level pressure to respect a tax treaty, whereas in practice the pressure to respect an investment agreement will depend upon its relative importance to the overall economy and a country's desire to attract future foreign investments.

Many tax treaties were negotiated a long time ago when the business landscape was different. Without a doubt, business has become more global and interconnected as improvements in logistics and communications have made it easier to take advantage of relative differences in climate, access to natural resources and labour, and to supply more diverse markets. Providing that externalities are correctly priced and responsibly managed, this should benefit everyone through increases in productivity. In the context of a multinational group, taking advantage of these efficiencies through activities such as centralised procurement, centralised marketing, and contracting out of non-core services have led to increased cross-border transactions between related parties.

These same improvements in logistics and communications mean that some businesses are more mobile, giving rise to issues of harmful tax competition. Clearly, an extractive investment is not mobile per se, although given that investment capital is finite extractive investors do need to choose between alternative investment options. However, other parts of the extractive supply chain may be best undertaken in a country other than the country of production. As discussed in the introduction, efficient global growth occurs where the mineral resources (wherever they are located) are delivered to the end consumer (wherever they are located) at the lowest all-in cost. This all-in cost includes the costs of financing, extraction, processing, manufacture, and distribution, including the correct pricing of externalities arising from these activities and including the taxes borne in the value chain from start to finish.

At the same time, with the notable exception of the United States, there has been a shift towards territorial taxation systems. This means that under their domestic law many developed-country treaty partners are giving up some (but not all) taxing rights over income earned offshore by their tax-resident companies. This does not so far seem to have been accompanied by a corresponding return to source country withholding taxes to the extent that may have been expected.

From the perspective of a developing-country tax treaty party, one way of looking at this is that the value of the tax treaty concession given to such a developed country is now worth less than at the time the tax treaty was negotiated. Perhaps – but given the expected longevity of the tax treaty – it is worth reflecting on what future changes may take place that would challenge that view. For example, given concerns around base erosion and profit shifting it is not inconceivable that the next phase of the move to territorial taxation is accompanied by an increase in withholding taxes to protect the source country's tax base. Why would this matter to a lower-income resource-rich country that expects mainly foreign investment inflows? This potentially matters a great deal in a number of areas. For a lower-income resource-rich country, one of the significant challenges is managing the impacts of the so-called resources curse. The creation of a fund that makes foreign investments can be a common part of an overall strategy to manage the resource curse as well as to manage the resource wealth for the benefit of future generations, and tax treaties can support this outbound foreign investment. Transformative economic development can flow from successful extractive investments and investments in related infrastructure. It may not be so many years before the relative balance of investments flows into and out of a lower-income resource-rich country becomes more nuanced. Furthermore, large mineral-producing countries are rarely also large mineral-consuming countries; in terms of realising taxable income they are therefore dependent on being able to export their production to a consuming country. Analysis of base erosion and profit shifting and the UN work on transfer pricing are also questioning the appropriate way in which to view the taxation rights that should accrue to a country by virtue of its large markets and large consumer populations. Viewed through this lens the bargain may start to look different again.

If tax treaties are not respected or are applied incorrectly in practice by the tax administration, this will contribute to the cost of doing business. The renegotiation or termination of tax treaties will increase the perception of country risk and will increase the cost of finance. Therefore any change in tax treaty policy needs to be carefully evaluated for (i) the impact it has on future investment and (ii) the impact on existing investment (which may in any event be stabilised by an investment agreement). From the extractive investor's perspective, the certainty and stability benefits provided by tax treaties are very valuable and have a direct impact on project funding costs. However, the tax result delivered by tax treaty benefits is just one factor in the post-tax project investment analysis. If there were no tax treaty, the higher – or the risk of a higher – tax burden would be taken into account in the project economics and will impact the investment decision, as well as the relative competitiveness of the investment opportunity versus a competing alternative. Therefore in the case of foreign investment tax policy the agreement of a tax treaty is as much a part of the policy framework as the domestic tax legislation.

Since tax treaties apply to investments in all business sectors, it makes sense to review the particular fiscal considerations of the extractives sector and to determine what aspects of these need to be addressed in the context of (i) foreign investment through a tax treaty and (ii) foreign investment not through a tax treaty, for example relying simply on domestic law or targeted investment incentives where the situation merits. So making clear policy choices rather than arriving haphazardly at an unexpected outcome with the potential for unintended political consequences is surely the preferred course of action.

7 Conclusions

Through consideration of the extractive investment life cycle, the factors impacting access to investment capital, and the competing interests of various stakeholders, we can see that a successful extractive investment requires the alignment of a great many variables. Indeed given the enormous obstacles to be overcome it almost seems surprising that any manage to make it to fruition at all. Many readers will recognise how difficult it is to deliver infrastructure investment within a single developed-country context, and arguably an extractive investment is even more difficult to realise with the added complexities of the one-time nature of the resource benefit (often an emotive issue) and a revenue stream that is determined by reference to a global price.

There is competition for extractive investment capital in two senses. First, there are more potential projects available in the world than the funds to finance them. Second, for a limited number of the more attractive "tier-one" projects it is also true that there may be more potential providers of investment capital than needed. However, in both cases the degree of competition is not static but responds to changes in the extractive investment cycle, which ebbs and flows as supply and demand for minerals changes. This cycle is accentuated due to the lagging effect of the long lead time for a new mine to come into production. This is further compounded by the fact that it is harder to access capital to pursue a counter-cyclical investment strategy. The simple reason for this is that the future is inherently hard to forecast, and more weight is always given therefore to the near term.

Some large extractive investments have associated infrastructure requirements in the form of roads, rail, air, and port facilities that can underpin an entire region's or a country's economic development. The scale of extractive investments like these can also have the side effect of accelerating improvements in local country institutional capacity. For example, the capital and raw material import requirements of a project may be so large that it represents a high percentage of a country's total imports. Practically speaking the extractive investor has a self-interest in ensuring that the country has the systems, the controls, and the administrative capability to properly deal with this volume of imports on a timely basis whilst incorporating appropriate safeguards against corruption. The same observation can be made with respect to the supply of contracted services and the administration of any VAT and withholding taxes, including the processing of refunds. These kinds of legacies will benefit all sectors of the country's economy.

As explained in the section dealing with the extractive investment life cycle, fiscal revenues from the extractive investment will be subject to considerable fluctuation, and this volatility presents challenges for governments in terms of planning and budgeting. There will also be considerable challenges for some tax authorities in terms of the capacity to administer large extractive taxpayers.

Therefore understanding the total economic impacts flowing from a large extractive investment is fundamental to developing the appropriate tax policy framework. This includes the broader benefits described earlier as well as the impact on other sectors of the economy. It includes an appreciation of the full spectrum of extractive investors and the way in which investment decisions are made and financed. A government must decide how much foreign extractive investment it wishes to attract as a proportion of the overall economy and on what terms, for example as an exporter or perhaps as a catalyst for regional economic development. Understanding the economy, the major financing, trade, and investment flows is key to understanding where support is needed and where tax policy decisions – including tax treaty policy decisions – could hinder or promote economic growth.

Tax treaties are simply one tool that can be used as part of the overall foreign investment framework (inbound and outbound). Tax treaties generally apply to all business sectors, and therefore the provisions of most relevance to the extractive sector will need to be considered in that context. Of course the reverse is also true, so that amending or terminating a tax treaty solely because of its impact on the extractive sector will also impact other business sectors.

The policy objective that is furthered by entering into a tax treaty and the related trade-offs need to be clearly understood. For example, imposing withholding tax on interest paid to a foreign lender will protect against tax base erosion, but as explained in the section dealing with financing, since lenders invariably require a tax gross-up, it also effectively makes the cost of borrowing higher. Where this gross-up is tax deductible, the additional cost will be partly financed by reduced corporate income taxes.

At its simplest, a tax treaty can help eliminate or minimise double taxation for an extractive investor. This in turn improves the project's post-tax returns to the investor and may improve the relative competitiveness of the project versus another competing investment. A tax treaty can also support a stable investment environment, as the tax treaty position should take precedence over future changes in domestic tax law and therefore effectively provide a known ceiling against future change of tax law risks. Through competent authority and mutual agreement procedures, a tax treaty can also provide a potential means to resolve tax disputes.

In conclusion, if the goal is to optimise the mineral production required to support global economic growth, there is a clear role for tax treaties to play as part of the overall tax policy framework for foreign investment. Since most major mineral producers are not also major mineral consumers, there is a collective interest in supporting a multilateral international tax framework – including tax treaties – that provides clear guidelines, supports efficient investment, and delivers benefits to all stakeholders.

Notes

1 The author of this chapter is the former global head of tax at Rio Tinto, and whilst the views expressed are strictly those of the author, the perspective and experience drawn upon are those of an international mining company investor.

2 Financing costs comprise the price for the provision of debt and equity capital, including any related financing and professional fees. It is the all-in cost of funding the investment expenditures and is incurred in addition to the expenses that the capital raised is spent on.

3 To learn more, visit http://www.taxtreatieshistory.org/, a not-for-profit joint project of the OECD, Institute for Austrian and International Tax Law Vienna (WU), IBFD, Università Cattolica del Sacro Cuore, IFA Canadian Branch, and the Canadian Tax Foundation, on the history of tax treaties and their provisions.

4 For more discussion on capital import neutrality, please refer to Chapter 5 in this book (Daniel and Thuronyi, 2016).

5 For a more detailed discussion on taxation of capital gains, please refer to Chapter 7 in this book (Burns, Le Leuch and Sunley, 2016).

6 Farm-in is the acquisition of a license for a consideration which, usually, is satisfied by an obligation to bear future costs connected with the license, although the consideration can take many forms, including cash. Earn-in is similar to a farm-in, but the license is not acquired until the consideration has been settled, usually by undertaking works in the license area.

7 Assume Investor A has a mining project that is worth \$100m. The project needs an additional \$100m of investment in order to begin production, when it will be worth \$200m. Investor A enters into an earn-in agreement with another unconnected person – Investor B. Under this earn-in agreement Investor B will earn a 50 percent share of the mining project provided that Investor B invests the \$100m capital needed to bring the mine into production. Investor A currently owns 100 percent of a mining project that is worth \$100m. Once the earn-in is completed Investor A will own 50 percent of a mining project worth \$200m, or \$100m. In other words, the value of what Investor A expects to have before and after the earn-in agreement is the same, and in that sense there is no disposal to tax. It is economically equivalent to and often takes the form of the mining company issuing new shares and using the capital proceeds to develop the mine. Shareholders who do not participate in such an equity raising see their interests in the company diluted but have not made a disposal.

8 For a good description of the purpose of tax gross-up clauses in lending documentation, see *The ACT Borrower's Guide to LMA loan documentation for Investment Grade Borrowers*, produced by Slaughter & May February 2010.

9 See this explanation on the IFC website: http://www1.ifc.org/wps/wcm/connect/Topics_Ext_Content/IFC_External_Corporate_Site/IFC + Syndications/Overview_Benefits_Structure/Syndications/B + Loan + Structure + And + Benefits/

10 For example, a copper mine may produce significant by-products such as gold, silver, molybdenum, and others.

11 International Accounting Standard 36 *Impairment of Assets* seeks to ensure that an entity's assets are not carried in the financial statements at more than their recoverable amount (i.e., the higher of fair value less costs of disposal and value in use). With the exception of goodwill and certain intangible assets for which an annual impairment test is required, entities are required to conduct impairment tests where there is an indication of impairment of an asset, and the test may be conducted for a "cash-generating unit" where an asset does not generate cash inflows that are largely independent of those from other assets. For examples in the mining sector, see the BHP Billiton financial statements for the year ended 30 June 2012, Rio Tinto financial statements for the years ended 31 December 2011 and 2012, and Anglo American financial statements for the year ended 31 December 2012.

12 A retained or overriding royalty can be used in the situation in which a seller and buyer may not agree on the value of a mineral asset. The seller may retain a royalty that pays in certain price scenarios as a practical way of bridging that valuation gap. The seller can then dispose of the retained royalty at a later time if it wishes. Another common scenario is when the seller wishes to insure against seller's remorse by using a royalty to preserve some upside interest.

13 Many large multinationals engage in periodic reviews of their corporate structure to eliminate companies that are inactive or superfluous to requirements, as these are costly to administer in terms of compliance and audit responsibilities.

14 I have deliberately *not* described these as non-renewable natural resources because many metals can be and are in fact recycled. However, from the perspective of the country where the minerals are extracted they may be a non-renewable source of income.

15 See the OECD Manual on Effective Mutual Agreement Procedure for a detailed description of best practice in this area – http://www.oecd.org/ctp/dispute/manualoneffectivemutualagreementprocedures-index.htm.

7 Taxing gains on transfer of interest

Lee Burns, Honoré Le Leuch and Emil M. Sunley[1]

1 Introduction

In the last decade, there have been a number of transactions involving the transfer[2] of an interest in a mining or petroleum right[3] (see Box 7.1). Many reported transfers have involved purchasers paying substantial consideration for such rights. This has brought into focus the income tax treatment of gains arising from such transfers.[4] The tax treatment of a transfer of mining or petroleum right is complex, and recent transactions have highlighted the inadequacy of the income tax laws of many countries (particularly developing countries) to tax gains arising on the transfer of such rights.[5]

In broad terms, there are two ways that a mining or petroleum right can be transferred, each with differing tax consequences. First, the entity holding the right[6] can transfer its interest in the right (referred to as a "direct transfer"), or, second, the owner of the entity holding the right can transfer its interest in the entity that holds the right (referred to as an "indirect transfer"). Moreover, these transfers may be structured in different ways. The income tax treatment of a direct or indirect transfer can be complex, involving issues relating to: (i) the structure of the transaction and character of the interest transferred (revenue or capital); (ii) the valuation of the consideration for the transfer; (iii) the timing of the transfer; and (iv) the geographic location of the gain derived. The taxing rules may apply specifically to mining and petroleum rights or, more likely, to immovable property (which usually includes a mining or petroleum right either under general law or through a specific tax law definition). The international norm is that the source country (referred to as the "host country") has full taxing rights in relation to income derived from the exploitation, or gains derived from the transfer, of immovable property located in the host country.[7] Even if the host country that has issued the mining or petroleum right has jurisdiction to tax a gain arising from a direct or indirect transfer of the right under domestic law, the application of domestic law to the gain may be restricted under a tax treaty.[8] Indeed, the transaction effecting the transfer may be structured so as to obtain treaty protection from host country taxation.

The purpose of this chapter is to outline the income tax issues relevant to the taxation of any gain arising on a direct or indirect transfer of a mining or petroleum right for both the transferor and transferee. The chapter begins by summarising the different conceptual options and issues that may arise for taxation of transfers of mining or petroleum rights. The main body of the chapter discusses the tax treatment of a direct transfer of interest, followed by a discussion of the tax treatment of an indirect transfer through the sale of an interest in an entity that derives its value principally, directly or indirectly, from a mining or petroleum right or rights. There is then discussion of the tax treatment of transfers of interest under overriding royalty and farm-out agreements. The last section considers the treatment of a transfer of interest when additional profits tax is payable or under a production sharing agreement.

2 Conceptual approach to taxation of the transfer of mining or petroleum rights

Transfers of mining or petroleum rights are quite common in the industry and may take many forms (see a few examples in Box 7.1). Indeed, a mining or petroleum right granted by the host country may be transferred a number of times during its life cycle. Even when a mining or petroleum right is originally granted to a single corporate entity, the right may be wholly or partly transferred, directly or indirectly, several times during its validity. There may be various reasons for such transfers, including spreading the risk associated with a potentially unsuccessful exploration or prospecting project or to raise funds to carry out further mining or petroleum operations. It may also be the case that the business activities of some entities are limited to exploration or prospecting, with these entities making their income from the transfer of rights relating to successful exploration or prospecting operations.

When a mining or petroleum right is held by more than one entity as a joint venture, the whole or partial transfer by one of the entities of its interest in the right will concern only the entity making the transfer and not the joint venture.[9] The decision to transfer an interest in a mining or petroleum right, therefore, is an individual decision and not part of the joint operations and accounts, and the accounting and tax consequences concern only the transferor and its transferee, not the other holders of the right.

Box 7.1 Examples of structuring direct and indirect transfers of mining or petroleum rights

Transfer during exploration and appraisal:

- **Farm-in/farm-out agreements**
  - Ireland (2013): acquisition of a 75 percent interest in an exploration licence in exchange for carrying the full cost of a 3D seismic program and reimbursement of a portion of previously-incurred costs.

  - Guinea (2012): sale by one entity of a part of its interest in a production sharing agreement in exchange for reimbursement to the farmor of $27 million of past costs and carrying farmor's future costs associated with an exploratory well and optional appraisal well up to a cost cap per well.

- **Overriding royalty**
  - Mongolia (2002): a Canadian company acquired a mining licence in Mongolia for cash consideration plus 2 percent of the gross revenue realised from any commercial discovery. In 2004, a Canadian company agreed to pay $37 million to acquire the royalty interest.

- **Purchase of an exploration company**
  - Norway (2012): acquisition of an exploration company holding interest in 28 exploration licences in the country for a purchase price of $372 million, plus a bonus payment up to $300 million depending on future discoveries. The transaction is subject to the approval of ministries for energy and finance.

- **Total transfer of interest in petroleum agreements**
  - Uganda (2010): acquisition of the entire 50 percent interest held by a company in two blocks covered by production sharing contracts where major discoveries were made and appraised, for a total cash consideration of $1.45 billion. A dispute on capital gains tax (CGT) and stamp duty liability with the seller and the purchaser involving the Ugandan courts and international arbitration was resolved in 2015 confirming the tax payment.

- **Partial transfer of interest in petroleum agreements**
  - Uganda (2012): two sales and purchases agreements on one third interest in three blocks (including the above two blocks), each one with a company, for a total cash consideration of $2.9 billion. The resolution of the related tax disputes between the seller and the tax authorities settled in 2015 upon agreement of the tax payable by the transferor of $250 million.

- **Indirect transfer by sale of a foreign-listed company holding interests in several countries**
  - Mozambique (2012): sale for $1.9 billion of all the shares of the listed company indirectly holding interests in several countries, mostly in Mozambique (8.5 percent in a deep offshore block where giant gas discoveries were made and 10 percent in an onshore block). In order not to postpone the sale, the selling

company "seeked clarity on a possible tax charge" and announced that the company is "subject to Mozambique corporate income tax on the imputed capital gains arising on its Mozambique assets as a result of the transaction", with the tax return to be submitted within 30 days of completion of the transaction.

- **Indirect transfer of a minority interest in a foreign company holding host-company mining rights**
    - Mozambique (2013): sale for $4.2 billion of 28.5 percent in a foreign company holding 70 percent of the mining right in a block with major gas discoveries subject to the approval of the authorities. After negotiation with the state, the seller accepted that tax was payable on the transaction.
- **Issuance of new shares**
    - Mongolia (2006): one of the world's largest mining companies acquired new shares (and a controlling interest) in a Canadian mining company in return for a payment of $1.5 billion. The value of the Canadian company's shares derived primarily from a mining licence in Mongolia.

Transfer during production:

- **Sale of the equity in a mining company**
    - Ghana (2011): indirect sale and purchase of 18.9 percent equity in two domestic mining companies by acquiring the shares in non-resident companies. For a total cash consideration of $661 million.

Source: Press releases from companies (amounts expressed in U.S. dollars)

The tax treatment of a transfer of interest depends on a number of factors including (i) the type of mining or petroleum right (an exploration or prospecting right, a mining lease or development licence, or a contractual-based right); (ii) the form of the consideration for the transfer (a single cash consideration or other types of consideration [such as combining work obligations, overriding royalty, production payments, or contingent cash payments depending on future events]); and (iii) the way the transfer is structured (such as a direct transfer of the mining or petroleum right, an indirect transfer of shares or other equity interests in the holder of the right, or through a corporate reorganisation, including merger or spin-off[10] arrangements). Direct transfers are generally taxable whatever the level of interest transferred,[11] while often indirect transfers of an interest may be taxable only if there is a change in control or, more commonly, a lower percentage threshold defined in the law as a "substantial change".[12]

Under a pure tax-royalty arrangement, the tax liability of the transferor of a mining or petroleum right depends on the host country's tax laws. The initial policy issue is whether the host country is going to tax the gain. The economic impact of imposing tax on a gain arising on transfer of interest is explained in Box 7.2. Assessing the impact of the transfer on the future tax payments to the host country, with or without the transfer occurring, is paramount when deciding tax policy, as illustrated in Box 7.3.

For a host country that has decided to tax the gain on transfer of a mining or petroleum right, there are three possible bases of taxation depending on the tax system. First, the gain (being the consideration received reduced by the written-down value[13] of the right at the time of transfer) may be assessable as income[14] subject to the ordinary corporate tax rate or to the specific corporate tax rate applicable to mining or petroleum activities when so provided. Second, the gain may be assessable as a capital gain under the capital gains tax (CGT), when a CGT exists and applies to mining or petroleum operations in the host country. Third, that part of the gain representing the recapture of depreciation or other deductions in relation to the cost of the right may be taxed under the ordinary corporate tax, and that part of the gain representing the excess of consideration received over the undepreciated cost of the right may be taxed under the CGT. Each of these possibilities is explained in sections 3.1 and 3.2.

Box 7.2 Economic effects of taxing gains on transfers of interest

- The market for rights is not perfectly competitive. There are few buyers and sellers, and information regarding future mineral or petroleum prices and production costs is limited.
- Transfers of an interest in a mining or petroleum right will only take place if there is a willing buyer and a willing seller.
- The agreed price for the transfer must fall between the reservation price of the seller (the lowest price the seller is willing to take) and the reservation price of the buyer (the highest price the buyer is willing to pay).
- If gains on transfers of interest are taxed, the reservation price of the seller will be higher (as the seller has the liability to pay the tax) and the reservation price of the buyer will also be lower (as the buyer may be a future seller). The tax on the gain could discourage some transactions, particularly when the buyer of an interest plans to flip it. The impact is likely to be much smaller if the buyer is making a long-term investment.
- The legal liability and the incidence of the tax may differ.
- The contractual arrangement between the buyer and the seller may specify a price net of any tax due on the transfer, with one party agreeing to compensate the other for the amount of taxes due.
- Buyers and sellers will structure transactions to minimize taxes payable.

Effective taxation of gains on a transfer of interest requires that the tax law is explicit in relation to the determination of the value of the transaction, the character of the gain as income or capital, and the tax treatment, liability, and payment related to transfers and their tax accounting – in particular for indirect transfers resulting from change in control in the entity holding an interest, a growing solution used for transfers – otherwise disputes may occur, with many recent cases of such disputes. Except when the tax law provides otherwise, the payment of the tax on the gain by the transferor may be deferred until the end of the tax year, although, ideally, the tax payment in respect of the transaction should take place earlier, as a condition for the country authorising the transfer.[15]

A few resource-rich countries have decided to exempt transfers from taxation, considering that such gains have been mostly re-invested in the country by the transferor and taking into account relatively high levels of taxation that may apply (such as Norway, where no step-up in depreciation is allowed to the purchaser to maintain tax neutrality), but such a treatment is exceptional.

If a country decides to exempt transfers, it is important to determine the scope of an exemption clause in the law or a mining or petroleum agreement as it applies to transfers, in particular, whether the tax exemption applies to the gain on transfer or only to the duties and fees (such as an exemption from registration or notary fees) related to the transfer. A number of mining or petroleum agreements contain a clause that may be interpreted as an exemption from transfer or stamp duties while remaining silent on the taxation of transfer gains. Taxation is the critical issue in relation to transfers, and such a clause should explicitly address whether the transfer is subject to tax.

When the tax-royalty agreement is subject to an additional profits tax (APT) or a surcharge tax supplementary to the corporate tax (as in the United Kingdom), the legislation has to determine whether the transfer gain, or capital gain, is also subject to the APT and the impact of the transaction on APT accounting. For example, is the consideration paid by the transferee deductible for its APT calculation in all cases or only if the value of the transaction has been subject to APT and the corresponding liability was paid by the transferor? One supplementary difficulty is that APT is often a joint liability borne by the joint venture involved in a mining project and not an individual liability of one entity constituting the joint venture, while the taxation on transfer is an individual liability for the seller. For the time being, many laws or agreements are still silent on this issue, while it should be explicitly provided for when defining the APT. This is discussed further in section 6.1.

The same determination has to be made under production sharing contracts (PSCs)[16] or service contracts[17] in the case of a transfer of an economic interest by one party constituting the contractor. Is the taxation on transfer under a PSC limited to corporate taxation of the gain or CGT (which appears to be the objective)? Or is the value of the transaction to be, in addition, recorded for the purposes of cost recovery and indirectly for profit oil sharing, which seems difficult to justify on the basis that a transfer is an individual decision and not a cost incurred by all the parties constituting the contractor. Checking PSCs, legislation, and agreements to determine the treatment of transfers and deciding on the tax policy in this respect is important.[18] This is discussed further in section 6.2.

3 Direct transfer of a mining or petroleum right

The first scenario considered is a transfer by the holder of the whole or part of a mining or petroleum right. A mining or petroleum right is an intangible asset of the holder. The tax treatment of any gain arising on the transfer of a mining or petroleum right depends on the interplay among (i) the rules for taxing business income; (ii) deduction recapture rules; (iii) the CGT rules; and (iv) the application of any applicable tax treaty. The tax treatment will depend also on the structure of the transaction. The discussion in this section focuses on a simple transfer of a mining or petroleum right. The tax treatment of a transfer under an overriding royalty or farm-out agreement is briefly discussed in section 5.

3.1 Deduction recapture

The cost of acquiring a mining or petroleum right is likely to have been allowed as a deduction under either (i) the normal operation of the depreciation rules[19] or (ii) a special deduction rule applicable to the capital costs of mining or petroleum operations.[20] In either case, the cost may be deducted outright (as may occur in the case of an exploration or prospecting right) or deducted over the expected life of the mining or petroleum operations or a shorter period as specified in the tax law. In both cases, the timing of the deduction may be deferred until the commencement of commercial production.[21]

If the transferor has deducted the acquisition cost of a mining or petroleum right under the depreciation regime, the normal rules applicable to transfers of depreciated assets will apply to the transfer of the right. In particular, when the consideration for the transfer of the right is more than the written-down value of the right at the time of transfer, some or all of the depreciation deductions have been recaptured on transfer of the right. The depreciation rules will apply to include the recaptured deductions in income. If a special deduction rule applies to mining or petroleum expenditure, it is usual for an amount representing a recaptured deduction to be included in income. Consequently, the outcome is similar to that under a comprehensive depreciation regime.

If the transferor is a non-resident, the host country will have jurisdiction to tax the transferor only on domestic source income. While not always clearly stated in the income tax law, a recaptured deduction should be treated as domestic source income.

Box 7.3 Possible impact of transfer on host country future tax revenues

The two following simplified examples illustrate the possible negative impact of certain tax rules on the future revenues of the host country when integrating the one-time tax payment on the transaction, if any, made by the transferor and the future tax liabilities of the transferee.

Case 1 of a direct transfer: Assumptions: (1) Transferor's gain subject to CGT (at a lower rate than the corporate tax [CT] rate). (2) The transferee can deduct the full purchase price (and not only the written-down value of the asset at the time of transfer) from its taxable base subject to CT. Such tax rules if adopted would indeed reduce the host country's revenues *versus* a "no-transfer scenario" by an amount equivalent to the difference between (i) the present value of the tax savings on the increased cost recovery deductions allowed to the transferee and (ii) the CGT paid on the gain by the transferor.

Case 2 of an indirect transfer: Assumptions: (1) Purchase by a host country's producer (P) of all the shares in a foreign company (S) holding several exploration and production rights in the host country. (2) The law does not explicitly deal with the taxation of the gain made by the shareholders of S, and they do not pay tax in relation to the transaction. (3) P takes advantage of uncertainties in the tax law of the host country and structures the transaction so as to deduct from its CT base in the host country the entire purchase price. This case, if accepted, would reduce the host country revenues *versus* a no-transfer scenario by an amount equal to the gain multiplied by the CT rate.

Today, the tax legislation of most countries ensures that the foreign transferor's shareholders are liable for tax and the cost of acquiring the shares is not deducted outright or amortised.

It is recommended to carry out this kind of dual analysis, looking at the integrated impact of the transfer on the transferor's and transferee's tax liabilities, when designing the tax policy and rules applicable by a host country to direct and indirect transfers or when approving a specific transfer.

3.2 Gain on transfer of a mining or petroleum right

If the consideration for the transfer of a mining or petroleum right is more than the original acquisition cost of the right, the tax treatment of the excess will depend on the scope of the depreciation regime and its interaction with the normal income tax or CGT rules.

3.2.1 Application of depreciation regime

A depreciation regime may include both the recaptured depreciation deductions and the gain above cost in income. This means that a gain derived on the transfer of a mining or petroleum right is effectively treated as income and taxed under the normal operation of the corporate income tax. This has the advantage of ensuring that the taxation to the transferor of the recaptured deduction and the gain above cost and the deduction of cost by the transferee are all at the same tax rate.[22]

3.2.2 Characterisation of the gain as income or capital

If the depreciation regime taxes only recaptured depreciation deductions, then the gain above cost is dealt with separately. In this case, taxation of the gain will depend on whether the gain is characterised as income or a capital gain.

There are two possible bases upon which a gain above cost may be characterised as income. First, the income tax law may make no distinction between income and capital gains in relation to business assets with the gain on disposal of any business asset treated as income. This is common in civil-law countries where there is alignment of tax accounting with financial accounting.[23] It will apply also in those common-law countries where the tax legislation defines business income to include gains on the transfer of all business assets.

Second, a mining or petroleum right might be held on revenue account either as trading stock (or inventory) or an asset that is acquired with an expectation that it will be disposed of for a profit. It would be an unusual case in which a mining or petroleum right is held as trading stock (or inventory), but it is certainly possible that a mining or petroleum right (particularly an exploration or prospecting licence) is held with the intention or reasonable expectation that it will be transferred for a profit.

For those countries that maintain the distinction between revenue and capital, and apart from the cases mentioned in the previous paragraph, a mining or petroleum right is likely to be characterised as a "capital" or "structural" asset of the holder's business and, therefore, a gain arising on the transfer of the right is a capital gain. Taxation of capital gains depends on whether the country has a CGT and, if it does, on the scope of capital gains taxation. While many countries have a comprehensive CGT applicable to a broad range of business and investment assets, CGT taxation in some common-law developing countries may apply only in relation to a few specific classes of asset. Importantly, even when there is only limited taxation of capital gains, it is likely to apply to capital gains on disposal of immovable property in the country (which should include a mining or petroleum right; see section 3.2.3).

If a gain arising on disposal of a mining or petroleum right is subject to CGT rather than the normal corporate income tax, the issue is whether any concessional tax treatment applies in relation to the gain (as compared to the normal income tax). While concessional treatment is common under a CGT,[24] today it is likely to be limited to individuals and not apply to companies. Importantly, if the gain is treated as a capital gain and is either untaxed because the country does not have a CGT or concessionally taxed under the CGT, then there will be asymmetric tax treatment, as between the transferor and transferee as the transferee's cost represented by the gain is likely to be deducted at the normal the corporate tax rate.

3.2.3 Jurisdiction to tax the gain

If the person holding a mining or petroleum right is a non-resident, then there is the additional issue of whether there is jurisdiction to tax the gain. For a gain that is taxed as income under the normal corporate tax, jurisdiction to tax will depend on whether the gain has a geographic source in the jurisdiction. Source may also be the basis for taxation under the CGT. Alternatively, the taxation of non-residents under the CGT may be limited to assets listed as taxable assets.[25]

The rules for determining the source of income or gains may be specified in the income tax law or, in the case of common-law countries, may be determined by reference to case law. For civil-law countries, jurisdiction to tax a gain on transfer of a mining or petroleum right is likely to depend on whether the gain is attributable to a permanent establishment of the transferor in the host country. This may be expressly framed as a source rule or simply as the basis for taxation of the business income of non-residents. The basic notion of a permanent establishment is a fixed place of business through which the business of an enterprise is carried on. Given that the holder of a mining or petroleum right will be obliged to undertake specified work commitments in the host country, the holder is likely to have a permanent establishment in the host country. The meaning of permanent establishment is discussed in section 3.2.4.

The concept of permanent establishment is a civil law concept that is used also in tax treaties. Traditionally, in common-law countries, the source of income has been determined through case law. However, a number of common-law countries now specify source rules in the income tax law, including using the permanent establishment concept so as to align domestic law with tax treaties. So for common-law countries that use the permanent establishment concept, the gain on transfer of a mining or petroleum right is likely to be sourced in the country.

For common-law countries that rely on case law, the determination of source is a practical hard matter of fact.[26] The source of income is determined having regard to all the facts and circumstances relating to the derivation of the income. Under case law, income arising from immovable property is normally sourced where the immovable property is located.[27] This applies to both rents and gains on transfer of the property. It is usually the case that mining and petroleum rights are treated as part of the immovable property to which they relate (see section 3.2.4). If this is not the case, then the determination of source is more problematic, as a court may be prepared to hold that a casual gain arising from the disposal of an intangible asset is sourced at the place of contract.[28]

If the jurisdiction to tax under CGT is based on a list of taxable assets, the list will normally include immovable property located in the jurisdiction. A similar issue arises as to the meaning of immovable property for this purpose (see section 3.2.4).

For those common-law countries that do not use the permanent establishment concept, the treatment of a mining or petroleum right as immovable property will ensure that the gain is taxable under either the normal income tax or CGT. If a mining or petroleum right is not considered immovable property, then there is the possibility that the gain may go untaxed, particularly if the transaction is between two non-residents with the place of contract outside the jurisdiction.

3.2.4 Application of tax treaties[29]

If a transferor[30] of a mining or petroleum right is a non-resident, jurisdiction to tax a gain on transfer of the right under domestic law may be affected by a tax treaty between the host country and the transferor's country of residence. The initial issue is whether Article 6, 7, or 13 applies to the gain. While the gain may be properly characterised as a business profit, Article 7 applies only if Articles 6 and 13 do not apply.[31] The starting point, therefore, is to consider whether Article 6 or 13 applies. Article 6(1) provides that

> Income derived by a resident of a Contracting State from immovable property . . . situated in the other Contracting State may be taxed in that other State.

This gives full taxing rights over the income to the country in which the immovable property is located. This is justified on the basis of the close economic connection between the income and the host country.[32] This taxing right is not exclusive so that the residence country may also tax the income provided relief is given for the host country's tax.[33]

In the present context, the issue is the meaning of "income derived . . . *from* immovable property" (emphasis added) in Article 6(1). This is intended to cover income from the "exploitation" of immovable property (such as rent) but not gains from the alienation of immovable property even if the gain is ordinary business income.[34] If Article 6 does not apply, then Article 13 may apply. Article 13(1) provides that:

> Gains derived by a resident of a Contracting State from the alienation of immovable property referred to in Article 6 and situated in the other Contracting State may be taxed in that other State.

As with Article 6, this gives full taxing rights over the gain to the country in which the immovable property is located.

The complication is that Article 13 is headed "Capital Gains" and, while the text of the Article refers to "gains", there is an argument that Article 13 applies only to capital gains. This would seem to be the interpretation of Article 13 by Canada, as it has included a reservation in the Commentary to Article 6 stating that Canada will apply Article 6 to revenue gains on the alienation of immovable property.[35] Other countries, such as the United States and Australia, do not limit Article 13 to capital gains but apply the article generally to gains on the alienation of property.[36] For these countries, Article 6 applies to income from immovable property (such as rent), and Article 13 applies to income or capital gains from the alienation of immovable property.

Articles 6 and 13 apply in relation to "immovable property". Article 6(2) defines "immovable property", and this definition applies also for the purposes of Article 13(1). "Immovable property" is defined in Article 6(2) to have the meaning under the law of the contracting state in which the immovable property is located. The reference to "law" in Article 6(2) is not confined to the tax law of the contracting state where the property is located but is a reference to the entire law of that state.[37] However, if there is a specific tax law definition of immovable property, this should have priority over the general law meaning.[38] Mining and petroleum rights may be treated as part of the immovable property to which they relate under general law principles[39] or through an extended tax law definition.[40] The definition in Article 6(2) also includes "rights to which the provisions of general law with respect to landed property apply", which should cover mining or petroleum rights. It may be, though, that a particular transaction is structured so that the value is not in the mining or petroleum right transferred but the transfer of information related to the right.[41] The only way that Article 6 or 13 could apply in this case is if there is specific tax law definition of immovable property in the host country that includes mining or petroleum information that then applies for the purposes of the treaty through Article 6(2).

If, for whatever reason, Articles 6 and 13 do not apply,[42] then Article 7 will apply as the transferor is carrying on business. Article 7 provides that the profits of an enterprise of a contracting state are taxable only in that state unless the profits are attributable to a permanent establishment of the enterprise in the other contracting state. The important difference between Articles 6 and 13 on the one hand and Article 7 on the other hand is that taxation is permitted under Article 7 only if the gain is attributable to a permanent establishment in the host country. The definition of "permanent establishment" is broadly stated in Article 5. The fundamental notion of a "permanent establishment" is stated in Article 5(1), namely a fixed place of business through which the business of an enterprise is carried on. The definition in Article 5(2)(f) expressly includes a "mine, an oil or gas well, a quarry or any other place of extraction of natural resources", so the holder of a mining lease or development licence will have a permanent establishment. While the reference to "extraction" will not include exploration,[43] it is expected that there would be a fixed place of business through which prospecting or exploration activities are conducted and, therefore, a permanent establishment within Article 5(1). Despite this, there may be a rare case when a person passively holding a prospecting or exploration right for, say, speculation purposes, disposes of the right without having a permanent establishment. For this reason, it is important that countries make clear in their treaty negotiations that either Article 6 or 13 applies to all types of gains on transfer of immovable property.

3.3 Rollover relief

An alternative to taxing the transfer of a mining or petroleum right is to "roll over" the transferor's written down value of the mining or petroleum right at the time of transfer to the transferee. This means that no gain is recognised to the transferor, and the transferee continues to deduct the original cost of the mining or petroleum right until exhausted. If the cost has already been fully deducted by the transferor (such as for a prospecting or exploration right), then no further deductions are allowed to the transferee.

Rollover relief recognises the potentially tax-neutral position on transfer of a mining or petroleum right when account is taken of the fact that the transferee will be entitled to a deduction for the cost of acquiring the right. If, for example, the right is a prospecting or exploration right the cost of which is deductible outright, then the tax on the gain to the transferor will be offset by the tax value of the deduction to the transferee for the cost of acquiring the right. For this reason, some countries may prefer to roll over the transferor's written-down value of the mining or petroleum right to the transferee rather than tax the transfer. The reality, though, is that the deduction for the cost of the mining or petroleum right may simply create a loss carried forward for the transferee that may take some years to be fully realised. For this reason, as well as for equity between investors,[44] governments have preferred to tax the gain knowing that the impact of the deduction to the transferee for the cost of the mining or petroleum right will be deferred. This has been particularly the case given the large amounts paid for mining or petroleum rights in recent years.

It is noted that rollover relief may apply when a mining or petroleum right is transferred between related companies as part of a corporate reorganisation. This is justified on the basis that there is no change in economic ownership of the assets (including a mining or petroleum right) that are the subject of a reorganisation.

4 Indirect transfer of a mining or petroleum right

As indicated, the shares or other equity rights in an entity derive their value from the assets held by the entity. Thus, for example, if the principal asset of a company is a mining or petroleum right, the value of the shares in the company will equate to the value of the right. This means that, instead of the company selling its interest in the mining or petroleum right, an equivalent gain could be made by the owners of the company selling their shares in the company. Indeed, it is a common form of tax planning for non-residents to invest through a multi-tier non-resident company structure so as to facilitate possible tax-free exit from the investment. This is illustrated by Figure 7.1.

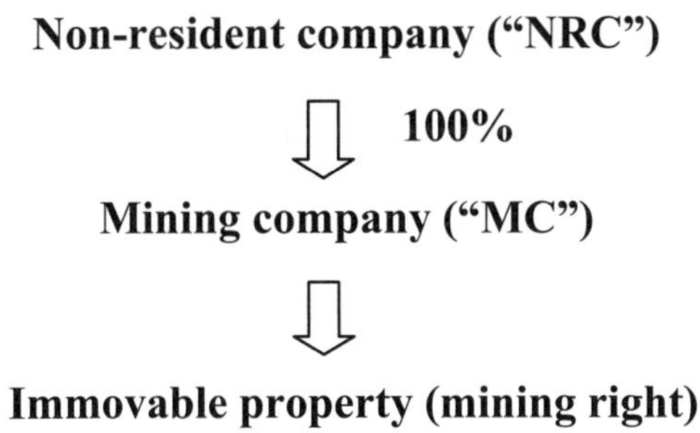

Figure 7.1 Indirect transfer of interest

In this example, there are two options for realising the mining right held by the mining company (MC). First, MC could sell the right. As explained, any gain on disposal of the right is likely to be taxable in the host country. Second, the non-resident company (NRC) could sell the shares in MC. The gain on disposal of the shares may or may not be taxable in the host country depending on the tax law in that country and the impact of any applicable tax treaty. Even if there is jurisdiction to tax, there is an issue as to how the tax is collected when the transaction takes place outside the host country between two non-residents. These issues are discussed in what follows.

4.1 Should indirect transfers be taxed?

The initial issue is whether indirect transfers should be taxed. There are two main arguments in favour of taxing indirect transfers. First, taxing indirect transfers protects the integrity of the host country's taxation of direct transfers. If there is no indirect transfer taxation rule, then it would be expected that foreign investors will use indirect transfers to avoid host country taxation of direct transfers. Second, host country taxation of indirect transfers is consistent with international norms as articulated in Article 13(4) of the OECD Model.

The main argument against taxing indirect transfers is that the taxing rule may be difficult to comply with and enforce, as the transaction is between two non-residents taking place outside the host country. The enforcement difficulties may be particularly acute for developing countries. Compliance and enforcement difficulties can be reduced through the use of thresholds that limit the scope of the taxing rule. However, in this regard, it is acknowledged that foreign investors may plan around these thresholds. Further, the taxing rule can be supported by information exchange and mechanisms to facilitate collection of the tax.

On balance, the integrity argument is a strong argument supporting the indirect transfer taxing rule.

4.2 Taxation of gains on transfer of an interest in an entity holding a mining or petroleum right

As with gains arising on direct transfers, there are several possible characterisations of the gain arising on an indirect transfer of a mining or petroleum right. The shares or other interest disposed of will be a business asset and, therefore, for those countries that do not make a distinction between revenue and capital gains in the business context, the gain will be ordinary business income. For those countries, particularly common-law countries, that do make the revenue/capital distinction, the gain may be either ordinary business income or a capital gain. It will be ordinary business income if the interest in the entity is held as trading stock or inventory or the interest was acquired with the reasonable expectation that it will be sold for a profit. The latter case is a more likely scenario, as the chain of companies may be specifically established to facilitate the making of an indirect transfer.

If the gain is ordinary business income of a non-resident, the critical issue is whether the host country has jurisdiction to tax the gain. If jurisdiction to tax is based on the gain being attributable to a permanent establishment in the host country, then it is unlikely that the gain will be taxed in the host country. For common-law countries that do not use the permanent establishment concept, the case law indicates that the source of a gain on a simple disposal of financial asset is likely to be the place of contract of sale.[45] In the example cited, the contract for the sale of the shares in MC by NRC is likely to be concluded outside the host country to ensure that the gain is foreign sourced.

For those common-law countries that treat the gain on an indirect transfer as a capital gain, taxation of the gain will depend, first, on whether the country has a CGT and, if it does, on the jurisdictional limits of the CGT in its application to non-residents. As discussed, this may be based on the source of the gain or on a specified list of taxable assets. While immovable property located in the jurisdiction will be on the list, shares in a company (particularly a non-resident company) may not be included.

In either case, taxation as ordinary business income or a capital gain will require a special rule giving the host country jurisdiction to tax. For common-law countries where the gain may be taxed either as ordinary business income or as a capital gain depending on the circumstances, the jurisdictional rule needs to be included in both the income tax source rules and CGT rules.

4.3 Designing the jurisdictional rule

Several issues must be considered in designing the jurisdictional rule. First, the jurisdictional rule is based on an interest in an entity that derives its value from immovable property in the host country. As with direct transfers of interest, the meaning of "immovable property" is critical to the operation of the rule. If the general law meaning of immovable property does not cover mining and petroleum rights, then a special tax law definition should include such rights.

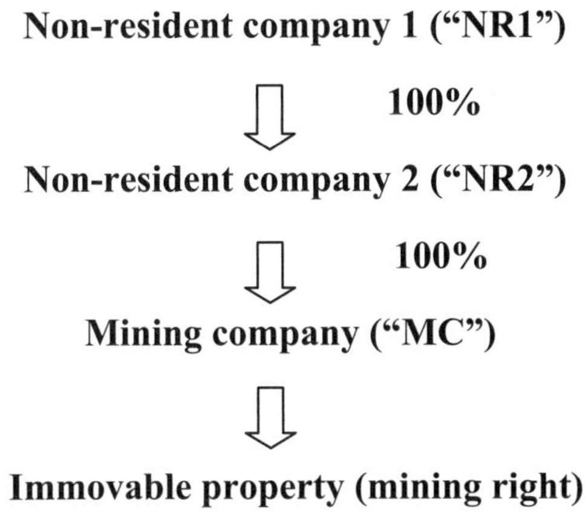

Figure 7.2 Multi-tiered indirect transfer of interest

As discussed, the definition of "immovable property" could be extended to counter-planning that allocates value to the mining or petroleum information associated with a mining or petroleum right rather than the right itself.

Second, a rule that applies up only one tier as in Figure 7.1 will be susceptible to tax planning that involves making the gain on the transfer of an interest in an entity higher up the chain of entities. This is illustrated by Figure 7.2.

The jurisdictional rule is commonly stated to apply to gains derived on the disposal of interests in entities the value of which derives, wholly or principally, *directly or indirectly*, from immovable property in the host country. The value is derived *directly* from immovable property if the interest disposed of is NR2's shares in MC. The value is derived *indirectly* from immovable property if the interest disposed of is NR1's shares in NR2. The value of the shares held by NR1 in NR2 is derived directly from the value of the shares held by NR2 in MC. As the value of the shares held by NR2 in MC is derived directly from the value of the immovable property of MC, the value of the shares held by NR1 in NR2 is derived indirectly from the immovable property of the MC. The reference to the value being derived indirectly should apply down an unlimited number of tiers of non-resident entities. This does involve the use of tracing rules, although a minimum threshold at each tier (such as 10%) may apply to limit complexity.

Third, the jurisdictional rule should not be limited to gains on the disposal of shares in a company but should extend to interests in any entity. If the rule is limited to shares in companies, then the rule may be avoided by the interposition of a non-corporate entity, such as a unit trust or limited partnership, and the gain made on disposal of the interest in the non-corporate entity. This is illustrated by Figure 7.3.

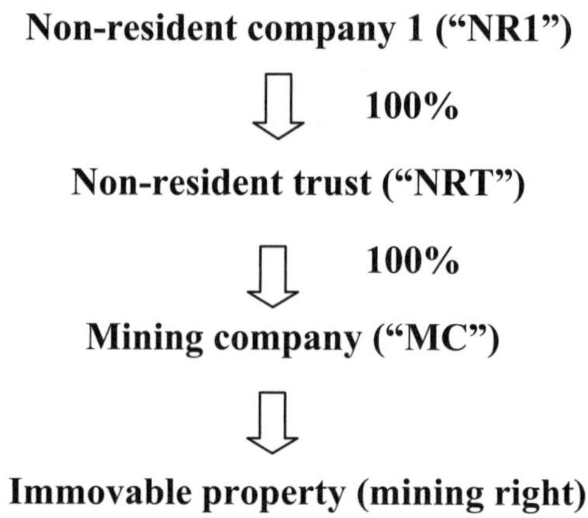

Figure 7.3 Indirect transfer of interest involving non-corporate intermediary

In this example, if the taxing rule is confined to the transfer of an interest in a company, then the rule will not apply to the gain that NR1 makes on the transfer of its interest in NRT.

Fourth, there should be a threshold-limiting taxation to cases when the non-resident has a substantial interest, directly or indirectly, in the entity holding the mining or petroleum right. In particular, it is not appropriate or feasible to apply the taxing rule to small investors in large public companies. The issue is determining the threshold for a "substantial interest". Given that 10 percent is the standard threshold for distinguishing a direct investment from a portfolio investment, a 10 percent or more interest would be an appropriate threshold for a substantial interest in an entity holding a mining or petroleum right. This could be supported by a back-up threshold based on the value of the interest in the entity holding a mining or petroleum right. Thus, the taxing rule could apply if the non-resident disposing the interest in the entity holding a mining or petroleum right has, directly or indirectly, either (i) a 10 percent or greater interest in the entity holding the right or (ii) an interest to the value of, say, $10 million or more in the entity holding the right.

Fifth, the threshold for applying the rule needs to be determined. The usual threshold is that the value of the assets of the entity comprises "principally" immovable property (including mining or petroleum rights). The threshold is based on the market value of the assets at the time of transfer and not the original cost of the assets. The "principally" threshold implies that the value of immovable property is more than 50 percent of the value of the total assets of the holder of the right. When this threshold is satisfied, the host country has jurisdiction to tax the whole of the gain even if the level of the interest is less than 100 percent. The "principally" threshold can be avoided by having an entity in the chain, directly or indirectly, holding interests in mining or petroleum companies in more than one country so that the "principally" threshold is not satisfied in relation to any country. This can be countered by lowering the threshold to, say, one third or twenty-five per cent, but this will only add complexity to the calculation, because the gain taxed in the jurisdiction would need to be prorated by reference to the value of immovable property in the jurisdiction.[46]

Finally, an issue arises as to whether the taxing rule applies whenever a person satisfying the thresholds specified (the holding and value of asset thresholds) disposes of any part of its interest (say 1 percent) or whether it is limited to the disposal of minimum level of interest (say 10 percent). In other words, is there also an alienation threshold? An alienation threshold will relieve some of the compliance burdens of the taxing rule but is subject to avoidance through staggered sell-down arrangements (i.e., selling the interest through several transactions, each of which is below the alienation threshold).

4.4 Impact of tax treaties

If a country has jurisdiction to tax under domestic law and a tax treaty applies, the treatment under the tax treaty needs to be considered. Article 13(1) will not apply in this case, as the interest in an entity (such as shares in a company) is not immovable property. Article 13(4) provides that

> Gains derived by a resident of a Contracting State from the alienation of shares deriving more than 50 per cent of their value directly or indirectly from immovable property situated in the other Contracting State may be taxed in that other State.

There are some issues with the application of Article 13(4).[47] First, unlike Article 13(1), there is no cross-reference to the definition of "immovable property" in Article 6. As the definition of immovable property in Article 6(2) is not expressly limited to the application of Article 6, there is some strength to the argument that the definition applies generally for the purposes of the treaty.[48] If this argument is not accepted, then the issue of whether immovable property in Article 13(4) includes mining or petroleum rights or mining information may depend on the application of Article 3(2) (dealing with undefined terms in the treaty). The meaning of "immovable property" in Article 13(4) can be clarified in treaty negotiations.

Second, Article 13(4) applies only to the alienation of shares in a company and not to interests in other entities, such as units in a unit trust. Consequently, if, for example, the gain is made on the disposal of units in a unit trust, Article 13(4) will not apply, and host country taxation is excluded by virtue of Article 13(5). This can be compared to Article 13(4) of the UN Model, which refers to "shares of the capital stock of a company, or of an interest in a partnership, trust or estate".

Finally, Article 13(4) is only a relatively recent addition to the OECD Model,[49] although an equivalent rule has been in the UN Model since it was first published in 1980.[50] It is possible that some of a host country's older tax treaties do not include Article 13(4) and, therefore, under these older tax treaties, there may be residence country–only taxation of a gain arising on disposal of shares deriving more than 50 percent of their value directly or indirectly from immovable property in the contracting state.

If a country has older tax treaties that do not include the equivalent of Article 13(4), this may encourage treaty-shopping practices. It may be necessary to put an anti–treaty shopping rule in domestic law to protect against such practices (see section 5.1).

4.5 Collection of tax

Even if a host country has jurisdiction to tax, as the transaction giving rise to the gain is likely to take place outside the jurisdiction between two non-residents, there is a further issue as to enforcement of the tax. This really has two aspects: (i) the tax administration discovering that the transaction has occurred and (ii) collection of the tax. It is becoming common practice for the sector legislation to require an entity holding a mining or petroleum right to notify the sector ministry and obtain prior approval for a substantial change[51] in the underlying ownership of the entity.[52] Such a provision is important, as it ensures that a country knows the beneficial owner of interests in the country's natural resources. It is necessary then to provide either in the sector legislation or income tax law that the sector ministry has an obligation to advise the revenue authority of the change so that the revenue authority can pursue any tax liability resulting from the change during the approval process. This addresses the information problem.

Once the revenue authority is aware of the transaction, there are a few ways in which the tax payable may be collected by the revenue authority.[53] First, the sector legislation could provide for withdrawal of the mining or petroleum right if tax is not paid in respect of a transfer of a substantial interest, directly or indirectly, in the company holding the right.

Second, the income tax law could provide that the holder of a mining or petroleum right is treated as agent of the non-resident person liable for the tax.[54] If the non-resident person liable for the tax does not pay the tax, the holder of the right is treated as personally liable for the tax. This would allow the revenue authority to collect any unpaid tax from the holder of the right using the normal debt-recovery rules applicable to unpaid tax.

Third, if there has been an indirect transfer of a mining or petroleum right, the income tax law could provide that the holder of the right is deemed to have made a transfer of the right on a proportionate basis by reference to the indirect transfer rule described earlier. The extent of the transfer depends on the level of change in the underlying ownership of the holder of the right. For example, if a company holding a 100 percent interest in the holder of a mining or petroleum right transfers 50 percent of that interest to another company, then the holder of the mining or petroleum right is deemed to have transferred

50 percent of its interest in the right. This goes further than simply treating the holder of the right as an agent of the non-resident taxpayer; rather, it shifts the primary liability to the holder.

As the primary liability is with the holder of the right and not the non-resident who actually derived the gain, it may be argued that this overcomes any treaty limitation on taxation of the gain if there is no equivalent of Article 13(4) in any relevant treaty. Care must be taken with this argument as, in substance, the relevant taxation in this case is source-country taxation, which is the subject matter of tax treaties. There is also the possibility of double taxation, as the home country of the person disposing of the shares or other interest is likely to tax the person on the gain, but no double tax relief may be allowed, as that person has no tax liability in the host country. This can be compared with the agency option under which the person disposing of the shares or other interest should still be entitled to double tax relief, as they have the primary liability for the tax.

4.6 Issuing of new shares[55]

As an alternative to a disposal of shares in a company holding a mining or petroleum right, the company, or another company higher up the corporate chain, could issue new shares to a third person in return for a cash contribution. This can effect a change in control of the mining or petroleum right if a sufficient number of new shares are issued.

The issuing of new shares may be done in conjunction with the passing of a resolution by the company to alter the rights attached to the existing shares so that they have little or no value in return for consideration. This will result in the value previously attached to those shares being effectively shifted to the newly issued shares.

Both the issue of new shares and the alteration of the rights attaching to the existing shares may not involve a disposal of an asset and, therefore, there may be potentially no tax consequences arising from the change in ownership. While sophisticated capital gains systems may include deemed capital gain rules in the case of value-shifting arrangements, this is unlikely to be the case in developing countries. Such arrangements may be countered through the deeming rule referred to earlier under which the holder of the right is to treated as having disposed of a proportionate interest in the licence if there is a substantial change in the underlying ownership of the holder.

It is noted that the same planning could be undertaken through the use of unit trusts.

5 Transfers of interest under an overriding royalty or farm-out agreement

The discussion in section 3 outlined the tax position in the case of a simple transfer of a mining or petroleum right. This section considers the tax position when an interest in a mining or petroleum right is transferred (i) under an overriding royalty agreement or (ii) under farm-out agreement.

5.1 Overriding royalties

The holder of a prospecting or exploration right may want to transfer the right before any commercial discovery is made. In this case, it is difficult to put a value on the right at the time of transfer. If, ultimately, no commercial discovery is made, the right has little or no value. On the other hand, if, ultimately, a commercial discovery is made, the right may be very valuable. For this reason, a person holding a prospecting or exploration right may dispose of the right for a nominal cash consideration and a periodic amount (referred to as an "overriding royalty") based on the gross revenues realised by the transferee from any commercial discovery in relation to the right. For example, a prospecting or exploration right might be transferred for $100 plus 5 percent of the gross revenue realised from any commercial discovery. Thus, the transferor retains a contingent interest, namely, a right to future income if a commercial discovery is made.

The transaction may be characterised for tax purposes as the disposal of an asset in return for an income stream (namely, the overriding royalty). Even if the prospecting or exploration right is a capital asset, the overriding royalties will be properly characterised as income. Thus, the payment of the overriding royalty will be deductible to the payer and taxable to the recipient.[56] However, in the absence of special rules, if the recipient is a non-resident, the overriding royalty may be untaxed. In this case, the payment may be deductible to the payer[57] but non-taxable to the recipient. The tax treatment to the non-resident recipient will depend on the character and source of the overriding royalty and the application of any relevant tax treaty.

The first issue is the character of an overriding royalty. While commercially the amount is usually referred to as a "royalty", it is not a royalty in a legal sense. The ordinary meaning of a royalty is:

> it is inherent in the conception expressed by the word [royalties] that the payments should be made in respect of the particular exercise of the right to take the substance and therefore should be calculated either in respect of the quantity or value taken or the occasions upon which the right is exercised.[58]

As the recipient of an overriding royalty has no right in the extracted resource, the payment does not qualify as a "royalty" within the ordinary meaning. The payment simply has its foundation in the contract providing for its payment and, therefore, in absence of a special tax rule, will be characterised as ordinary business income. There are two possible tax characterisations to avoid this outcome. First, an overriding royalty may be included in an expanded tax law definition of "royalty", in which case it will be characterised as a royalty for tax purposes. Second, the tax law may provide that an overriding royalty will be its own class of income. For example, an overriding royalty may be referred to as a "natural resource amount" and defined as

> an amount calculated in whole or part by reference to the quantity or value of minerals or a living or non-living resource taken from land or sea.[59]

The second issue is the geographic source of an overriding royalty. This will depend on how the overriding royalty is characterised for tax purposes. If an overriding royalty is simply characterised as ordinary business income, then it may not have a source in the host country. It is unlikely that the recipient of an overriding royalty will have a permanent establishment in the host country. For common-law countries that do not use the permanent establishment concept, the source of an overriding royalty will depend on all the facts and circumstances. If a court is prepared to look at the economic substance of the arrangement, the court may conclude that what gives value to the overriding royalty is the resource in the ground in the host country and, therefore, the overriding royalty is sourced in the host country. It is possible, though, that a court may conclude that, as there is no underlying property supporting the payment and the overriding royalty has its basis in a contract, the source of the overriding royalty may simply be the place of contract. The transaction can be easily structured so that the place of contract is outside the host country, particularly if the overriding royalty agreement is between two non-residents.

If an overriding royalty is characterised as a royalty or has its own characterisation, then it is more likely that it will have a source in the host country. Royalties are commonly sourced based on the residence of the payer. If the overriding royalty is its own class of income (such as a natural resource amount), the tax law may provide that it is sourced at the place where the natural resource is located.[60]

If there is jurisdiction to tax an overriding royalty, it is usual to apply the same non-resident withholding tax rule as applies to standard royalties. Consequently, it is likely that the amount will be deductible at the normal corporate tax rate but taxed at the non-resident royalty withholding tax rate (which may be lower than the corporate tax rate), thereby resulting in a reduction in the overall host country revenues when such an arrangement is adopted.

Jurisdiction to tax an overriding royalty under domestic law is likely to be excluded by a tax treaty. Article 6 will not apply, as an overriding royalty is not an amount derived by the recipient from immovable property; rather, as explained, it is simply a contractual-based amount. Article 12 will not apply, as an overriding royalty is not within the definition of "royalty" in Article 12(2). While, as explained, an overriding royalty may be ordinary business income (i.e., business profits), Article 7 will exclude host-country taxation if, as is likely to be the case, the recipient does not have a permanent establishment in the host country.

Even if there is no tax treaty between the host country and the country where the recipient of the overriding royalty is resident, the recipient may establish a conduit company in a third country that does have a tax treaty with the host country to obtain treaty protection for the payment of overriding royalties. This sort of international tax planning is referred to as "treaty shopping". Some countries have included an anti–treaty shopping rule in domestic law to protect against such practices.[61]

5.2 Farm outs

A farm-out agreement[62] may be entered into when a holder of a mining or petroleum right wants to bring in a "partner" to secure additional capital and mitigate risks of exploring or developing the project on its own. The new partner may also bring special expertise to the project. When a commercial discovery has been made, the new partner will have to pay a premium over costs already incurred. Joint ventures are common in the petroleum sector and are becoming more common in the mining sector.[63]

Under a "farm-out" agreement, the holder of a mining or petroleum right ("farmor") may transfer a percentage interest in the right to another person ("farmee") in exchange for value that may comprise a cash amount and the farmee agreeing to meet some or all of the farmor's future work commitments under the right (the "earning obligations"). The farm-out agreement may relate to specified work commitments or work commitments up to a specified amount. The transfer of the interest in the right may be immediate on signing of the agreement (an "immediate transfer farm-out agreement") or deferred to a later point in time, usually when the farmee has fulfilled its work commitments under the agreement ("deferred transfer farm-out agreement" often referred to as an "earn-in agreement"). From a tax perspective for the farmor and farmee, a farm-out agreement raises characterisation, timing, and valuation issues. Importantly, though, the tax treatment of a farm-out agreement will depend on the terms of the agreement and the tax law of the host country. For this reason, only a few generalised comments are made in what follows about the tax treatment of transfers of interest under a farm-out agreement.[64]

In broad terms, a farm-out agreement may be characterised as a transfer of interest in return for the farmee meeting the costs of the farmor's future work commitments. A farm-out agreement may also oblige the farmee to pay a cash amount, usually on signing the agreement. In this case, an important issue is the tax treatment of the cash amount. The amount may be characterised as a pro-rata reimbursement by the farmee of the past costs incurred by the farmor that relate to the interest in the mining or petroleum right transferred to the farmee. As these costs are likely to have been deducted by the farmor, the cash reimbursement may be properly characterised as reimbursed tax deductions and includible in income. In turn, the farmee should be allowed a deduction under the normal rules for deduction of mining or petroleum expenditure to the extent that the cash amount paid by the farmee is includible in the farmor's income as a reimbursement of the farmor's costs.

If the cash amount paid by the farmee exceeds that amount reasonably characterised as a reimbursement of the farmor's past costs, the excess should be included in income as a gain on the transfer of the interest in the mining or petroleum right to the farmee under the rules discussed in section 3.

While the future work commitments undertaken by the farmee that relate to the interest in the mining or petroleum right retained by the farmor may be characterised as either in-kind income of the farmor or consideration for the transfer of the interest to the farmee, some countries may, as an incentive to encourage exploration or development, expressly exclude the value of work commitments from being included in income or treated as consideration for the transfer of the interest in a mining or petroleum right.[65] This means that only the cash amount is taxed under the principles outlined earlier.

The deduction for costs of the farmor carried by the farmee under a farm-out agreement should be deductible only to the farmee.

6 Treatment of transfer of interest under APT and PSC arrangements

The previous sections of the chapter essentially deal with the taxation of gains arising from direct or indirect transfers of mining or petroleum rights under the normal operation of the income tax or CGT. There are, however, other fiscal issues to be addressed regarding the treatment of transfer of interest transactions and resulting gains when the holder of the right is liable to APT or has obtained the right under a PSC or a risk service contract. In particular, does a transfer of a mining or petroleum right have an impact on the APT liability or on production sharing? Is the related gain of the transferor also liable to APT? How does the gain impact cost recovery and profit petroleum sharing between the parties to a PSC?

Globally, the most frequent structure used for exploration and exploitation ventures, especially regarding the holding of petroleum rights, is that the holder of a licence or an interest in a PSC is an unincorporated consortium constituted by more than one legal entity (often a company), with each entity being jointly and severally liable to the state under that licence or PSC, except for income tax purposes under which their liability is individual. Therefore, in reality, a transfer of interest should only concern the transferor and transferee involved in the transaction and not the licensee or the holder of the PSC in its entirety.[66] APT tax laws and petroleum contracts are still often silent on this basic reality in the industry considering the licensee or holder as a person, not referring explicitly to the frequent situation of a consortium formed by several persons.

6.1 Application of APT to transfers of interest

There are two main design options for the application of the APT to transfers of interest. Which option applies depends on who is the taxpayer under the APT.

Under the first option, the APT is a *separate* tax liability of each entity constituting the licensee and not a joint liability of the licensee. This is the simplest case and applies, for example, in the UK (to the 10 percent supplementary charge payable in addition to the corporate tax) or in Australia (to the 40 percent petroleum resource rent tax or PRRT levied on an individual petroleum project in addition to the corporate tax). However, the fiscal treatment of gains arising from a transfer of interest differs between these two countries. In the

UK, since December 2011, chargeable gains have been included in the profits subject to the supplementary charge, except when the transfer is a swap of licenses or is reinvested in the sector. Having chargeable gains liable to both corporate tax and APT is relatively rare. On the contrary, in Australia, the transfer of an interest does not trigger PRRT consequences. Since the enactment of the PRRT in 1987 several amendments to the law and rulings were necessary to progressively clarify the PRRT treatment of a transfer for the transferor and the transferee with the objective of being neutral in terms of PRRT liability. Thus, the consideration received by the transferor is not subject to PRRT and is not deductible by the transferee for PRRT purposes. However, the transferee is entitled to make deductions for the cost transferred from the transferor in proportion to its acquired entitlement for corporate tax.

Under the second option, the APT is a *joint* tax liability of the licensee and not an individual liability of each entity constituting the licensee. This is the case under most resource rent tax schemes based on the effective profitability achieved by a petroleum project. Only some of those schemes today clarify in detail the treatment of transfer of interest for APT purposes either in the law enacting the APT or in the petroleum agreement. Generally, the principle developed by Australia for the PRRT liability of a company, intended to remain neutral regarding the APT consequence of a transfer of interest, is followed but at the difference of Australia applied jointly to all the entities constituting the licensee, not individually.

With the increased prevalence of transfers of interest, it is important that APT regimes clearly set out the treatment of transfers of interest.

6.2 PSCs and transfers of interest

PSCs were introduced more than 40 years ago and are now widely used globally. While PSCs generally provide for the approval of a transfer of interest, the accounting consequences on cost recovery and the tax obligations arising from such a transfer have been only recently clarified in more and more PSCs. The following rules are becoming commonly applied when the legislation or the PSC deals with transfer of interest issues.

(1) A transfer of interest is generally not considered as part of the petroleum operations jointly performed under the PSC but is an activity incidental to petroleum operations because the decision to enter into a transfer of interest agreement is made by only one entity constituting the contractor and not all of them collectively. The immediate consequence under this approach is that the transaction has no impact on cost recovery and profit petroleum sharing in order to maintain neutrality among the various PSC holders. Therefore, the consideration paid by the transferee is not considered as a recoverable cost under the PSC, and the consideration received by the transferor is not assimilated to revenue, reducing its balance

of unrecovered costs. The transferee inherits the unrecovered cost incurred by the transferor in proportion to the acquired interest in the PSC. However, any gain derived by the transferor is subject to tax under the income tax or CGT as explained previously.[67]

The stated rules apply, for example, in Angola, where the Law N°10/04 of November 12, 2004, provides that capital gains arising from transfer under PSCs are profits subject to the 50 percent petroleum income tax. A new law in Mozambique[68] provides for the taxation of gains related to direct and indirect transfers under PSCs at the corporate tax rate of 32 percent. Transactions prior to this law have been liable to tax under specific negotiated deals using as a basis the general law (see detailed examples in Box 7.1). In Indonesia, government regulation N° GR97 of 2010 clarified that the transferor income arising from a transfer of interest is immediately liable to a final income tax equal either to 5 percent (during the exploration period) or 7 percent (during the exploitation period) of the consideration gross amount.[69]

(2) A few countries using PSCs have developed a transfer clause providing that a transfer of interest has an impact on cost recovery. Thus, in Gabon, the consideration received by the transferor is considered revenue reducing the balance of its recoverable costs, while gains are liable to the corporate income tax. This approach is relatively exceptional.

It is recommended that any tax law and PSC should address in detail such provisions to prevent difficulties in case of transfers.

7 Conclusion

It is important that host countries have adequate rules to ensure effective income taxation of direct and indirect transfers of an interest in a mining or petroleum right. Developing these rules requires consideration of the fundamental features of the income tax, namely (i) characterisation (revenue or capital); (ii) timing of the taxable event; (iii) valuation of the consideration received; and (iv) the source of income (domestic or foreign). Explicit rules may need to be included to ensure effective taxation of overriding royalties, farm outs, or indirect transfers through the disposal of an interest in an upper-tier entity. Further, the application of the domestic law rules needs to take account of the application of any applicable tax treaty. Importantly, host countries need to ensure that the negotiation of any future tax treaties preserve the country's right to tax gains on the transfer of interest no matter what form the gain takes. Moreover, the consequences of a transfer in case of payment of an additional profits tax or of a PSC have also to be explicitly addressed in the law or the agreement, in coordination with the income tax or CGT treatment of the gains.

Notes

1 Research assistance was provided by Ms Nikki Teo, PhD student, University of Sydney. The authors wish to thank Richard Krever, Joseph Guttentag, Stephen Shay, Philip Daniel, Artur Świstak, Michael Keen, and Victor Thuronyi for their comments on the chapter. However, all errors and omissions are the sole responsibility of the authors.
2 The reference to "transfer" in this chapter is a reference to any form of transfer or alienation of ownership of a mining or petroleum right or an interest in an entity, directly or indirectly, holding such a right, including a sale or assignment.
3 A reference in this chapter to a "mining or petroleum right" includes an exploration or prospecting licence or permit, a mining lease, development licence, or an interest in a petroleum agreement (which may be a production-sharing agreement or a risk service contract).
4 While the transfer of an interest in a mining or petroleum right may involve value-added tax (VAT) or goods and services tax (GST) issues, this chapter focuses on the income tax treatment of gains arising on such transfers.
5 See, generally, IMF (2012) at paragraph 74 and Appendix III.
6 A reference in this chapter to the holder of a mining or petroleum right is a reference to the holder of an exploration or prospecting licence or permit, a mining lease or development licence, or a party to a petroleum agreement (contractor).
7 See Vann (2000) at p. 743.
8 A tax treaty is an international agreement between two or more countries (referred to as "Contracting States") providing for the avoidance of double taxation and the prevention of fiscal evasion. Tax treaties are usually bilateral. In broad terms, a tax treaty allocates taxing rights between the Contracting States in relation to income or gains arising from economic activity between the States. The general pattern of a tax treaty is to limit or exclude the taxing rights of a Contracting State as host country. Generally, a Contracting State as residence country (referred to as the "home country") has full taxing rights but with an obligation to provide double tax relief in relation to host country taxation. Tax treaties generally follow the OECD Model Double Tax Convention on Income and Capital (referred to as the "OECD Model"). The United Nations has also prepared a model tax treaty entitled Model Taxation Convention Between Developing and Developed Countries (referred to as the "UN Model"). The UN Model is largely based on the OECD Model but includes broader source-country taxing rights in relation to some classes of income. Unless indicated otherwise, the article references in this chapter are to those in the most recent version of the OECD Model (released in August 2014).
9 This assumes that the joint venture is not a partnership. Classification of a joint venture as a partnership is usually avoided by the joint venturers sharing output rather than profits.
10 In broad terms, a "spin-off" is a form of corporate reorganisation under which a division or part of a company ("parent company") is separated (or "spun off") into a new company, with the parent company distributing the shares in the new company to its shareholders on a *pro rata* basis. The outcome is that the parent company has divested itself of ownership of the division or part that has been spun off into the new company but in a way that its shareholders retain their interest in that division or part through their shareholding in the new company. One reason for a mining or petroleum company to enter into a spin off arrangement is to separate assets having different risk profiles.
11 The income tax could provide for tax-free transfers, with the transferee taking over the transferor's cost of the mining or petroleum right (including a nil cost). This may apply generally or only when the transfer is made under a farm-out agreement when the only consideration is work commitments (see sections 3.3 and 5.2).
12 A change in control is usually designated as a change, directly or indirectly, of *more than 50 percent* of the membership interests in the entity holding the right. The threshold for a "substantial change" may be as low as 10 percent.

13 The written-down value of a mining or petroleum right is the cost of the right reduced by any depreciation or other deductions allowed in respect of the cost of the right.

14 If the cost of acquiring a mining or petroleum right is depreciated for tax purposes, then taxation of the transfer of the right may be, wholly or partly, under the depreciation rules (see sections 3.1 and 3.2.1).

15 This is discussed further in section 4.5.

16 Under a PSC, the contractor bears all costs of exploration and development in return for a share of any resulting production. The PSC will usually specify a portion of total production that can be retained by the contractor to recover costs ("cost oil"). The remaining production (including any surplus of cost production over the amount needed for cost recovery) is termed "profit oil" and is divided between the government and contractor based on a formula set out in the PSC. "Cost oil" and "profit oil" may be termed "cost gas" and "profit gas" or "cost petroleum" and "profit petroleum" – depending on the circumstances.

17 Under a services contract, the contractor is paid a fee for services performed (such as drilling services). The fee may depend on the success of the project.

18 It is possible that the tax provisions will be in a PSC. While it is considered best practice for tax provisions to be provided for in legislation, if they are in the PSC, the PSC must provide for direct and indirect transfers of interest.

19 The reference to "depreciation" in this chapter is a reference to any form of capital allowance in relation to capital expenditure, including amortisation (a term commonly used in relation to intangible assets and expenditure).

20 In civil-law countries, the close alignment of tax accounting with financial accounting means that the financial accounting depreciation rules applicable to the cost of a mining or petroleum right apply also for tax purposes subject to any acceleration in the rate of depreciation for tax purposes. There is usually greater separation of tax accounting from financial accounting in common-law countries. One reflection of this is that the income tax law in common law countries usually includes a comprehensive depreciation regime. Traditionally, the depreciation regime in common-law countries was confined to tangible assets (such as plant and equipment), leaving the deduction of the cost of acquiring intangible assets to general principles. Even if that is still the case in some common-law countries, it is common for a special deduction rule to apply to mining or petroleum expenditure. For a general discussion on the relationship between financial and tax accounting, see see Burns and Krever (2000) at pp. 599–602 and 673–678.

21 In this case, it is possible that no deduction may have been allowed for the cost of the right at the time of the transfer.

22 This is relevant when capital gains are either untaxed or taxed at a different (usually lower) rate to that applicable under the normal corporate income tax.

23 See Lee Burns & Richard Krever, *supra* note 20.

24 Examples of concessional treatment of capital gains include: (i) indexation of the cost of the asset for inflation; (ii) partial inclusion of the gain; or (iii) application of a lower tax rate than under the normal income tax.

25 See, for example, section 2(3)(c) and the definition of "taxable Canadian property" in section 248(1) of the Income Tax Act 1985 (Canada) and sections 855–10 and 855–15 of the Income Tax Assessment Act 1997 (Australia).

26 *Nathan v FC of T* (1918) CLR 183, at pp. 189–190.

27 *Liquidator, Rhodesia Metals Ltd (in liquidation) v Commissioner of Taxes* [1940] AC 774.

28 *Australian Machinery & Investment Co Limited v DCT* (1946) 180 CLR 9.

29 It is important to emphasise that each tax treaty is the result of a negotiation between the Contracting States and will not necessarily exactly replicate the OECD Model (or UN Model), so regard must be had to the terms of the particular treaty in question. Further, many countries do not exactly follow the OECD's interpretation of the articles of the OECD Model as set out in the Commentary to the OECD Model. Interpretational differences are set out in the reservations or observations in the Commentary to

the OECD Model. Also, the OECD Model has been amended over time, and older tax treaties will be based on earlier iterations of the Model.

30 Often the contractor under a petroleum agreement is incorporated outside the host country and only registered as a branch in the host country.

31 Article 6(4) (Article 6 priority) and Article 7(4) (Article 13 priority).

32 Paragraph 1 of the Commentary to Article 6 of the OECD Model.

33 The residence country is obliged to give relief from double taxation under Article 23.

34 Paragraph 3 of the Commentary to Article 6 of the OECD Model.

35 Paragraph 8 of the Commentary to Article 6 of the OECD Model.

36 See paragraph 85 of the Technical Explanation to the United States Model Income Tax Convention of November 15, 2006. Generally, Article 13 of Australia's tax treaties is headed "Alienation of Property" and refers to "gains" rather than capital gains.

37 Klaus Vogel et al., Klaus Vogel on Double Taxation Conventions: A commentary to the OECD, UN and US Model Conventions for the avoidance of double taxation on income and capital with particular reference to German treaty practice, London/Boston, Kluwer Law International, third edition, at p. 376.

38 Ibidem.

39 *Government of the Republic of South Africa v Oceana Development Investment Trust Plc* [1989] 3 All SA 661.

40 See, for example, section 855–20 of the *Income Tax Assessment Act* 1997 (Australia).

41 See, for example, *Resources Capital Fund LP v Commissioner of Taxation* [2014] FCAFC 37.

42 For example, the gain on disposal of immovable property is ordinary business income and, under a particular tax treaty, Article 6 does not apply to the alienation of immovable property, and Article 13 applies only to capital gains, or a mining or petroleum right is not immovable property, or the value is allocated to associated information rather than the right transferred.

43 Some countries may expressly include "exploration" in their tax treaty equivalent of Article 5(2)(f). See, for example, Article 5(2)(f) of the Australia–United Kingdom tax treaty (2003).

44 If the gain made by the transferor is not taxed, the transferor's effective tax rate on its overall profits derived from the venture will become considerably lower than anticipated.

45 *Australian Machinery & Investment Co. Ltd v DCT* (1946) 180 CLR 9.

46 See, for example, section 83(1)(lc)(ii) and 143H of the *Income Tax Act* 1997 (Cook Islands).

47 See generally, Stefano Simontacchi, "Immovable Property Companies as Defined in Article 13(4) of the OECD Model", (2006) *Bulletin for International Taxation* 29.

48 *Id.* at pp. 30–31. It is noted that the U.S. Model Tax Treaty deems an interest in a land-rich entity to be immovable property for the purposes of Article 13. See United States Model Tax Convention, November 15, 2006, Article 13(2)(b) reference to "United States real property interest". The Technical Explanation to the US Model explains the term as defined in section 897(c) of the Internal Revenue Code to include "shares in a US corporation that owns sufficient US real property to satisfy an asset ratio test on certain testing dates": Technical Explanation of the 2006 US Model Income Tax Convention, paragraph 216.

49 Article 13(4) was included in the OECD Model in 2003.

50 Article 13(4)(a) of the UN Model effectively limits the scope of Article 13(4) to property management companies. Consequently, the source country taxing rights are broader under the OECD Model. If two Contracting States are proposing negotiating a tax treaty based on the UN Model, it is important that paragraph (a) of Article 13(4) is deleted so that the taxing rights under the indirect transfer rule are broadly stated.

51 The definition of substantial change can vary between 10 percent and 25 percent.

52 In old mining and petroleum laws, the obligation to notify a transfer or assignment and obtain approval from the minister did not explicitly mention "indirect" transfers. Many such laws were amended to deal with the approval of direct and indirect transfers.

53 These suggestions are based on proposals currently under consideration in several countries.

54 See, for example, section 143H(4) of the *Income Tax Act* 1997 (Cook Islands).
55 An example is included in Box 7.1.
56 The recipient may have incurred prospecting or exploration expenditure that can be offset against the income received.
57 The host country may characterise the payments as recurrent outgoings of the transferee and, therefore, revenue in nature.
58 *Stanton v Federal Commissioner of Taxation* [1955] HCA 56; (1955) 92 CLR 630, at p. 642.
59 See, for example, section 2(tt)(ii) of the Income Tax Act (Cap. 340) (Uganda).
60 See, for example, section 79(n) of the Income Tax Act (Cap. 340) (Uganda).
61 See, for, example, section 88(5) of the Income Tax Act (Cap. 340) (Uganda).
62 See, generally, Charles Birch. (2002), "Choosing the Right Joint Venture Structure for a Farmin or Farmout," *Journal of Australian Taxation*, 5(1), 60.
63 For example, the Morobe mining joint ventures in Papua New Guinea, which are 50–50 joint ventures between Harmony Gold Mining of South Africa and Newcrest Mining of Australia.
64 The potential complexity of the tax treatment of a transfer of interest under a farm-out agreement is highlighted by the approach taken by the Australian Taxation Office to such transfers in two taxation rulings: Australian Taxation Office, Miscellaneous Taxation Ruling MT 2012/1 *Application of Income Tax and GST Laws to Immediate Transfer Farm-out Arrangements* ("MT 2012/1") and Australian Taxation Office, Miscellaneous Taxation Ruling MT 2012/2, *Application of Income Tax and GST Laws to Deferred Transfer Farm-out Arrangements* ("MT 2012/2"); see Ian Murray. (2013), "The Tax Treatment of Farmouts: Do Rulings MT 2012/1 and MT 2012/2 Chart a Path to Revenue Nirvana or Hades?," *Australian Tax Review*, 42, 5.
65 See, for example, section 143G of the *Income Tax Act*, 1997 (Cook Islands).
66 The only exception deals with the preemptive rights that may be exercised by the other entities.
67 When the PSC arrangement provides for an "after-tax profit petroleum sharing" as in a number of countries, the PSC should explicitly provide that the transferor is individually liable for taxation on gains, because the after-tax sharing only deals with taxation of joint petroleum operations, excluding individual tax liabilities derived from a transfer. Many PSCs are silent on this issue.
68 Law No. 27/2014 of September 23, 2014. See, in particular, Articles 18(d), 25 and 29.
69 This mechanism of taxation on the gross amount was decided to minimize the possible impact of double tax treaties on the taxation of transfers.

References

Birch, C. (2002), "Choosing the Right Joint Venture Structure for a Farmin or Farmout," *Journal of Australian Taxation*, 5(1), 60–113.

Burns, L. and R. Krever. (2000), "Taxation of Income from Business and Investment," in V. Thuronyi (ed.), *Tax Law Design and Drafting* (The Hague: Kluwer law International), pp. 597–681.

International Monetary Fund. (2012), *Fiscal Regimes for Extractive Industries: Design and Implementation*, August 15, 2012, Available at http:// www.imf.org [Accessed August 15, 2015].

Murray, I. (2013), "The Tax Treatment of Farmouts: Do Rulings MT 2012/1 and MT 2012/2 Chart a Path to Revenue Nirvana or Hades?," *Australian Tax Review*, 42(1), 5–32.

Vann, R. (2000), "International Aspects of Income Tax," in V. Thuronyi (ed.), *Tax Law Design and Drafting* (The Hague: Kluwer law International), pp. 718–810.

Vogel, K. M. Engelschalk, M. Görl, A. Hemmelrath, M. Lehner, R. Pöllath, R. Prokisch, M. Rodi, F. Stockmann, and W. Tischbirek. (2005), *Klaus Vogel on Double Taxation Conventions: A Commentary to the OECD, UN and US Model Conventions for the Avoidance of Double Taxation on Income and Capital with Particular Reference to German Treaty Practice*, 3rd edition (London and Boston: Kluwer Law International).

8 Fiscal issues for cross-border natural resource projects

Joseph C. Bell and Jasmina B. Chauvin

1 Introduction

Natural resource projects located in one state requiring transport across another to access world markets present special challenges for effective fiscal regimes, particularly for low-income countries. For example in the case of large mining projects, typically the investor will have responsibility for the development of the required rail and port infrastructure as part of the project. This in turn requires the governments in the transit and mine jurisdictions to develop models for the determination of taxes, royalties, and other government charges in their respective jurisdictions.

Although the project's total expected return can be calculated, there are no economic principles commanding a particular allocation of revenues and profits between the parts of the project – the mine and the transportation infrastructure – and hence the two governing jurisdictions. There would be no investment in the rail and port absent the mine; similarly without the rail and port, the mine would not be developed. In the case of one integrated project with the same owner, there is only a single rent or return to be taxed by the two sovereigns. This issue is, of course, not specific to mining. It is also applicable to oil or gas produced in one country and piped through another or for that matter to any integrated project straddling national borders.

Compared to traditional single-country projects, cross-border natural resource projects impose additional burdens on both governments and investors, making already complex transactions even harder to bring to fruition. For investors there are the added costs of negotiating and coordinating with multiple governments and additional political risk. For governments there is the need to coordinate infrastructure and operations as well as to manage differing development interests, which may affect project costs and benefits. Finally, there is the need to agree explicitly or implicitly on a division of project returns and associated tax revenues between the two countries.

Figure 8.1 provides a simple illustration of the revenue flows from an integrated project including a mine and rail and port facilities. In one case, all are located in a single country. In the other case the mine and part of the rail are located in Country A (the "mine jurisdiction") and the port and other part of the rail are located in Country B (the "transit jurisdiction").[1] The real economics of the

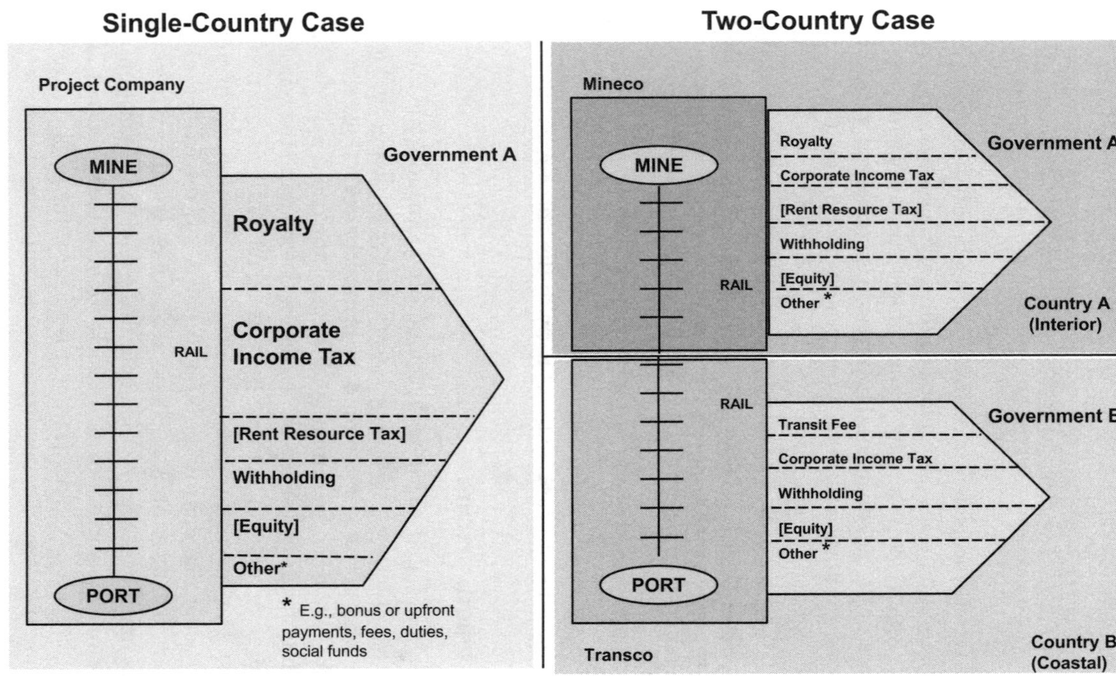

Figure 8.1 Illustration of a single-country versus cross-border resource project

project absent the border in the two cases are the same, but the existence of the border and two sovereigns adds considerable complexity and may add real costs.

In this analysis, we examine a number of approaches to allocating taxable income or tax revenues between the two countries including the arm's length principle endorsed by the OECD as well as other alternatives such as the use of a formulary basis or a special fiscal regime with the states "bargaining" over their respective shares. In some cases the tax issues may be resolved through structuring solutions in which transportation is provided by a separate operating entity with a different ownership structure. Each presents its own set of problems, and in all cases care must be taken to preserve for the mine jurisdiction a real return for its depletable resource while also fairly compensating the transit jurisdiction for its value added to the project economics.

It is also important to recognize the complexities associated with the three-party nature of the negotiations. The investor is concerned with the total burden of taxes, royalties, and other government charges on the project. In the process of negotiations the investor will also be sensitive to tax concessions in one jurisdiction that can be picked up and mirrored in the second (or elsewhere). In turn each of the governments is concerned with getting a "fair" share of the revenues consistent with its own tax and social and economic policies. Depending on the degree of coordination of the two tax regimes, the gain of one may come at the cost of the other. In some cases, a coordinated strategy may increase the total gain for both. Our hope is that making the complexities more transparent will lead to better-structured agreements that maximize economic benefits and allocate them fairly to the relevant parties.

2 Arm's length pricing

The situation in Figure 8.1 is hardly a unique tax situation. It is inherent in any multinational enterprise operating across taxing jurisdictions or more locally for enterprises operating in multiple sub-national jurisdictions as in the United States. In theory, the government and the investor could negotiate and determine the transfer price (or the principles for determining the transfer price) in the course of an audit or advance pricing agreement *after* the investment has been made. But given the investor's interest in determining its potential tax exposures when making the decision to invest and the existence of multiple jurisdictions, the investor is likely to seek some assurances from the taxing authorities up front regarding the applicable principles of taxation and for the determination of taxable income in each country. This need not be an agreement regarding actual charges; rather it is an agreement of how they would be calculated on the basis of expenditures actually incurred.[2]

The classic OECD approach for income tax purposes (and note that income tax is only one element) is to act as if the two national operations are separate entities and then to determine taxable income for each based on assumed transfer prices determined according to the arm's length principle. In this context that means determining the charges that an independent transportation company ("Transco") would impose on the mining company ("Mineco") for the rail and port services provided in the transit jurisdiction.

This starting point is in fact an artificial division of the project. In a large mining development the mine and the infrastructure that transport the resource form an integrated whole. Typically management and operation of the transportation network and its careful integration with the mining operation are critical to the success of the investment and are one of the reasons separation of the logistical network from the mine is rare in large-scale investments. In fact, while the main driver of the investment is the presence of the natural resource, frequently the rail and port facilities constitute the larger part of the capital investment and an even larger part of operating costs than the mine. The division of the project among political jurisdictions is even more artificial since only a part of the delivery infrastructure is located in the transit jurisdiction, the other part being in the mine jurisdiction.

Once a project is thus apportioned among political jurisdictions, the OECD guidelines for determining arm's length prices use a hierarchy of methods beginning with the comparable uncontrolled price (CUP). Applying the CUP requires identification of what independent companies would charge for the services in comparable circumstances, that is, what an independent rail and port operation would charge for the services being provided in the transit jurisdiction. For the reasons set out, however, most projects are developed on an integrated basis. In fact there are no comparable fully independent rail and port operations serving mining operations, especially within Africa, to provide comparable prices.[3]

The lack of comparable transactions leads one to the second traditional OECD method, the cost-plus method. The OECD guidelines (2010) for the cost-plus approach read:

> [The cost-plus method is] a transfer pricing method using the costs incurred by the supplier of property (or services) in a controlled transaction. An appropriate cost plus mark up is added to this cost, to make an appropriate profit in light of the functions performed (taking into account assets used and risks assumed) and the market conditions. What is arrived at after adding the cost plus mark up to the above costs may be regarded as an arm's length price of the original controlled transaction.[4]

While the formula may appear straightforward, determining the costs incurred and, more importantly, correctly accounting for the "risks assumed" and the local "market conditions" requires judgment calls in practice. Even minor differences in the assumptions that are made can significantly affect the pro forma financial results of the project and, consequently, the estimates of the corporate income taxes due to different fiscal authorities. The OECD acknowledges that

"because transfer pricing is not an exact science, there will also be many occasions when the application of the most appropriate method or methods produces a range of figures all of which are relatively equally reliable."[5]

Unfortunately, as our analysis will show, the range of figures that the method can produce is so wide as to undermine the credibility of the method itself for these purposes.

2.1 Cost-plus method overview

To model the cost-plus approach one can think about the charges an independent transportation company ("Transco") would charge an independent mining company ("Mineco"). In various regulated industries and project finance structures these are usually rendered as two-part charges: one part to recover the cost of capital with appropriate return on the investment and one part to recover the operating expenses. The first charge is frequently referred to as an "access fee" – a fixed annual charge that reimburses Transco for its capital investment. If the parties were unrelated this access fee almost certainly would be accompanied by some form of a take-or-pay provision under which Mineco would be required to pay the access fee whether or not it shipped the product.[6] The effect of this is to transfer to Mineco the project risks of Transco.

The second charge, a "variable fee," is a volume-based charge based on the operating costs incurred in providing the shipping services elevated by a markup that provides some return to the operating activities. The analogy to rate setting in the context of regulated industries is obvious, but there are also some differences. Regulatory rate setting is usually conducted in the context of historical data, often for a group of highly comparable entities, and importantly is usually accompanied by a highly developed set of regulatory institutions to make the necessary determinations.[7] More fundamentally there is usually no identity of carrier and shipper.

While the overarching principle of the two-part fee appears to be a reasonable way to generate a transfer price between the related entities, each of these fees is composed of a number of elements for which various choices are plausible and which can significantly affect the estimate of taxable income.

2.2 Elements of the access fee

Broadly stated, determining the access fee requires the parties to make an estimate of all capital expenditures (capex) that will be incurred in the construction and ongoing maintenance of the rail, port, and rolling stock to calculate the net present value (NPV) of the capital expenditures and then to allocate the recovery of those costs over the project's lifetime to arrive at the annual charge that would allow the investor to recover the cost of the investment (including the assumed required return on capital).[8] Formally, the NPV of the capital expenditures would be calculated as:

$$NPV_{Capex} = \sum_{t=0}^{N} \frac{Capex_t}{(1+r)^t}$$

where t is the time period in which a capital expenditure is incurred, N is the total number of periods (usually years) in the project's lifetime, $Capex_t$ is the capital expenditure incurred at time t, and r is a discount rate (which is discussed at significant length in what follows).[9] Next one must calculate the required annual access fee that would ensure that all capital expenditures are recovered, including a minimum return on capital. The access fee must satisfy the following equation:

$$NPV_{Access\ fee} = \sum_{t=0}^{N} \frac{Access\ Fee_t}{(1+r)^t} = NPV_{Capex}$$

where the $Access\ Fee_t$ is the pre-tax annual access fee. The formula makes it clear that the access fee is set so as to recover the present value of capital expenditures for a given discount rate and that the only difference between the two is in the timing of the inflows and outflows. While the capex tends to be lumpy and front-loaded, the annual access fee is a fixed per period charge.

The challenge of the exercise is that all of these variables have to be estimated by the parties up front, while each element of the calculation is highly uncertain. For example, the numerator in the NPV_{Capex} formula, $Capex_t$, will depend on the unique environmental, geological, and engineering features of the project. While companies with significant expertise in construction and operation of large-scale infrastructure projects use their best judgment to assess the likely costs, each environment carries unique risks that may lead to cost overruns, delays, and other unexpected expenses. In the world of project finance, a 10 to 15 percent cost-overrun "cushion" would typically be added to the numerator to account for this likely volatility in actual project costs.

To counter this uncertainty, the tax authorities could agree on a methodology for determining the access fee and ultimately calculate the access fee according to actual capital costs incurred prior to operation.[10] However, even then the formula would need to take into account the subsequent capital expenditures that will be incurred during the lifetime of the project. Alternatively and preferably, the access fee will have to be adjusted periodically to account for the additional capital expenditures.

An even more important source of variation in estimates of the access fee will come from the choice of the discount rate r that appears in the denominator of both of the formulas shown. The higher this discount rate, the higher will need to be the dollar amount of the access fee. The rate most commonly used to discount expected cash flows in project NPV calculations is the weighted average cost of capital (WACC). The WACC is the estimate of the return that debt and equity investors would require to invest in a given project, taking into account the specific risks and market conditions of the country, the project, the industry, and so on. In the case in which a company is financed by debt and equity, the WACC or r is calculated as:

$$WACC = \frac{E}{V}K_e + \frac{D}{V}K_d(1 - T_{mc})$$

where E denotes the value of equity, D the value of debt, $V = D + E$ is the total value of the firm, K_e is the cost of equity, K_d the cost of debt, and T_{mc} is the marginal corporate tax rate.

Like the access fee itself, the computation of WACC requires estimating a number of ambiguous parameters: E, D, K_e, K_d, and T_{mc}. For each of these parameters a range of seemingly plausible proxies are available. Indeed, according to the Association for Financial Professionals "providing the 'right' answer about how to estimate each of these variables is a difficult, if not impossible, task."[11] In practice, for most financial transactions that firms undertake, they consider outcomes under various plausible WACC values that often include a range of about 10 percentage points. Such a range of WACC values would result in considerable variation in the computed access fee, which in turn leads to a highly magnified variation in taxable income.

We now consider each assumption that is used in calculating the access fee.

2.2.1 Capital structure

The WACC will be sensitive to the assumed ratio of debt and equity that is funding the project. Since debt is typically less costly than equity and because of the beneficial tax effects of using debt (deductibility of interest payments), a higher debt/equity ratio will ordinarily lower the WACC and hence the computed access fee. For the purpose of considering an "arm's length" price that would be charged between unrelated parties, one would want to consider what the typical capital structure would be for an independent company providing transport services without the benefit of a throughput contract or other third-party credit support.

To do so, we can look for data on the capital structure of other local transportation companies; however, in many settings few or no comparable companies will exist. Moreover, in such environments, debt markets will likely be relatively underdeveloped, and a typical company will largely be funded by equity, resulting in low debt/equity ratios. For example, according to a widely used data source the average debt-to-capital ratio for railroad companies in emerging markets is 19.8 percent.[12] In reality Transco may be largely funded through an intercompany loan from the parent or a third-party loan guaranteed by the parent. This would permit a higher debt/equity ratio (but should also result in the use of a lower interest rate).[13] Thus, the range of justifiable value for the debt/equity ratio could be as low as 20/80 when relying on comparables for truly independent projects or as high as 60/40 (when relying on a guarantee from a credit-worthy parent).

2.2.1.1 COST OF EQUITY

The cost of equity is arguably the parameter with the widest range of plausible estimates because of the number of parameters that go into calculating it. While several alternative methods for calculating K_e exist, the most common is the Capital Asset Pricing Model (CAPM).[14] It calculates the cost of equity as:

$$K_e = \left(R_f + CRP\right) + \beta\left(R_m - R_f\right)$$

where R_f is the return on a risk-free security, CRP is a country risk premium, R_m is the return on the market portfolio (the difference, $R_m - R_f$, is known as the equity market risk premium) and beta measures the volatility of the particular issuer relative to the market.

Risk-free rate: While a number of choices are possible, the most commonly used estimate of R_f is the rate of return on a U.S. Treasury bond. However, there are differences in views as to what the correct underlying Treasury security should be (e.g., a short-term bill, a 5- or 10-year note, or a 30-year bond). Given that the historically the difference in returns between 90-day Treasury bills and 30-year Treasury bonds is approximately 3 percentage points, the choice for the risk-free rate will have real effects on WACC. Moreover, once the reference security is agreed, it is far from clear what the time period is from which the rate should be quoted. On the one hand, one can argue that the rate should be the one quoted on the date that the decision to invest in the project is made. However, given that the project would unlikely borrow at a 20- or 30-year horizon and would face refinancing risk, another reasonable argument is to use a smoothed rate, such as a 5- or 10-year average. These estimation differences can impact the bottom line, especially if the spot rate differs significantly from the long-run average.

Country risk premium: If the U.S. Treasury is used as reference for R_f, then a CRP should be added to it in order to compensate investors for the risk associated with operating in countries with less developed markets and more volatile conditions than those prevailing in the U.S. The CRP can usually be gauged from sovereign credit ratings published by ratings agencies or from actual spreads on sovereign bonds. However, many emerging-market countries (including the majority of Sub-Saharan African countries) are not yet included in such standardized ratings and may not have rated sovereign debt outstanding. For such countries, estimates of the appropriate CRP could vary widely, from a range of 8 percent (based on credit ratings of low-grade but rated countries) to upward of 14 percent (based on actual sovereign spreads of certain high-risk countries).

Equity market risk premium (EMRP): The EMRP is the additional return that investors require in order to invest in equity as opposed to a risk-free security. The EMRP is usually calculated by averaging the historical differences in the returns on equity investments and risk-free investment across global markets. But the historical premia that are calculated by academics and practitioners around the world are acknowledged to be extremely imprecise with large standard errors.[15] Moreover, these premia may be time varying, and there is no consensus on what the correct rate in a given time period is or whether geometric or arithmetic historical averages should be used for future forecasts. The EMRP remains a highly contentious issue not only in the finance literature – in practice, firms use EMRP estimates ranging from below 3 percent to upward of 7 percent (AFP, 2011). These differences in estimates can lead to large differences in WACC and affect decisions regarding investment projects.

Asset Beta: In mature equity markets, the asset beta is typically calculated as the historical volatility of the price of a company's stock relative to the market in which it operates. Even for companies with available volatility data, however, different estimates can arise from the use of different time series. Although frequently a 3- to 5-year historical times series is used, there is no agreement in the finance literature or in practice on what the "correct" approach is (AFP, 2011; Fama and French, 1997). For unlisted companies or greenfield projects, the exercise is even more complicated, as there is no existing volatility data. Here, it is common to use the beta of comparable companies operating in the same industry. Again, the lack of readily available comparables in many emerging markets will complicate the analysis, requiring reference to comparables from other markets/regions or from somewhat different industries. Each of the choices can affect the final result. For example, standard calculations of "railroad" industry betas may lump shipping companies together with urban mass-transportation systems, railroad equipment manufactures, and other businesses with different risk profiles, leading to beta estimates ranging from 0.5 to 1. Moreover, in an integrated project in which the primary offtaker is a mine, it may be more relevant to use the asset beta of mining companies, which have historically been higher than those of transportation companies.[16]

2.2.2 *Equity tax adjustment*

The return on equity in the WACC formula is intended to be a net equity return, that is, the distribution to equity holders after payment by the project entity of all corporate income taxes and other taxes and fees. Thus in applying the formula to determine the access fee it is necessary to take account of the corporate income tax that would be applied to Transco's pre-tax income by the transit jurisdiction.[17] If K_e is 14 percent but the average corporate tax rate on Transco's earnings in the transit jurisdiction is 30 percent, the required pre-tax equity return for calculating the access fee would be 20 percent (0.14/(1.00–0.30)). Substituting this into the earlier equations gives the following for the determination of the tax-adjusted WACC or r to be used for the computation of the access fee where T_{ac} equals the average effective corporate tax rate:

$$\text{WACC}_{tax\ adj.} = \frac{E}{V}\frac{K_e}{(1-T_{ac})} + \frac{D}{V}K_d(1-T_{mc}) = r_{tax\ adj.}$$

Alternative Estimates of K_e. Depending upon the assumptions made, in our example for Transco the CAPM yields a range of possible estimates for K_e even before adjustment for corporate tax (see Table 8.2). While the most optimistic estimate of 12 percent appears unrealistic for many emerging market projects, the highest estimate is above 20 percent, a level frequently cited (but also disputed) as the minimum rate of return an investor would expect for a mining investment in a low-income, low-capacity country.

2.2.3 *Cost of debt*

The cost of debt should reflect current market conditions and the perceived riskiness of the particular borrower. K_d is typically determined by reference to a risk-free rate such as the London Interbank Offered Rate (LIBOR)[18] or the rate on U.S. Treasury securities plus a risk premium that is based on the credit rating of the borrower (usually a company credit rating available from credit ratings agencies). In data-poor environments where many companies are unrated and in the case of greenfield projects, assessing the cost of debt is more difficult. If one were looking at debt from an independent third party with no affiliate support, one can consider the rate at which the local government borrows and adjust upward/downward based on the perceived credit risk of the project relative to the government. Another method is to look to data of the average borrowing rate of local companies and adjust in reference to that average.

There is an interaction between the assumed debt–equity ratio and the assumed cost of debt. The higher rates calculated on country-specific experience should only be applied in conjunction with the lower debt–equity ratio that would typically apply in such cases. If the debt is guaranteed or supported by contractual commitments or directly provided by an affiliate, then a higher debt–equity ratio may be appropriate, but the rate used for the debt should be related to the actual cost of debt to the affiliated entity or the entity providing the contractual guarantee, for example, the parent company.

2.2.4 *Debt tax adjustment*

Finally, the pre-tax cost of debt needs to be adjusted to account for the tax benefits of debt in the cost of capital calculation. In principle it should be project and country specific, as it should represent the likely tax rate that will apply to the project for which the access fee is being calculated.

To sum up this part of the discussion, Table 8.1 lists all the parameters that would enter the access fee calculation and the plausible range of variation for estimates of each of the parameters for a hypothetical greenfield port and rail project in an emerging-markets country. We will later show the implications of these ranges for any effort to compute the access fee and in turn taxable income.

Table 8.1 Ranges of parameters in determining the access fee

Parameter	*Justifiable range*	*Sources of variation*
NPV_{capex}	+ /− 10–15%	Cost estimates, environmental, engineering, geological, political risk factors affecting construction
Weighted average cost of capital (WACC):		
Capital structure	20–60% debt	Reference to actual versus hypothetical capital structure, choice of comparables for hypothetical arms-length lender
(i) Cost of Equity:		
Risk-free rate	2–5%	Underlying risk-free security, time period over which the risk-free rate is quoted
Country risk premium	8–14%	Determining reasonable comparables in absence of credit ratings and sovereign spreads
Equity market risk premium	3–7%	Choice of historical estimate, choice of baseline risk-free security, averaging methodology (geometric vs. arithmetic), timeframe of underlying data
Asset beta	0.5–1.0	Determining reasonable comparables in absence of historical returns data (which industries and regions are most comparable)
(ii) Cost of Debt:		
Risk-free rate	+/−1%	LIBOR or U.S. Treasury rate. Reference time period can vary.
Risk adjustment	+/−4%	Depends on availability of sovereign spreads, cost estimates of comparable companies, existence of third-party guarantees
Tax rate	25–30%	Choice of expected versus target tax rate, actual versus marginal

2.3 Elements of the variable fee

In contrast to the access fee, which if agreed in advance may be based on a number of estimated factors, the variable fee should be based on the actual costs that are incurred in operations. To permit budgeting and planning, the variable fee in any year could be based on estimated or historical costs subject to a "true up," that is, reconciliation of estimate with actual after the close of the period. This is a procedure used in many regulated industries or project structures in which costs are passed through.

Still, at least two elements need to be decided: first, what costs are to be allowed. Second what is the appropriate "markup," if any, by which actual expenses will be elevated in order to arrive at the variable fee and a reasonable profit.

Allowable costs should include all direct costs of operations including materials, labor, insurance, third-party services, and other expenditures that are not of a capital nature. For clarity and to minimize disputes, a schedule of allowable costs should be developed. Where acquisition is from an affiliated entity, accounting may be more difficult. One approach would be to allow affiliated purchases only at cost, relying on the markup to account for any profit that the affiliate entity might have otherwise earned.[19] Note any transit fee (see discussion that follows)[20] should be an allowable cost for purposes of determining the variable fee.

In the spirit of the OECD transfer pricing guidelines, a cost markup is to be applied to costs in order to provide an "appropriate profit" to the service provider for its activities. Although not so characterized in the OECD transfer price guidelines, the markup might also be viewed as administrative overhead or indirect costs to recognize management services provided by the home office if those services are not recovered otherwise.[21] Unfortunately, neither in theory nor in practice is there a consensus on what constitutes an appropriate profit markup for service providers.

There are two other aspects of the variable fee worth noting. The costs used to build up the fee could be the same costs allowed as deductions in determining taxable income in the transit jurisdiction, but that does not necessarily have to be the case. There would be some administrative advantage in preserving this identity, as that would facilitate auditing and would assure the transit jurisdiction that the access fee would preserve some taxable income in all periods.[22] Second, to the extent that the variable fee is recognized as a cost to Mineco deductible in the mine jurisdiction, the mine jurisdiction has a strong interest in the elements permitted as recoverable costs and the markup. Of course, as noted throughout, the mine jurisdiction need not necessarily recognize the transfer price negotiated by the transit jurisdiction. In particular the access fee may incorporate elements of a nature or magnitude, for example, a high management fee or markup that is not consistent with the mine jurisdiction's tax laws.

2.4 Gross income to taxable income

Determining transfer prices or formulas for the access and variable fee is only the first step in determining taxable income. The agreed prices together with actual shipments will generate gross revenues and costs. Then it is necessary to compute taxable income utilizing all of the rules generally applicable to determining taxable income. A couple of points are worth noting. The computation of the access fee, if agreed up front, will embody an assumed debt/equity ratio, but the actual capitalization utilized by the taxpayer may differ from the assumed ratio. Further, the revenue code itself may set limitations on the debt/equity ratio and amount of interest expense that may be deducted pre-tax, giving rise to additional differences between earnings before interest and taxes (EBIT) and taxable income.

Similarly, some expenses used in the computation of the variable fee may be subject to limitations or may not be deductible for purposes of income tax. Conversely, there may be other expenses, for example, a management fee that the taxpayer might claim even though they may not have been used in the buildup of the variable fee. Finally, expenses may differ due to capitalization practices. Capital costs used to calculate the access fee (if negotiated in advance) will differ from actual capital costs incurred, and depending on the particular capitalization and depreciation rules used, the return to capital to may be spread through time quite differently than the timing of returns implicit in the financial model used to build up the access fee. In addition to these complexities, many of the deductible operating costs or those costs embodied in capitalized assets will be incurred in transactions, with affiliated entities raising transfer price issues of their own.[23] In short, net income implied by the transfer fee and taxable income may differ significantly.

Therefore even if one were to apply the cost-plus approach to derive the project's revenues, there still remains much uncertainty and administrative complexity in arriving at taxable income and tax liabilities, as the revenues are only the first element of the calculation.

2.5 Illustrating the impact on tax revenue

To further illustrate the issues set out in the prior section, we have put together a simple model to show the effect that the choices of the various parameters can have on the computed transfer prices, the access and variable fee, and in turn on the income tax revenue of the downstream government. The example assumes a US$1 billion hypothetical rail and port project with a lifetime of 30 years located in a high-risk emerging-markets country where few or no alternative transport modes are available. The income tax computations are simplified but sufficient to illustrate the fundamental points.[24]

Table 8.2 summarizes how different but plausible ranges of the various input parameters discussed yield a range of values for the WACC and hence the imputed access and variable fees and, ultimately, the taxable income. The main financial results are shown in Figure 8.2.

The "low case" in which each parameter is chosen to be least favorable to the project EBIT yields a WACC of 9 percent and the lowest taxable income and tax revenue. Meanwhile, the "high case" in which parameters are chosen to be most favorable to the project EBIT yields a WACC of 23 percent and the highest revenue to the government. The "mid case" is an arithmetical average to the two extreme cases. What is remarkable is the wide range of outcomes that results from the different choices of parameters. Across the scenarios, average taxable income ranges from $37 million annually in the low case to $196 million in the high case, yielding tax revenues that range between $11 million and $59 million – a range of more than 500 percent![25] These results and in particular their wide variance should give no one comfort.

Table 8.2 Key assumptions and financial results under three scenarios

Values in US$ millions unless specified	*Low Case*	*Mid Case*	*High Case*
ASSUMPTIONS			
Up front capex	1,000	1,000	1,000
Replacement capex (per year)	50	50	50
Weighted average cost of capital (WACC)	**9%**	**14%**	**23%**
Capital structure (% debt/equity)	60%	40%	20%
Cost of equity, K_e:	12%	18%	26%
Risk-free rate, K_f	2%	4%	5%
Country risk premium (*CRP*)	8%	11%	14%
Equity market risk premium (*EMRP*)	3%	5%	7%
Beta	0.5	0.75	1
Effective (after tax) cost of debt, K_d:	7%	8%	10%
Cost of debt (nominal)	12%	14%	16%
Inflation adjustment	2%	2%	2%
Tax rate	30%	30%	30%
Operating expenses	100	100	100
Operating cost markup	3%	7%	10%
FINANCIAL RESULTS			
Access fee	146	196	278
Variable fee	105	108	110
Operating expenses	100	100	100
Depreciation	70	70	70
EBIT	**81**	**133**	**218**
Interest expense	44	36	22
Taxable Income	**37**	**97**	**196**
Income Tax	11	29	59

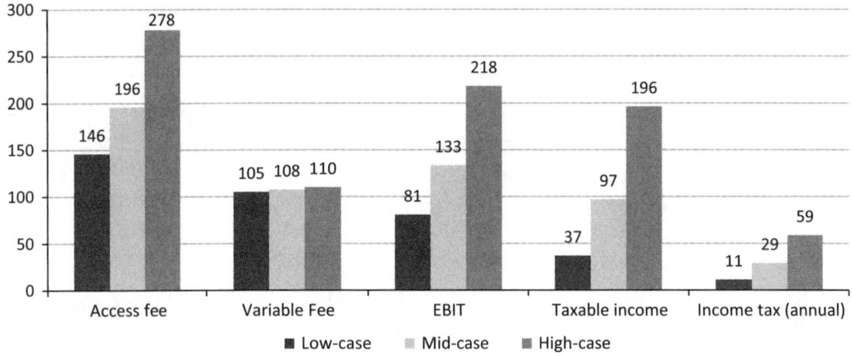

Figure 8.2 Summary of key results

3 Derived or negotiated tax liability

Although the OECD has chosen to try to allocate income on the basis of the arm's length principle, it is not the only possible approach. We now lay out a number of alternative approaches that may prove more appropriate than the cost-plus approach in some cases.

The first is what we term a negotiated tax liability. It would be possible using the model to directly negotiate tax revenues as a function of capital investment and operating costs, simplifying administration and reducing uncertainty about future revenue flows.

The first step would be to use a simple economic model (such as that used in the computations of Table 8.2) to calculate the annual access fee and the variable fee. The second step would be to calculate the tax liability in any year as the sum of three elements: (1) the tax on the imputed return on equity assumed in the calculation of the access fee, (2) the tax rate times the markup embodied in the variable fee, and (3) the tax rate times the net miscellaneous income from any activity not included in the core infrastructure functions subject to the access or variable fees.

For the first element, one could calculate a levelized access fee without adjusting for tax on equity capital, that is, using K_e without adjustment for tax. The difference between the fee so calculated and the higher annual access fee calculated using $K_e/(1 - T_{ac})$ would be the amount of the annual tax payment.[26] This still requires the parties to have agreement on all the variables determining WACC, including K_e, the permitted debt/equity ratio, and the cost of debt. The second element, the variable component, would be simply equal to the tax rate times the agreed mark up on allowable costs. As before, agreement would have to be reached on what costs would be used to determine the base for the markup. Finally, it would be necessary to take account of any incidental income of the project or income earned from third-party use of the infrastructure.[27] Operating cost deductions against the latter should only be allowed for costs not included in the deductions subject to the variable fee markup and in any case would have to be limited to costs that would not have been incurred except for such incidental activity. Losses from the third component should not in principle be allowable against the income tax liability attributable with respect to the fixed and variable streams.[28]

While this suggested approach suffers from the same computational uncertainties inherent in determining the access fee and the variable fee under the cost-plus approach, it avoids the additional uncertainties related to the difference between gross income and taxable income and would provide much more certainty in administration.

Alternatively, in light of the wide range in estimated tax liability coming out of the model, authorities might consider simply negotiating a fixed annual amount payable to the government in lieu of income tax. The payment might also include any transit fee that the government imposes. This may seem primitive and inconsistent with the notion of an income tax, but it may be more honest to the situation and could greatly simplify tax administration for the transit jurisdiction. Negotiating the fee would require some considerable sophistication on the government's part.

A negotiated income tax or income tax plus transit fee could also present the mine jurisdiction with some interesting tax alternatives. Rather than calculate a transfer price between Mineco and Transco, the mine jurisdiction could (if agreed) treat the project as a unitary entity, calculating taxable income for the project as a whole, allowing deduction of expenses incurred in both jurisdictions. The tax payment made to the transit jurisdiction could be treated either as a deduction in calculating the tax owed to the mine jurisdiction or perhaps more properly as a credit against the tax due to the mine jurisdiction to the extent that the negotiated tax reasonably approximates the income tax that would have otherwise been due.[29] The tax-and-credit approach is obviously analogous to the system employed in which a government taxes residents on world-wide income but allows full or partial credit for income tax paid on activity outside of the taxing jurisdiction.

Such a system would have interesting risk-sharing properties between the mine and transit jurisdictions. The transit jurisdiction would have a relatively certain and secure tax stream, while that of the mine jurisdiction would remain more volatile, reflecting both market volatility and cost risks. On the other hand, the mine jurisdiction would capture the full upside of more profitable projects and in particular would not be subject to any indirect sharing of rents or resource payments with the transit jurisdiction through the tax system. Despite these intriguing properties, the authors know of no examples of such schemes being applied in practice.

4 Formulary system

A second alternative for allocating income for income tax purposes is to use a formulary system to allocate the income of the combined enterprise among tax jurisdictions (or to the jurisdiction utilizing the system) on the basis of various items such as the percentage of property, payroll, or sales of the total enterprise within the tax jurisdiction. The formulary system is used within the United States[30] to allocate enterprise income to particular states and is being advocated by the European Commission for use in Europe.[31] Even the OECD has recognized the formulary approach in the use of the split profit for highly integrated activities, although it still purports to do so within the context of the arm's length principle (discussed earlier).

To apply a formulary system, one would treat the entire enterprise (mine, rail, and port) as a single entity, just as if it were in a single jurisdiction. One would then compute the taxable income for the entity using either common rules agreed to by the two governments and the investor or using the particular rules of the tax jurisdiction applying the system. Once taxable income was so calculated, one would apply the formula to allocate it among the two jurisdictions.

In theory this could be done on a unilateral basis by either the transit or mine jurisdiction computing taxable income before allocation on the basis of its own tax system and using its own system for allocation, just as different states in the United States may apply different allocation formulas and calculate enterprise income differently. Alternatively, the computation could be done in a three-party agreement among the investor and both jurisdictions. The latter would have the advantage of appearing to tax all but not more than all of the income, avoiding no taxation or double taxation. But it also makes matters considerably more complicated since it is necessary to have agreement among the two jurisdictions concerning both the rules for calculation of taxable income and the formula for allocating income.

Among factors usually considered for allocation – assets, labor (payroll), sales – only assets and possibly labor would seem relevant, since sales are being made to persons in third-party jurisdictions. Using assets requires addressing many definitional issues. Assets might be limited to fixed tangible assets (including rolling stock). Intangible assets, including particularly the value of the mine concession itself, are much more problematic. Fixed assets would be assigned to the jurisdiction in which they are located. Assets shared by the two jurisdictions, such as rolling stock, would have to be allocated among operations in the two jurisdictions, perhaps simply on the basis of mileage, but more complex factors could be imagined.[32] Valuation would be further affected over time by the depreciation rules used, for example, economic depreciation per financial statements, tax depreciation (particularly distorted because of accelerated depreciation of expensing), or some agreed common rules.[33] The purpose of using assets is to *allocate* taxable income not to determine it. Given this, book values (original cost less economic depreciation) may be the best among the measures readily available.

An especially knotty problem may exist in the taxation of gains when an interest in the project is sold directly or indirectly.[34] This is a problem no matter what system is being used for the allocation of income, but if the two jurisdictions are employing some sort of formulary system for the division of income tax revenues, arguably the same formula should apply, since the gain is presumably attributable to some acceleration of income. On the other hand, the mine jurisdiction and the seller, depending upon the circumstances, may argue that the larger part of the value is attributable to the capitalized value of the resources, which would not be reflected in the invested capital.

Although dependent upon the particular facts and the definitions used, a formulary system and the allocation on the basis of assets in many instances could lead to the transit jurisdiction having higher income tax revenue than the mine jurisdiction, as the capital investment in rail and port will often exceed the investment in the mine. For instance, the investment in the downstream infrastructure for the Rio Tinto Simandou project in Guinea may be several times the value the investment in the mine itself. This somewhat uncomfortable result may be better understood and accepted by noting that the mine jurisdiction should also be recovering a royalty to capture the value of its resources. Nevertheless, one problem with utilizing a formulary system even if all of the parameters can be specified is that "taxable income" of the enterprise is likely to contain some element of rent or payment for the resource value. The interaction of the royalty and income tax streams and the capture of the resource value by the host country is discussed further in what follows.

Using a formulary system for allocating income between the two jurisdictions does not avoid the normal problems in determining taxable income. For the project as a whole, the issues of debt/equity ratios, cost of debt, and transfer prices all remain. Even the values of assets used to allocate income between the jurisdictions (if assets are used) are the result of capitalizing expenditures for services, equipment, and goods, some portion of which are acquired from affiliated entities (e.g., rails made from steel acquired from affiliated steel producer, as is the case of ArcelorMittal in Liberia).[35]

To avoid or mitigate these larger problems would require the application of the formulary system to the parent itself, including downstream activity and other segments not being part of the mine and its rail and port infrastructure. This larger application of the formulary system has some intriguing possibilities, but it raises a whole other level of discourse, including the need in a mining jurisdiction to have any formulary system for income tax coupled to a strong and independent royalty.

Although application of the formulary system requires careful definitions and faces all of the problems associated with taxation of an investment located in a single jurisdiction, it does not depend upon a set of values as widely dispersed as the estimates for the parameters used in the cost-plus method, and in that important particular is a superior method of calculation.

5 Royalties and transit fees

The interactions of the two jurisdictions are more complicated than simply determining and then allocating taxable income among them. The mining jurisdiction also expects and is entitled to a royalty for payment of the natural resource itself. In theory one can separate the royalty payment attributable to the "rent" element or the value of the resource as a factor of production from the income tax or other payments. Indeed, there ordinarily would be a royalty payment whether one or two jurisdictions are involved.

In principle the royalty payment should represent the rent or resource payment so that net income after subtracting the royalty payment would only be the normal return to capital. But royalties are at best an approximation and cannot be expected in practice to correspond to anything but a rough value of the rents or resource value. Thus some component of the income may be attributable to rent or the resource value, especially for highly profitable mines or during "high" price periods. Of course, the opposite can also be true especially during "low" price periods, and perhaps one could argue for their equaling out roughly. Still, proposals such as resource rent taxes, variable royalties, or other mechanisms to capture additional revenue during high-profit periods strongly suggest the belief that income net of royalty will often contain a component of rent. This belief is further supported by the wide range of ad valorem royalties that we see in practice.

The use of a resource rent tax[36] in the mine jurisdiction in lieu of or in addition to an ad valorem royalty attenuates but does not fully eliminate this problem. In application a resource rent tax should only reach profits in excess of those necessary to provide a market return on the deployed capital. In that sense the tax is properly targeted only on the rent or resource value, although determination of the threshold used to divide the normal return to capital from the return to the resource (rent) in practice is more a matter of art or convention. Unless the tax captures the full rent or value, any profits above the threshold will also be subject to income tax, and through the income tax both jurisdictions will be capturing part of the rent or resource value.

The royalty problem has an analogue in the transit jurisdiction and the imposition of a "transit" fee. Transit fees, not to be confused with tariffs paid by shippers or the access and variable fees used to set a transfer price, are not universal, but in our limited experience in West Africa, both governments and investors expect the payment of such fee. Like a royalty, the higher the transit fee, the smaller the income for the project as a whole. In addition, when the royalty is calculated on the mine mouth value or other point in the mine jurisdiction, the transit fee will reduce the royalty payment. Thus a transit fee, like a royalty, can (against any agreed split and treatment of income tax) shift tax revenue from one jurisdiction to the other. Transit fees and examples are discussed in more detail in Chapter 9 of this volume at section 8 (Le Leuch).

In the first instance the transit jurisdiction may appropriately charge for leasing the right of way and land for the rail and port facilities. There is, however, a more subtle factor that also may be taken into account in computing a transit fee. The in-place value of the resource depends upon expected future market prices and the nature of the deposit (e.g., grade, impurities, or geology). Yet another part of the determination of the in-place value of the resource is locational, the cost of moving it to markets, and a principal component of that is its proximity to the sea. In the single-jurisdiction case, one does not need to take too refined an approach to the matter since the royalty, land rentals, and to some extent other taxes capture both the nature of the deposit and the location. There is a single "source" country. However, value determination is more complicated when two jurisdictions are involved.[37]

The importance of location can be illustrated by a case in which the mine jurisdiction does have an outlet to the sea but when shipping through a neighboring country is cheaper. This is the case for mining deposits located in southeast Guinea near the Liberia border, where shipment through Liberia (in part through established transport corridors) could be much cheaper. Some estimates indicated savings in the neighborhood of 40 percent in capital costs and 40 percent in operating costs for the rail and port.[38] Where such an alternative in-country route exists, cost comparisons (including fiscal burdens) of using the in-country (or third-country) versus alternative route allow one to estimate an upper limit on location value of the alternative route.[39] Where the mine country is landlocked and there is only one feasible exit country, the upper limit on the transit charge is the amount taking account of the royalty and other charges of the two governments that would otherwise make the project uneconomic (i.e., that would drive the return below the minimum rate of return on capital investment or, more realistically, the next best call on the resources of the potential investor).

These economics, which are due to simple monopoly power,[40] do not imply that the transit jurisdiction should capture all the "location" value any more than that the mining jurisdiction should expect to capture through royalty all of the theoretical rent or resource value. However, they do illustrate that location affects project economics just as the characteristics of the deposits and that the transit jurisdiction does have some equitable claims to share in the overall project benefits. Geology or geography, both create claims, and within some range there is no principled approach to determining the allocation. Some view rail and port transport as simply a cost element, but extraction is also simply a cost item. Labels alone do not solve the problem.

6 Effect of third-party interests

Both tax and structure issues may be affected by third-party ownership or use of the infrastructure. There is a strong interest in utilizing infrastructure established for mining in broader economic development, although actual success in doing so has been limited.[41] The efforts to do so have focused on either requirements for third-party access or separation of operation and ownership of the assets. Any effective access for third parties will generate additional revenues and costs. In some cases, for example, local passenger service, the service may be more a condition of getting the concession or right of way and certainly not intended to be profit making. In others the host government may attempt to force third-party access for other resource developments within either the transit or mine jurisdictions.[42] Establishing third-party charges or tariffs may require the government and other parties to address in the context of the cost of service and cost recovery many of the same issues and items discussed in the cost-plus section. And while one could speculate on interrelationships, in the end for tax purposes it is probably simply a matter of recognizing and allocating revenues and additional costs when two jurisdictions are involved.

A more complicated situation arises when third-parties have ownership or operational rights to the infrastructure, especially when ownership in part or whole is vested in the host government.[43] In addressing the matter, one must look at the economic reality and not focus on labels. Where the investor is responsible for capital costs and operating expenses and has full control over operations, for tax purposes "ownership" of parts of the infrastructure may not matter. Two other cases are of interest, however. In the first case the rail and port infrastructure is held by two or more independent investors, only one of which is the operator. If the ownership interests are not adjusted to reflect use, then the pricing for transport and port services is likely to have significant economic substance, and the prices will no longer be "transfer" prices. To the extent that the transport entity covers more than one jurisdiction, there would still be the issue of allocation but in a simpler form.

The second case, a variant of particular interest, is when the government holds an interest.[44] The government then has a dual interest in the transport charges, which will determine both the value of its equity, as well as the size of its tax base. This must lead to a negotiated agreement about rates, a debate that may center on the same elements discussed earlier with respect to the use of cost-plus method for transfer pricing, at the risk of repetition, a debate for which governments may be ill prepared.

7 Conflicting interests

Most of the discussion has been framed as a negotiation between the transit taxing authority and the investor. But obviously the upstream taxing authority, the mine jurisdiction, has also a strong interest in the imputed charges. The investor will seek to deduct from its income in the mining jurisdiction the costs incurred in transportation in the transit jurisdiction. If both jurisdictions in fact accept the same calculation, higher transfer prices will shift income and tax revenue to the downstream jurisdiction; conversely, lower prices will shift income and tax revenue away.

The project as a whole has a single rent, and the project's realization is dependent upon the cooperation and assent of both jurisdictions. Subject to the investor being satisfied, with the post-tax return for the project as a whole, the tax issues shift to a debate between the two governments with a focus on three items: the royalty regime of the mine jurisdiction, any transit charge by the transit jurisdiction, and the division of the income tax burden. The governments are not unconstrained in their bargaining. Royalty rates, tax rates, and the definition of taxable income may already be set by statute and subject to limited variation. Moreover, governments are subject to investment treaties and other legislation requiring them to act on a non-discriminatory basis or to observe other standards.

Although there is an assumed view that symmetrical treatment is required to avoid over- or undertaxation, that is not strictly speaking necessary given that many other factors unique to each tax system will affect the actual tax liability of the whole enterprise, for example, tax rates, allowable expenses, capitalization and depreciation rules. In any case, both jurisdictions have an interest in the total tax liabilities of the enterprise given the impact on the investment as a whole, and both jurisdictions have a common interest in the integrity of cost and revenue reporting, especially when transactions with affiliated entities are involved, as well as other necessary coordination.

8 Conclusion

The unitary nature of the mine and its cross-border infrastructure, each fully dependent upon the other, means that any exercise to separate the two into independent entities for tax purposes has a high degree of arbitrariness. The wide range of possible results is illustrated by our analysis of the cost-plus method and the assumptions required for its application. Notwithstanding the OECD's commitment to the arms-length principle, a better approach is to recognize the unitary nature of the project and to apply a profit-split or formulary allocation to apportion income between jurisdictions. The success of this approach requires as an ancillary matter that the mining jurisdiction apply a strong royalty or resource rent tax recognized in the computations of both jurisdictions. All of the traditional issues for determining taxable income, including the possibility of different calculations by each jurisdiction, remain.

Notes

1 Although we use the labels "transit jurisdiction" and "mine jurisdiction," it is important to remember that part of the transportation infrastructure lies in the mine jurisdiction, a factor that is particularly important if consideration is given to treating the transportation infrastructure as a separate entity.
2 Compare to the role of the host government agreements for multi-jurisdiction pipelines discussed in Le Leuch (2016), Chapter 9 in this volume.
3 For a survey of rail and port operations serving mining, see Toledano (2012). For experience in West Africa, see Strong (2004).
4 OECD Transfer Pricing Guidelines for Multinational Enterprises and Tax Administrations, OECD (July 2010), p. 26.
5 Ibid., p. 124.
6 Such a clause could also be a way to preserve income to the transit jurisdiction even if actual operations are suspended temporarily or permanently.
7 For more discussion on tariff rate setting, see Le Leuch (2016), Chapter 9 in this volume.
8 For this purpose, the project's lifetime is the number of years during which the investor will own and operate the infrastructure. In many projects this period is specified in the contract up front; thereafter, ownership of the infrastructure often transfers to the government. To the extent that this period is renegotiated ex post, the access fee may need to be adjusted.
9 In the discussion that follows, we will assume annual discounting, such that the discount rate r is an annualized discount rate, giving rise to a per-annum access fee.
10 Actual capital expenditures incurred prior to the date that the access fee becomes effective would have to be adjusted upward using the agreed discount rate, r.
11 "Current trends in estimating and applying the cost of capital," Association for Financial Professionals, 2011. In another illustration of this conundrum, a recent working paper constructs 440 different ways of calculating WACC based on 11 different measures of the cost of equity, 4 measures of the tax rate, 2 measures of the cost of debt, and 5 measures of the leverage ratio (Frank and Shen, 2012).
12 See http://pages.stern.nyu.edu/~adamodar/. Data from the same source suggests an average debt-to-capital ratio for "Metals & Mining" companies in emerging markets of 20.8 percent and for "Transportation" companies of 27.6 percent. Debt ratios are lower for industries in regions with less developed capital markets, such as the "Africa and Middle East" category.
13 See discussion in Shay (2016), Chapter 3 in this volume, regarding the problems in determining the appropriate treatment of debt when the debt is from or directly or indirectly guaranteed or supported by a related entity.
14 Other methods for calculating the cost of equity include the Fama-French three-factor model and the Carhart four-factor model, both of which are extensions of the CAPM that allow for more than one beta parameter. In addition, there is a class of equity valuation models such as the Gordon growth model that take the value of equity to be the discounted sum of expected future cash flows (dividends). In addition, numerous studies

have found that various other firm characteristics not included in CAPM (such as firm size, the earnings-to-price ratio, the book-to-market value of equity, and others) also have power to predict equity returns (Da et al., 2012). Despite these challenges to the CAPM, it remains the most widely used model for calculating cost of equity in practice. Da et al. cite that about 75 percent of finance professors recommend using the CAPM to estimate the cost of capital for budgeting and that a survey of chief financial officers indicates that 74 percent of the respondents use the CAPM. They also argue that despite some problems with the use of the CAPM in estimating cross-section stock returns, it remains useful in estimating the cost of capital for projects.

15 For example, one paper quotes an annualized average market premium for 1963–1994 of 5.16 percent per year with a standard error of 2.71 percent (Fama and French, 1997). This standard error implies that the risk premium for a project with a beta equal to 1.0 could be anywhere from 2.45 percent to 7.87 percent.

16 Based on data compiled by NYU finance Professor Aswath Damodoran, the average beta of emerging markets metals and mining companies is 1.4, compared to 0.9 for transportation companies and 0.8 for railroad companies (data as of January 2013, available at http://pages.stern.nyu.edu/~adamodar/).

17 We note but do not analyze the interesting case in which the investment is in pass-through form so that the only tax is imposed at the level of the investor.

18 Despite recent controversies surrounding the accuracy and possible misrepresentation of the LIBOR rate in financial markets, it remains the widely used benchmark for pricing securities. Proposals to increase regulatory oversight of the LIBOR determination process are underway.

19 See Shay (2016), Chapter 3 in this volume, for a fuller discussion of transfer pricing issues.

20 See discussion in Section 4; also in Le Leuch (2016), Chapter 9 in this volume.

21 Compare a markup permitted to an operator for indirect costs in the context of joint operating agreements, commonly used in the petroleum sector between partners to a joint unincorporated venture to allocate responsibilities and liability.

22 This conclusion assumes that any allowable deduction for management fees would be less than the permitted markup.

23 See Shay (2016), Chapter 3 in this volume.

24 For simplicity of illustration, the calculations assume the project investment of US$1 billion occurs in one period, followed by a constant annual maintenance capital investment of US$50 million, fixed volumes with a simple estimate of operating expenses (of US$100 million annually), 30-year straight-line depreciation of capex and 15-year depreciation of rolling stock, full deductibility of interest, and taxable income equal to financial income less interest deduction (i.e., no loss carry-overs and other differentials).

25 All calculations presented here are in real terms. The actual amounts payable would be subject to inflation adjustment.

26 Again, because all calculations are done in real terms, the amount actually payable would be subject to an inflation adjustment.

27 An implicit assumption is that the project is "ring-fenced" for tax purposes.

28 Although the negotiated formulas and amounts would in effect be an effort to negotiate net income and the tax structure, we do not attempt to address arguments as to whether such a tax could be credited in a resident jurisdiction as a tax on net income.

29 Conceptually, any portion of the payment due as a transit fee should be a deduction, and the portion due as a payment for income taxes should be a credit. The size of the allowable deduction by the mine jurisdiction of the income tax payment to the transit jurisdiction would also require consideration of the implicit tax rate and some notion of the reasonableness of the imputed income in the transit jurisdiction. The latter could lead the mine jurisdiction and investor back into the same transfer pricing debate that the negotiated figure was intended to limit.

30 See generally Hellerstein (2012).

31 Proposal for a Council Directive on a Common Consolidated Corporate Tax Base, COM(2011) 121/4, 2011/0058 (CNS)("EU Council Directive").

32 In the proposed Nabucco gas pipeline in Europe (now cancelled, possibly to be restricted in simpler form), the parties provided for the allocation of net revenue (gross revenues less original costs) for national tax purposes on the basis of the proportional share of the total length of the pipeline falling in the particular jurisdiction – Article 11.2 of the Agreement Among the State Parties Regarding the Nabucco Project (July 13, 2009) available at http://www.mfa.gov.hu/NR/rdonlyres/8B0D4EA0–8FF1–46C3–8772-E16905FE29E9/0/090714_nabucco_agreement.pdf. Assuming equal costs, this is equivalent to allocation on a net asset basis.

33 Some of the factors that would need to be considered are identified in the EU Council Directive Articles 92–94.

34 For a general discussion of the issues associated with the taxation of capital gains, especially where indirect transfers of interest are involved, see Burns, Le Leuch and Sunley (2016), Chapter 7 in this volume.

35 A variation of the formulary system would be to have the governments and the investor agree to treat the entire project as a stand-alone entity for tax purposes subject to an agreed contractual regime, something like is done with joint development zones in which income is computed and allocated according to some agreed system – for more discussion, see Daniel, Veung and Watson (2016), Chapter 11 in this volume. The governing document could also deal with royalties, duties, transit fees (if preserved), customs, VAT, withholding, tax exemptions, exchange rights, employment, local procurement, and other issues typically dealt with in development agreements. The authors are not aware of any examples.

36 For the principles and issues affecting design of resource rent taxes, see generally Land (2010).

37 Within jurisdictions, the application of the royalty rate on the mine mouth basis partially takes account of the location aspect of valuation for royalty purposes. See generally Otto et al. (2006).

38 Calculations can be much more complicated. For instance, an investor in Guinea offered to construct a light rail to a port in Guinea from its Guinean mine location provided that it could have the right to export its ore across Liberia. The savings from the shorter route through Liberia, including the reduction in capital costs for engines and rolling stock and the reduced operating costs, would have more than offset the additional cost of the light rail across Guinea, but the capital savings is significantly reduced.

39 There is an intermediate case in which a mine in a country whether landlocked or not may have the possibility of exporting through either of several neighbors, for example, Guinean ore could move to the sea through Ivory Coast or Liberia. The potential location rent is then limited to the cost of the next best alternative.

40 Control of the monopoly power of the transit state and the right of landlocked states to access transportation has long been a subject of international concerns. For a brief summary of relevant international conventions, see Le Leuch (2016), Chapter 9 in this volume.

41 For a full discussion of the issue and impediments in practice, see Toledano (2012).

42 Even in economically advanced jurisdictions, the successful requirement of third-party access has been difficult. There are many operational problems with expanding local service, for example, high-density unit train traffic may not be readily compatible with more localized service that also has to be addressed but are outside of the scope of this discussion.

43 See Toledano (2012), Table at fn. 14 for a sample of ownership and operational arrangements.

44 The Simandou project in Guinea has such a structure. Rio Tinto holds the mining concession, but the rail and port infrastructure is to be held by a joint venture of Rio Tinto and the government.

References

Association for Financial Professionals. (2011), *Current Trends in Estimating and Applying the Cost of Capital.*

Da, Z., R.J. Guo and R. Jagannathan. (2012), "CAPM for Estimating the Cost of Equity Capital: Interpreting the Empirical Evidence," *Journal of Financial Economics*, 103(1), 204–220.

Fama, E.F. and K.R. French. (1997), "Industry Costs of Equity," *Journal of Financial Economics*, 43(2), 153–193.

Frank, M.Z. and T. Shen. (2012), *Investment, Q, and the Weighted Average Cost of Capital*, Available at SSRN 2014367 (2014).

Hellerstein, J.R., W. Hellerstein and John A. Swain. (2012), *State Taxation* (Warren Gorham Lamont).

Land, Bryan (2010), *Resource Rent Taxes: A Re-Appraisal,* in Daniel, Philip, Michael Keen and Charles McPherson (eds) *The Taxation of Petroleum and Minerals: Principles, Problems and Practice* (Routledge, London and New York), pp. 241–262.

Organisation for Economic Co-operation and Development. (2010), *OECD Transfer Pricing Guidelines for Multinational Enterprises and Tax Administrations.*

Otto, J., Craig Andrews, Fred Cawood, Michael Doggett, Pietro Guj, Frank Stermole, John Stermole and John Tilton. (2006), *Mining Royalties: A Global Study of their Impact on Investors, Government, and Civil Society* (Washington, DC: World Bank Publications).

Strong, J. (2004), "The Development of Railway Concessions in West and Central Africa," *The Journal of Structured Finance*, 9(4), 66–91.

Toledano, P. (2012), *Leveraging Extractive Industry Infrastructure Investments for Broad Economic Development*, Available at http://academiccommons.columbia.edu/catalog/ac:154081.

9 International oil and gas pipelines

Legal, tax, and tariff issues

Honoré Le Leuch[1]

1 Introduction

International transportation of oil and gas is a major element of international trade. Oil-producing areas are often located at a distance from growing petroleum markets; transportation occurs via ships, rail, or increasingly, pipelines. These extend beyond the territory of a producing country and frequently cross several countries before reaching final destinations.

Cross-border petroleum pipeline projects encompass technical, economic, contractual, regulatory, and tax issues. Differing approaches to these diverse issues stem from diverging objectives of neighboring countries, as well as of sponsor pipeline companies (Stevens et al., 2003, 2009; Vinogradov, 2001). Each single project is specific to a geopolitical context. The differences extend to corporate structure, taxation regime, transportation tariffs, and other terms and conditions. International law provisions concerning cross-border petroleum pipelines remain relatively limited. Several international conventions helped landlocked countries[2] to gradually obtain basic rights, allowing for transit of their natural resources to ports. However, the enforceability and implementation of such rights are problematic for countries, investors, and lenders.

This chapter focuses on the main issues regarding cross-border pipelines:

- Importance of international pipeline transportation
- Categories of cross-border petroleum pipelines and examples of existing projects
- Applicability of international law to pipeline projects
- Legal and contractual solutions generally adopted and how to streamline the corporate, contractual, and tax structures of such projects
- Tax issues
- Determination of international pipeline tariffs, and the differences between tariffs and transit fees, as well as the main principles and methods of designing pipeline tariffs
- Recommendations on structuring and fostering development of new international petroleum pipelines.

2 Importance of international oil and gas transport

Having access to transportation infrastructure and minimizing international transport risk and cost are primary objectives for both petroleum producers and consumers.

Large volumes of crude oil and natural gas are internationally traded from producing to consuming countries – 64 and 29 percent of world's production, respectively. In the case of crude oil, where most of the trade is shipped by sea, reliance on international pipelines is less pronounced, although not insignificant. Internationally traded natural gas, however, is largely transported by international pipelines (69 percent); the remaining 31 percent is transported by ships as liquefied natural gas (LNG).

Petroleum exploration in basins located on shore far from the coast is often at a disadvantage in the absence of pipeline facilities. Such a disadvantage stems from the distance to an export port in another country and results in higher costs for the petroleum companies and lower revenues for the countries. A lengthy and complex process of negotiation with the transit country to allow the construction and operation of a pipeline across its territory adds to these costs.

3 Categories and objectives of cross-border pipelines

The two main categories of cross-border pipelines are the export pipelines from landlocked countries and the transit pipelines that cross borders. Each category has its own distinct objectives and legal basis. Accordingly, identifying the proper category of a cross-border project when analyzing international pipeline legal frameworks is critical. Unfortunately, many publications dealing with international pipelines do not consider or delineate these essential differences.

Each category is subject to a specific body of international law, rights, and obligations. The general expressions "transit pipelines," "transnational pipelines," or "international pipelines" and often used without qualification. Their application to a specific category of cross-border pipeline remains vague. "Transmission pipelines" is primarily used for domestic pipelines, including those in federal states. "Transit" is a well-known concept in international law and refers to the freedom of transit of goods by authorized means of transport in other countries.

3.1 Export pipelines from landlocked countries

The first category is designed to cover oil or gas production exported from a landlocked state to a coastal port by crossing the territory of one or more transit states. In most cases, the pipeline transportation system is built and operated by a special-purpose pipeline company or by a consortium of companies, generally majority owned by the companies holding an exploration and production interest in the initial petroleum discoveries and fields in a landlocked country and willing to continue exploration activities to identify additional resources in that country.

Several options may exist in terms of ownership and exploitation of a pipeline transportation system. The simplest option is that in which only one company owns and operates the entire multi-country system; the more complex option is one in which distinct companies are established in each state for the ownership or operation of the pipeline in each country segment, though managed as an integrated project. In all cases, each country segment is subject to the jurisdiction of that country, under the umbrella of an interstate governmental agreement or treaty for coordinating the integrated transnational project between and among the concerned states.

When commencing exploration in a landlocked country, oil and gas companies assume that, when necessary, they will be able to negotiate arrangements for an international pipeline with both the landlocked country and the transit country. They further assume that a minimum threshold of reserves is reached to justify the costs of construction and operation of a pipeline.

A cross-border pipeline project can be mutually beneficial to landlocked and transit countries. Identifying and developing mutually beneficial interests can facilitate the negotiation of the project; in the long term, doing so can mitigate political risks by aligning the respective interests of the states. Creating a balance of interests helps establish long-term stability that supplements the general rights and obligations derived from international law.

A transit country has at least three major goals in hosting an export pipeline from a landlocked country, in addition to complying with its obligations of cooperation under international law. The first is to boost its domestic economic activity, since the project is capital intensive during its construction and generates local employment. Moreover, the pipeline company will be liable to corporate taxes and other taxes in relation to its activity in the transit state during the project's life. The second goal is to obtain an equity participation in the project, since the transit state may negotiate a right to acquire a minority participating interest in the pipeline, at least in the segment crossing the country. The third goal is to stimulate petroleum exploration and production in its own acreage located along the pipeline route by negotiating the right for its upstream contract holders to access a part of the available transportation capacity of the export pipeline on attractive commercial terms.

Another goal of the transit state is the possible right to purchase part of the production transported by the export pipeline to cover its domestic requirements. Generally speaking, this is not necessarily a significant advantage for oil or gas, which are traded at international market prices adjusted to the point of delivery; exceptions may arise in those cases in which the transit country bears high costs for importing its energy.

3.2 Cross-border transit pipelines

The second category of cross-border pipelines consists of international oil or gas pipelines other than those originating from a landlocked state. Their objective is the transit in one or more countries of oil and gas for export from a producing country. This category differs from the first with respect to the international law applicable to each category and the degree of flexibility in selecting among several routes. In most cases, several alternative routes for transit at relatively comparable costs may exist for this second category; the alternative routes for exporting petroleum from a landlocked country, if any, may be significantly more expensive than the shortest or more cost-effective export routes, strongly limiting the bargaining power of the landlocked country. This geographical disadvantage explains why international law has provided special transit rights to landlocked countries.

The simplest cross-border transit scheme of the second category of cross-border pipelines corresponds to a pipeline built between two countries. It may involve onshore or offshore systems, for example, transit pipelines from the Norwegian offshore fields to the British or continental European coasts. More complex international projects link several countries. They may be located on the same continent, such as the long intra-continent oil and gas transportation systems from Russia to Western Europe, or between two continents. The pipeline transit systems may be entirely onshore or constitute onshore and offshore segments. For example, several gas pipeline systems connect the Algerian fields to Europe, with the objectives of diversifying gas clients and minimizing transportation costs.

3.3 Cases of export pipelines from landlocked countries

There are few cases of export pipelines from landlocked countries. Out of 44 landlocked countries, only 7 currently export oil or gas: Azerbaijan, Bolivia, Chad, Kazakhstan, South Sudan, Turkmenistan, and Uzbekistan. Two African countries – Niger and Uganda – may soon join this group. Other landlocked countries produce for domestic consumption only.

The most representative examples of export pipelines from landlocked countries are the Chad/Cameroon oil pipeline system and all the oil or gas export pipelines from Azerbaijan to Turkey across Georgia (in particular, the oil Baku/Tbilisi/Ceyhan pipeline, or BTC, and the South Caucasus gas pipeline, or SCP). The export gas pipelines to Argentina and Brazil are different because the transported gas is entirely purchased by the transit countries. Details on existing landlocked export projects are summarized in Box 9.1.

The major challenge of the Chad/Cameroon oil pipeline project was the negotiation of all of the arrangements and authorizations that commenced in 1993. The negotiation of many operational and funding agreements and the award of the pipeline licenses followed these agreements. At the time, the project arrangements represented one of the most advanced legal, contractual, and financing schemes for an export pipeline from a landlocked country. The project came into operation in 2003. The pipeline exported more than 500 million barrels of Chadian oil from 2003 to 2013. Extensions to the main pipeline have been built to connect new fields and operators located in Chad; a possible extension to Niger is under consideration. The original bilateral agreement envisaged such potential extensions.

Box 9.1 Examples of existing landlocked export pipelines

Africa

- *Chad/Cameroon export oil pipeline.* Its main original objective is to export oil from the landlocked Chadian Doba basin to the port of Kribi located on the Atlantic coast of Cameroon; this is a distance of 1,070 km, of which 170 km are in Chad and 900 km are in Cameroon. The pipeline has been in operation since 2003. The pipeline is owned by two companies: COTCO incorporated in Cameroon and TOTCO in Chad. The investment for the pipeline system amounted to US$2.2 billion. The bilateral agreement was signed in 1996, followed by the signing of the other arrangements, including those for financing, until 2000. Pipeline tariffs are paid to COTCO and TOTCO.
- *New projects in East Africa related to South Sudan and Uganda.* Since its independence, South Sudan has been looking for a new oil export pipeline alternative to supplement the two existing pipelines crossing Sudan to the Red Sea. Landlocked Uganda is considering an oil export pipeline project to the Indian Ocean crossing Tanzania.

Latin America

- *Bolivia/Argentina pipelines.* A first pipeline was built in the 1970s to export gas from Bolivia to Argentina. The exported gas is purchased by Argentina to cover its internal demand.
- *Bolivia/Brazil gas pipeline.* This 3,000-km gas system is owned and operated by two companies: GTB SA in Bolivia and TBG BA in Brazil. Brazil purchases all of the gas transported for its internal consumption.

Central Asia

- *Kazakhstan/Russia. The Caspian Pipeline Consortium (CPC)*, consisting of 11 companies or states, is involved in a 1,510-km oil pipeline from Kazakhstan to the Russian Black Sea. CPC was established in 1992; after several changes to the CPC structure, the system was built and put into operation at the end of 2001 and is operated by Chevron. Two separate pipeline companies, one for each country, were established, both incorporated in Bermuda: CPC Kazakhstan and CPC Russia.
- *Azerbaijan to Black Sea terminals.* There are two oil export systems: the 1,330-km *Northern Route Export Pipeline* (NREP) from Baku to the Russian Novorossiysk terminal, and the 883-km *Western Route Export Pipeline* (WREP) from Baku to the Georgian Supsa terminal.

- *Azerbaijan/Georgia/Turkey.* The two pipelines from Baku were supplemented by the new and larger 1,768-km *Baku/Tbilisi/Ceyhan* (BTC) oil pipeline. This major US$3.6 billion investment was put into operation in June 2006. The BTC consortium consisted originally of 11 companies that owned the transportation system; BP manages the pipeline. The intergovernmental arrangements related to the project were made under the umbrella of the European Energy Charter Treaty of 1994.
- *Azerbaijan/Georgia/Turkey.* The South Caucasus Pipeline (SCP) is a project similar to BTC and uses the same corridor, but it does so to export gas instead of oil from the Baku area to the Turkish border. Seven companies originally constituted the SCP consortium. SCP exports began in September 2006. The SCP consortium agreed to an expansion project called SCPX in December 2013, and construction is underway.
- *Other pipelines from Kazakhstan, Turkmenistan, Uzbekistan, etc.*

The BTC oil pipeline came into operation in June 2006, allowing exports from Azerbaijan and some from Kazakhstan through two transit countries, Georgia and Turkey. As with the Chad/Cameroon project, it took nearly 10 years to move from the first studies to pipeline operation. The intergovernmental agreement was signed in 1999 under the umbrella of the Energy Charter Treaty of 1994. The system transported 2 billion barrels from 2006 to mid-2014.

3.4 Cases of cross-border transit pipelines

In contrast to the limited number of export pipelines from landlocked countries, numerous cross-border transit pipelines exist, built for transporting oil or gas between two or more countries or adjacent continents. The most significant ones are listed in Box 9.2.

Several examples of long-distance transit pipelines demonstrate their growing economic and geopolitical importance for increasing gas export capacities from large producing countries, supplying gas-importing countries at lower costs than the LNG alternative, or minimizing the potential political risk posed by transit countries by preferring lines laid in international waters when feasible. Algeria progressively built three intercontinental offshore gas lines linking Algeria to southern Europe across the Mediterranean Sea, the third one direct to Europe. The first one transits across Tunisia for the Trans-Mediterranean Pipeline to Italy and has been in operation since 1983; the second one crosses Morocco for the Maghreb-Europe Gas Pipeline and has been in service since 1996. The third one goes offshore from Algeria to Spain for the MedGas Pipeline and was commissioned in 2011.[3]

Box 9.2 Selected cross-border transit pipelines

Africa

- From Algeria to Italy across Tunisia and the Mediterranean Sea: the gas Trans-Mediterranean Pipeline
- From Algeria to Spain across Morocco and the Mediterranean Sea: the gas Europe-Maghreb Pipeline
- From Algeria to Spain across the Mediterranean Sea: the MedGas Pipeline
- From Libya to Italy across the Mediterranean Sea: for gas exports
- From Mozambique to South Africa: for gas exports
- From Nigeria to Ghana across Benin and Togo: the offshore West African Gas Pipeline

Latin America

- From Argentina to Chile: for gas exports
- From Colombia to Venezuela: for gas exports

North America

- From Canada to the United States: many oil and gas export pipelines
- From Mexico to the United States, and from the United States to Mexico: for gas exports

Europe

- From Russia to eastern and western Europe: many oil and gas export pipelines, on shore and recently off shore, the Blue Stream crossing the Caspian Sea, and the Nord Stream in the Baltic Sea
- From offshore Norway to the United Kingdom and continental Europe (Belgium, France, and Germany): several oil and gas export pipelines from Norwegian offshore fields
- European connectors and inter-country pipelines: several gas interconnector systems
- From Central Asia/Turkey to European countries: several gas transmission lines under consideration, in addition to the Trans Adriatic Pipeline under construction

Middle East

- From Iraq to Turkey, from Iraq to Saudi Arabia: several oil export pipelines

Asia and Australia

- From Myanmar to Thailand, or China: several gas export pipelines
- From Russia, Kazakhstan, Turkmenistan, or Uzbekistan to China: several recent gas or oil export pipelines
- From Timor-Leste (offshore JPDA) to Australia: a gas export pipeline to an LNG plant

Several trans-Europe pipeline systems were developed in the past four decades by Russia to increase its oil and gas exports. Russia initially selected only onshore routes, but in recent years it built several new offshore lines to supply gas to Europe. First was the Blue Stream pipeline to Turkey via the Black Sea, in operation since 2003, built in a joint venture with ENI; second were the Nord Stream lines across the Baltic Sea, in service since 2011 and owned and operated by Gazprom and four European companies.

4 International law applicable to cross-border pipelines

4.1 The principle of freedom of transit

Although domestic law applies to the section of a transnational pipeline located in a specific country, provisions of international law are also applicable. This is important for ensuring the principle of freedom of transit provided in several international conventions, some dealing specifically with the rights of landlocked countries or submarine pipelines. However, international law does not govern the determination of the pipeline tariff scheme; the transit fee, if any; or the tax regime applicable to the segment of an international pipeline under the jurisdiction of a state. Exceptions exist when bilateral tax treaties for the avoidance of double taxation and the prevention of fiscal evasion or ad hoc bilateral treaties concerning the project may apply.

The basic international conventions applicable to cross-border pipelines are the General Agreement on Tariffs and Trade (GATT) of 1947 and the related 1994 World Trade Organization (WTO) Agreement, which contains an article dealing with the principle of freedom of transit for goods and means of transport that is applicable in most countries.

Transit rules for energy apply to the 52 member countries of the Energy Charter Treaty (ECT) of 1994.[4] Article 7 focuses on the freedom of transit in those countries, as follows:

ECT Article 7 Transit:

(1) Each Contracting Party shall take the necessary measures to facilitate the Transit of *Energy Materials and Products* consistent with *the*

> *principle of freedom of transit* without distinction as to the origin, destination, or ownership of such Energy Materials and Products or discrimination as to pricing on the basis of such distinction, and *without imposing any unreasonable delays, restrictions or charges.*[5] [Emphasis added.]

4.2 Specific rights of access to the sea for landlocked countries

The issue of protecting the rights of export and access to the sea for landlocked countries is specifically addressed in two conventions: the New York Convention on Transit Trade of Landlocked States of 1965 and Part X of the Right of Access of Landlocked States to the Sea of the United Nations Convention on the Law of the Sea (UNCLOS) of 1982. The New York Convention was important because it affirmed, for the first time, the specific rights awarded to landlocked countries: the principles of the free right of access to the seas; the freedom of transit without restriction; and the right of concerned states to consider oil and gas pipelines in the definition of the "means of transport." Part X of UNCLOS dealing with the right of access of landlocked countries to and from the seas reinforced the principles of the New York Convention with the same right to include by mutual agreement "pipelines and gas lines" in the definition of "means of transport." UNCLOS provides that "landlocked States shall enjoy freedom of transit through the territory of transit States by all means of transport" (Article 125.1) and that "traffic in transit shall not be subject to any customs duties, taxes or other charges except charges levied for specific services rendered in connection with such traffic" (Article 127.1). This wording does not refer to any transit fee due in relation to the transit. Moreover, Article 129 of UNCLOS implies an established obligation for cooperation between transit states and landlocked states regarding the construction of the means of transport, including pipelines.

4.3 Right to lay pipelines on the continental shelf or high seas

UNCLOS stipulates the right and freedom to lay and operate a pipeline on the continental shelf in Part IV and on the high seas beyond the continental shelf in Part VII. Coastal states may not impede a pipeline project on the continental shelf and may not impose fees or charges on the transit pipeline other than any applicable income taxes.

5 Legal, corporate, and tax framework of cross-border pipelines

Cross-border pipeline systems raise more complex legal, regulatory, corporate, and tax issues than pipelines under a single jurisdiction.[6] Different national laws apply to the transportation system laid over several countries, and they are complemented by international law. International law, however, remains limited in this domain. The corporate structure, tax framework, and agreements related to cross-border projects are still designed and negotiated largely on a case-by-case basis, both for the intergovernmental agreements and the agreements among individual countries and investors, shippers, and lenders. The European Union, under the umbrella of the Energy Charter Treaty and with a view to facilitating energy supplies to Europe, has developed model agreements since 2001 for cross-border pipeline projects, but these model agreements have met with limited success.[7]

5.1 Intergovernmental agreement

A cross-border pipeline is generally governed by a bilateral or multilateral intergovernmental agreement (IGA) signed between the concerned countries as a foundation for the transportation project. Investors, however, are not signatories of such an agreement.[8]

The IGA defines countries' commitments to authorize planning, design, construction, and operation of the project; transit countries have a key obligation that they shall "not interrupt or impede the freedom of transit of petroleum." The signed IGA is then ratified by each national parliament to become effective as an international treaty with a status above domestic laws. Such a treaty mitigates the perception of political risk by investors, shippers, and lenders.[9] IGAs give the support of international law to the project's legal and commercial terms negotiated separately with each country. IGAs generally have long duration, recognizing the operational life of the project – sometimes more than 50 years.[10] The end of operations more usually results from the exhaustion of the petroleum reserves to be transported by the specific project than for technical reasons.

When an IGA deals with a landlocked export project, its preamble refers explicitly to the main international conventions protecting the rights of landlocked states and awarding specific rights of access to the sea for the export of their natural resources. That category of IGA also deals with the characterization of petroleum resources that are the subject matter of the export pipeline from the landlocked country, especially in terms of the location of the resources to be transported. The objective of a pipeline may either concern all of the resources of a landlocked state[11] or only those produced from one or more identified basins.

The rules of priority and conditions of access to the pipeline, depending on the origin of the petroleum extracted within the producing country, may be agreed to under an IGA.[12] The IGA may define special rights of access to the pipeline project, within the agreed priority rules, in favor of existing or future petroleum producers active in the transit country, when such rights are part of the negotiation. The potential to extend the pipeline to other landlocked countries may be included.

In principle, an IGA also addresses tax issues. In most cases, each country involved in the project decides the pipeline taxation of the section crossing its territory and under its jurisdiction, with the requirement that such a tax regime may not impede the freedom of transit. The IGA may clarify or amend any tax treaties in effect between the concerned states. The IGA deals also with the main principles for tax liabilities in each country.

When countries agree under an IGA that a transit fee is payable in the transit country, which is not obligatory, the IGA must stipulate the principles and conditions for imposing such a fee; the fee has to be negotiated so that it cannot be interpreted under international law as an impediment to the freedom of transit. Pipeline tariffs are not addressed in the IGA; they are subject to commercial transportation agreements designed under the applicable host government agreements or regulations and approved by the respective states.

5.2 Host government agreement

An IGA is supplemented by a series of agreements signed separately between each country involved in the project and its pipeline investors. Figure 9.1

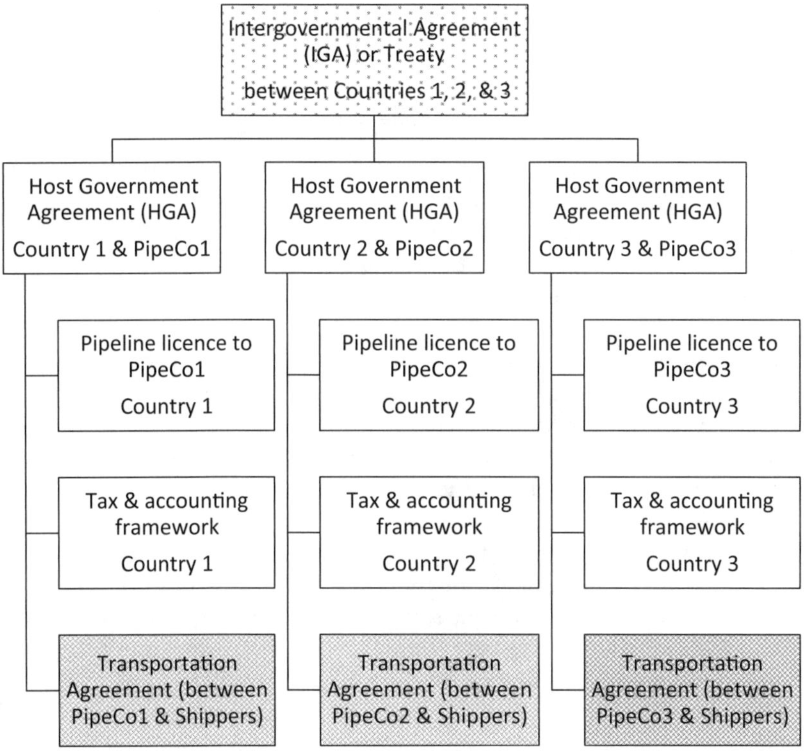

Figure 9.1 Schematic arrangements of cross-border pipeline projects

Source: the author.

Note: The example is illustrative only, assuming three countries involved in the project and one company per country. It shows the three levels of arrangements: the multi-country agreement, the separate country agreements, and the commercial transportation agreements.

illustrates an example of the main agreements required on the assumptions that a pipeline project crosses three countries (Country 1, 2, and 3), and the pipeline project involves three pipeline companies (PipeCo 1, 2, and 3), each one owning and operating the related country pipeline segment. The corporate structure has to be agreed on in each case.

The main agreement in each country is the one between the country and the pipeline company, often called a host government agreement (HGA). The agreement is governed by the IGA and the national laws of the country. It defines the rights and obligations of each party, as well as the tax regime applicable to the pipeline company and its shareholders in the country of activity; the tax regime is consistent with the general tax code, except for any justified tax exemptions or specific tax rules for determining the taxable income.

The HGA determines the conditions for obtaining the necessary "pipeline licence" and permits in the country, prior to beginning construction and operation. The conditions include the procedures for carrying out the relevant environmental and social impact assessments (ESIAs) and obtaining the right-of-way for laying the pipeline in the agreed corridor. It also specifies the rights and conditions of use by the pipeline company, its shareholders, and third parties.

5.3 Corporate structure of the transnational pipeline project

Several alternatives exist for establishing the structure of a special-purpose pipeline company or companies responsible for the integrated transportation project.[13] The first solution, which corresponds to the simplest corporate structure of the multi-country project, is to establish a single corporate entity or joint venture to design, finance, build, own, and operate the entire transnational pipeline system and register the entity or joint venture in each country. This option is rarely used; this should nevertheless be a preferred option since it would considerably simplify the number of arrangements required for implementation, accounting, taxation, and financing.

The second solution is to constitute a separate legal entity, for each country, that is responsible for all of these activities: this solution is more common. The third solution increases the complexity by creating distinct companies in each country, each one in charge of a specific activity, for example, one owns the segment and another operates[14] the transportation system in the country.

The business structure of a pipeline project may also be established as an unincorporated joint venture between the co-owners, where one entity is designated as the operating company. Each entity constituting a joint venture is, in general, individually liable to income taxation in the country of activity. This structure is commonly used in upstream exploration and production activities to facilitate the transfer and assignments of rights by each co-owner; it is rarely selected for pipeline projects.

The place of incorporation of each company participating in the project has to be decided, preferably in the country of its main activity, or in a country not related to the project. This decision is often made to benefit from a low taxation regime or a favorable network of double taxation treaties. It is generally not politically acceptable to all government participants, even for establishing the operator of the system; however, many cases of this scheme exist for transit pipelines. For example, the company established for the offshore and onshore Nord Stream project is based at Zug in Switzerland. The places of incorporation of the entities involved in the project are generally subject to the prior approval of the governments under the IGA or HGA. When one company only is established for a multi-country project, the selection of the place of its incorporation is sensitive, because each country involved is interested in being selected for incorporation. A compromise is needed, keeping in mind that whatever the place of incorporation, the company must be registered in each country of activity.

5.4 Transportation Agreements

The "transportation agreement" is a commercial contract entered into under the IGA and the HGAs, between the pipeline company (the "carrier") and each of the users (the "shippers") of the transportation system. It deals with the terms and conditions of transportation, including the committed volumes, quality, and specifications of the petroleum to be transported, and the determination and payment of tariffs and any other applicable fees. Often, the agreement covers only the transportation services for a country segment of the project, but other options may be applied for reducing the number of agreements to be entered into by a shipper using the entire pipeline. The transportation agreement has to be consistent with the relevant HGA and the other transportation agreements entered into for the other country segments of the project. Transportation agreements are signed for long periods and frequently contain a "ship or pay" commitment"; this commitment specifies the annual capacity of the pipeline reserved by the shipper and the obligation to pay even when the shipper does not fully use the reserved capacity during a year. Lenders often require such a commitment by shippers as a guarantee for financing the pipeline.

5.5 Other agreements

Depending on the pipeline project structure, shareholders and lenders may require other agreements for such issues as project management, operation, and financing before the pipeline company makes a final investment decision. In most cases, the period for negotiating the structure of the project, agreements, and financing is considerably longer than the construction period.

This timeline explains why a key objective for all interested parties should be the streamlining of the business structure and arrangements, ideally through a single pipeline company. The common objective should be limiting the number of entities created for the integrated project to prevent the multiplication of requisite agreements, reduce the total length of the agreements (in words), and facilitate their implementation. Harmonizing the fiscal and regulatory regimes applicable to the transnational pipeline and defining appropriate tax rules for allocating revenues and costs may limit the customary need for a pipeline company per country.

5.6 Transparency in agreements, tariffs, and revenues

Generally, the IGA agreement is public when it becomes a treaty. By contrast, many HGAs are not public, except when they are promulgated as law or for other reasons.[15]

Transportation agreements, which detail the tariff provisions, often contain a confidentiality clause preventing publication. Detailed information on pipeline tariff schemes is not easily available unless the country regulations so provide. There is, however, a trend to publish at least the government revenues obtained from the pipeline construction and operation through the payments of taxes, fees, and participation in the project. An excellent example is the Chad/Cameroon pipeline, for which the revenues collected by each host country, including the transit country, have been published annually.[16] As part of its policy of encouraging energy transit and nondiscrimination, the European Union is willing to promote voluntary transparency for all pipeline tariffs and transit fees, but it does not create any binding obligation to publish details.

6 Tax issues related to cross-border pipeline projects

6.1 Guiding principles for taxation of cross-border pipelines

Cross-border pipelines are international infrastructure for transporting petroleum across several countries from producers to consumers. This fact explains why their tax regime is not comparable to the taxation of extractive industries, where high rents may occur. An international pipeline should be liable to the customary taxation of any infrastructure project in a country. Sometimes, specific tax benefits or exemptions may be awarded, when fully justified, to encourage the project and reduce the tariff payable by the users.

The respective right of each country regarding taxation of international pipelines is often addressed in bilateral tax treaties in a manner similar to the treatment of transnational cables, as provided for under the Organisation for Economic Co-operation and Development (OECD) Model Tax Convention on Income and on Capital. In other cases, the IGA may specify tax provisions, applicable bilateral treaties, and any ad hoc bilateral treaty dealing with the pipeline project.[17] Differences between bilateral treaties may exist, particularly regarding whether a pipeline in a country, territory, or offshore is a permanent establishment for tax purposes; tax rules may differ between the submarine pipelines laid in the continental shelf or the high seas and on-shore lines. In all cases, each country must comply with the key principles of international law not to impede the transportation of petroleum when designing its pipeline fiscal regime within the framework of its general tax regime. This compliance includes not imposing unfair, non-transparent, or discriminatory charges on cross-border pipelines.

The principles for the determination and apportionment of the total revenues and costs between each of the countries and entities are treated in the IGA and approved by the governments. These principles should be consistent with the principles and guidelines of the OECD on application of the arm's length principle to transfer pricing within a legal entity or related entities. In some cases, priority is given to simplicity when determining appropriate allocation rules, for example, using a formulary apportionment for revenues and costs based on distance, volume shipped, or capacity,[18] when the characteristics of the project, facts, and circumstances justify doing so in a fair and equitable manner. The exchange of information between countries is always stipulated for two reasons: first, to mitigate the risks of taxable base erosion and profit shifting to third countries and second, to efficiently coordinate cost control and tax audits by the states.

6.2 Implementation of tax principles for cross-border pipelines

Whatever the business structure and place of incorporation, the pipeline company or entity is liable to taxation of each segment of the pipeline in the country of location, even when the entity is incorporated abroad. This liability applies because the ownership or operation of a pipeline usually creates a permanent establishment in the country of location or offshore.

Each country decides the tax regime on profits, capital gains, and property applicable to the pipeline within its boundaries, but it does so in conformity with relevant IGA provisions. The tax regime may vary from one country to another involved in the project, as long as the result is not considered an impediment to the freedom of transit or discriminatory. The tax regime for the pipeline company, its shareholders, personnel, subcontractors, and lenders should be generally applicable to any economic activity related to an infrastructure project. However, when provided for in the HGA, such a regime may contain tax incentives and/or exemptions, but only when the tax or pipeline legislation so provides.[19] Thus, the shipper using a cross-border pipeline is not liable for petroleum export duties and taxes.

Taxable income for the pipeline activity in the country is determined by the rules generally applicable in defining the assessable income of an entity subject to corporate income tax at the relevant rate, except for specific rules related to pipelines, such as the eligibility for deductions and for depreciation of capital costs. Any other taxes, including property tax on the assets, withholding taxes on dividends, interest, royalties, or service fees, as well as import duties on goods and the value-added tax (VAT), may apply under an individual country's laws, unless the legislation or the IGA/HGA provide for specific exemptions regarding the project. Transfers and assignments of rights by entities holding interests in the pipeline company may be subject to taxes on gains, unless an exemption is granted.[20] For some projects, tax incentives may be negotiated for minimizing taxes and indirectly transportation costs, but there is no such requirement under international law. The BTC project benefits from several exemptions reducing the effective tax rate.[21] Some submarine pipelines are subject to lower taxes.[22] The 2007 ECT model IGA contains in Part III on Taxes (Article 13.1 to 13.10) and in Non-discrimination (Article 14) a long series of tax exemptions and benefits regarding, among other things, the VAT, customs duties and other levies, and payment of interest or dividends. Some HGAs may provide a tax stabilization clause or a larger contract stabilization clause, implying compensation by the state to the pipeline company should the "economic equilibrium" of the agreement be modified by a "change in law." Any tax benefit, exemption, or holiday should only be granted after a detailed examination of the reasons to grant it; any stabilization clause should be properly drafted to ensure balance and to limit any potential impact on state revenues.

The allocation of the revenues and costs between the countries involved in the integrated project is of paramount importance to achieve a fair, reasonable, and transparent allocation of the revenues and costs generated by the project in each country – especially when the applicable income tax rates differ from one country to another. Unless a formulary apportionment rule is adopted, the "functionally separate entity" approach and OECD transfer pricing guidelines are generally followed, supplemented by any specific pipeline tax provisions in the IGA and HGA. The main principles retained for revenue and cost allocation are the following:

- Allocation of the revenues of the project, when they are not directly identified by country, in a fair and reasonable manner, and ensuring that the total of those revenues allocated to each country for a year in a proportionate share is equal to the overall revenues of the project;
- Allocation of the costs and expenses of the project under the same principle;
- Allocation of the costs and expenses not identified for each country by consistently applying methods generally accepted in the pipeline transportation industry.[23]

Even if a pipeline may be considered as "immovable property," debates on whether a transnational pipeline creates separate permanent establishments in each country, each one liable to national taxation, continue to exist.[24] The reason is that Article 5 of the OECD Model Double Tax Convention on Income and Capital and its Commentaries does not deal definitively with cables and pipelines on all these issues. For example, the tax treatment of submarine pipelines may be different. Accordingly, under specific bilateral treaties dealing with pipelines, Belgium, France, and Germany have granted to Norway the exclusive taxation rights on all the pipeline activities originating from that country, up to and including the land terminals at destination countries. In contrast, in similar cases, the United Kingdom may tax the profits and capital gains related to the segment in its territory, considering the segment to be a permanent establishment subject to taxation. Therefore, it is recommended that the IGA and the respective HGAs address in detail the tax treatment of the project segment per country. Possible tax risks include the following (Olsen, 2012):

> The OECD Commentaries are inconsistent in this regard, as they suggest in one paragraph that a pipeline might be of preparatory or auxiliary character according to Art. 5(4), but then in the next sentence suggest that a pipeline creates a PE or an immovable property without giving a clear guideline or recommendation, which creates uncertainty, inconsistent characterization, possible taxation in the wrong jurisdiction, disputes and even double taxation or less than a single taxation.[25]

The main source of revenues for the transit country, while relatively low in absolute amounts due to the nature and profits of transportation activities, is often derived from corporate income tax payments. Rare exceptions arise when a transit fee is payable or when the state is a participating investor in the project.

7 Determination of cross-border pipeline tariffs and transit fees

Cross-border pipeline tariffs are provided for under the transportation agreements, negotiated and entered into between the pipeline company and the shippers, unless the national law or regulations applied to the concerned pipeline segment, and the IGA or HGA impose rules for the determination of such tariffs. Often, the tariffs or transportation agreements are subject to the prior approval of the government, because such tariffs have an indirect economic impact on the upstream sector and the determination of the assessable income of the pipeline company. Moreover, the interests of the countries involved in a cross-border pipeline may not be aligned; an exporting country seeks lower tariffs, while the transit country prefers higher tariffs. In accordance with international law, the tariffs in all cases must remain reasonable so as not to be considered as impeding transit.

The transport tariff due by each shipper under the transportation agreement or regulations may consist of two components: the "pipeline tariff" itself, which is payable to the pipeline company; and the "transit fee," which is payable to the government when such a fee is agreed under the applicable IGA or HGA. When a transit fee is payable, its amount in most cases is significantly lower than the tariff; otherwise, such a payment could be considered an impediment to the freedom of transit. The expression "transit tariffs" is sometimes used; this can be misleading in the absence of a definition clarifying whether the amount is a pipeline tariff only or whether it includes a transit fee element.[26]

7.1 Differences between pipeline tariffs and transit fees

By definition, the pipeline tariff is designed to give the company the revenues required for (1) the recovery of all expenses incurred and paid during construction, financing, and operation and (2) an element of profit to achieve a post-tax return on capital during a given period; this profit should be seen as a fair remuneration on the invested capital, calculated as either an agreed rate of return on equity capital only (ROE) or a rate of return on investment (ROI), aggregating equity and debt.[27]

Several methodologies may be applied to comply with these two objectives assigned to tariffs.[28] Whatever methodology is followed, a tariff includes compensation for the actual taxes paid by the pipeline company under the applicable tax regime, such as the corporate tax on its profits and any other taxes or fees, to achieve the agreed post-tax rate of return for the period of determination. The higher are the taxes payable, then the higher the tariff charged is likely to be. The level of taxation of a transit pipeline project should remain reasonable so as not to impede transit, at a rate lower than the effective tax rate applied to an upstream project.

In contrast, a transit fee, when applicable, is a payment charged by the government of the transit country. It may be justified on different grounds that do not include the need to provide a pipeline company with a minimum return on investment. Its applicability and amount mainly depend on the category of export pipeline, the political context, and the negotiation.

- First, the transit fee may be justified as compensation for the costs directly borne by the transit country in relation to the pipeline project, such as those for the right of way on the pipeline corridor when the state directly provides access to land or those for the provision of safety and protection services to the project by the state or as compensation for any environmental disruption.
- Second, the transit fee may be justified in the IGA as compensation for any specific tax exemptions or benefits granted to the pipeline company, or, in rare cases, designed as an advance payment of corporate income tax or a minimum income tax, as with the BTC project.
- Third, the transit fee may result solely from negotiation without direct reference to any other principles when the countries involved in the project so agree.

Payment of a transit fee remains, however, relatively uncommon; no standard principles, rules, practices, or methodologies exist for its determination.

When the transit fee for a cross-border pipeline is negotiated, the main reason is often that the transit country desires to execute a natural monopoly power against the exporting country; by accepting a transit fee, the exporting country seeks to mitigate the risk to transit rights for its petroleum in future. In the absence of sufficiently clear international law, the initial negotiating strategy of the transit country is often to obtain a share in the additional benefits received by the exporting country as a result of using the route across that transit country instead of an alternative route that would be more costly to investors, shippers, and the exporting country.

In very specific cases only, a comparative cost/benefit analysis of several alternative routes may be conducted to assess the relative bargaining power of the transit country. The most prominent case in which such an approach can be justified is for a gas project in which the gas can be exported either via a pipeline crossing a third transit country or directly from the producing country to the purchasing country by ships as LNG. The major difference between the two alternatives, when both are economically justified, results from the value of the energy savings realized during the entire life of the transportation project because higher consumption of gas during processing and transportation under the LNG solution than with a pipeline. The sharing of such savings between the parties explains, for example, the level of the transit fee paid to Morocco or Tunisia, assessed as a percentage of the volume shipped (see Box 9.3).[29]

7.2 *Specific right of landlocked countries regarding transit fees*

Absolute rights for export and access to the sea are given to those countries by international law, and those rights should be the basis for the negotiation of an IGA with the transit country. Because of the intrinsic geographic disadvantage of a landlocked country and the possible monopoly power of a transit country, the approach of comparing alternate export route to justify the rationale and amount of a transit fee would be detrimental to this category of countries because there is often no cost-effective export alternative.

The purpose of a transit fee when countries agree to negotiate it should not be to allocate to the transit country any share in the upstream petroleum economic rent generated in the exporting landlocked country by the domestic production of petroleum.[30] The sharing of the upstream rent should be an issue between the sovereign producing country and its producers only. This is not to say that a transit fee has no impact on the producing country. Clearly, payments of pipeline tariffs and any transit fee, as any other cost legitimately borne by the producers, reduce the size of the producing country's upstream rent and revenues.

7.3 *Impact of international law on transit fee liability*

There is no international law imposing transit fees. Considering the key objective of the freedom of transit, international law limits the situations in which a transit fee is due. This principle is particularly clear for landlocked countries seeking access to the sea and for pipelines laid on continental shelf. Interpretation of Article 127 of UNCLOS stating that "traffic in transit shall not be subject to any customs duties or other charges *except charges devised for specific services*" [emphasis added] could be that a transit fee not justified as a compensation for costs of services is not allowed in the specific case of an export pipeline from a landlocked country. In contrast, for pipelines other than export lines from landlocked countries, offshore lines, and those subject to regional treaties dealing with the freedom of transit by pipelines, a transit fee may be negotiated – but only when so agreed.

Despite the intent of international law, some transit pipelines have been liable to payments of transit fees resulting from long negotiations, while many others are not liable. There is a need for international law to clarify the situations in which a transit fee is due and how it is determined, exempting from such payments the export pipelines originating in landlocked countries. Box 9.3 summarizes information on transit fees for each category of cross-border pipeline system. It highlights the fact that transit fees are not always applied, particularly for transit pipelines, and that when applicable, their amounts and rationale vary. It also shows that when transit fees are payable in relation to a landlocked export project, they are mainly designed as a compensation for services or for special tax benefits from the transit country.

Box 9.3 Examples of pipeline transit fees

Export pipelines from landlocked countries

- *Chad/Cameroon oil pipeline:* a fixed negotiated unit fee of US$0.41 per barrel [increased to US$1.40 per barrel in October 2013 following renegotiation] paid to Cameroon, in part for compensation of services. The transit fee is only one of the revenue sources derived by Cameroon. From 2004 to 2013, the country received total revenues amounting to US$410 million, or US$0.82 per barrel transported; of this amount, US$203 million (50 percent of the total revenues) was for transit fees, US$50 million (12 percent) was for corporate income tax, US$42 million (10 percent) was for other taxes and fees, and US$115 million (28 percent) was for dividends as a return on its equity in the pipeline company.

Source: Chad/Cameroon Development Project, Update N° 34 (update end 2013).

- *BTC oil pipeline via Georgia:* a unit fee, indexed, from US$0.125 per barrel the first year. The fee is payable as a compensation for services and tax benefits. It is treated as an advance payment for corporate income tax and other taxes, corresponding to a minimum amount of income tax. Each participant is responsible for its corporate income tax.
- *SCP gas pipeline via Georgia:* a unit fee, indexed, from US$2.5 per 1,000 m^3 (or 5 percent of the contractual gas price under the HGA) for the first year. The fee is payable in cash, with an option to take 5 percent of the gas transported in kind. The fee is payable as compensation for services and tax benefits. It corresponds in the HGA to a minimum tax and is treated as an advance payment for corporate income tax and other taxes.

- *Oil pipelines from South Sudan to Sudan:* a transit fee has become payable since the creation of South Sudan.
- *Gas pipeline from Bolivia to Brazil:* no transit fee.

Other cross-border pipelines projects, onshore or offshore

- *Gas intercontinental pipelines from Algeria to Europe:* a transit fee negotiated as a percentage between 5 and 7 percent of the quantities transported payable in kind or in cash to the concerned transit country, respectively Tunisia and Morocco; it is primarily based on the sharing of the cost benefit of the pipeline route versus the LNG alternative. In contrast, no transit fee applies to the latest offshore pipeline direct to Europe.
- *Gas pipeline from Timor-Leste to Australia*: no transit fee.
- WAGP project, offshore West Africa: no transit fee.
- *Oil and gas pipelines from Canada to the United States*: no transit fee.
- *Oil and gas pipelines from Norway to the United Kingdom or continental Europe*: no transit fee.
- *Gas and oil pipelines in European Union countries*: no transit fee.
- *Gas and oil pipelines from Russia to European Union countries:* the tariff may include the equivalent of a transit fee or special benefits to the transit country. However, no transit fees apply to the recent offshore Nord Stream and Blue Stream lines.

7.4 Main principles and methodologies for designing pipeline tariffs

The principles adopted for the determination of domestic pipeline tariffs generally apply to the design of international cross-border pipeline tariff schemes. The existence of a pipeline in a region may create a situation of natural monopoly, because the construction of additional pipelines to increase competition in transport is generally not economically justified. Both the pipeline tariffs and the terms and conditions governing transport system access by third parties are regulated and subject to the approval of a relevant authority that controls and monitors whether the rates are "fair and reasonable" to the shippers. Thus, the rate of return on the equity capital employed for the project, or alternatively, the rate of return on the investment (total funds outlaid), is often limited to the low rate generally applicable to utility companies. This rate is increased by a risk element, when appropriate, and is one of the most critical factors to be regulated or agreed to in the design of the tariffs.

The determination of the tariff has two main components. The first element is the recovery of all eligible costs, interest, taxes, and charges borne by the pipeline company; this recovery is made at cost and depends on the definition of the allowable costs and expenses. The second element is the return on investment or on equity generating the profit. Since the required return on equity is significantly higher than the effective post-tax interest on debt, pipelines are generally funded using a high debt-to-equity ratio – approximately three to one; the debt covers 75 percent of the investment, allowing a lower weighted average cost of capital (WACC) on the investment to minimize the unit tariffs. This approach requires prior approval of the financing plan and its terms, particularly to ensure that financing by debt is intended for minimizing the tariff and not for profit shifting. Another supplementary way to minimize the unit tariff is to increase the effective throughput of a transport system by having third parties use the transportation system when spare capacity is available. Such a third-party access (TPA) rule should provide for nondiscriminatory tariffs, encouraging third parties to use the existing pipeline instead of building another one.

There are a number of different detailed methodologies for determining pipeline unit tariffs used. The most traditional one is the cost of service (COS) methodology initially developed in Canada and the United States to regulate the tariffs of pipeline networks. The computation of the annual required COS amount follows two objectives:

- To recover all reasonable incurred costs and taxes, such as (1) the operating, maintenance, administrative, and general costs; (2) the depreciation of the investment, often on a straight-line basis over a relative long period (for example, 20 years);[31] and (3) the corporate income tax and other taxes and fees payable to the host country.
- To get a return on the remaining non-depreciated asset rate base, using the relevant WACC percentage on investment derived from the effective equity-debt structure.

The annual COS amount is then converted into a unit tariff constituted of two parts, as defined in the relevant regulations or transportation agreements:

- A "capacity reservation charge," representing fixed costs. The transportation agreements often provide for a ship-or-pay commitment; this refers to the reserved capacity contracted by the shipper, under which it undertakes to pay that charge even if the reserved capacity is not entirely used.
- A "commodity charge" per effective volume transported, representing the variable usage costs only.

The standard COS tariff model, initially designed for companies owning and operating multiple pipeline networks in a country and subject to regulated tariffs periodically revised, may be improved when dealing with a new pipeline transportation project funded under a specific financing plan by considering the following:

- First, by using the actual terms of the approved financing plan for interest, financial charges, and reimbursements of the principal for the determination of the tariffs, and by agreeing on the rate of return on equity for the investors in lieu of using the traditional WACC approach on the total asset base of the pipeline company.
- Second, by determining a fixed unit amount, subject to indexation, computed as a constant capital cost allowance (excluding variable costs) under a discounted cash flow (DCF) analysis, using as discount rate the targeted rate of return on equity.[32] The objective of this approach for a new project is to level the annual unit tariffs during the period for which the DCF analysis is performed. The traditional COS approach would lead to tariffs decreasing each year, relatively high in the first years, while the shippers prefer to pay a relatively constant unit tariff over time,[33] with lower tariffs in the first years and higher amounts later. In the same fashion, a unit tariff ceiling may be agreed to, with a carry-forward of costs not recovered during a year.
- Third, by differentiating or not differentiating the tariffs between the initial shippers having undertaken the ship-or-pay obligation for facilitating the financing of the project and the new third-party access users.

8 Conclusions

Cross-border pipelines are critical to increase international trade of oil and gas to meet growing world demand. They are also necessary to continue to develop petroleum resources in new basins. However, many specific legal, contractual, tax, and economic issues have to be addressed before concerned investors, states, and financial institutions decide on new transnational pipeline projects.

Not many transnational pipelines allow landlocked countries access to the sea. Those pipelines raise specific issues when the landlocked country and the pipeline company negotiate with transit countries, and these issues are imperfectly addressed by international law. In particular, international law should clarify the respective rights of landlocked and transit countries, and, if a transit fee is payable in special circumstances, should stipulate how it may be determined without impeding the freedom of transit. Such improvements would reduce the perceived risks by investors and lenders and shorten the negotiations of the multiple agreements needed for a new project.

For any pipeline system, the transport tariffs should remain fair, reasonable, transparent, and nondiscriminatory. Encouraging more shippers to use the system and funding such projects by an appropriate ratio of debt to minimize tariffs – provided that such leverage is not intended for profit-shifting reasons – are key objectives to reduce unit tariffs.

Another key objective to shorten the protracted negotiation period is a common effort to streamline the corporate, contractual, and tax structures of an integrated cross-border pipeline project and render loan agreements less complex. Finally, it is essential to clarify the tax regime applicable to each segment of a pipeline under the jurisdiction of a country or offshore, as well as the interaction of the regime with international taxation and tax treaties, to prevent tax uncertainties and profit shifting to third countries.

Notes

1 The author acknowledges helpful comments on an initial draft from Philip Daniel and Artur Świstak.

2 There are 44 landlocked countries, of which 32 are developing countries without direct access to the sea. Sixteen are located in Africa (including South Sudan), 19 are in Europe (including Central Asia), 7 are in Asia, and 2 are in South America.

3 The transit countries involved in the two first pipelines receive a transit fee in the form of a royalty. Under the third pipeline, no fee is applicable because the line is entirely offshore; this solution was rendered possible by the technological progress allowing a direct pipeline in ultra-deep waters over 2,000 meters.

4 As of January 2015, 47 countries have ratified the treaty. Russia provisionally applied the treaty until October 18, 2009, when it notified its withdrawal from the treaty. The treaty contains favorable provisions on investment protection, such as the "fair and equitable treatment" clause, frequently used by investors in investment disputes not related to energy transit issues.

5 Those principles are reinforced in the Energy Charter Draft Transit Protocol, which has been under negotiation since 2003 without success. Negotiation on a new draft Transit Protocol prepared in 2010 has been suspended. Its draft Article 10 deals with transit tariffs based only on "on operational and investment costs, including a reasonable rate of return," and excluding any transit fee.

6 In federal countries, such as Canada or the United States, special domestic rules may apply differently to intrastate pipelines and interstate pipelines, particularly with respect to the regulations of tariffs and approvals of activities.

7 The Energy Charter Secretariat published two versions of a model IGA and a model HGA (see Energy Charter Secretariat, 2003 and Energy Charter Secretariat, 2007). Both models were designed within the framework of the Energy Charter Treaty. The first one, in 2003, appears relatively close to the two BTC agreements signed in 1999 and 2001. The second version, in 2007, is more original and addresses in detail the pipeline tax issues, with a policy objective to (1) largely limit the tax liabilities for the project investors, subcontractors, and lenders and (2) provide for tax exemptions beyond the applicable general tax legislation. This special and favorable tax scheme under those models cannot be easily transposed in other environments.

8 In parallel with the negotiation of the IGA, a preliminary framework agreement may be entered into by all the parties, including the project investors, to deal with the principles applicable to the project.

9 Under the theory of "obsolescing bargain" applied by several authors to international pipelines, when the pipeline transportation system is built, the power of the country of transit becomes high due to the economics of a pipeline project characterized by large up-front capital costs and small operating costs. There is a possible risk that the transit country may decide to unilaterally change the terms agreed for the transit, as with pipelines in the Middle East or Ukraine for the gas transit from Russia to supply Europe. Landlocked countries have limited alternative routes in case of a conflict initiated by the transit country. Therefore, the policy is to mitigate these possible risks by obtaining

satisfactory protection rights under international law and by designing appropriate intergovernmental agreements to align the interests of concerned countries.

10 As an example, the IGA between Azerbaijan/Georgia/Turkey concerning the Baku/Tbilisi/Ceyhan pipeline project is entered into for the duration of the project, while the respective pipeline licenses under the HGAs are awarded for a primary term of 40 years, with two possible 10-year extensions for the continuation of the exploitation.

11 Such as for the Baku/Tbilisi/Ceyhan pipeline project, where the project is defined as the transportation of any petroleum extracted in Azerbaijan or abroad from the city of Baku to the city of Ceyhan.

12 Such as for the Chad/Cameroon pipeline project.

13 The following examples illustrate possible corporate structures of recent projects. For the Chad/Cameroon oil pipeline project, two separate related companies have been constituted for the ownership and operation, each one subject to a distinct HGA: COTCO under the law of Cameroon, responsible for the Cameroonian section, and TOTCO under the law of Chad, responsible for the Chadian section. Each company is liable to tax in the relevant country. For the Baku/Tbilisi/Ceyhan project across Azerbaijan/Georgia/Turkey, a single company, the BTC Company, was originally constituted for the entire project by 11 participants, mostly incorporated outside of the project countries. Each individual participant is a party to the HGAs and remains individually liable to profit tax under the HGA applicable in a country for the activities in that country. The main participant (BP, with an interest of 30.1 percent) is also the operator of the entire pipeline on behalf of the company. The international Nord Stream gas pipeline across the Baltic Sea between Russia and Germany, mostly laid down in the offshore economic exclusive zones of five countries, is owned and operated by a single company, Nord Stream AG, incorporated in Switzerland, a country not directly involved in the project, except by the location of the control room at Zug in Switzerland, where it has offices. The company is subject to a 10.1 percent income tax only.

14 The duties of an operating company are to manage, coordinate, and conduct the day-to-day activities on behalf of the pipeline company. By design, this operating company generates very low profits, its costs being reimbursed by the pipeline company.

15 The texts of the non-executed HGAs related to the BTC or SCP project have been published because they are annexed to the executed IGA made public. This process was followed to give more legal security to the investors and lenders, each country recognizing the provisions of the applicable HGAs so annexed.

16 See Chad/Cameroon Development Project, Project Update N° 34, year-end report 2013, available at www.essochad.com.

17 Thus, the Framework Agreement between the United Kingdom and Norway Concerning Cross-Boundary Petroleum Co-operation of 2005 contains tax provisions empowering each respective country to tax profits and capital gains related to offshore pipelines, under the obligation of not impeding petroleum transportation.

18 Such a simplified approach was selected for the WAGP transit pipeline project linking four countries offshore West Africa, where an ad hoc "agreed fiscal regime," defined at length under the IGA, applies to each of the four countries for determining the income tax payable by the single company responsible for the project. An apportionment percentage based on distance and reserved capacity in each state is defined to allocate revenues and costs.

19 Some HGAs, however, contain tax exemptions not provided for in the law, as well as a clause giving precedence to the HGA, which may raise an issue of enforceability when the HGA does not have the force of law.

20 In most countries, the taxation of capital gains related to the sale or transfer of an interest in a pipeline project is not clarified. For details on taxation of gains, see Burns, Le Leuch and Sunley (2016), Chapter 7 in this volume.

21 Thus, the HGAs related to the BTC project provide that the co-owners of the pipeline are only subject to a specific list of taxes (namely, corporate income tax at a fixed rate),

benefit from a list of tax exemptions (including on dividends, interest, withholding tax on foreign subcontractors, property, and transfers), and are exempt from other taxes. They also benefit from a tax stabilization clause.

22 According to a document of Nord Stream AG ("General Background Paper on Nord Stream," November 2013, available at www.nord-stream.com), the project is "subject to fewer taxes and transit fees as most of its route is . . . beyond territorial waters."

23 The IGA of the BTC project provides for the following: "any costs and expenses which are related to the entirety of the applicable Transportation System are to be allocated among the States in accordance with any reasonable allocation method which is selected by the Project Investor and applied consistently by the Project Investor from year to year, in a manner such that the aggregate amount of such costs and expenses reportable to the States for a calendar year is equal to the aggregate actual amount of such costs and expenses associated with the . . . Project for such calendar year. Any such allocation method selected by a Project Investor shall be based upon the relative length of the Transportation System located in the Territory of each of the States, the relative amount of capital expenditures or expected capital expenditures incurred or to be incurred with respect to the portion of the Transportation System located in the Territory of each of the States or any other method consistent with practices which are generally accepted in the international Petroleum transportation industry."

24 For example, the SCP's HGA states that the pipeline does not create a permanent establishment; however, the participants to the project are individually liable under the HGA to a special tax regime.

25 Olsen (2012), "Characterization and Taxation of Cross-Border Pipelines," pp. 119–120, IBFD.

26 For example, see Energy Charter Secretariat (2006). The use of the expression "transit tariffs" is explained by the purpose of the study willing to assess the full transit tariffs, which in some studied countries includes a transit fee not disaggregated under the study.

27 An ROE is always greater than an ROI, the latter determined on the basis of a weighted average capital cost (WACC) combining the respective rates for equity and debt, or another methodology.

28 For further discussion on tariff design, see Bell and Chauvin (2016), Chapter 8 in this volume.

29 The difference in internal energy consumption between the two technical alternatives may reach 10 percent, depending on the distance. The last pipeline from Algeria to Europe is a direct offshore pipeline, eliminating any transit fee.

30 In the same fashion, when a transit fee is payable, the unit amount is often escalated using an inflation index and not an index based on the variations of oil or gas prices.

31 The depreciation rules for tariff determination are often different from those that apply to tax depreciation (which may provide for a shorter depreciation period) or to company financial reporting.

32 By an iterative process, the discounted cash flow analysis performed over a given period allows the determination of the constant capital cost allowance necessary to grant to the investors the agreed after-tax rate of return on equity, after taking into account the assumed throughput as well as the estimated investment, financing plan, equity, and taxes and fees. Variable costs are then added to the constant allowance to obtain the tariff.

33 Subject, however, to an indexation formula to reflect inflation.

References

Energy Charter Secretariat. (2003), *Model Intergovernmental and Host Government Agreement for Cross-Border Pipelines*, 1st edition (Brussels: The Energy Charter Secretariat).

Energy Charter Secretariat. (2006), "Gas Transit Tariffs in Selected Energy Charter Treaty Countries," Study prepared by the Directorate for Trade, Transit, and Relations with Non-Signatories of the Energy Charter Secretariat. Brussels: The Energy Charter Secretariat.

Energy Charter Secretariat. (2007), *Model Intergovernmental and Host Government Agreement for Cross-Border Pipelines*, 2nd edition (Brussels: The Energy Charter Secretariat).

Olsen, Knut. (2012), *Characterisation and Taxation of Cross-Border Pipelines* (Amsterdam: IBFD).

Stevens, Paul. (2009), *Transit Troubles: Pipelines as a Source of Conflict*. A Chatham House Report (London: Royal Institute of International Affairs).

Stevens, Paul, Robert Bacon and Ralf Dickel. (2003), "Cross-Border Oil and Gas Pipelines: Problems and Prospects," ESMAP Report, World Bank and United Nations Development Programme.

Vinogradov, Sergei. (2001), "Cross-Border Oil and Gas Pipelines: International Legal and Regulatory Regimes," Research paper prepared for the Association of International Petroleum Negotiators, University of Dundee, Scotland, United Kingdom.

10 The design of joint development zone treaties and international unitization agreements

Peter Cameron

1 Introduction

In this chapter, I examine two ways in which states can work together and develop hydrocarbons resources to their mutual benefit. The opportunities for peaceful exercise by coastal states of sovereign powers over very extensive maritime spaces have never been greater, but the combination of political will and economic aspiration still presents significant challenges. It is in this setting that there is scope for using mechanisms such as joint development zones (JDZs) and international unitization agreements (IUA). These legal instruments have assumed an important role in the past few decades as states have sought to interpret and implement the evolving international law of the sea to their advantage.[1]

Both instruments are a response to distinct situations in which cooperative development of natural resources by states is problematic, whether the resources are located off shore or on land. The first of these has rightly attracted considerable attention from scholars and commentators: how to secure cooperative management of hydrocarbon resources by sovereign states in areas that are subject to overlapping claims. The reasons for this interest are easy to glean from the fact that there are several dozen maritime delimitation disputes going on around the world. A further group of disputes apply to inland lakes or seas such as the Caspian Sea and tracts of land that cross present national borders. The potential for armed conflict arising from such disputes is illustrated by the recent conflicts in the South and East China Seas. However, the discovery of oil and gas is a great incentive to states to negotiate a solution, even if it is only on a provisional basis so as to leave the disputed boundary out of the provisional settlement in order to allow development to commence.[2] With an ongoing dispute it is very hard to attract serious, reputable investors. Should an agreement on a JDZ be reached in such circumstances, it would not only resolve this impasse but at the same time would represent a victory of economics over politics.

The second situation in which cooperative development becomes problematic is when the resource crosses or is believed to cross *established* borders and states have to agree on the next steps if exploration or development is to take place. While this situation, usually formalized as an IUA, lacks the element of an inter-state dispute over borders, many other challenges are likely to face the parties: for example, what kind of cooperative IUA structure is appropriate; how do the parties, not only states but also any international or national oil and gas companies already involved or having an interest, reach agreement on sharing the deposit, and what action can be taken by one state if the other(s) lacks a similar enthusiasm for resource development?

Much of the writing on the subject of cooperative development is characterized by one or both of two features: first, there is a preoccupation with the rules of international law and the framework they provide to states to develop their resources; second, there is an interest in describing and reviewing the various legal structures which states design for cooperative development. Although these concerns have resulted in valuable and pioneering work, the notion is rarely present in this body of writing that the legal frameworks themselves point to wider problems that make cooperative development difficult. For example, in many states there is a lack of institutional capacity to implement complex legal structures. There may also be a lack of confidence in certain kinds of legal arrangements, particularly ones that appear to entrust significant powers to international energy companies. In such situations, formal legal structures may be preferred on the grounds of transparency even though they offer challenges in operational terms against those that might offer a pragmatic, ad hoc and informal approach. The diversity of interests among states is also very wide, with the result that natural resource development gives rise to diverging policies about the rate and manner of development. Legal frameworks have to make allowances for reaching agreement among states with sometimes radically different policies on such matters; these are after all policies that are a response to distinct constellations of national priorities, pressures and interests.

This chapter argues that since international law has developed substantially in this area, it offers states a wide latitude for their choice of instrument in addressing cross-border development. However, this freedom to shape options to particular circumstances has to be set against policy constraints at the national level; these in turn may encourage the adoption of formal (i.e., legal) responses even where flexible ones are available and more appropriate. In its approach, the chapter discusses the structural design of JDZs and IUAs while not discussing tax issues inherent to their design.

2 The basis for any state action

While boundaries of states on land generate disputes and sometimes lead to armed conflict, for the most part such boundaries are securely established. Relative to maritime areas at least, they present a sharp contrast to the very recent efforts to delimit jurisdiction over what was once treated as common space. Disagreements over such boundaries are common. This is where the role of international law could prove significant and helpful.

Any action by a sovereign state to reach agreement with a neighbor or with neighboring states needs to take as its starting point an analysis of the relevant international law relating to its maritime areas. The framework set out by successive conventions on the law of the sea contains several key principles. The most recent and most influential of these is the United Nations Law of the Sea Convention (UNCLOS), which replaces four earlier treaties and to some extent codifies customary international law on this subject.[3] Under Article 83(1) of UNCLOS, states are required to cooperate toward reaching agreement regarding their delimitation disputes. Under Article 83(3) they are also required to make every effort to enter into practical *provisional* arrangements pending agreement on delimitation of the Exclusive Economic Zone (EEZ) or Continental Shelf. Moreover, the same provision requires states not to jeopardize or hamper the negotiation of a final agreement over the disputed area. The exact nature of the provisional arrangements envisaged under Article 83(3) is not specified in the Convention. It simply imposes a general obligation to cooperate when a deposit is found to cross boundary lines which are already delimited or which are situated in an area that is subject to overlapping claims. The substantive content of such a general requirement to cooperate is likely to be highly uncertain. One scholar notes that "the negotiating governments are not constrained, either by international law or by deadlines, to reach agreement".[4]

From the foregoing the conclusion is that while the parties appear to be required by international law to notify, inform and consult other interested states and to negotiate with them in good faith, there is no duty following from this to reach a specific type of agreement, such as one establishing a JDZ and related institutions. The existence of procedural rules requiring cooperation is distinct from a requirement that the shared petroleum deposit be developed jointly.

If one were to refer to good practice in cooperation between states on these issues, it quickly becomes clear that there are two principal ways of proceeding with a proposal for a collaborative relationship, the JDZ and the unitized structure. The question then arises of what the key differences are. For the JDZ, the area over which it applies is a stand-alone one, agreed between or among the parties and comprehensive in its scope. It transfers operational management of petroleum resources to an international body. The joint right and risk structure is shared between nation states and not companies. Allocation of production between states is a result of prior knowledge of geology and negotiation power (traditionally 50–50).

By contrast, unitization of a structure arises when the holders of separate licenses or contracts decide to develop jointly a geological structure that lies under several of these grants of rights. When the deposit straddles international boundaries, an IUA may result from discussions among the respective governments. Under this government-to-government agreement, there will be a commercial agreement on unitization involving the private or state companies responsible for petroleum operations.[5]

The key difference between the JDZ and a unitized structure lies in that the boundary between states is usually settled in a unitized development, whereas a JDZ circumvents an unsettled boundary issue. In other words, the structure it adopts is self-consciously a *transitional* device. There are other differences: the JDZ carries the risk of political interference and a duplication of state oversight and control; it is a form of governance through a treaty between states; in the JDZ, the key features are a legally binding 'constitution'; a distinct managerial structure and a dedicated support staff or administration; in a unit which is the subject of an IUA, allocation of jurisdiction is made to existing institutions, rather than to a newly established one where material and procedural rules will govern supervised conduct.

Neither instrument is, strictly speaking, entirely new; in various forms each has been used for a very long time. This chapter compares and contrasts the design of these two different forms of cooperative development when applied to disputed areas. It pays particular attention to their use in West Africa and the Pacific and North Sea regions. Some conclusions will then be drawn about the way forward for the many states that have these problems on their policy agendas.

The sheer diversity of geological, political and historical circumstances among states means that whatever the form of cooperative agreement is chosen, differences will result. There can be no such thing as a 'one size fits all' solution for cooperation if that is the goal being sought. Even with apparently 'standard' forms like a JDZ or unitization, adaptation is almost inevitable, and the final outcome will depend upon choice and negotiation by the states concerned. This is much more than a challenge to classification. It means that if an international arbitral tribunal or court were to attempt to mandate a form of joint development on states in a case before it, it would face an impossible task.

3 The JDZ: overview

Although more than two dozen legal arrangements have been concluded for joint development of hydrocarbons and other resources, it is striking how diverse the agreements and structures have been to date.[6] There has been no uniformity of approach, with some permitting the parties to adopt separate forms of licensing and others not even specifying precisely what the zone or area for cooperation is. For a JDZ as understood here (where some effort is made to institutionalize cooperation), it is useful to distinguish three basic models (see Table 10.1). Model 1 gives the leading role to a single party: one state with oil and gas expertise manages the development of the JDZ, with the other state's participation confined to revenue sharing according to a pre-agreed formula and monitoring. The early joint development arrangements adopted by Bahrain and Saudi Arabia (1958), Abu Dhabi and Qatar (1969) and Sharjah and Iran (1971) are examples of this. Model 2 develops a structure on a joint party axis: the states retain authority over the JDZ and delegate minimal or no power to the joint authority, or together they may elect to out-source its management to a third party, usually an expert/consultant. An example of this is the Malaysia–Vietnam arrangement for a joint party regime under which each state nominated its national oil companies (NOCs) to undertake hydrocarbons

Table 10.1 Joint development arrangements – sample of models

Countries	*Year*	*Model*
Bahrain–Saudi Arabia	1958	1
Abu Dhabi–Qatar	1969	1
Sharjah–Iran	1971	1
Sudan–Saudi Arabia	1974	2
Japan–South Korea	1974	2
Malaysia–Thailand	1979	2
North–South Yemen	1988	2
Guinea Bissau–Senegal	1993/1995	2
Nigeria–São Tomé e Príncipe	2001	3
Timor-Leste–Australia	2002	3

activity in the 'defined area'.[7] Model 3 is highly complex and formal. A strong joint authority with licensing and regulatory powers is charged with the development of the JDZ. It has legal personality and can therefore enter into binding contracts with prospective contractors on behalf of the states concerned. This involves some surrender of sovereignty over the zone of cooperation to a supranational entity and is therefore a matter of some sensitivity. Examples of this include the Timor-Leste–Australia JDZ (known as the Joint Petroleum Development Area or JPDA) and the Nigeria–São Tomé e Príncipe JDZ (the former is examined in Daniel, Veung and Watson, Chapter 11 of this book; the latter is described in what follows).

Common elements in JDZ frameworks do exist of course. Typically, two states will agree to share resource revenues and costs for a specified period of time (probably in the region of 30 to 50 years). There will be varying degrees of form and complexity, but all will require party agreement. Examples are: Saudi Arabia–Bahrain JDZ (1958) defined in a single article and the Australia–Indonesia Timor Gap JDZ (1989) with 34 articles and four extensive annexes. Other common provisions include delimitation of the JDZ; provision for the sovereign and jurisdictional status of the JDZ; identification of the authorizing entity; taxation; reconciliation of municipal law in both states; treatment of 'common deposits' extending beyond the JDZ area; a dispute settlement mechanism; and health, safety and environmental regulation.

4 The JDZ: Nigeria–São Tomé e Príncipe as a case study

Many years ago, in anticipation of an emerging trend in the international law of the sea and particularly the idea that coastal states would be permitted to claim a 200-nautical-mile EEZ,[8] Nigeria passed an EEZ Law in 1978 and modified it in 1998 by Decree No 41. The Democratic Republic of São Tomé e Príncipe ratified its Official Maritime Claims Law in 1998. Since that time, the EEZ concept has become established as a defined feature of UNCLOS. Cooperation between these two states was stimulated by the fact that there was considerable overlap between the territorial claims of each country based on the law of the sea; the states merely had to decide how to proceed, and ultimately they agreed to establish a JDZ.

The outcome was far from certain at the outset of negotiations.[9] There were important differences between the two states. Although neighbors, each one had a very different colonial history, and neither shared the same dominant language. Nigeria had decades of involvement in the oil and gas industry and is far larger in size than its tiny neighbor. This asymmetry did not affect its sovereignty under international law but could hardly be ignored by its smaller neighbor and partner. Moreover, São Tomé e Príncipe had also awarded acreage to companies prior to the formation of the JDZ, so the issue of pre-existing interests of foreign companies was on the table. What such acreage would yield was shrouded in uncertainty too: seismic coverage was limited. Another factor that underlines the differences is that while for São Tomé e Príncipe this was its first experience with any form of maritime boundary dispute settlement, Nigeria had already tested the formal process of adjudication by referring a disputed boundary with Cameroon to the International Court of Justice in The Hague and had tested unitization with Equatorial Guinea in the Ekanga/Zafiro fields. The confidence with which Nigeria approached such negotiations can be imagined. Its large land mass and population of 120 million had given it the opportunity to manage boundary issues before even if they were largely on land and internal in character. As a small island nation, São Tomé e Príncipe had little experience of boundary issues to date. The risk of being overwhelmed by Nigeria was therefore significant.

In responding to this context, it appears that political will to reach agreement existed at the highest level and was crucial to achieving the resulting JDZ in line with Article 74(3) of UNCLOS. At the same time it was clear to all that the JDZ was to be a temporary solution which did not settle the underlying claims to maritime space by the states. To address the imbalance referred to earlier and improve São Tomé e Príncipe's leverage in the relationship, the treaty scope was extended to include fisheries as well as oil and gas resources, perfectly compatible with the UN Law of the Sea Convention but unique in the world's JDZ treaty arrangements. Another key element was the management of popular expectations. In São Tomé e Príncipe in particular, these were high despite the time required to develop the resources; the first licensing round in 2003 included a signature bonus element which generated benefits at a very early stage. So far, around US$350 million has been received in signature bonuses and concession rentals (Yabo, 2013).

The JDZ was established by treaty on February 21, 2001, after brisk but thorough negotiations. It is located in deep offshore waters in the Gulf of Guinea, with an overall size of approximately 35,000 sq km, lying 150 km south of the coast of Nigeria and 90 km west of São Tomé e Príncipe, in water depths from 1,500 m in the north to more than 4,000 m in the southwest. The legal regime comprised a package of instruments such as a treaty; petroleum regulations; tax regulations; environmental regulations; a development contract (production sharing contract or PSC) and a choice of law for 'unresolved matters'. The treaty covers a 45 year period and allocates benefits and obligations (Nigeria 60%; São Tomé e Príncipe 40%). A governance structure is set up, comprising a Joint Ministerial Council to exercise overall political responsibility and supervise the Joint Development Authority (JDA), charged with managing the JDZ on behalf of the two states. Both bodies are required to reach decisions on a consensual basis. Notably, the treaty contains transparency provisions supplemented by a Joint Declaration on Transparency and Governance signed by the heads of state and governments. The JDZ is also a member of the Extractive Industries Transparency Initiative. Although the treaty was executed in both English and Portuguese, the official language of the JDZ is English.

The first licensing round was held in 2003; the first block was awarded in April 2004; and a second round was held in November 2004, leading to the award of 6 out of the 11 blocks so far delineated. The first PSC was signed in February 2005, and five had been concluded by 2013. By any comparable JDZ standard, this is a rapid process.

Experience with the Nigeria–São Tomé e Príncipe JDZ already points to some wider lessons about this form of cooperation. The idea that a legal regime, however comprehensive, can provide rules for every contingency in the life of a JDZ is illusory. Modifications to the existing regime will be required to deal with a variety of problems that arise in the implementation of the JDZ treaty. For example, the regulations will require some further development, not least as new problems arise which may be unique to the JDZ context. Moreover, the JDZ institutional structure does not replicate the institutions of a state. It will have to interact with existing national institutions and with legal competences that remain rooted in the states themselves. Indeed, support from the respective state departments and agencies, such as tax authorities, police, customs and immigration will be an almost continuous feature of their operation. In this case, the treaty prescribed joint security and policing in Article 42, but this was difficult since it touched upon important issues of sovereignty. Yet the need for such action has been clear due to poaching and illegal fishing in the JDZ, for example. Powers vested in the respective states can have a negative impact on the JDZ institutions, such as state decisions making frequent changes in the JDZ council and authority leading to a lack of continuity in political leadership. Unexpected demands on funding have also put strain on the operation of joint structures: contrary to agreements on budgeting, operational issues have arisen such as cost overruns and delays at times when it became difficult and expensive to secure drilling rigs to operate in the JDZ water depths at a peak stage in drilling activity. Prior to oil and gas production, there were also issues relating to the funding of the joint institutions themselves.

The influence of national policies on the JDZ's operational functioning can be seen in two areas that have emerged as key planks of resource development policy: local content and the maximization of wider impacts in the local economy such as infrastructure provision. In the former area the general aim is to promote employment for local people and to support local business in providing goods and services to the resource project. In the Nigeria–São Tomé e Príncipe JDZ, local content was promoted by awarding small percentages during the bid rounds to qualified domestic firms to build up their capacity in hydrocarbons operations; training and supply of goods and services were also encouraged. However, the scope of local content measures was limited in São Tomé e Príncipe's case by the absence of skilled oil and gas staff since the country was new to the oil and gas business. The JDZ itself contributed to training new personnel for the national structures by supporting the recruitment of former and serving JDZ staff to serve in ministries and presidential advisory roles in each of the states. With respect to critical infrastructure and social amenities, special projects have been carried out in communities by operating companies in both of the JDZ states, with a view to sharing the benefits more widely. More than 61 projects have been initiated in different parts of the two states (Yabo, 2013).

In another respect, national interest rather than policy has had a role in JDZ organization. Inevitably, it has been necessary to balance the mix of employees from each state and to manage the social and cultural diversity among staff in the JDA. These practical concerns have had the side effect of creating delays in decision making due to the need for referrals to higher or outside authorities. There is a contrast here with the kind of rapid response typically found in many international oil and gas operating companies when faced with a problem. The structure itself tends toward a bureaucratic approach.

These critical remarks on the Nigeria–São Tomé e Príncipe JDZ should not detract from the undoubted successes it has had in its first decade. Investment levels in oil and gas operations have reached US$400 million. If oil and gas had been discovered in greater amounts, this figure is likely to have been much higher. This underlines a fact of life for any JDZ structure: an assessment of its value will ultimately turn on the commercial prospects of its geology. If the geology disappoints, then no matter how high the quality of design and operation, investment and its impacts will be modest. In this case, the two states' commitment to the JDZ treaty over a 45-year period means that sustained exploration efforts are likely to be encouraged and more discoveries are possible, an outcome that could not be expected without their commitment to a cooperative approach. Whether it can be seen as a model is harder to argue. It remains the only JDZ of its kind in Africa, and indeed it is one of the few functional JDZs in the world.

5 Unitization

The technique called unitization has long been used within a single state when a field straddles two concession areas. The purposes of unitization are to permit economically efficient development of the entire field as a unit by the licensees, sharing costs and production, to avoid wasteful duplication of effort and competition on two sides of the boundary and protect the respective, or in legal terms 'correlative', rights of the parties. Its practice has generated a body of literature in its own right.[10] In cases where a field straddles an international boundary or boundaries, a state-to-state unitization agreement is necessary – an IUA. Treaties between states on unitization tend to follow the approach adopted in domestic unitization. This is a less complex approach to joint development than a JDZ and is best understood as a technique that may be applied in many contexts rather than a structure in a single area in the way that a JDZ is. The central feature and key difference with joint development is that the boundary between the states on which the geological formation has been found has already been delineated by the states themselves. Hence there are parallels between on-land unitization within a single state and unitization off shore between states. Even so, provisions do exist for JDZs to unitize with other, non-JDZ concession areas or within a JDZ itself. There is provision for this in for example the Nigeria–São Tomé e Príncipe Treaty (Article 30).

The design of an IUA is a process facilitated by the existence of a great deal of government–industry practice within national borders. Since matters of detail about operations will often be left to the industry in a commercial agreement, the number of provisions required in an IUA between governments can be reduced. States may conclude a short treaty in which they provide for certain companies to enter into a cross-border unitization agreement (as is common in the North Sea), or they may choose to conclude a unitization agreement themselves. An example of the latter is the agreement between Trinidad and Tobago and Venezuela for the Loran-Manatee Field made in 2010.[11] Typical elements in such IUAs are the definition of a field and/or unit area to which the agreement will apply; the applicable laws; the roles of the respective governments; rules on sharing of petroleum produced and associated costs; and determination of the way in which the commercial exploitation of the unit area is to be undertaken. Prior to the conclusion of any such agreement it is necessary to obtain some idea of the reserve base and make a determination of the total reserves in place within the area. The agreement itself will provide for the apportionment of production from the unit area but may also provide for redetermination at a later date. This mechanism is designed to allow a party or parties to call for a readjustment of shares as knowledge of the geological base increases and can take into account shifts in the deposit itself as a result of drilling activity.

6 Unitization in practice

Several regions provide examples of international unitization. The oldest – at least outside of the Middle East on-land unitizations – are in the North Sea. Asia and Latin America can also provide examples. One such example is the Sunrise International Unitization Agreement in the Timor Sea area in South-East Asia. Several of these will be examined in what follows.

6.1 Norway and the United Kingdom

The cooperative approach of Norway and the UK to the development of common offshore petroleum deposits was path breaking in the 1970s. It initiated a body of literature that has encouraged the idea that inter-state cooperation in the development of a common resource deposit is an emerging rule of customary international law. Since that time, the view has gained ground among states that economic pragmatism should take precedence over political differences. In retrospect, however, the early treaty instruments adopted in the North Sea to promote cross-border unit development appear rather clumsy, overly formal in a legal sense and, as a result of the lengthy times required to negotiate them, likely to undermine the very pragmatism that they were designed to encourage.

For almost 30 years, the approach adopted by the governments of Norway and the UK to the development of a shared petroleum deposit has been to conclude a customized treaty for each new cross-border field. When the licensee companies discovered a petroleum deposit that was thought to extend across a national boundary, negotiations commenced between the governments on joint development of the resource. This resulted in the conclusion of an inter-governmental agreement (IGA). It became the typical legal response by the North Sea states when deposits were found to straddle the international boundaries between, for example, Norway and the UK, the Netherlands and the UK and Norway and Denmark. In each case, the aim of the negotiations was to conclude an international treaty between the two governments and to let the licensee companies reach a separate unitization agreement between themselves, subject to the approval of the respective governments. This pattern began in the North Sea with the negotiation of a treaty for the Frigg gas field in the 1970s and subsequently became familiar in other parts of the world.[12]

The inter-governmental negotiations took place respecting the existing international maritime delimitation agreements, such as the one between Norway and the UK concluded on March 10, 1965.[13] They addressed specific matters in relation to a particular field, on the basis of established international borders: a point of difference between this context and that of many other cross-border disputes around the world. In addition, such agreements usually contained a common 'unity of deposit' clause. Essentially, this stated that, in the event of a single petroleum reservoir extending across the dividing line and being exploitable "wholly or in part" from the other side, "the two States are obliged, in consultation with the licensees, if any, to seek to reach agreement as to the manner in which the petroleum reservoir shall be most effectively exploited and the manner in which the proceeds deriving therefrom shall be apportioned".

The wording of this clause is significant. The trigger for cooperation in developing the reservoir is not the mere existence of a cross-border deposit but rather the technical exploitability of one part from the other side of the dividing line. It does not require the states to develop any shared resource as a unit. Indeed, "the only firm condition imposed is apparently the condition that the proceeds of exploitation should be shared" (Taverne, 1994, p. 155). Such a narrow focus has to be understood in the context in which it was negotiated (even though such clauses can still be found today, as in Australia and New Zealand). Since that time, governments have been much more sensitive to the need to develop the common deposit in a sustainable manner: to ensure maximum recovery of the deposit and to ensure from the outset that the companies entrusted with the task are technically and financially qualified to do so.

Between 1975 and 1992 four bilateral treaties were concluded between Norway and the UK and the Netherlands and the UK[14] on specific cross-border unitizations. Although there was a large measure of standardization in the four agreements, there were also some differences among them. The agreements for Statfjord, Murchison and Markham fields all followed the pattern set by the Frigg Agreement of 1976. They start from the boundary delimitation established in the respective Norwegian–UK and Netherlands–UK Agreements of 1965[15] and the undertaking in those agreements by both governments that if a petroleum field crossed the dividing line and was exploitable from either side, the governments would seek to reach agreement on how the field could be most effectively exploited and how the reserves would be apportioned. In the Statfjord and Murchison Agreements between Norway and the UK, for example, both signed on the same day in Oslo in 1979, there were also provisions which looked to the future when greater geological understanding of the deposit might reveal that the initial division was unfair. Provisions for a subsequent review (or 'redetermination' as it is known in the petroleum industry) and reapportionment of reserves among the parties addressed this in a manner that was more detailed than in the Frigg Agreement. There were also provisions that required installations within 500 meters of the dividing line to be jointly determined by both governments, provisional apportionment was no longer to begin at 50–50, there was to be free movement between installations, greater freedom for inspectors in inspecting installations, the implementation of a program for exploitation, an improved measuring system and the introduction of certified production records of petroleum and emergency provisions. In the Murchison Agreement there were only minor changes: a government's right to call a redetermination schedule was included, as was room for a government request in reassessment of the field, more precise measures for pollution prevention were included and greater clarity over jurisdiction of installations positioned on either side of the maritime boundary. Further modifications were made in the treaty applied to the Markham field. It distinguished for example between redeterminations made at the request of the licensees and those initiated by one of the governments.[16] While these differences can be seen as incremental improvements in the governments' approach to the problem, they also created a patchwork, in which jurisdictional and regulatory responsibilities differed from one treaty to the next, especially when cross-border pipelines were involved.[17]

Each of these treaties related to an identified geological structure that crossed the dividing line and could be exploited from either side. The respective governments had already granted exploration and production licenses over part of the area under well-established and broadly similar regulatory regimes. The starting point for the governments and their licensees was not therefore very different from a familiar situation in the petroleum industry, where, within a single jurisdiction, licensees discover a petroleum bearing structure which crosses a border line between one license area and another. In that situation, unitization is normally a requirement of the regulatory regime,[18] and the key issue is an apportionment of the reserves between one licensed area and another. Apportionment in that context is essentially a technical matter determined by reports provided by reservoir engineers chosen by agreement to exercise an objective judgment. The North Sea Treaties established an analogous framework in the cross-border context. Apportionment of the reserves is again the key issue. When agreed by the two governments, it determines the share of the licensees on either side of the border and the base from which the tax take of the two governments is to be calculated. Otherwise, these treaties deal with a range of regulatory matters that need to be addressed in the context of joint operations, which are in fact similar to matters that would need to be dealt with under a separate jurisdiction if there were no cross-border context.

The driver behind cooperation was and remains a clear economic self-interest. Moreover, alongside the establishment of cooperative arrangements, both governments were scrupulous in preserving what they considered to be their respective sovereign rights, as is clear from the statement of principle which concludes the substantive provisions in the Norway–UK Agreement on the Frigg gas field:

> (1) Nothing in this Agreement shall be interpreted as affecting the jurisdiction which each State has under international law over the Continental Shelf which appertains to it. In particular, installations located on the Continental Shelf appertaining to the United Kingdom shall be under the jurisdiction of the United Kingdom, and installations located under the Continental Shelf appertaining to the Kingdom of Norway shall be under the jurisdiction of the Kingdom of Norway. (2) Nor shall anything in this Agreement be interpreted as prejudicing or restricting the laws of either State or the Exercise of jurisdiction by their Courts, in conformity with international law.[19]

This wording has appeared *mutatis mutandis* in every agreement made since.

6.2 Timor Sea

The IUA that was concluded between Australia and the Democratic Republic of Timor-Leste was unusual in being closely linked to the other mode of cooperative arrangement, the **joint petroleum development authority** (JPDA), a form of JDZ, which had established a three-tiered administrative structure. Its aim was to permit the exploitation of the Sunrise and Troubadour oil and gas fields, known together as the Greater Sunrise field. These fields straddled the border between the JPDA set up by the Timor Sea Treaty (2002) and the territorial waters of Australia, which had been delimited several years before in the Timor Gap Treaty between Australia and Indonesia (which claimed Timor as part of its territory at the time). Within that JPDA there had already been a substantial gas discovery in the Bayu–Undan field and oil and gas discoveries in the Elang fields.[20]

7 The pragmatic use of law: frameworks

In recent years a number of states have experimented with a new form of legal instrument to address the need for cooperation in the event of cross-border deposits being in prospect or already discovered. This is the framework approach. It has been applied to contexts in which there is already agreement on the boundary between the states concerned. Examples are the Framework Agreement on Petroleum Co-operation between UK and Norway (2005) (hereinafter 'Framework Agreement'); the agreement between Canada and France relating to the Exploration and Exploitation of Transboundary Hydrocarbon Fields (2005); the Framework Treaty relating to the Unitization of Hydrocarbon Reservoirs that extend across the delimitation line between Trinidad and Tobago and Venezuela (2007); the Treaty between Norway and Russia concerning Maritime Delimitation and Cooperation in the Barents Sea and Arctic Ocean (2010) (Annex II) and the Agreement between the United States and Mexico concerning Trans-boundary Hydrocarbons Reservoirs in the Gulf of Mexico (2012). The elements of such framework agreements vary considerably, with wide differences in the scope and depth of commitment made by the respective states. So far, the Framework Agreement between the UK and Norway is the most innovative and is therefore analyzed below at some length.

They can be summarized as being more amenable to the use of discretion by the authorities in specific cases than the structures and techniques discussed so far, designed to facilitate speedy approval of cross-border unit developments proposed by energy companies and including some delegation to the companies themselves, whether they are state or privately owned. Most of them prohibit hydrocarbon production from a cross-border deposit without prior agreement between the states.

For states that are currently considering the adoption of legal forms of cooperation for the development of common resource deposits, the framework approach is worthy of study.[21]

7.1 The Norway–UK Framework

In February 2005 the two major oil- and gas-producing states in the North Sea area, Norway and the UK, cast aside three decades of cooperation in cross-border petroleum projects in favor of an entirely new approach based on a Framew ork Agreement.[22] The express aim of the agreement is "to deepen further" the co-operation between the UK and Norway "with respect to petroleum cross-boundary projects and to achieve optimal exploitation of the petroleum resources on the continental shelves appertaining to the two States". While this agreement does not replace or modify any of the existing treaty instruments between the two states on cross-border petroleum development, it rejects a key assumption on which these bilateral agreements were negotiated and concluded: the idea that a distinct inter-governmental treaty is required for each field that is to be developed on a cross-border basis. The considerable influence which the practice of these states has had elsewhere in the world makes this new orientation of more than regional interest. In addition, the bilateral arrangements they have put in place over several decades probably constitute one of the most pragmatic forms of inter-state co-operation on cross-border unitization in operation anywhere in the world. However, the new legal arrangements raise the question of why a change in established practice was considered necessary.

The Framework Agreement sets out an inter-governmental framework within which particular projects may be approved without going through the lengthy procedure of negotiating a separate treaty for each cross-boundary reservoir. When these treaties were concluded in the 1970s and 1980s, the North Sea was at a quite different stage of development, and the respective states had different expectations from future resource development. The UK has become a net importer of petroleum and is preparing for a future of significant gas (and oil) import dependence. Norway, by contrast, will have a growing ability to export petroleum to the UK due to expanding pipeline infrastructure. From a geological point of view, there has been another significant change. At the present time, cross-border projects that are proposed for development are more likely to be for small and medium-sized fields. The traditional approach of concluding a separate treaty for each cross-border development is ill suited to this context, and its complexity and unpredictability are likely to act as disincentives to companies seeking to bring cross-border discoveries forward for development. The Framework Agreement, by encouraging the development of industry confidence about inter-governmental cooperation and simplifying the arrangements for cross-border cooperation, is designed to act as an incentive to the planning and execution of such projects. On one estimate, the simpler procedure could stimulate an investment of up to US$2 billion in the so-called Cooperation Corridor (a 60-km zone extending either side of the trans-boundary line) within the next eight years (Pilot-Kon-Kraft, 2002).

The Framework Agreement states that in the event that a petroleum reservoir is deemed by both governments, following consultations with their respective licensee companies, to be a 'Trans-Boundary Reservoir' which should be exploited, it will be exploited as a single unit under the terms of the Framework Agreement. In that case, each government shall issue the authorizations required according to their national law.[23] Separate provision is made for a situation in which the exploitation is to take place from infrastructure located on one side of the boundary. The trigger for a cooperative approach is simpler than that provided in the common deposit clause of the delimitation agreement between Norway and the UK, which refers to the field's exploitability "wholly or in part". The authorized licensees will conclude *inter se* a licensees' agreement, which is to be submitted to the governments for their approval. This is one of three key approvals that each of the governments is responsible for granting. The licensees' agreement will resemble a typical Unitization and Unit Operating Agreement and will set out the main terms for joint operations.[24] Simplicity is a key requirement in the way that licensees address these topics. This is evident in the single, integrated unitization agreement. It contrasts with other framework agreements such as those between Venezuela–Trinidad and Tobago and Norway and Russia, which envisage two separate agreements: the unitization agreement that is drawn up by the respective states and a unit operating agreement that is negotiated and signed by the licensee companies. In the UK–Norway version, the unitization agreement will include provisions for arrangements following a one-off determination of the apportionment of reserves between the licensees ("to apply for all time to all activities") or procedures ("including a timetable") for carrying out and applying the outcome of redeterminations (a choice is therefore offered to the licensees on this very delicate issue), and procedures for the settlement of any disputes related to the distribution of the hydrocarbons across the boundary, as well as disputes between the licensees. If the authorization extends into licensed or non-licensed areas, there are provisions to deal with this. A unit operator is appointed by the licensees, but the approval of the two governments is required, as is any proposed change in the operator. This unit operator is responsible for the submission of a development plan to the two governments for approval (and any amendments to the plan). This has to cover both exploitation of the deposit and transportation of the petroleum. This is the third and last of the key approvals required before any petroleum may be produced from the reservoir. Other matters to be agreed between the two governments include the timing of the cessation of production and the use of infrastructure on one side of the delimitation line to explore for or to exploit a hydrocarbon reservoir on the other side or to process hydrocarbons from such a reservoir.

The Unit Operator is responsible for preparing a decommissioning plan for the field and for its installations and facilities. This has to be approved by the competent authority of the state where the installations and facilities are located, but the competent authority of the other state has to be consulted. Where these are located on both sides of the border, a joint plan may be submitted.

Three forms of dispute settlement procedure are provided in the Framework Agreement:[25] first, implementation of the Agreement is to be facilitated by a consultative mechanism, the Framework Forum, which meets twice a year and comprises representatives of each government. A principal objective is to try to ensure that any potential disputes are resolved before it is necessary to invoke the formal channels set out in Chapter 5 of the Agreement. The Framework Forum is the primary dispute resolution body. It is very similar to the Consultative Commissions set up under all the earlier Norway–UK agreements[26] but has a clearer mandate to act as a dispute resolution body. The second channel for disputes is the procedure involving a Conciliation Board, to which disputes may be submitted by either government. The Board's decision has to be made "within a reasonable time limit", and its decisions are binding on both governments. This is in practice little different from the arbitration provisions in earlier agreements except that the Board will consist of five members, and if the two governments wished to agree to different arrangements they may elect to do so under Article 5(1) of the Framework Agreement. Third, an expert determination process is provided for matters relating to field determinations or apportionments, under Article 3.4, subject to procedures to be agreed between the two governments. The expert's decision is binding on the two governments.

The Framework Agreement is of recent origin, but its initial impact has been very encouraging. Two small oil fields and a gas transmission project (the 'Langeled' line) were initiated 'on the back' of the treaty process in a spirit of cooperation and were announced at the time of signing the Framework Agreement. In the case of the two oilfields, Boa and Playfair, which span the median line between the two states, each was deemed to be in one country or another to make it easier for field development to proceed. The Boa field is almost entirely on the Norwegian continental shelf with a small extension into the UK. The Playfair field lies almost entirely on the UK continental shelf but has a small extension into Norwegian waters. The governments deemed that Boa should fall entirely within Norwegian jurisdiction and Playfair entirely within UK jurisdiction. Essentially, this is a pragmatic solution in favor of exploitation (but not joint development) rather than an outcome of the treaty itself. The first genuine results of the Framework Agreement were two cross-border fields approved in July 2005, called Enoch and Blane. These were discovered in 1985 and 1989, respectively, but were not developed because of perceived cross-border complications and the difficulty of reaching agreement between UK and Norwegian partners. The projects were approved by relying upon existing infrastructure, and no separate treaty was required in either case for development to go ahead.

7.2 Other examples

The recent Transboundary Hydrocarbons Agreement between Mexico and the U.S.[27] establishes a framework that expressly promotes the unitization of maritime transboundary reservoirs. It facilitates the conclusion of voluntary arrangements (unitization agreements) between U.S. leaseholders and the Mexican state company, Pemex, for the joint exploration and development of transboundary reservoirs. Incentives are provided to encourage parties to conclude such arrangements if the reservoir is proven to be a cross-border one and if a unitization agreement does not yet exist. However, if the parties cannot reach agreement on authorizing joint production, each one can authorize its licensee to proceed; the only condition being a duty to exchange production data on a monthly basis.[28] This provision "is unique and unlike other transboundary hydrocarbon agreements in effect globally".[29] A recent example of the majority, contrasting approach is found in the Norway–Russia Agreement for the Barents Sea.[30]

All unitization agreements under the Agreement have to be reviewed and approved by the respective states. The Agreement removed one obstacle in particular. Under Mexican law Pemex was prohibited from jointly developing resources with leaseholders on the U.S. side of the boundary. In 2008 an energy reform law was adopted to change this but only if cooperation takes place following an international agreement on transboundary resources. The framework Agreement removes that obstacle.

A few years earlier, in 2007, the Framework Agreement between Trinidad and Tobago and Venezuela was signed. It established a general legal framework for hydrocarbon reservoirs that extend across the delimitation line so that they could be exploited in the most effective and efficient manner. It established a Ministerial Commission as the supervisory body.

7.3 Is the framework approach a new model?

The 'framework' approach is significant as a new stage in the evolution of cooperation agreements for cross-border resource development. It is one that seeks to go beyond the cumbersome IGA approach that has become common around the world since it was first concluded between Norway and the UK in 1965. As an example of bilateral state cooperation in resource development, the framework approach – certainly in its current North Sea form – may be the most pragmatic form of cross-border agreement yet seen. In that case, the tensions latent in any bilateral relationship on this sensitive subject have been carefully subordinated to the aim of securing the economic benefits for both states. However, the peculiarities of the circumstances to which it applies mean that it may not perhaps be capable of functioning as a model. This is a mature hydrocarbons province, with extensive cross-border infrastructure already in place and its future determined by policy concerns about maximizing efficient recovery. For areas that have little exploration or little production and where there is a need to provide investors with signals about the stability of the legal framework (as in the South China Sea, for example), there may be few lessons from the framework approach.

By contrast, the 'model effect' of the early North Sea unitization agreements is beyond doubt. Their core idea spread to various parts of the globe, partly because of the dearth of alternative models at that time,[31] partly because they were pragmatically designed to capture the new economic potential offered by offshore petroleum production and partly because they were the next logical step beyond the 'unity of the deposit' clause in the early delimitation agreements. Where states were able to reach agreement on delimitation issues, the wording used in their bilateral agreements often followed *verbatim* the 'unity of the deposit' idea in Article 4 of the Norway–UK Delimitation Agreement of March 10, 1965 (for example, in the cases of Iran and Bahrain; Trinidad and Tobago and Venezuela). This set the scene for the bilateral treaty instrument used extensively and discussed earlier.

With respect to the 'framework' approach, a similar degree of international influence may occur, but a note of caution should be sounded first. To succeed, this approach requires an agreed boundary, a high level of willingness to cooperate and a commitment to maximizing recovery of the resource on the part of the states concerned. This has been evident in the North Sea region and in parts of the Americas, especially among the major producing states. Not all states would have the same trust in the international oil companies or even in their own state companies. It is hard to see such an approach finding much support in emerging African producer states, where memories of oil company–state asymmetries are still vivid. Moreover, when progress is slow or lacking altogether, the familiar question will tend to appear: when presented with evidence of a commercial petroleum deposit, can one state unilaterally initiate development? In this sense, the enhanced cooperation offered by the framework agreements to date may not provide a failsafe insurance against the risk that neighboring states with widely different circumstances will take up a confrontational stance on cross-border resource development. It is certainly a very encouraging step, however, in the direction of peaceful resolution of differences.

8 Conclusion

The development of a co-operative framework for petroleum resource development can be seen as the rational choice of sovereign states since the sources of potential conflict in a long-term petroleum resource project are considerable. They include not only those that can arise in a bilateral relationship between states but also those arising from relations with third states, as well as the interface with international (and national) oil companies and the occasional uncertainties arising from an often complex and changing geological database. If one looks to the future, states will need to develop forms of cooperation that provide predictability and simplicity in a context of strong, continuing interest in petroleum resource development and the inevitable uncertainties that arise in managing diverse rights and claims in a particular setting. International law offers scope and support for such cooperation, which need not diminish the sovereign rights and powers of the states involved.

This is an area in which there is a growing body of international experience. What is clear from the examples presented here is the extent to which national policy considerations will play a major role in shaping and limiting the choices that states make with respect to cooperation. This was very evident in the Nigeria–São Tomé e Príncipe JDZ regime, where local content and wider development policies played a role. The recent evolution of cooperation in the 'framework' approach demonstrates a willingness to subordinate potentially troublesome considerations to a commercial logic in this area without compromising the sovereign rights of the states concerned. By contrast, not many joint development structures have yet been attempted. The scale of their design and management would seem to disqualify them as options for many new and emerging producing states given their limits in capacity. The more straightforward unitization agreements have been tested in many settings, but a 'framework' approach of some kind is likely to become highly attractive to those states with national companies on which they can rely. Where such domestic agencies are lacking to counter the perceived influence of the international oil and gas companies, there is a risk that states will be wary of such pragmatic approaches and instead favor a more formal, rules-based structure. If so, that would be an ironic development, since a number of countries with established production – such as those in the North Sea and in the Caribbean – seem to be moving away from this approach in favor of more flexible, informal arrangements designed to achieve more rapid but also sustainable results than the formal structures seem able to deliver.

Notes

1 Detailed fiscal matters for JDZ are addressed in Daniel, Veung and Watson (2016), Chapter 11 in this volume.
2 The idea is not unique to hydrocarbon development. The Model Intergovernmental and Host Government Model Agreements for Cross-Border Pipelines (second edition, 2008) developed by the Energy Charter Secretariat includes a provision on 'isolation of any boundary or territorial disputes'. It includes the statement: "No Boundary or Territorial Dispute between or amongst any of the States shall interfere in any manner with any Project Activities": http://www.encharter.org/fileadmin/user_upload/document/ma-en.pdf.
3 The Convention has been ratified by 166 states, giving it very considerable authority: http://www.un.org/depts/los/convention_agreements/convention_overview_convention.htm.
4 D.M. Ong. (1999), "Joint Development of Common Offshore Oil and Gas Deposits: 'Mere' State Practice or Customary International Law?," *AJIL*, 93, 771–804, 771. For a comprehensive review of the literature on this subject of cooperation and its limits in relation to hydrocarbons, see Cameron, P.D. (2006), "The Rules of Engagement: Developing Cross-Border Petroleum Deposits in the North Sea and the Caribbean," *ICLQ*, 55, 599–626 at 614.
5 The various terms typically found in an international unitization agreement are the subject of a model form published by the AIPN, intended to work with PSCs (www.aipn.org). Other models have been published by the Petroleum Joint Venture Association of Canada (www.pjva.com), the American Petroleum Institute (www.api.org) and the Rocky Mountain Mineral Law Foundation (www.rmmlf.org).
6 Without regard for the many significant differences among their arrangements, the countries involved in such joint development schemes include: Bahrain–Saudi Arabia (1958); Czechoslovakia–Austria (1960); Netherlands–Germany (1962); Kuwait–Saudi Arabia (1965); Abu Dhabi–Qatar (1969); Sharjah–Iran (1971); France–Spain (1974); Japan–Korea (1974); Sudan–Saudi Arabia (1974); UK–Norway (1977); Malaysia–Thailand (1979); UK–Norway (1981: Statfjord); UK–Norway (1981: Murchison); Norway–Iceland (1981); Tunisia–Libya (1988); North–South Yemen (1988); Malaysia–Vietnam (1992); Colombia–Jamaica (1993); Netherlands–UK (1993); Guinea Bissau–Senegal (1993) and (1995); UK–Argentina (1995); Cambodia–Vietnam (2001); Nigeria–São Tomé e Príncipe (2001); Timor-Leste–Australia (2002); Tunisia–Algeria (2002); Barbados–Guyana (2003).
7 Memorandum of Understanding between Malaysia and the Socialist Republic of Vietnam for the Exploration and Exploitation of Petroleum in a Defined Area of the Continental Shelf Involving the Two Countries, June 5, 1992.
8 The UN Convention on the Law of the Sea set out provisions on the Exclusive Economic Zone in Part V (Articles 55–75): the EEZ is an area beyond and adjacent to the territorial sea reaching a maximum of 200 nautical miles from the landward edge of the territorial sea. The coastal state has sovereign rights (not full sovereignty) for the purposes of exploring and exploiting, conserving and managing natural resources in the seabed and subsoil. In carrying out its rights and performing its duties, the coastal state is required to have due regard to the rights and duties of other states.
9 The following paragraphs have benefited from a paper presented by A.M. Yabo, Head of the Legal Unit at the Nigeria–São Tomé e Príncipe JDZ at the Regional Workshop, 'Managing Offshore Oil & Gas Resources: Reservoir Management, Unitization & Approaches to Trans-boundary Issues', organized by the Energy Governance and Capacity Initiative of the US Department of State in Accra, Ghana, March 14–15, 2013: 'Issues that were overcome in the Formation of the Nigeria–São Tomé e Príncipe Joint Development Zone (JDZ) & Ongoing Issues in the Management of the JDZ.

10 For example, Terence Daintith's comprehensive account of unitization in 'Finders Keepers? How the Law of Capture Shaped the World Oil Industry' (2010), Resources for the Future Press, Washington DC; and J.L. Weaver and D. Asmus. (2006), "Unitizing Oil and Gas Fields Around the World: A Comparative Analysis of National Laws and Private Contracts," *Houston J of Int'l Law*, 28, 3–197.

11 Unitisation Agreement for the Exploitation and Development of Hydrocarbon Reservoirs of the Loran-Manatee Field that extends across the Delimitation Line between the Republic of Trinidad and Tobago and the Bolivarian Republic of Venezuela, August 16, 2010.

12 Agreement relating to the Exploitation of the Frigg Field Reservoir and the Transmission of Gas therefrom to the United Kingdom, May 10, 1976, UK-Nor., Gt. Brit. TS No.113 (Cmnd. 7043), 1098 UNTS 3. For a detailed account of the Frigg Agreement, see J.C. Woodliffe. (1977), "International Unitisation of an Offshore Gas Field," *ICLQ*, 26, 338–353. The field ceased production in October 2004.

13 Agreement between the Government of the United Kingdom and Northern Ireland and the Government of the Kingdom of Norway relating to the Delimitation of the Continental Shelf between the Two Countries (March 10, 1965) Gt Brit TS No. 71 (1965), Cmnd. 2757; UNTS 214.

14 Frigg, see note 12 above; Agreement relating to the Exploitation of the Statfjord Field Reservoirs and the Offtake of Petroleum therefrom, October 16, 1979, Gt Brit TS No 44 (1981) (Cmnd. 8282); Agreement relating to the Exploitation of the Murchison Field Reservoir and the Offtake of Petroleum therefrom, October 16, 1979, Gt Brit TS No. 39 (1981) (Cmnd. 8270); Agreement relating to the Exploitation of the Markham Field Reservoirs and the Offtake of Petroleum therefrom, May 26, 1992, UK–Neth., 1993 Gt Brit TS No. 38 (Cmnd. 2254). In each case the agreements have been amended by Exchanges of Notes and, in the case of the Frigg Agreement, by a further Agreement of August 25, 1998 (see Framework Agreement, Annex E). Other agreements have been concluded with Norway on pipelines (Agreement of November 21, 1985, amended by the Agreement of 1 November 2004, between the Two Governments relating to the Transmission by Pipeline of Liquids from the Heimdal Reservoir and other Reservoirs to the United Kingdom, and the Framework Agreement of August 25, 1998, relating to the Laying, Operation and Jurisdiction of Inter-connecting Submarine Pipelines) and the Ekofisk Field (Agreement of May 22, 1973, as amended by an Exchange of Notes dated July 27, 1994, relating to the Transmission of Petroleum from the Ekofisk Field and Neighbouring Areas to the United Kingdom).

15 Agreement relating to the Delimitation of the Continental Shelf between the Two Countries, March 10, 1965, UK–Norway, 1965 Gr Brit TS No 71 (Cmnd. 2757), 551 UNTS 214; Agreement relating to the Exploitation of Single Geological Structures Extending across the Dividing Line on the Continental Shelf under the North Seas, October 6, 1965, UK–Netherlands, Article 1, 1967, Gt Brit TS No 24 (Cmnd 3254).

16 However, the idea of a redetermination is echoed in Article 3 of the Frigg Agreement and Article 3 of the Statfjord Agreement. For a discussion of this practice in the international petroleum industry, see Nwete, B. (2005), "Mitigating Redetermination Problems in Unitised Hydrocarbon Fields," *IELTR*, 9, 228–233.

17 'Building UK–Norwegian Cooperation in the North Sea: A Statement by UK and Norwegian Energy Ministers', October 2, 2003, 2: http://www.ag.dti.gov.uk/upstream/infrastructure/overarching.doc

18 A unitization agreement will normally be made by the owners of a single field which extends into more than one license area to develop that field as a single unit: see English, W. (1996), "Unitisation Agreements," in M.R. David (ed.), *Upstream Oil and Gas Agreements* (London: Sweet and Maxwell), pp. 97–115.

19 Frigg, see note 12 above, Article 29(1) and (2). The same wording is found *mutatis mutandis* in Article 22 of both the Statfjord and Murchison Agreements, Article 24 of the Markham Agreement, and Article 1.3 of the Framework Agreement.

20 For further details, see Daniel, Veung and Watson (2016), Chapter 11 in this volume.
21 For a recent overview of five of these framework agreements, see 'Recent Framework Agreements for the Recognition and Development of Transboundary Hydrocarbon Resources', by Nigel Bankes in 'Energy from the Sea: An International Law Perspective on Ocean Energy' (2015), edited by N. Bankes and S. Trevisant, pp. 106–129.
22 Framework Agreement between the Government of the United Kingdom of Great Britain and Northern Ireland and the Government of the Kingdom of Norway concerning Cross-boundary Petroleum Co-operation, signed on April 4, 2005 (http://www.og.dti.gov.uk/upstream/infrastructure/nfa_2005.doc). The agreement covers a variety of potential cross-border projects, including the development of new fields that straddle the maritime boundary, the use of installations on one side of the delimitation line to exploit resources on the other side (host facility development) and the construction, laying and operation of a range of pipelines including landing pipelines. Its origins lie in a joint industry–government report, "Unlocking Value through Closer Relationships", authored by Pilot-Kon-Kraft in 2002 (available at www.pilottaskforce.co.uk).
23 Article 3.1(1) and (2).
24 Department for Energy and Climate Change/Norwegian Petroleum Directorate (2005), 'UK-Norway. Trans-Boundary Oil & Gas Fields: Guidelines for Development of Trans-Boundary Oil & Gas Fields: https://www.gov.uk/government/uploads/system/uploads/attachment_data/file/15574/nor-guide.pdf
25 A separate procedure is provided for disputes concerning pipeline access: Articles 2.7 and 5(2).
26 Frigg, Articles 27–28; Statfjord and Murchison Articles 20–21; for a similar approach in the Markham Agreement, see Articles 22–23 (the Markham Commission).
27 Agreement Concerning Transboundary Hydrocarbon Reservoirs in the Gulf of Mexico, U.S.–Mex., February 20, 2012, T.I.A.S. No. 14–718, Available at http://www.state.gov/documents/organization/231802.pdf. For a detailed assessment of the Agreement, see Sanchez McLaughlin (2015), especially Parts VI and VII.
28 Article 7(5) of US–Mexico Treaty (see Note).
29 *Houston J of Int'l L*, p. 780.
30 Treaty Concerning Maritime Delimitation and Cooperation in the Barents Sea and the Arctic Ocean, Norway-Russia, Annex II, Article 1(8), September 15, 2010; 50 ILM 1113: this states that the parties have an obligation to refrain from permitting production without a jointly approved unitization agreement.
31 In Europe there was the treaty between Austria and Czechoslovakia, 1960, 495 UNTS No. 7242, 125; the agreement between the Federal Republic of Germany and the Netherlands, supplemental to the Ems-Dollard Treaty 1969, 509 UNTS No. 7404, 104. In the Middle East there were several such agreements, but their relevance to a study of cooperative arrangements is mixed. For example, the Agreement between the Kingdom of Saudi Arabia and the Government of Bahrain, signed on February 22, 1958 (http://www.un.org/Depts/los/legislationandtreaties), is a revenue-sharing agreement, in which the parties do not envisage any cooperation with respect to the exploration or exploitation of the deposit or field. By contrast, the 1969 agreement on maritime boundaries and sovereign rights between Qatar and Abu Dhabi envisages the joint exercise of sovereign rights over the al-Bunduq oilfield.

References

Bankes, N. and S. Trevisant, eds. (2015), *Energy From the Sea: An International Law Perspective on Ocean Energy* (Leiden: Brill).

Cameron, P. (2006), "The Rules of Engagement: Developing Cross-Border Petroleum Deposits in the North Sea and the Caribbean," *ICLQ*, 55, 599–626.

Daintith, T. (2010), *Finders Keepers? How the Law of Capture Shaped the World Oil Industry* (Washington, DC: Resources for the Future Press).

English, W. (1996), 'Unitisation Agreements," in M.R. David (ed.), *Upstream Oil and Gas Agreements* (London: Sweet and Maxwell), pp. 97–115.

Framework Agreement between the Government of the United Kingdom of Great Britain and Northern Ireland and the Government of the Kingdom of Norway Concerning Cross-Boundary Petroleum Co-operation, signed on April 4, 2005. Available at http://www.og.dti.gov.uk/upstream/infrastructure/nfa_2005.doc.

Garcia Sanchez, G.J. and R.J. McLaughlin. (2015), "The 2012 Agreement on the Exploitation of Transboundary Hydrocarbon Resources in the Gulf of Mexico: Confirmation of the Rule or Emergence of a New Practice? *Houston Journal of International Law*, 37(3), 681–792.

Model Inter-Governmental and Host Government Agreement for Cross-Border Pipelines (2007) (second edition), Energy Charter Secretariat.

Nwete, B. (2005), "Mitigating Redetermination Problems in Unitised Hydrocarbon Fields," *IELTR*, 9, 228–233.

Ong, D.M. (1999), "Joint Development of Common Offshore Oil and Gas Deposits: 'Mere' State Practice or Customary International Law?," *AJIL*, 93, 771–804.

Pilot-Kon-Kraft (2002), Unlocking Value through Closer Relationships: www.pilottaskforce.co.uk

Taverne, B. (1994), *An Introduction to the Regulation of the Petroleum Industry: Law, Contracts and Conventions* (Deventer, the Netherlands: Kluwer).

Weaver, J. and D. Asmus. (2006), "Unitizing Oil and Gas Fields Around the World: A Comparative Analysis of National Laws and Private Contracts, *Houston Journal of International Law*, 28, 3–197.

Woodliffe, J. (1977), "International Unitisation of an Offshore Gas Field," *ICLQ*, 26, 338–353.

Yabo, A.M. (2013), 'Managing Offshore Oil & Gas Resources: Reservoir Management, Unitization & Approaches to Trans-boundary Issues', Regional Workshop organised by the Energy Governance and Capacity Initiative of the US Department of State in Accra, Ghana, 14–15 March: 'Issues that were overcome in the Formation of the Nigeria-São Tomé e Príncipe Joint Development Zone (JDZ) & Ongoing Issues in the Management of the JDZ'.

11 Fiscal schemes for joint development of petroleum in disputed areas

A primer and an evaluation

Philip Daniel, Chandara Veung and Alistair Watson[1]

1 Introduction

Significant amounts of petroleum lie in areas of disputed sovereignty or absence of agreed boundary delimitation.[2] Many, but not all, such areas are maritime and lie beneath seas that countries can claim as their Exclusive Economic Zone (EEZ) (for exploitation of water column, seabed, and subsoil resources, though not for navigation) in terms of the United Nations Convention on the Law of the Sea (UNCLOS).[3] UNCLOS came into force only in 1974, and techniques of exploring for and extracting petroleum in offshore areas have become efficient and widespread only in more recent times. Delineation of maritime boundaries in earlier times thus may not have seemed important or was made according to older legal principles.

UNCLOS itself provides for the adoption of "interim arrangements" where, for some reason the parties cannot delineate or agree a permanent maritime boundary (Article 33). In the case of petroleum areas, the most common form of arrangement has become the joint development zone (JDZ). JDZs also exist onshore, where UNCLOS is not relevant. Under a JDZ, the parties put aside the sovereignty issue, usually for a defined period, thus also putting aside the question of title to resources in the ground or under the seabed. Instead, they agree to attribute petroleum produced from the JDZ, or the revenues raised under a joint fiscal scheme, in percentages to each country. Prominent JDZ examples include Bahrain–Saudi Arabia, Malaysia–Thailand, Timor-Leste–Australia, and São Tomé e Príncipe–Nigeria.[4]

In a number of places, disputes over boundaries continue, as sometimes do negotiations over a possible JDZ. Contentious areas include the South China Sea, Venezuela–Trinidad and Tobago, Cameroon–Nigeria, Angola–DRC, the Caspian Sea, and Cambodia–Thailand. The new prospects in basins off the coasts of a number of West African countries have been identified, in some cases, before formal delimitation and agreement on maritime boundaries, raising the possibility of new sets of overlapping claims for EEZs. The Arctic Ocean – considered to hold a significant proportion of the world's yet-to-be-discovered hydrocarbons – is subject to a series of overlapping claims.

The field of public international law on maritime claims, principles of delimitation of maritime boundaries and JDZs carries an enormous literature (see, for example, Becker-Weinberg, 2014; Hestermeyer et al., 2012; Nordquist and Moore, 2012, and the exposition in Crawford, 2012). That cannot be said for the economic and fiscal issues presented by interim solutions to unresolved maritime claims, despite the growing significance of these issues.[5] Cameron in this volume explains the legal challenges involved in creating a JDZ and how a JDZ differs from a unitization scheme, even one that extends across maritime boundaries.

This chapter aims to document some key examples of the JDZ and evaluate the types of fiscal arrangements that occur. These fiscal arrangements consist, first, of the attribution of petroleum production or proceeds among the partner states and, second, as in any national scheme, of the tax, production sharing, state participation and pricing rules applied to companies operating in the JDZ; then third the "architecture" of the fiscal arrangements – meaning the specific ways in which each country's regime and institutions blend with each other and with joint arrangements specially created, and, fourth and finally, the provisions for projects where resources either straddle the perimeter of the JDZ or require infrastructure extending beyond the JDZ to achieve export of petroleum (see also Le Leuch in this volume).

Fiscal terms in JDZs may differ from those in, say, neighbouring areas under exclusive jurisdiction. Do they differ in any systematic way – for example in average effective tax rates? And would a JDZ work differently on international oil companies' (IOC) perceptions of risk from a sovereign national scheme?

This chapter presents in detail the specific example of the interim arrangements made between Australia and Timor-Leste. This is an especially complex case, one which illustrates virtually all the issues that need to be addressed and frictions that may arise in designing and implementing a JDZ.

The chapter outlines some practical lessons and policy conclusions, intended as helpful to those designing and negotiating interim arrangements, to those operating within them, and to civil society interests seeking to appraise the impact of these schemes.

2 Maritime disputes and joint development zones

According to data available in Pawlak (2012) by 2009 there were 170 formal agreements or treaties establishing maritime boundaries, but 365 known potential maritime boundaries were yet to be delineated and decided. (See also Cameron in this volume.) Only a minority of the parties to undecided or disputed maritime boundaries have entered agreements establishing joint development zones.

This simplest way to explain the characteristics of JDZs is by examples. After discussing the architecture of JDZs, we outline the arrangements in two of the best-known JDZs: Malaysia–Thailand and Nigeria–São Tomé e Príncipe. Then in section 3 we proceed with quantitative evaluation and in section 4 with detailed analysis of the case of Australia and Timor-Leste.

2.1 The fiscal architecture of joint development zones

2.1.1 The rationale for JDZs

A JDZ under UNCLOS applies to an offshore area[6] subject to overlapping maritime boundary claims by the countries with adjacent or opposing coastlines where known deposits of or prospects for petroleum exist. (See also Cameron in this volume.) The countries cannot agree on a delimitation but also do not want to hold up the exploration and development of any petroleum resources, so for pragmatic reasons they agree to a joint approach and defer formal boundary delimitation for a defined period of time. The JDZ usually involves (1) shared jurisdiction; (2) an agreed regulatory architecture; (3) sharing of petroleum produced; or (4) sharing of revenues under a jointly administered fiscal regime.

2.1.2 Attribution of petroleum produced

JDZs differ from international unitisation agreements in that a JDZ may cover areas with no discoveries. Under unitisation, the boundary is usually not disputed; rather what is addressed is attribution of petroleum across an agreed boundary according to knowledge of location of reserves in discoveries.[7] Redetermination of reserves and attribution occurs periodically under agreed rules, usually on the basis of technical analysis. Countries establish JDZs, on the other hand, in order to put aside competing claims and allow exploration or extraction (usually both) to go ahead in spite of the absence of a maritime boundary. The extent of the zone and the division of any petroleum discovered are determined by relative negotiating power.

Fifty–fifty sharing has proved appealing many cases in which no other basis exists for a different attribution. Nevertheless, examples of other attributions occur: the special area favouring Nigeria within the Nigeria–São Tomé e Príncipe JDZ or the zones B and C under the old "Timor Gap" treaty. Differences from 50% attribution might arise when the parties recognize that one party may have a stronger claim than the other over parts of the total area in dispute, but neither party wishes only a partial permanent delineation.

In principle, the rules of the zone might do no more than attribute any petroleum found and extracted. In practice, JDZs need a much more sophisticated architecture of rules and administrative structure governing activities and of fiscal terms to implement the attribution. Peter Cameron in this volume analyses the legal architecture. The parallel fiscal architecture covers the mechanisms for sharing physical petroleum, proceeds, or revenues earned under a joint fiscal regime, both between the states and with private parties engaged in petroleum activities. It must also cover the fiscal treatment of activities related to petroleum exploration or development, occurring whether or not production occurs, and those for exporting petroleum from the JDZ.

2.1.3 *Concept of the fiscal scheme*

The precedent from fiscal terms of the participating countries strongly influences the design of fiscal terms in a JDZ, but usually with an element of purpose-built fiscal terms for the zone. The detailed examples in this chapter all rely on a core fiscal mechanism (whether production sharing or otherwise) from which the countries then share proceeds. What remains to the private participants after this core mechanism may be taxed, either according to common rules or under each country's national scheme with revenues and costs apportioned using the JDZ attribution percentages.

Thus even where one country operates a licensing system and the other does not, the JDZ might rely upon a single contractual scheme. A production sharing contract, for example, may determine the initial sharing of production between the JDZ governments collectively and any private investor, even where that PSC model does not reflect practice in either participating state. As with most such systems when used nationally, a hybrid emerges in which taxation applies to residual income of the "contractor" after production sharing.

Similarly, where the parties agree to a tax and royalty system – not contractual and not with production sharing – the core charge for the resource could be a combination of bonus, royalty or fees, charged collectively and distributed to the partner states. Again, tax would follow on the residual income. The Nigeria–São Tomé e Príncipe and Timor-Leste schemes reflect this approach.

By contrast, if the parties cannot agree a core fiscal scheme, jointly operated, then each country's own fiscal system could apply to the gross proceeds of petroleum production in the attribution percentages. This would bring the JDZ closer to a unitisation scheme. Private investors face more challenges under this alternative because they lack the assurance of a common scheme agreed by the parties: the partner states have the usual incentives arising from time inconsistency to seek to secure a higher share of their own attribution percentages after production starts, though the JDZ architecture would usually place some constraint on any unilateral attempt to modify terms by one party.

2.1.4 *National oil companies*

Where the partner states have strong national oil companies with privileged positions in their own exclusive jurisdictions, these positions often carry over to the JDZ. An automatic role for the respective NOCs, for example, prevails in Malaysia–Thailand but not in Nigeria–São Tomé e Príncipe, or in Timor-Leste–Australia. In some respects, NOC dominance simplifies matters since the direct attraction of private investment by the JDZ regimes becomes irrelevant: the NOCs take full responsibility for the financing of exploration and development.

In a mixed system, the NOCs could function as recipient of production shares for the governments, obviating the need for a separate collection agency. Malaysia–Thailand, for example, contrasts with Timor-Leste–Australia in this respect. Many JDZs have a joint authority that functions not only as regulator but also as collector of significant revenues via fees or production sharing. In principle, the regulatory authority could deal with taxes designed specifically for the JDZ, though national tax authorities generally retain this role.

2.1.5 Taxation

JDZs have adopted either a single tax system for the JDZ or application of each country's tax system in attribution percentages. Common direct taxation by assessment with separate applications of indirect taxes or taxes by withholding represents a combination. The system of unified resource taxation (the resource charge or production sharing) with separate application of normal business and indirect taxation is common.

Application of national taxes, however, requires the equivalent specifically for the JDZ of an international double taxation agreement or code for the JDZ. The existence of the JDZ raises specific complications over source and residence for income tax purposes – commonly resolved by deeming the JDZ to be the tax territory of both countries but with rights to tax only in the attribution percentages. Limitations on withholding taxes on payments to non-residents become part of the mechanisms to limit competitive appropriation of revenues beyond the attribution percentages.[8]

Most countries now specify a treatment for capital gains purposes of transfers of interest in petroleum rights and in assets associated with those rights. Again the harmonisation or integration of these rules in a JDZ presents significant challenges.[9]

2.1.6 Unitisation beyond a JDZ

The fact that perimeters of a JDZ are usually arbitrary means that discoveries are possible that lie across these perimeters. The parties then face, if willing, unitisation of fields applying a JDZ regime to one part and a national regime to another. Just as likely – and represented by Greater Sunrise between Timor-Leste and Australia – the JDZ itself may have temporarily settled only part of a dispute. If areas outside the JDZ also remain contested the parties may require still further "interim arrangements", exactly as happened between Australia and Timor-Leste. This phenomenon serves only to emphasise the incompleteness and temporary nature of JDZ schemes.

2.1.7 Petroleum infrastructure

At the time of UNCLOS and then the first establishment of JDZs in disputed maritime areas the exploration target was oil (not natural gas) and the expectation was for infrastructure located within the JDZ close to any producing field. Upstream operations would terminate, and fiscal value would arise "at the point of tanker loading". Subsequently, however, interest in gas raised the challenge of jurisdiction and taxation of transportation and processing facilities for JDZ products that might be located outside the JDZ (Calder, this volume). The Timor Sea Treaty, for example, provides that a pipeline commencing in the JDZ but landing in one of the contracting states comes under the jurisdiction of the destination state.[10]

Crude oil loaded onto a tanker at facilities within the JDZ has a specific value (when not sold at arm's length) at the closest reference price adjusted for quality and transportation cost differentials. Oil and more especially gas transported out of a JDZ by pipeline requires valuation for upstream fiscal purposes after deduction of the transportation costs. How are those to be assessed? The answer requires transfer pricing rules that may benefit from no established point of reference and hence no comparable uncontrolled price. Similarly, natural gas transported by pipeline then processed into LNG outside the JDZ has an upstream "price" that may reflect a series of affiliate transactions with owners of transportation and processing infrastructure. This infrastructure requires planning, construction, and operation, all of which under a national jurisdiction would give rise to taxable income. Attribution of taxing rights for such income is far from straightforward in the case of a JDZ.

2.2 Malaysia–Thailand joint development zone

Malaysia and Thailand have no agreement on the continental shelf border in the Gulf of Thailand. The disputed border results from the two countries with adjacent coasts using different coastal baselines in calculating the equidistant line for a boundary. The two neighbours signed a memorandum of understanding in 1979 to create a joint development area where non-living natural resources can be explored. The Joint Authority established in 1990 issues licences and regulates the JDA.[11] The JDA comprises three blocks (Figure 11.1). Blocks B-17 and C-19 are fully owned and operated by subsidiaries of Petronas and PTT. Block A-18 is a joint venture between Petronas's subsidiary (50%) and Hess Company of Thailand (50%). Gas discoveries leading to production were made in the joint zone.

The discussion of each country's national terms that follows illustrates how the JDZ regime derives from and compares with the partner countries' national regimes.

2.2.1 Fiscal framework for petroleum activities in Malaysia

Malaysia has a long history of petroleum exploration and production. Shell made the first commercial discovery in 1909 in the state of Sarawak and started producing oil a year later. Companies that produced oil at the time assumed all risks and operating responsibilities from exploration to production, paying the Malaysian government royalty at fixed percentages and also income taxes. As commercial production accelerated in the early 1970s, the government sought to strengthen control over hydrocarbon activities in Malaysia. Petronas, the state-owned company, was thus established, endowed with the rights to explore and develop Malaysia's hydrocarbon resources under the Petroleum Development Act of 1975. Contractors were no longer solely required to pay a royalty and income taxes but to operate under a production sharing contract (PSC), and to partner with Petronas in joint ventures. For marginal fields, the contractors have an option to operate under a risk service contract (RSC) and receive compensation for the services provided to Petronas instead of a share of production.

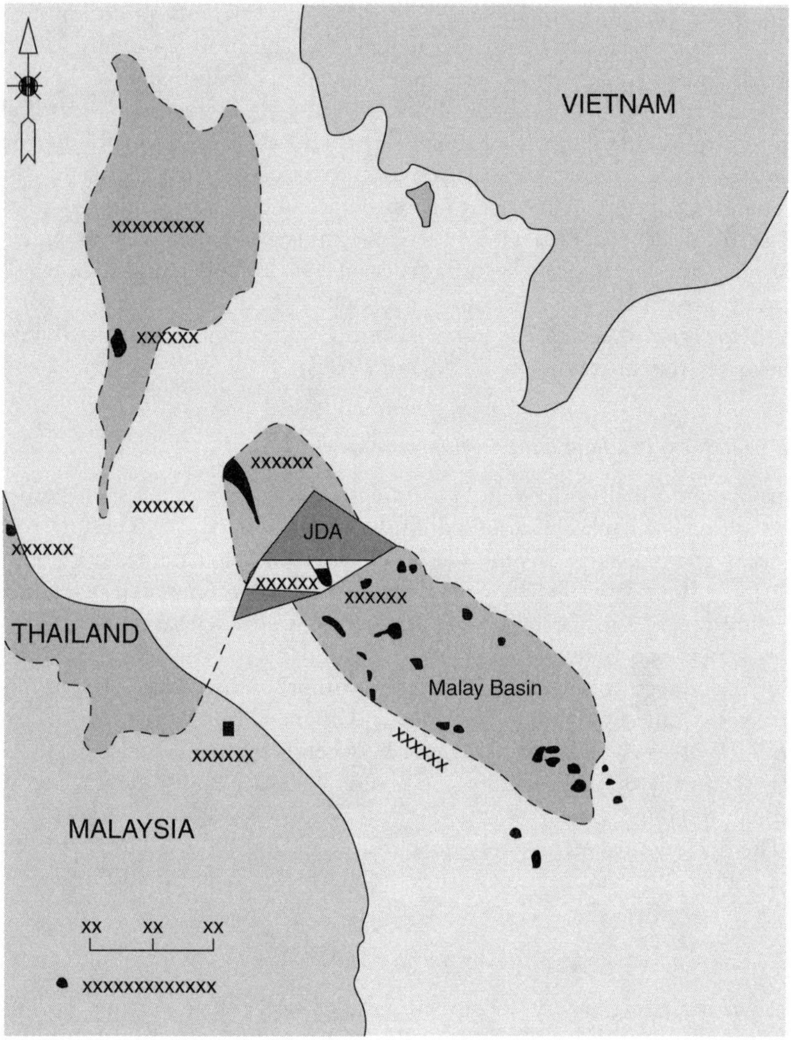

Figure 11.1 Malaysia–Thailand JDZ

Source: Malaysia–Thailand Joint Authority

The PSC regime was first patterned after the Indonesian PSC until a new model PSC was developed in 1987. The model PSC went through several revisions up to 1997 with several agreements post-dating the model. Under this PSC regime, a contractor pays an explicit royalty of 10% of total production to the government and then recovers its costs from a share of remaining production. Profit petroleum remaining after royalty and cost recovery is shared

Box 11.1 The Malaysia–Thailand JDZ production sharing contract

Cost recovery is linked to project profitability as measured by the contractor's revenue to cost ratio (R/C ratio) – commonly known as the R-factor. The higher the R/C ratio, the lower the cost recovery limit, which ranges from 30% to 70%. If in any quarter the cost recovery limit exceeds the actual cost eligible for recovery, the difference, known as excess cost recovery, is shared between the contractor and Petronas according to a specific scale.[1] The R/C ratio and cumulative total hydrocarbon value (THV) determine the sharing of excess cost recovery and profit petroleum. THV is determined by individual field and equals the lesser of 300 MM Bbl for oil or 0.75 trillion cubic feet (TCF) for gas and the size of the field's proved recoverable reserves. This amount is adjusted as more information about the field becomes known. Cumulative THV is the sum of all individual THVs from a contract area. If THV equals 300 MM Bbl, realised cumulative production from a contract area may exceed the cumulative regulatory THV, especially toward the final stage of production. Table 11.1 summarizes the sharing rates of excess cost recovery and profit petroleum as stipulated in the 1997 model PSC.

Table 11.1 Cost recovery limits and shares of excess cost recovery and profit petroleum to contractors

R/C Ratio	*Cost Recovery Limit*	*Excess Cost Recovery if cum. Production ≤ cum. THV*	*Excess Cost Recovery if cum. Production > cum. THV*	*Profit Petroleum if cum. Production ≤ cum. THV*	*Profit Petroleum if cum. Production > cum. THV*
0.0 ≤ R/C < 1.0	70%	NA	NA	80%	40%
1.0 ≤ R/C < 1.4	60%	80%	40%	70%	30%
1.4 ≤ R/C < 2.0	50%	70%	40%	60%	30%
2.0 ≤ R/C < 2.5	30%	60%	40%	50%	30%
2.5 ≤ R/C < 3.0	30%	50%	40%	40%	30%
R/C ≥ 3.0	30%	40%	20%	30%	10%

1 This is a relatively unusual approach; in most PSCs unused cost recovery simply forms part of profit petroleum.

according to a sliding scale determined by the revenue-to-cost (R/C) ratio. An export tax of 10% is imposed on any petroleum exported out of Malaysia.

The contractor pays petroleum income tax of 38% on the revenues it derives from its share of cost recovery, excess cost recovery and profit petroleum, less eligible deductions. Losses from prior periods are carried forward indefinitely. When the oil price exceeds $25/Bbl, escalated by 4% from the date of contract, the contractor pays an additional profit tax. The government takes 70% of the profit arising from the difference between the base and actual prices. Petronas Carigali, an exploration and production company wholly owned by Petronas, can elect to take a minimum 15% participation interest carried through exploration. Past costs are not repaid but are cost recoverable. Participation in actual contracts has varied between 15% and 50%. Figure 11.2 graphically represents the revenue to the government of Malaysia from a stylized 900 million barrel oil project, the assumptions for which are set out in Figure 11.4. The average effective tax rate (AETR) is also shown as a measure of government share.

2.2.2 Fiscal framework for petroleum activities in Thailand

Petroleum exploration in Thailand commenced in the early 1920s in the northern part of the country. Government agencies exclusively undertook these activities, with no participation by the private sector. All that changed in 1954, when the government implemented a new policy that allowed the private sector to explore and develop petroleum resources. The Petroleum Act (PA) and Petroleum Income Tax Act (PITA) of 1971 were then enacted to regulate and tax petroleum activities in the kingdom.

The PA and PITA have gone through several amendments. Contracts awarded before 1982 were regulated and taxed by the Thailand I Regime. The Thailand II Regime took effect in 1982 during the hike of oil prices but was amended in 1989 to become Thailand III Regime. Legislation was revised again in 2007, PA (No. 6) and PITA (No. 6), for the bidding round of that year.[12] A state-owned company PTT Public Company Limited (PTT), formerly known as the Petroleum Authority of Thailand, became one of the Fortune 500 Global Companies during the oil boom years. PTT Exploration and Production (PTTEP), a subsidiary of PTT, accounts for about 30% of total domestic oil and gas production, with operations overseas. In the private sector, Chevron remains the largest player, producing about 70% of oil and condensates from its offshore fields in the Gulf of Thailand in 2010.[13]

Thailand III is a royalty and tax regime. The contractor pays a royalty at rates on a sliding scale of monthly sales volume as summarized in Table 11.2. The royalty falls to 70% of the regular rates for deep-water blocks. After deducting royalty at the prescribed rate the contractor pays petroleum income tax at 50% but is not required to withhold tax when dividends are distributed to investors. A reduction of income tax to 35% is possible through a royal decree, but a remittance tax of 23.08% is then payable, making an effective tax rate of 55% on remitted profits.[14] The contractor must withhold 15% on the payment of interest to lenders in either case. The legislation makes no explicit provision for

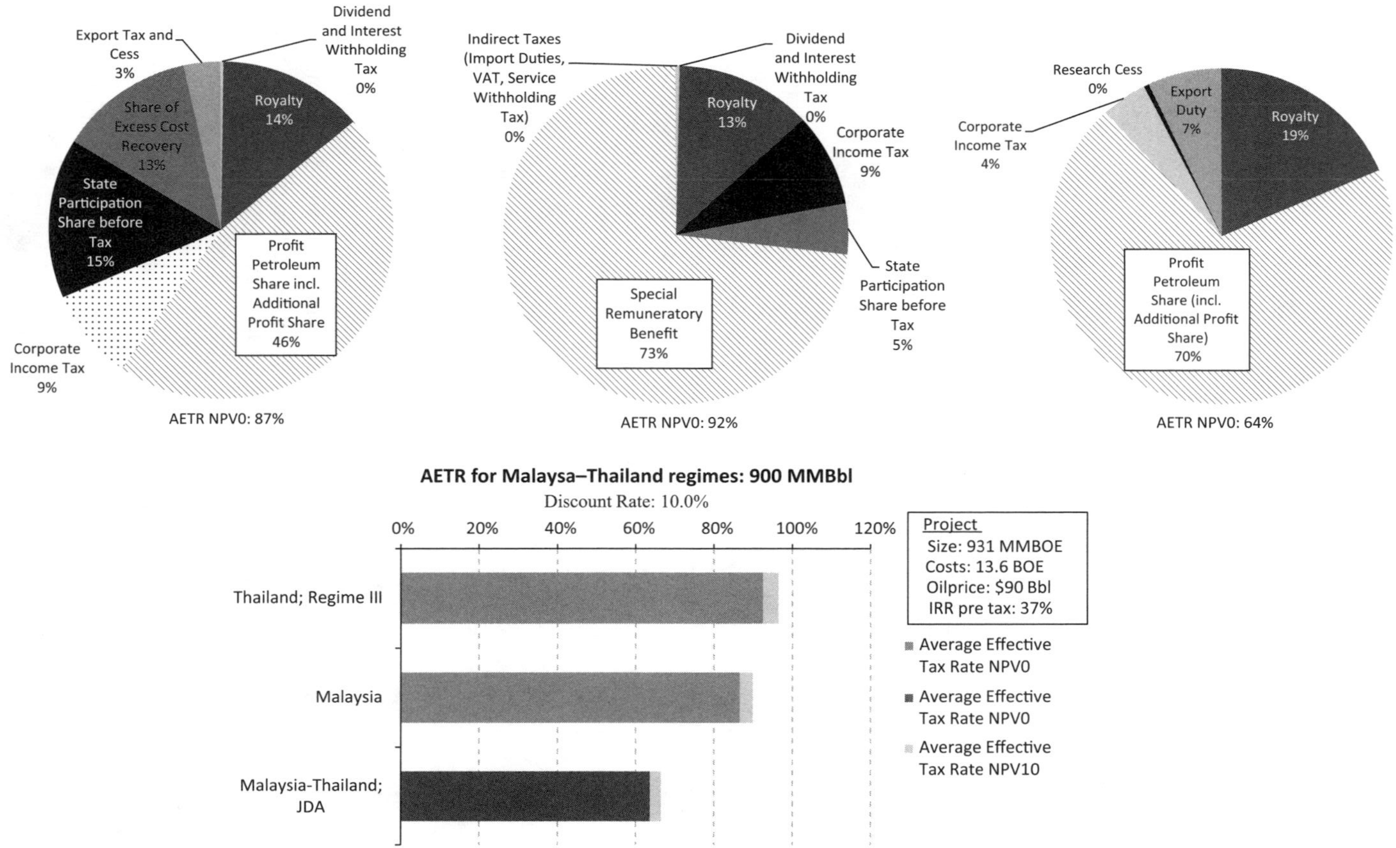

Figure 11.2 Malaysia–Thailand project life revenues and AETR from a stylized 900 MMBbl field

Source: Authors' calculations

Table 11.2 Royalty rates for Thailand III

Monthly Sales Volume	*Royalty Rates*
Up to 60 MMbbl	5%
60–150 MMbbl	6.25%
150–300 MMbbl	10%
300–600 MMbbl	12.5%
Over 600 MMbbl	15%

Table 11.3 Rates of special remuneratory benefit using Thai Baht

Income per metre of well	*SRB*
Up to THB 4,800	0%
THB 4,800–14,400	1% per each THB 240 increment
THB 14,400–33,600	1% per each THB 960 increment
Over THB 33,600	1% per each THB 3,840 increment (max. 75%)

state participation; however, the Invitation to Bid of May 23, 2007, included a provision for participation by a Thai national entity (usually the state company) in the petroleum concessions of at least 5%. The contractor carries the state entity through development but receives reimbursement for the state entity's share of past costs.

Unique to the Thailand III fiscal regime is a form of additional profits tax known as "special remuneratory benefit" (SRB) introduced by the amendment to the Petroleum Act in 1989. The contractor's income per metre of well drilled sets a scale for SRB rates. Income for this purpose is the revenue from the petroleum before royalty and other payments to the government, adjusted for inflation and exchange rates. Metres of wells drilled is the cumulative total metres of all wells drilled during the licence period, beginning at exploration, plus a geological constant which is intended to reflect the relative risks and difficulties associated with drilling the block. The geological constant varies from 300,000 metres for onshore blocks to 600,000 metres for deep offshore blocks in the Andaman Sea for the 19th and 20th bidding rounds: the higher the figure, of course, the lower the resulting income per metre of well. The rates of SRB are determined according to a sliding scale in Table 11.3, with a maximum rate of 75%.

The SRB rates are applied to the petroleum profit, calculated as revenue less capital expenditure with uplift, operating expense, and petroleum loss carried forward from prior years. Each contract specifies a rate of uplift. The Petroleum Regulation of 1989 stipulates the maximum rate of such uplift to be 35%. Negative petroleum profit (i.e., loss) is carried forward to the next period. The SRB is deductible for petroleum income tax purposes. Figure 11.2 presents the revenue streams to the government from a stylized petroleum project.[15]

2.2.3 Fiscal regime for the Malaysia–Thailand joint development area

The fiscal regime for the JDA is patterned largely on Malaysia's PSC, but with a simpler profit sharing mechanism between the contractor and the Joint Authority. From total production, a royalty of 10% is payable to the Joint Authority. Petroleum exported outside of both Malaysia and Thailand incurs export tax at 10%. Customs authorities of both countries collect the export tax individually but reduce the amount due by the contractor by 50% in accordance with the percentage attribution to each state. Cost recovery is limited to 50% of petroleum produced, and unused cost recovery forms part of profit petroleum. Profit petroleum is split equally between the contractor and the Joint Authority. The contractor pays income tax on remaining petroleum income. An income tax exemption applies for the first 8 years of production, after which the contractor pays income tax at 10% for the next 8 years and 20% thereafter. The contractor pays income tax to the tax authorities of both countries, but the amount is reduced by 50% by each country. Tax losses can be carried forward indefinitely. The contractor pays additional profits tax of 50% (similar to the Malaysian device) where the petroleum price exceeds US$25 per barrel, escalated by 5% every year from 1994. No withholding tax applies to dividends or interest payments.

2.2.4 Discussion

For the assumed example the JDA regime emerges as significantly less tough on the contractor than either of the national fiscal regimes. The share to the states in aggregate, however, would include the proceeds to the national oil companies in each case. Assuming those are no different from cases under exclusive national jurisdiction, then the explanations for the more generous regime would include less favourable geological conditions and prospectivity in the zone, an intention of both countries to accelerate development in the joint zone relative to other areas, and an awareness that risk of future change in the JDA rules might add to investors' perceptions of risk. Some combination of these probably applies.

2.3 Nigeria–São Tomé e Príncipe joint development zone

2.3.1 Fiscal framework for petroleum activities in Nigeria

Nigeria is the largest producer of petroleum in Africa and is a member of OPEC.

The first commercial discovery in Nigeria was made in the Niger Delta in 1956, where production commenced 2 years later. The oil industry has remained concentrated in the Niger Delta, with a daily production rate of about 2.5 MM Bbl. Nigeria also holds the largest reserve of natural gas in the continent, in addition to a vast amount of coal and renewable natural resources.[16]

Two separate fiscal regimes apply to oil in Nigeria – the joint venture (JV) regime, essentially a tax and royalty system applies onshore/in shallow water, and production sharing applies in deeper waters offshore.[17] Both regimes, however, were to be modified under the terms of the new Petroleum Industry Bill (PIB), originally proposed in 2008 but not enacted by the National Assembly by the time of the change of government in 2015. The PIB has gone through several versions. This chapter illustrates the terms included in the July 2009 Memorandum on the PIB prepared by the Inter-Agency Committee (the Inter-Agency Memorandum, IAM), the last major revision prior to the 2015 election. Table 11.4 provides summaries of 1993 and 2005 PSCs and IAM terms for both fiscal regimes. The terms for the latest 2007 PSC are presented in Appendix 1, where they are compared with regimes of other countries.

JV arrangements are between the holder(s) of an oil mining licence and the federal government as represented by the Nigerian National Petroleum Corporation (NNPC). In the first instance the JV partners are entitled to 100% of production. Each JV partner, including NNPC, then sells its share of production, pays its share of costs, and is separately liable for royalty and taxes. The JVs operate under a royalty/tax system originally specified in legislation but modified since enactment by a memorandum of understanding (MOU) between the companies and the government, which has undergone several revisions. The government receives a royalty payment between 0% and 20% of total production depending on the location and water depth of the field. Petroleum profits tax applies to petroleum income at 85%.

Under PSCs, the government, represented by NNPC, appoints the investor as "contractor" to assist the government in developing the resources. The parties agree that the contractor will meet the exploration and development costs in return for a share of any production to recover cost and a share of profit oil in excess of the cost. The contractor will have no right to be paid in the event that discovery and development do not occur. If production goes ahead, the government receives a royalty payment from the contractor at a rate that ranges from 0% to 16.67% depending on location and water depth of the block. The contractor is allowed to recover cost from a maximum 80% of total production after royalty. Profit petroleum is split between the government and the contractor according to a scale using the cumulative post-tax revenue-to-investment ratio – the R-factor.[18] The contractor pays corporate income tax on its income at 50% and withholds 10% of dividends and interest payments before remitting them to shareholders and lenders. Figure 11.3 shows the revenue streams that make up the total government revenue from the 900 MMbbl field example.

2.4 *Fiscal framework for petroleum activities in São Tomé e Príncipe*

The presence of hydrocarbon in São Tomé e Príncipe (STP) was known from the middle of the 19th century. However, it was not until 1972 that Texas Pacific drilled the first exploration wells. At the end of 2015, no commercial discovery had been declared in the exclusive economic zone. Nevertheless, because of its location in a region where major oil plays have been found, the country has potential to become a large producer of hydrocarbons.

Table 11.4 Summary of Nigeria fiscal terms

	Current terms – Oil projects			*IAM terms*	
	1993 PSC	2005 PSC	JV	PSC (deep water)	JV/onshore
Royalty	Royalty on production 0–200m 16.67%,	Royalty on production 200–500m 12%,	Royalty on production 0–100m 18.50%,	Royalty on production 0–25Mbpd 5%	Royalty on production 5%/12.5%/25% varying with production rate and location (see Table 11.1)
	200–500m 12%,	500–800m 8%	100–200m 16.5%,	25–50Mbpd 12.5%	Max. for existing 20% onshore
	500–800m 8%,	800–1000m 8%	200–500m 12.5%,	>50Mbpd 25%	Max. for existing 18.5% shallow
	800–1000m 4%, > 1000m 0%	>1000m 8%	800–1000m 4%, > 1000m 0%	Royalty on price $70 — $110; 0.4% per $1 $110–140; 16% + 0.2% per $1	Royalty on price $70 — $110; 0.4% per $1 $110–140; 16% + 0.2% per $1
			On shore: 20%	$110–170; 22% + 0.1% per $1 >170; 25%	$110–170; 22% + 0.1% per $1 >170; 25%
Valuation point	volume of oil lifted/delivered to terminals (shipments)			oil production (wellhead)	
Valuation basis	Posted price or actual price, whichever higher			Official swelling price, as determined by Inspectorate and adjusted for quality and transportation costs	
Production sharing	Cost recovery limit 100%	Cost recovery limit 100%	n/a	Cost recovery limit 80%	n/a
	Sharing using cumulative production	Sharing using R-factor		Sharing basis unchanged	
	Govt. share 20%–60%	Govt. share 25%–75%			
	Profit petroleum shared after PPT	Profit petroleum shared after PPT		Profit petroleum before NHT	
PPT/NHT[1/]	PPT 50%		PPT 85%	NHT 30% (deep water and frontier)	NHT 50% (on shore and shallow water)

(*Continued*)

Table 11.4 Continued

	Current terms – Oil projects			*IAM terms*	
Investment tax credit/ allowance	50% tax credit for PPT	50% tax allowance for PPT	Tax allowance 5% on shore; 10–20% offshore	n/a	n/a
Depreciation	20% yr 1–4; 19% yr 5 from date incurred; intangible drilling expensed immediately			20% yr 1–4; 19% yr 5 from commercial production; intangible drilling depreciated	
Small field allowances (NHT)	not applicable			Separate oil, condensate and gas allowance. Volume cap, $ per barrel/$ per MMBtu cap and proportion of realized price cap. Different limits for on shore, shallow water, off shore	
CIT rate	not applicable			CIT 30%, consolidated by company	
CIT depreciation				25% per year from production	
Cost deductibility	Wholly, Exclusively, Necessarily test for PPT			Benchmarked, Verified, Approved test for NHT; Wholly, Exclusively, Necessarily and Reasonably for CIT Non-deductible: non-Nigerian overhead, 20% other non-Nigerian costs; interest and certain other costs (demurrage)	
Withholding tax	nil for PPT			nil for NHT; 10% for CIT (intention is to exempt)	
Industry levy	not applicable			2% of revenues	
NDDC levy	3% of costs			3% of costs	
Education tax	2% of assessable profit			2% of assessable profit	
Ring-fence	PPT by company			NHT consolidated by company for upstream but separately for deep water and on shore/shallow. Midstream subject to CIT only. CIT consolidated by company	

1/ Petroleum Production Tax (PPT); National Hydrocarbon Tax (NHT)

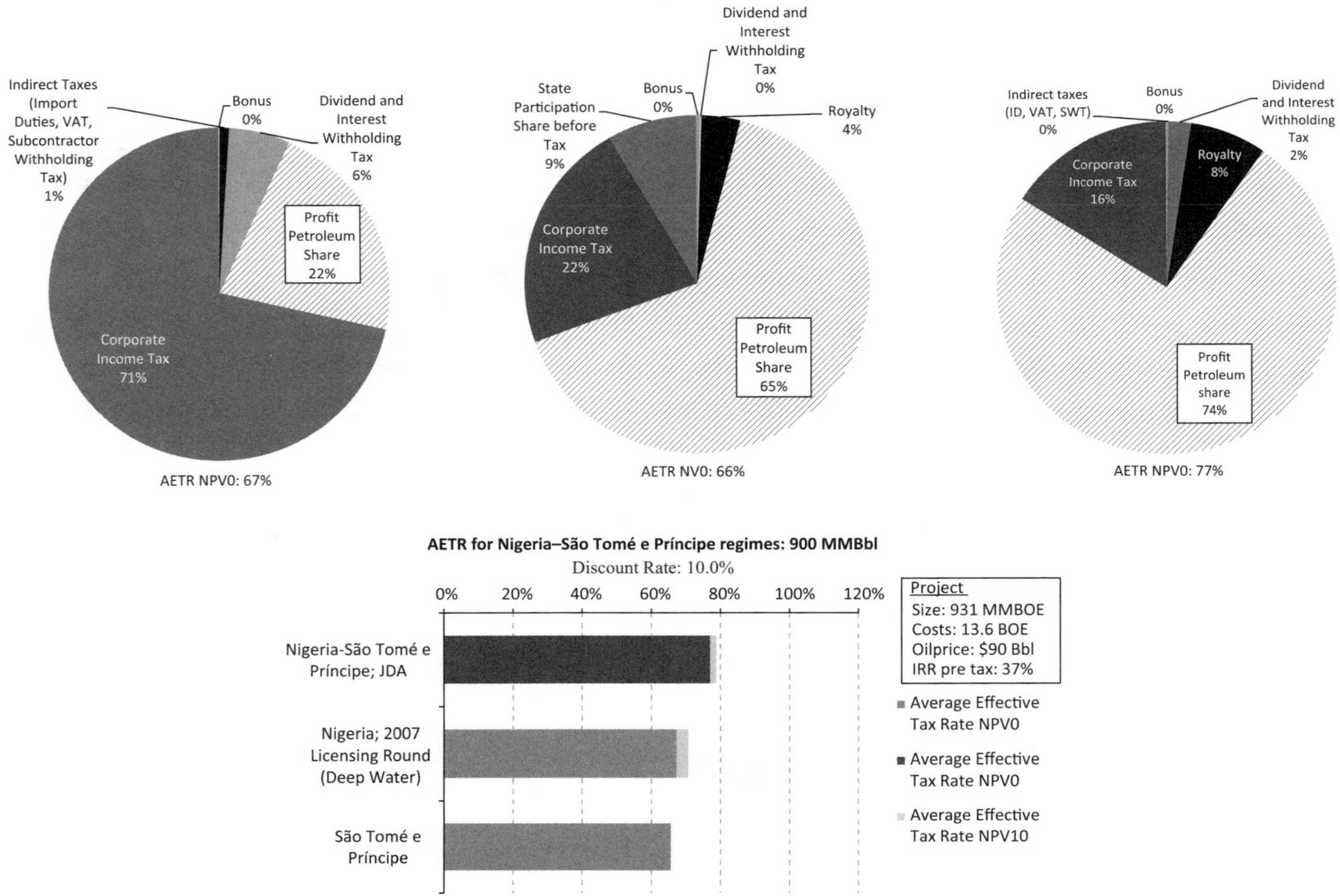

Figure 11.3 Nigeria–São Tomé e Príncipe project life revenues and AETR from a stylized 900 MMBbl field

Source: Authors' calculations

Table 11.5 Contractor profit share in STP PSC

Contractor's Rate of Return	*Contractor's Profit Share*
ROR < 16%	100%
16 % ≤ ROR < 19%	90%
19 % ≤ ROR < 23%	80%
23 % ≤ ROR < 26%	60%
ROR ≥ 26%	50%

Hydrocarbon activities in STP's exclusive economic zone would operate under either a production sharing (PSC) system or a risk service contract (RSC) system and be taxed according to the petroleum taxation legislation. If a development went ahead the government would receive 2% of total production in royalty payment under the PSC system. Up to 80% of total production (the cost oil or gas limit) after royalty can be taken to recover the costs of petroleum operation and development.[19] The government and the contractor share profit petroleum according to a sliding scale of pre-tax nominal rates of return (Table 11.5). The contractor pays 30% on its profits to the government. Losses from prior periods can be carried forward indefinitely. The model PSC does not stipulate the level of state participation in the project. However, the first Licensing Round Presentation in 2010 indicated a 10% minimum participation by the state in the form of free venture interest in the contractor group.

In the RSC system, instead of sharing production, the contractor would be compensated for its "service" with a portion of the revenues derived from petroleum production as agreed between the two parties. The government retains ownership of the resources under both PSC and RSC systems. The National Petroleum Agency (ANP) and Petroleum Oversight Commission together manage and oversee petroleum activities in the country. Figure 11.3 shows the government revenue breakdown from a stylized project example under the PSC system.

2.4.1 Fiscal framework for petroleum activities in Nigeria–São Tomé e Príncipe JDZ

Nigeria and São Tomé e Príncipe did not agree on the maritime boundary but acknowledged the importance of natural resources lying beneath the disputed area. The two countries established a joint development zone in February 2001, where Nigeria and STP have 60% and 40% of interests in the zone, respectively.[20] The treaty will last for 45 years but will be reviewed 30 years after the date of signature. The JDZ Petroleum Regulations and the JDZ Tax Regulations, along with the model PSC, govern petroleum activities in the joint jurisdiction under the Nigeria–São Tomé e Príncipe Joint Authority. The first licensing round in the JDZ took place in 2004. A total of five blocks were available for licensing. All blocks were explored to some extent. In December 2011,

Table 11.6 Contractor profit share from PSC

R-Factor	*Contractor Profit Share*
R < 1.2	80%
1.2 ≤ R < 2.5	25% + ([(2.5 – R)/(2.5 – 1.2)] × (80% – 25%))
R ≥ 2.5	25%

the government of São Tomé e Príncipe confirmed the existence of commercial quantities of oil in the JDZ in Block 1, where the French oil company Total was the operator.[21] Total relinquished Block 1 in 2013, however, while companies in Blocks 2, 3, and 4 had withdrawn in 2012. A new contract with a Hong Kong–based company for Block 1 was subsequently signed.

The fiscal regime for the JDZ has the overall structure of a Nigerian PSC, including R-factor production sharing, in contrast to STP's internal rate of return (IRR) mechanism. If development is successful, the contractor pays a royalty to the Joint Authority at a rate that depends on the daily rate of production. The royalty rate is 0% if production is less than 20 Mbpd and 5% if production exceeds 70 Mbpd. When daily production falls between these two thresholds, the royalty rate is determined by the formula: 5% × (1 − [(70 − P)/(70 − 20)]), where P is production in Mbpd. As in Nigeria's and STP's EEZs, the contractor recovers investment and cost of operations from a maximum of 80% of production after royalty. Petroleum after royalty and cost recovery divides between the contractor and the Joint Authority according to the post-tax R-factor as set out in Table 11.6. Profits to the contractor are subject to 50% tax, with indefinite loss carry-forward. Each country imposes its own rules with regards to dividend and interest withholding taxes, with Nigeria taxing 60% and STP taxing 40% of the total amounts. Where the imposition is joint, Nigeria takes 60% and STP 40%; where the imposition is according to national rules the effective base is reduced to each country's attribution percentage. There is no requirement for the Joint Authority to have an equity interest in the projects.

3 Evaluation of fiscal regimes in JDZs

This section reports results from quantitative simulations of the fiscal regimes for exclusive economic and joint development zones.[22] In practice, investment decisions depend on a variety of factors that go beyond the fiscal regime – such as perceived geological potential, stability of institutions, and companies' diversification strategies. This analysis focuses exclusively on the characteristics of the fiscal regime and thus assumes all other factors constant and neutral with respect to the investment decision.

Appendix 1 presents a summary of fiscal terms for regimes simulated. JDZ fiscal regimes change in successive licensing rounds or offers of acreage. For the purpose of comparing exclusive and joint development zones and of detailed analysis, only one actual and recent fiscal regime is simulated for each JDZ scheme. For example, the fiscal terms for the 2007 PSC bidding round in Nigeria are simulated, but not the terms for 1993 and 2005 PSCs. Moreover, to simplify, minor taxes and levies are left out of the analysis unless they make up a material contribution to government revenues. Such additional items may include surface rentals, social development contributions, or local government taxes and levies.

The simulations employ two stylized project examples: a 300 million barrel (MM bbl) offshore field with a relatively high total cost per barrel of recoverable reserves, and a relatively larger 900 MM bbl offshore field with lower total cost per barrel. Figure 11.4 shows the project economics for the two fields. Note that these project examples do not reflect a particular field in a particular country but nevertheless represent fields that are broadly realistic in production profiles and costs. This is not to argue that these fields would have been viable or profitable in a low-price environment such as that prevailing early in 2016:

Offshore 300 MMBbl		
Production oil	275	MMbbl
Production gas	-	MMBOE
Production BOE	275	MMBOE
Years	21	
constant 2013 dollars	$ million	$/Bbl
Exploration costs	280	1.0
Development costs	1,500	5.5
Development drilling	2,033	7.4
Sustaining capital	-	0.0
Operating costs	2,387	8.7
Decommissioning	250	0.9
	6,450	23.4

Offshore 900 MMBbl		
Production oil	931	MMbbl
Production gas	-	MMBOE
Production BOE	931	MMBOE
Years	22	
constant 2013 dollars	$ million	$/Bbl
Exploration costs	380	0.4
Development costs	2,000	2.1
Development drilling	2,500	2.7
Sustaining capital	-	0.0
Operating costs	7,313	7.9
Decommissioning	450	0.5
	12,643	13.6

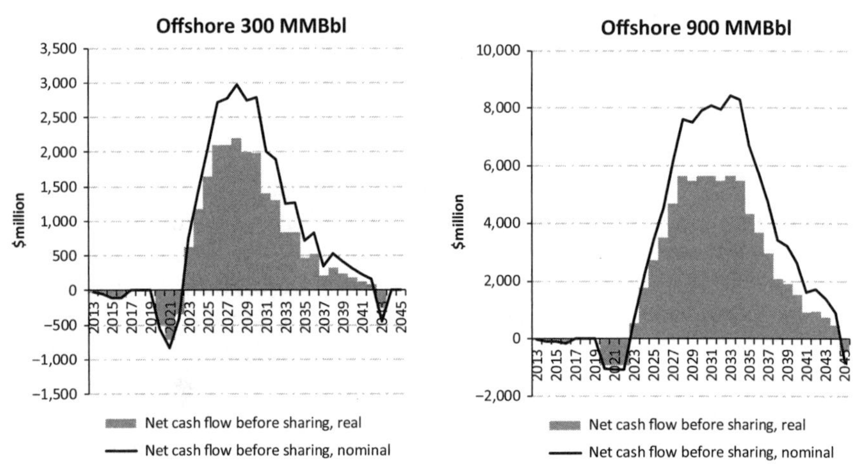

Figure 11.4 Project economics: stylized petroleum project examples

Source: Authors' estimates

in common with many other new prospects (and existing fields) their feasibility may depend on higher long run average prices. Moreover, measures such as the average effective tax rate (AETR) represent a division of rent – meaningful only where rent (as a surplus over minimum acceptable returns to capital) occurs – hence the use of high prices in our simulations to evaluate circumstances where there is material rent.

The evaluation uses simple economic assumptions. An oil price is assumed at US$90 per barrel in the base year, in order to demonstrate regime effects in above-average conditions of potential profitability, and the price escalates every year at a rate of 2%.[23] For debt finance, the real risk-free interest rate is 1%, to which is added a margin of 3.5%. Government, and the oil company investor results are presented using a discount rate of 10%. Equity finance meets all exploration costs, with development costs 70% debt financed. Finally, both fields are assumed to be located in offshore areas at depths of 1,200 metres. The last assumption only affects the results for Nigeria and Thailand where royalty rates vary according to water depth and location of the fields.

The average effective tax rate (AETR) presents a project-specific measure of "government take" in a success case. The AETR consists of the government's share of pre-tax net present value (NPV), usually measured at the government's assumed discount rate. For alternative fiscal regimes, alternative prices, and other circumstances, the AETR provides a comparative benchmark. Figure 11.5 reports estimated AETRs for the regimes studied.

Several observations emerge from the simulations. First, the ranking of fiscal regimes according to AETRs in this high-price case is consistent between both field examples (offshore 300 MM Bbl and offshore 900 MM Bbl), with Thailand on the top and Australia at the bottom of the charts. Second, no consistent pattern exists as to whether exclusive zone national regimes are "tougher" than joint regimes or *vice versa*. While exclusive zone regimes for Thailand and Malaysia yield higher AETRs than the joint regime, the opposite is true for Nigeria and São Tomé e Príncipe.[24] The Australia–Timor-Leste joint regime is tougher than Australia's exclusive zone regime but less tough than Timor-Leste's under both scenarios. The rankings may well change with different oil price assumptions.

Thailand's national regime is tougher than the joint regime as a result of the special remuneratory benefit (SRB, outlined earlier in this chapter) and a higher income tax rate (50% in the exclusive zone compared with a maximum of 20% for the JDZ). Recall that SRB is applied on profit petroleum at a rate that is progressive with income per metre of well. In the simulations, income per metre ranges between US$600 and US$3,000 for the 300 MM Bbl case and between US$900 and US$6,500 for the 900 MM Bbl case; thus SRB is imposed at or close to the maximum 75% rate for much of the project's production period. Combined with royalty, profit tax, and other fiscal terms, the SRB makes the government take very high on the assumptions used here. The Malaysian EEZ regime is considerably tougher than the joint regime because of the higher corporate tax and supplementary tax rates and the presence of interest withholding tax and state participation in the projects.

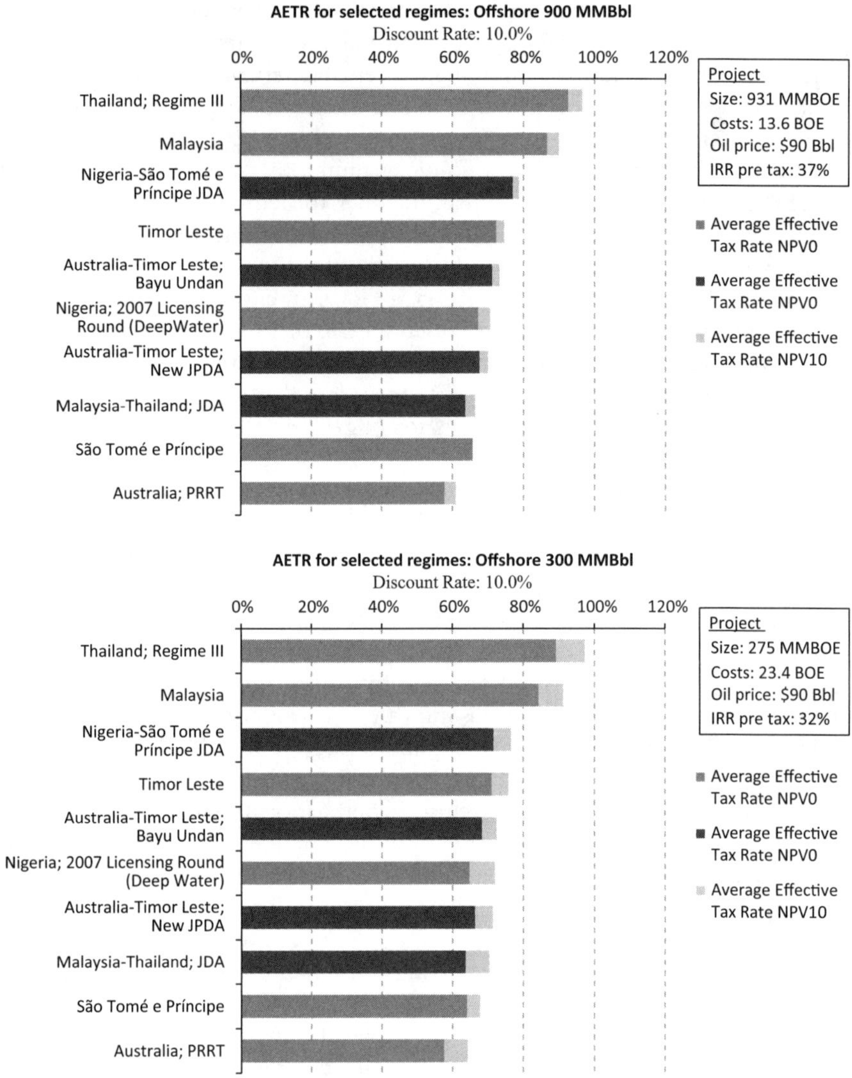

Figure 11.5 Average effective tax Rates for EEZs and JDZs

Source: Authors' estimates

The fiscal terms for the Nigeria–São Tomé e Príncipe JDZ produce a somewhat higher AETR than the assumed terms for the Nigerian EEZ. The deepwater assumption translates into 0% royalty rate for Nigeria but not for the JDZ. The Joint Authority also receives a higher share of profit petroleum. Similarly, the JDZ regime is tougher than the São Tomé e Príncipe regime because the JDZ guarantees a minimum 20% share of profit oil to the government while the national regime does not. The joint regime also imposes a higher rate of petroleum income tax (50% compared with 30%). However, the effects of these fiscal terms are offset in the national regime by a 10% free share in the contractor group.

Terms for the Timor-Leste–Australia JDZ are described in section 4. The government take for Timor-Leste is higher than those for the regimes applicable to Bayu-Undan and the new JPDA mainly because of the 15% state-carried interest assumed, given that other fiscal terms are broadly comparable. The first tranche petroleum in the Bayu-Undan regime acts as a pre-allocation of profit share, making an implicit royalty at the same rate as in the Timor-Leste national regime. Initial profit share to the government is less for the Bayu-Undan JDZ regime but would be higher for a large field. Australia does not impose royalty but has a resource rent tax in its national regime that is not applicable to profits from the JPDA since production sharing applies instead. The combined effect of the difference in fiscal terms results in a lower government share for the Australian jurisdiction than under either the joint regimes or the Timor-Leste national terms.

4 The case of Australia and Timor-Leste in the Timor Sea

4.1 Legal and fiscal framework for petroleum activities

Timor-Leste and Australia have no final maritime boundary in the Timor Sea. The two governments put in place a complex set of interim arrangements for the sharing of petroleum extracted from two overlapping joint development zones in the Timor Sea: (1) the Joint Petroleum Development Area (JPDA) under the Timor Sea Treaty (TST) and (2) the Greater Sunrise Unit Area (governed by the International Unitisation Agreement [IUA] and the Treaty Concerning Certain Maritime Areas in the Timor Sea [CMATS]). (See Figure 11.6.) These treaties result from long negotiations from 1999 to 2007 over replacements for arrangements made between Indonesia and Australia, during the period when Indonesia controlled East Timor. In sum, all these arrangements illustrate the full range of challenges in making interim arrangements in lieu of a full maritime boundary determination; hence the separate focus on this case in this chapter.[25]

Indonesia and Australia ratified an agreement in 1972, establishing a frontal maritime seabed boundary between the two countries in the Timor Sea and beyond. Portugal then ruled Timor-Leste and declined to participate in negotiations over a maritime boundary in the area. As a result, Australia and Indonesia left a gap in the frontal line (the "Timor Gap"), pending future negotiations with Portugal.

Indonesia's annexation of Timor-Leste as a province of Indonesia, following the occupation of late 1975, was not internationally recognized (UN Security Council Resolutions 384 [1975] and 389 [1976]). Australia, however, entered into negotiations with Indonesia about petroleum rights in the Timor Sea after Indonesia signalled unwillingness simply to "join the dots" across the gap in the 1972 frontal line. The "gap" lies between points A16 (east) and A12 (west) in the Australia–Indonesia maritime boundary (see Figure 11.6). The "Timor

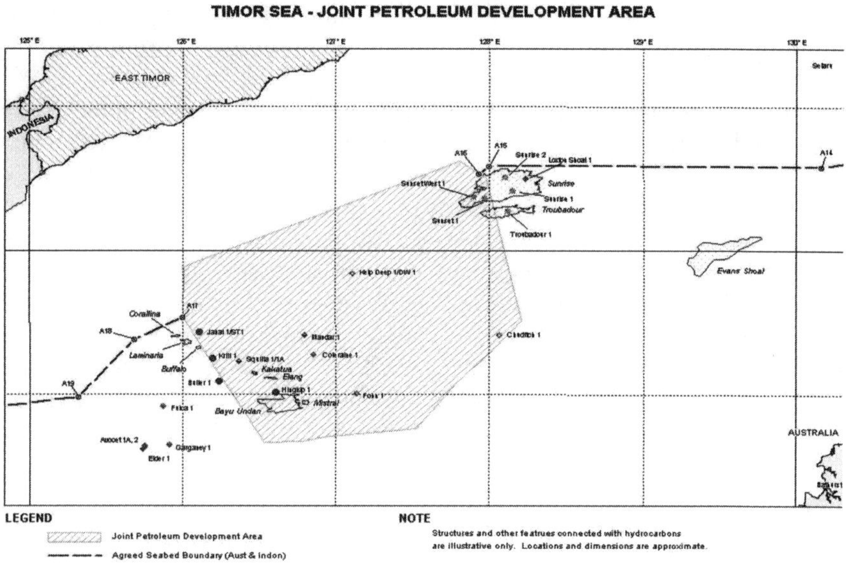

Figure 11.6 Timor Sea – joint petroleum development area

Gap Treaty" of 1989 resulted (ratified 1991), creating "Zone of Cooperation A" (ZOCA), where petroleum produced was attributed 50% to Australia and 50% to Indonesia. The ZOCA required the drawing of lateral lines intersecting the end-points that marked the Timor Gap in the 1972 treaty, and of further frontal lines to the north, and to the south at the median line between the opposing coasts.[26] Exploration had commenced earlier under both Portuguese and Australian authorizations and accelerated within the ZOCA. By 1999 there were major discoveries at Bayu-Undan, and at Sunrise and Troubador ("Greater Sunrise"), where the fields extended beyond the eastern perimeter of the ZOCA. Other smaller discoveries resulted in oil production at Elang Kakatua-Kakatua North.

Following the UN–sponsored referendum of 1999, Indonesia withdrew from Timor-Leste, and the UN established a transitional administration in East Timor (UNTAET). UNTAET declined to adopt the Timor Gap Treaty on behalf of Timor-Leste, continuing the arrangement only by means of an Exchange of Notes with Australia enabling existing activities to continue. In July 2001, UNTAET and Australia agreed the text of a new Timor Sea Treaty (TST). The ZOCA was renamed the Joint Petroleum Development Area (JPDA), and the treaty once again created an interim arrangement without prejudice to any future maritime boundary delimitation.

The TST attributed 90% of JPDA petroleum produced to Timor-Leste and 10% to Australia. Annex E of the TST called for unitization of Greater Sunrise, attributing 20.1% of Sunrise petroleum to the JPDA and 79.9% to Australia, following available technical information at the time about the likely reserve proportions in each jurisdiction. The TST was ratified by Timor-Leste in 2002 and then by Australia in 2003 after completion of negotiations over the international unitization agreement (IUA) for Greater Sunrise and the approval of arrangements for gas production at Bayu-Undan.[27] Australia ratified the IUA in 2003, but Timor-Leste declined to ratify pending a settlement of its wider maritime claims in the Timor Sea. A permanent maritime boundary was not delineated, but the dispute was resolved for the time being by a further interim arrangement, the Treaty on Certain Maritime Areas of the Timor Sea (CMATS): CMATS preserved the TST and IUA, but all the taxation and production-sharing revenue derived by both governments from the Sunrise unit area would be pooled and shared equally between the countries. CMATS and the IUA entered into force in 2007. If no development plan for Greater Sunrise had been approved by 2013, the parties were entitled to terminate CMATS. By 2016 neither Australia nor Timor-Leste had done so, though Timor-Leste had once again called for negotiations or arbitration under UNCLOS to delimit permanent maritime boundaries.[28] CMATS contains a provision that, even if terminated, it returns to operation if and when a development plan for the Greater Sunrise fields is approved.[29]

A combination of production sharing and taxation generates revenue for Timor-Leste and Australia in the JPDA. As a result of the treaties, however, there are four variants of the production sharing contract (PSC) operation in the JPDA and areas outside it exclusively granted under contract by Timor-Leste. Further, the tax rules applied by Timor-Leste also differ among projects, mainly because certain rights for pre-existing PSC holders were preserved under the Timor Sea Treaty and because there are some differences in terms between the JPDA and areas of Timor-Leste exclusive jurisdiction. Australia applies its own oil and gas fiscal regime in areas it has licensed outside the JPDA but takes proceeds from production-sharing contracts within the JPDA in lieu of its own petroleum resource rent tax (PRRT). The implementation of these fiscal regimes therefore carries unavoidable administrative complications.

4.1.1 The JPDA general regime

The TST calls for agreement between Timor-Leste and Australia over a joint "fiscal scheme" for each petroleum project in the JPDA (Article 5), covering the sharing of petroleum between investors and the two governments. The contract incorporating the fiscal scheme is also the form of licence for petroleum activities. The two governments agreed a new Petroleum Mining Code (PMC)[30] for the JPDA, and set out a model PSC as the general "fiscal scheme"; in addition, under the terms of the Treaty and the Tax Code,[31] Timor-Leste and Australia impose national taxation on their respective shares of revenues from and relevant activities in the JPDA. Timor-Leste incorporated its Petroleum Taxation Act of 2005 into its Taxes and Duties Act of 2008. This overall scheme applies to PSCs granted following the first post-TST licensing round for the JPDA held in 2006.[32]

4.1.2 The Bayu-Undan regime

The TST (Annex F), however, preserved the pre-existing PSCs setting out the regulatory and fiscal terms for the Bayu-Undan area (extending across two PSCs) and the part of Sunrise located in the JPDA (also two PSCs). Timor-Leste also preserved the inherited taxation terms for these PSCs while Australian taxation applies in accordance with prevailing law. In the period prior to final ratification of the TST, the Bayu-Undan PSCs (and taxation terms) were renegotiated, so that the rules applying to the Bayu-Undan project consist of the original PSCs,[33] as amended by "Appendix X", the inherited Indonesian Law on Income Tax (as at October 25, 1999), UNTAET Regulation 2000/18 and the Taxation of Bayu-Undan Contractors Act (2003). The taxation terms for the Timor-Leste portion of Bayu-Undan were fixed under a Tax Stability Agreement – this is symmetrical, so that Bayu-Undan contractors do not benefit from general tax reductions.

4.1.3 The Sunrise regime

The PSC and tax rules for the Sunrise contract areas were not amended after the TST came into force – thus, in practice, creating a third regime. As of 2016, this was relevant only to the Sunrise joint venture partners and taxation of subcontractors working in the JPDA on Sunrise. It consists of the inherited PSCs, the inherited Indonesian Law on Income Tax, and UNTAET Regulation 2000/18.

The fourth PSC regime is that for areas outside the JPDA where Timor-Leste applies its own exclusive jurisdiction. The PSC terms have been similar to those for the JPDA but included an option for a Timor-Leste national oil company to take up to 20% of a development at the time a commercial discovery is declared. Taxation of activities under these PSCs in Timor-Leste is set out in the Taxes and Duties Act (2008) but is not, of course, subject to the TST Taxation Code. For areas where Australia applies its exclusive jurisdiction the Australian offshore petroleum fiscal regime applies.

The fiscal terms that result from these four regimes are summarized in Table 11.7 for the PSCs and Table 11.8 for the tax regimes. The scheme of the PSC and tax is illustrated in Figures 11.7 for Bayu-Undan and 11.8 for Sunrise and the split by revenue type in Figure 11.10. Bayu-Undan and Greater Sunrise both allocate an initial tranche of petroleum, which is shared between the contractor and the designated authority (DA).[34] This first tranche petroleum is, in effect, a limit on cost petroleum, as it ensures that some production will be shared between the contractor and the DA, as soon as production commences. In contrast, the PSCs not covered by Annex F (and PSCs in Timor-Leste's exclusive jurisdiction) allocate 5% of production to the government, and this allocation is, in effect, a 5% royalty.

All the PSCs allow generous recovery of costs, by permitting an uplift of certain costs. In the case of the preserved PSCs, the uplift is equal to 127% of exploration costs and tangible capital (the investment credit). This device was inherited from the old Indonesian PSC regime for "remote areas" but during the period of the "Timor Gap Treaty" was even more generous. In the case of

Table 11.7 Timor-Leste: PSC fiscal terms and sharing between governments

	JPDA PSCs			*PSCs in Timor-Leste's Exclusive Jurisdiction*
	Bayu-Undan (Annex F Preserved PSCs)	*Sunrise (Annex F Preserved PSCs)*	*PSCs not covered by Annex F*	
First tranche petroleum (FTP) or royalty	10% of production; shared in same proportions as profit oil and gas between DA and contractor	10% of production rising to 20% after 5 years; shared in the same proportions as profit oil and gas between DA and contractor	5% of production to government (a royalty payment)	5% of production to government (a royalty payment)
Cost petroleum	Permits recovery of investment credit (equal to 127% of exploration costs + tangible capital) plus operating costs (includes current-year exploration costs, non-capital costs, depreciation and allowable operating costs in previous years that have not been recovered).	Permits recovery of investment credit (equal to 127% of exploration costs + tangible capital) plus operating costs (includes current-year exploration costs, non-capital costs, depreciation and allowable operating costs in previous years that have not been recovered).	Petroleum less royalty but not more than recoverable costs (exploration, appraisal, capital, and operating costs plus decommissioning reserve allowed that year). Unrecovered costs uplifted by the U.S. 30-year bond rate plus 11 percentage points.	Petroleum less royalty but not more than recoverable costs (exploration, appraisal, capital, and operating costs plus decommissioning reserve allowed that year). Unrecovered costs uplifted by the U.S. 30-year bond rate plus 11 percentage points.
Government share of profit petroleum	Any remaining petroleum after FTP and cost petroleum is split between the DA and contractor. For oil (inc. condensate): the government share increases from 50 to 70% as bpd increases; for gas, the government share is 40%.	Any remaining petroleum after FTP and cost petroleum is split between the DA and contractor. For oil: the government share increases from 50 to 70% as bpd increases; for gas, the government share is 50%.	Any petroleum remaining after the royalty and cost petroleum is split between the DA and the contractor. The DA's share is 40%.	Any petroleum remaining after the royalty and cost petroleum is split between the government and the contractor. The government's share is 40%.

(*Continued*)

Table 11.7 Continued

	JPDA PSCs			*PSCs in Timor-Leste's Exclusive Jurisdiction*
	Bayu-Undan (Annex F Preserved PSCs)	*Sunrise (Annex F Preserved PSCs)*	*PSCs not covered by Annex F*	
Decommissioning	Detailed agreed provision (Appendix X) that permits a decommissioning cost reserve. Undiscounted costs recovered (UOP) over 15 years.	No provision	Decommissioning reserve permitted, but costs discounted at the uplift rate.	Decommissioning reserve permitted, but costs discounted at the uplift rate.
Ring-fencing	Bayu-Undan project ring-fenced by development area	By contract area	By contract area	By contract area
Sharing between governments	90% of DA's FTP and profit petroleum to Timor-Leste; 10% to Australia	Under CMATS, 50:50 sharing of JPDA and non–JPDA upstream revenues (sharing and tax revenue)	90% of DA's royalty and profit petroleum to Timor-Leste; 10% to Australia	Not applicable
State participation	No	No	No	At the time of a commercial discovery, election for participation (up to 20%) through a state-owned contractor, required to pay its share of future costs.

Table 11.8 The tax regime applying to Timor-Leste's PSCs

	JPDA PSCs			*PSCs in Timor-Leste's Exclusive Jurisdiction*
	Bayu-Undan (Annex F Preserved PSCs)	*Sunrise (Annex F Preserved PSCs)*	*PSCs not covered by Annex F*	
Timor-Leste Income tax	Frozen Indonesian law modified by TBUCA, with 30% fixed rate; no branch profits tax	Frozen Indonesian law with 30% rate; 15% branch profits tax if Treaty tax code applies; (total tax 40.5%).	Imposed by the Tax and Duties Act, petroleum rate 30%	Imposed by the Tax and Duties Act, petroleum rate 30%
Depreciation and amortization for income tax purposes	All exploration and development expenditure, including tangible assets: Useful life 1–4 years: 25% SL Useful life >4 years: 20% SL Pro rata depreciation in first year of production EKKN residual losses on closure amortized against Bayu-Undan income over 5 years, SL	Frozen Indonesian law rules: Tangible assets: Election of SL or DB methods over useful lives. Asset classes: < 4, 8, 16, or 20 years. Intangible assets: amortized by units of production method (includes exploration and intangible development expenditure).	Exploration expenditure – SL 5 years; Development expenditure (other than depreciable tangible assets) – SL 10 years, or project life; Depreciable assets other than buildings – SL (individually) or DB (pool) over useful life. Asset classes: < 4, 8, 16, or 20 years. Option for depreciation by units of production method for small fields.	Exploration expenditure – SL 5 years; Development expenditure (other than depreciable tangible assets) – SL 10 years, or project life; Depreciable assets other than buildings – SL (individually) or DB (pool) over useful life. Asset classes: < 4, 8, 16, or 20 years. Option for depreciation by units of production method for small fields.
Ring-fencing	Bayu-Undan project ring-fenced by development area	By contract area	By contract area	By contract area

(*Continued*)

Table 11.8 Continued

	JPDA PSCs			*PSCs in Timor-Leste's Exclusive Jurisdiction*
	Bayu-Undan (Annex F Preserved PSCs)	*Sunrise (Annex F Preserved PSCs)*	*PSCs not covered by Annex F*	
Withholding tax on payments to non-residents	20% withholding tax on interest and dividends, subject to reduction under the Timor Sea Tax Code if payee is Australian. 8% on services, with some special categories calculated under frozen Indonesian rules	20% withholding tax on interest, dividends and services, subject to the Timor Sea Tax Code if payee is Australian, with some special categories calculated under frozen Indonesian rules.	6% final withholding tax on all payments for services. 10% withholding tax on other payments to non-residents (except where taxed as permanent establishment).	6% final withholding tax on all payments for services. 10% withholding tax on other payments to non-residents (except where taxed as permanent establishment).
Additional profits tax	Imposed by TBUCA: net 22.5% after 16.5% rate of return	No	Imposed by the Tax and Duties Act (as Bayu-Undan), termed Supplemental Petroleum Tax (SPT)	Imposed by the Tax and Duties Act (as Bayu-Undan), termed Supplemental Petroleum Tax (SPT)
Fiscal stability	Yes – tax law frozen; contractors do not benefit from tax reductions	No	No	No

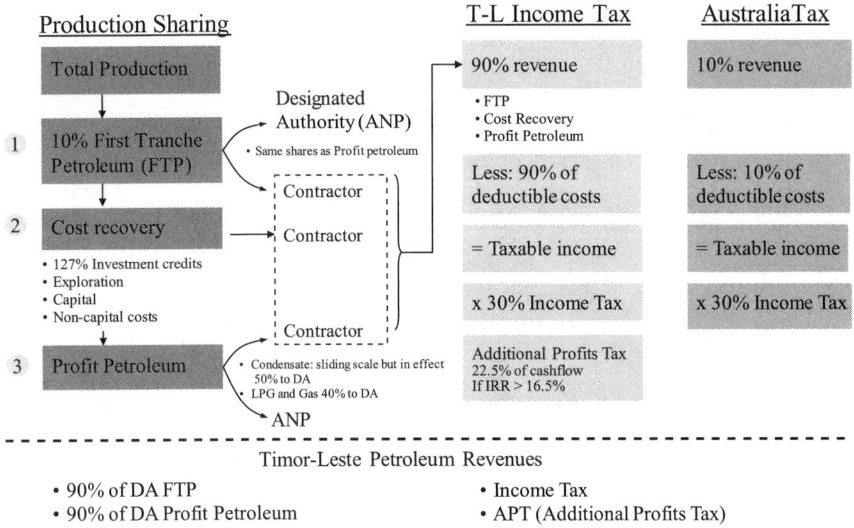

Figure 11.7 Fiscal regime for Bayu-Undan

the PSCs not covered by Annex F (or those in in Timor-Leste's exclusive jurisdiction),[35] unrecovered costs are uplifted annually by the U.S. 30-year bond rate plus 11 percentage points.

The split of profit petroleum is generally fixed percentages of remaining production. For oil production from the preserved PSCs, the fixed sharing varies within defined increments of the level of daily production, with three tranches: 0 to 50,000 bpd, DA share 50%, 50,000 to 150,000 bpd 60%, and greater than 150,000 bpd 70%. As JPDA PSCs cover the joint development area, the government's share of petroleum production is shared between Timor-Leste and Australia. The sharing is 90% for Timor-Leste and 10% for Australia. The JPDA share of Greater Sunrise petroleum is first shared 90:10 in favour of Timor-Leste, but under CMATS the governments then share equally in total upstream revenues collected from the entire unitised field (both production and tax revenue) including the petroleum not attributed to the JPDA.

The preserved PSC contractors pay income tax to Timor-Leste under Indonesian law frozen at October 25, 1999. However, the Indonesian law for the Bayu-Undan PSC is modified by the Taxation of Bayu-Undan Contractors Act (TBUCA). Thus for Bayu-Undan there is no branch profits tax but there is an additional profits tax. In general, withholding tax on payments to non-residents is higher under frozen Indonesian law than under the Tax and Duties Act. Except for Greater Sunrise, all the PSCs are subject to a supplemental petroleum tax (SPT) at a net rate of 22.5% of after-tax cash flows after the contractor has earned a 16.5% rate of return.[36]

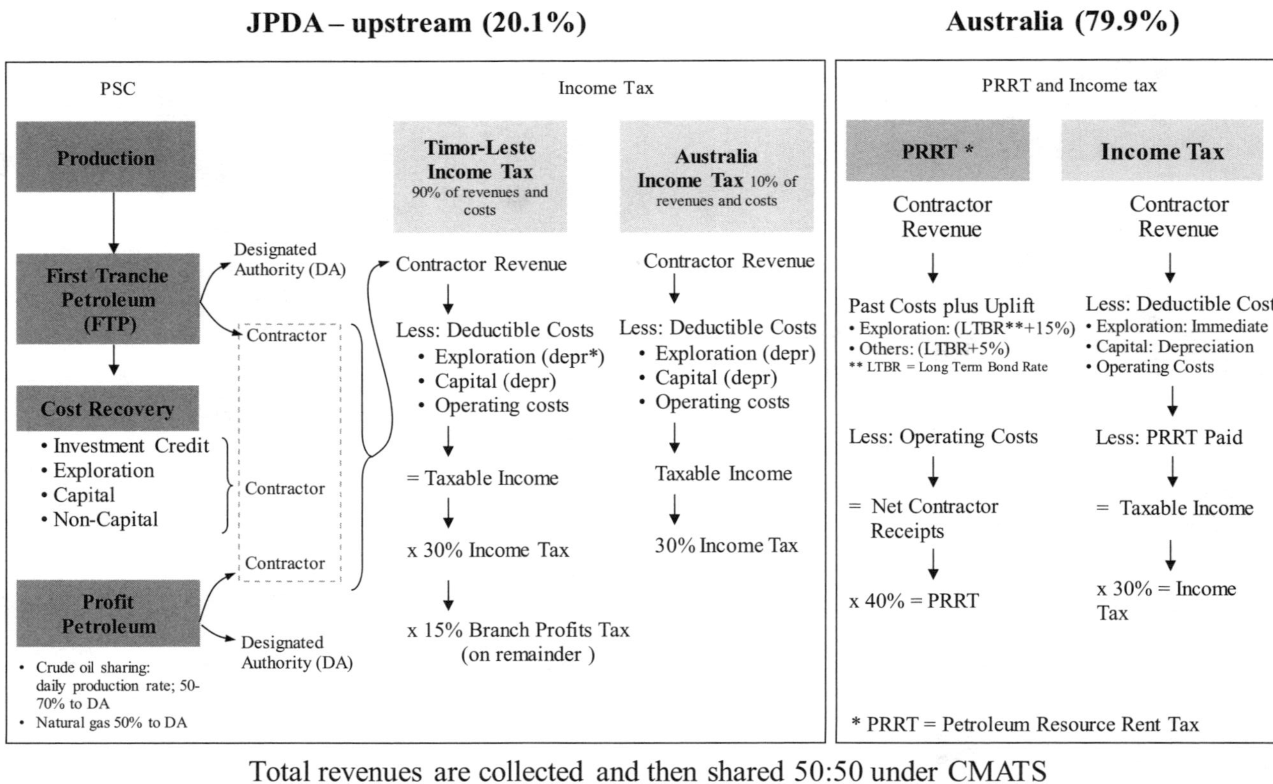

Figure 11.8 Sunrise fiscal regime

The treatment of interest deductions for tax and PSC purposes also differs. Under the Annex F PSCs the use of interest-bearing debt to finance operations must be approved by the DA. The new JPDA and Timor-Leste PSCs do not permit cost recovery of interest on debt. Under frozen Indonesian income tax rules, interest deductions are restricted to interest on debt that does not exceed a debt–equity ratio of 3:1. Under the Timor-Leste Taxes and Duties Act (2008),

Box 11.2 Petroleum exploration and development in treaty areas[37]

Following the closure of the small Elang Kakatua-Kakatua North (EKKN) oil fields in 2007, Timor-Leste's sole producing projects were the Bayu-Undan gas and condensate[38] project within the JPDA, operated by ConocoPhillips (with other venture partners) and the small Kitan field (35 million barrels), which started production in 2011 and was expected to stop in December 2015. Bayu-Undan consists of fields unitised from two PSC areas (Figure 11.9) and commenced commercial production of liquids (condensate and LPG) in July 2004 and of gas sales for LNG production in April 2006. Gas is piped to Darwin, Australia, through a pipeline owned by the same joint venturers and processed into LNG at Darwin LNG, a company again owned by the same parties. The LNG is sold under a long-term contract to Tokyo Gas and Tokyo Electric, who purchase it FOB Darwin and ship to Japan in their own LNG tankers. Condensate and LPG are essentially sold at spot prices, though under term contracts with selected buyers.

Bayu-Undan production has reached up to 110,000 barrels per day (bpd) of liquids and one billion cubic feet of gas per day (half exported to Darwin LNG and half re-injected into the reservoir in order to maintain gas exports at LNG plant capacity). Lifetime recoverable reserves of the project are estimated at 4 trillion cubic feet of dry gas and 500 million barrels of liquids, permitting a project life that extends beyond 2020. Bayu-Undan accounted for the vast majority of Timor-Leste government revenues after production commenced.

The Greater Sunrise project consists of the Sunrise and Troubador fields, straddling the JPDA perimeter to the east. The fields lie partly in two JPDA PSC areas and partly in two license areas granted by Australia (Northern Territory). The operator is Woodside Energy (of Australia), in partnership with ConocoPhillips, Shell, and Osaka Gas.[39] The joint venture has a commercial unitization agreement for the unit area, which is also the subject of the IUA and CMATS. A development concept for Greater Sunrise had not been decided, nor was a market for gas secured, by early 2016. The fields were estimated by Woodside to contain 5.1 tcf of dry gas and 226 million barrels of condensate.

interest is deductible but only to the extent of the taxpayer's interest income plus 25% of the taxpayer's non-interest income. Any excess interest expense can be carried forward for 5 years.

4.2 Issues

The architecture of the Treaties constrains both Timor-Leste and Australia in making overall policy and legal changes in the JPDA and in the Sunrise area. In addition, Bayu-Undan has a stabilized tax regime under Timor-Leste law. If companies consider the geological prospects in the JPDA worthwhile, then past successful investment (Bayu-Undan) and the stable framework probably act positively to encourage investment.

This chapter does not address the boundary delimitation issues facing both countries. The preoccupations of both countries on those issues, however, have profoundly influenced the interim arrangements made in both the Timor Sea and CMATS treaties, since (understandably) neither country wished to set a precedent that might conceivably work to its disadvantage in any eventual determination of a maritime boundary. In addition, although the treaties

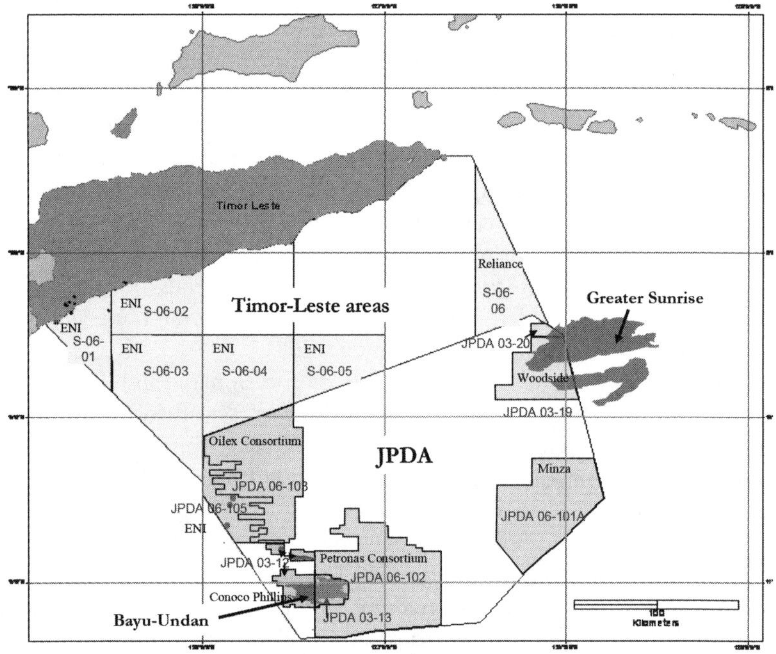

Figure 11.9 Timor-Leste and JPDA PSCs

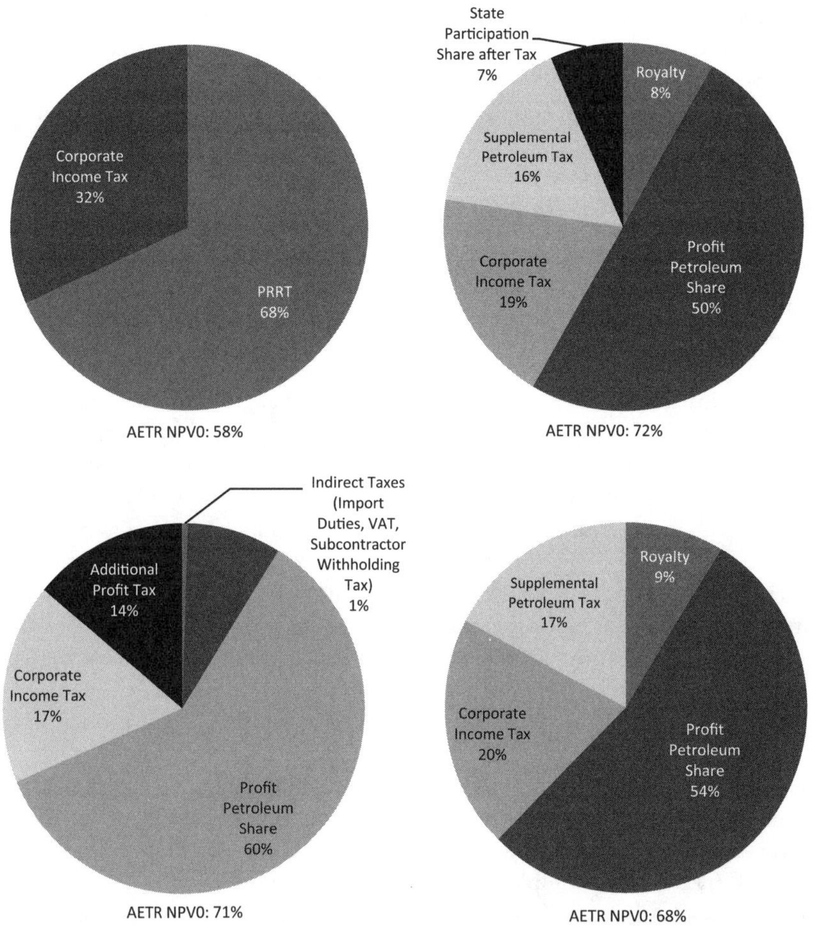

Figure 11.10 Australia and Timor-Leste: fiscal regimes; 900 MMBbl field

Source: Authors' calculations

establish joint development schemes, that does not mean the interests of both countries coincide with respect to individual petroleum development projects where the resource is located in a joint zone or is subject to a joint scheme.

Four circumstances make clear the extent to which interim arrangements of this kind present challenges that national jurisdiction does not face.

The first and most obvious is the existence of Greater Sunrise as a project that straddles the JPDA and areas outside it. Despite the TST, the Unitisation Agreement, and CMATS, the project had not progressed to development by 2015. The two governments, together with the private petroleum rights holders, had so far not found sufficient alignment of interests to reach a development concept and regulatory endorsements that they could agree and which would give buyers of gas sufficient confidence in security of supply.

The second is jurisdiction over pipelines and the associated transfer pricing questions. The TST provides, in effect, for extra-territorial jurisdiction in the control of the destination country for any pipeline.[40] Because regulatory authority over the JPDA for petroleum matters remained joint and carried out by a joint institution, the possibility of confusion and disputes was inherent. Most of these were resolved, though only after skill-intensive and time-consuming negotiations over, for example, the tariff scheme for the Bayu-Undan pipeline, which, in turn, was critical to the upstream transfer price of gas at the delivery point in the JPDA. Others, notably over taxing rights, resulted in arbitration proceedings involving investing companies and the Timor-Leste authorities – not finally resolved by early 2016.

The third concerns commercial decisions over location of petroleum-processing and spin-off activities. The issue was exacerbated by Australia's status as a mature petroleum-producing country with a substantial skills base in the industry, mature infrastructure, and a record of continuity of supply of oil and gas in export markets, while Timor-Leste had independence only newly restored in 2002 after more than a generation's experience of invasion, occupation, and violence. The instinct of petroleum companies was not to source inputs from Timor-Leste or to locate processing facilities there. Taking the second and third together, therefore, provides a persistent basis for conflict of interest between the joint zone partners over, for example, the portion of overall revenue accruing in the JPDA and the possibility for each country to use the production to stimulate ancillary industries in Timor-Leste or in the Northern territory (in the case of Australia). This remained a key point of difference on the Sunrise project: Timor-Leste prefers development through an LNG plant onshore in Timor-Leste, while the investors prefer a floating LNG development.

The fourth is the complexity of the joint schemes that emerged in this case. Layers of joint schemes – the TST, the IUA, and CMATS – have to be read together and interpreted. The schemes also gave rise to multiple different regimes applicable to private companies, which proved especially demanding upon the limited regulatory and administrative capacities of Timor-Leste. Timor-Leste has both absolutely and relatively the most at stake in terms of upstream revenues.

In practice, the Timor Sea Treaty effectively became a joint scheme for the development of just one major project – Bayu-Undan. This was not wholly due to the complexity of the arrangements: significant exploration took place in the JPDA both before and after the implementation of the TST but with limited success. The existence of the layers of joint schemes had not, by early 2016, removed the obstacles to development of the Greater Sunrise fields. On the other hand, the TST regime overall (including the applicable domestic tax provisions in both countries) permitted the Bayu-Undan project to go ahead by affording regulatory and fiscal assurances to the investors. Although the agreements concerning Greater Sunrise became entwined with the implementation of the Treaty and the Bayu-Undan project, they were not in themselves essential to the progress of the Bayu-Undan project itself.

5 Conclusions

Joint Development Zones clearly work as pragmatic devices to enable offshore petroleum exploration and production where the relevant countries cannot agree a permanent maritime boundary. Leaving aside the long-standing joint zones in the Middle East, both the Malaysia–Thailand JDZ and the Timor-Leste–Australia JDZ have supported significant production. In Malaysia–Thailand the production consists of a diverse portfolio of fields; that, at 2016, seems less likely for Timor-Leste–Australia where the complex architecture in practice supports a single major project. The varying outcomes must to some degree reflect the underlying motivations of the parties and whether the JDZ is seen by all sides as a satisfactory long-term solution even if technically "interim". Where both sides favour 50/50 and regard that as fair, the chances of success seem higher than when one party retains just a toehold for whatever reason.

Where there has been a maritime delimitation dispute, agreement on a JDZ with accompanying fiscal instruments does make a difference to private investor confidence. The JDZs do appear to have permitted exploration and development where it might not otherwise have occurred.

Fiscal devices in use in exclusive national jurisdictions also work in JDZs. They do, however, encounter added complications unless the parties decide to implement a single fiscal scheme throughout – whether production sharing or tax/royalty. The Timor Sea arrangements suggest that the implementation of national tax terms for a project, in the attribution percentages, carries unavoidable complications and potential for disputes. Nevertheless, the case for levying regular national taxes on income remaining after the charge for the resource (production sharing or royalty) stands up on grounds of ease of national administration.

We found no systematic differences between JDZ fiscal regimes and neighbouring national regimes in terms of the overall effective tax rates they are likely to imply. The JDZ regimes examined draw from international and local precedent but always with adaptations to the specifics of the joint area. Timing of when the JDZ regime was established relative to the domestic regimes – and hence consequently different perceptions of prospectivity and risk – are likely important determinants of relative fiscal take.

With the increasing importance of gas in world petroleum trade, pipeline and processing facilities have higher importance, together with their associated transfer pricing challenges (see, for example, the chapters by Calder and Le Leuch in this volume). In this area, JDZ architecture itself has so far been relatively weak, though the parties have in most cases developed practical solutions by negotiation. Similarly, the obstacles to development of "straddling fields" seem exacerbated if one part of the field is already in a JDZ. These experiences in the Timor-Leste–Australia case suggest that developing a purpose-built unit development approach for an individual project may prove more tractable, at least in fiscal terms, than the attempt to fit the special case within a much wider treaty or JDZ framework.

That observation leads to the final point. JDZ schemes arise because a dispute or disagreement has arisen in the first place. The effort to promote development while not prejudicing the parties' pre-existing maritime claims can result in excessive complexity in the schemes, making them hard both to interpret and to administer. Such complexity may sometimes outweigh the incentive to invest in petroleum exploration and development underpinning the rationale for a JDZ.

Appendix 11.1

Petroleum fiscal terms in simulated countries and their joint development areas (JDAs)

Table 11A.1 Petroleum fiscal terms in simulated countries and their joint development areas (JDAs)

Jurisdiction	*AUS-TML JDA – Bayu-Undan*	*AUS-TML New JPDA*	*Australia (AUS)*	*Timor-Leste (TML)*	*Nigeria – STP JDA*	*Nigeria (Deep Water 2007)*	*São Tomé e Príncipe (STP)*	*Malaysia–Thailand JDA*	*Malaysia*	*Thailand*
Regime type	PSC	PSC	Tax/Royalty	PSC	PSC	PSC	PSC	PSC	PSC	Tax/Royalty
Signature/ production bonus	Nil	Nil	Nil	Nil	SB, PB	SB	SB, PB	Nil	Exempt in practice	Nil
Royalty rate	10% first tranche petroleum (FTP)	5%	Nil	5%	0%–5%; daily rate of production (DROP)-based	0%–16.67% depending on onshore/offshore and water depth	2%	10% + 10% export duty[2/]	10% + 10% export duty	5%–15%; 70% of regular rates for deep water; sales volume-based
Cost recovery limit	100%	100%	N/A	100%	80%	80%	80%	50%	30%–70%; Revenue/cost (R/C) ratio-based	N/A
Profit sharing (% profit oil to contractor)	50%	60%	N/A	60%	25%–80%; post-tax R-Factor-based	25%–70%; post-tax R-Factor-based	50%–100%; ROR-based	50%	30%–80% if cumulative production < = CTHV; 10%-40% if cumulative production > CTHV[4/]; R/C ratio-based sliding scale	N/A
Corporate income tax	30%	30%	30%	30%	50%	50%	30%	0%/10%/20% (first 8 years of production; next 7 years; thereafter)	38%	50% (modelled) or 35% + dividend WT
Depreciation rule	1/5 years (expl./other capex); straight-line (SL)	1/10 years (expl./dev.); SL	1/15/5 years (expl./dev./replacement); SL	1/10 years (expl./dev.); SL	5 years; SL	Oil: 5 years; Gas: 4 years; SL	5 years; SL	1/10/5 years (expl./dev./replacement); SL	Varied methods and rates for asset classes	10 years (expl.&drilling cost shallow water); 5 years (other capex); SL

(*Continued*)

Table 11A.1 Continued

Jurisdiction	*AUS-TML JDA – Bayu-Undan*	*AUS-TML New JPDA*	*Australia (AUS)*	*Timor-Leste (TML)*	*Nigeria – STP JDA*	*Nigeria (Deep Water 2007)*	*São Tomé e Príncipe (STP)*	*Malaysia–Thailand JDA*	*Malaysia*	*Thailand*
Loss carry-forward	Indefinite	Indefinite	Indefinite	Indefinite	Indefinite	Indefinite	Indefinite	Indefinite	Indefinite	10 years
Supplementary profit tax	22.5% once IRR reaches 16.5%	22.5% once IRR reaches 16.5%	40%; PRRT	22.5% once IRR reaches 16.5%	Nil	Nil	Nil	50% on profit oil when price >$25/ bbl, escalated by 5% from 1994	70% on profit when price exceeds $25/ bbl, escalated by 4% from date of contract	0%–75% SRB progressive with income per meter of well[5/]
Dividend WT	Nil	Nil	0% (franked)	Nil	6% (weighted avg. of both countries)	10%	Nil	Nil	Nil	23.08%
Interest WT	Nil	Nil	Nil	Nil	14% (weighted avg.)	10%	20%	Nil	15%	15%
State participation	Nil	Nil	Nil	15% carried through exploration[1]/	Nil	Nil	10% free equity	Nil[3/]	15% carried through exploration[1/]	5% carried through dev. with reimbursement[6/]

Source: FAD's Fiscal Analysis of Resource Industries (FARI) database.

1/ This is the minimum rate. Carried costs are not reimbursable but are cost recoverable.

2/ Malaysia and the Kingdom of Thailand collect export duties under their respective legislation but reduce the applicable rates by 50%.

3/ There is no provision for state participation in the JDA. However, Petronas's wholly-owned subsidiary has 50% working interest in all of the three blocks. Thailand's state-owned PTTEP has 50% in two of the three blocks.

4/ Cumulative total hydrocarbon volume (CTHV): the sum of the individual THVs from a contract area. An individual THV is the lesser of 30 MMBBL or 0.75 TCF or the size of the individual field's approved proved ultimate recoverable reserves, as adjusted or redetermined from time to time. 30 MMBBL is used in the modelling.

5/ Special remunerator benefit (SRB).

6/ After a production area has been first correctly defined in the concession block, the applicant must propose in its special advantages to have a Thai legal person (established under the laws of Thailand with Thai nationals holding more than 50% in it), with the approval of the Petroleum Committee, to acquire an undivided participating interest of not less than 5% under the concession. Such juristic person shall reimburse the applicant the expenditures incurred from the block prior to the date of its participation according to its participating interest share and bear its participating interest share of all the expenditure incurred in the block from the date of its participation.

Notes

1 The authors are grateful to Michael Keen for comments on an earlier draft and to Nate Vernon for assistance with checking of calculations.
2 This chapter addresses the mechanics of joint development zones; nothing in the chapter should be taken to imply any view on the part of IMF staff or the present authors concerning the positions of any states that are partners to a JDZ on ultimate delimitation of maritime boundaries.
3 Crawford (2012) pp. 255–280 succinctly explains the rights of states in their territorial sea and other maritime zones.
4 For further explanation of the legal principles, with examples, see Cameron in this volume, Hestermeyer et al. (2012), Nordquist and Moore (2012), Becker-Weinberg (2014).
5 Pawlak (2012) p. 242 comments that "the newest maritime treaties concentrate more on economic cooperation than on the dispute-solving procedure."
6 The authors know only of one joint development scheme on land: that is the Saudi Arabia–Kuwait "neutral zone", which includes both jointly managed on-shore and offshore areas. https://en.wikipedia.org/wiki/Saudi%E2%80%93Kuwaiti_neutral_zone
7 The case of Timor-Leste and Australia, discussed in what follows, is exceptional in that unitisation took place across the perimeter of a JDZ rather than an agreed maritime boundary.
8 At early 2016, imposition of withholding taxes on charges for a pipeline that takes gas out of the JDZ was the subject of an unresolved dispute between Timor-Leste and petroleum contractors in the Bayu-Undan gas project.
9 The capital gains issue on assets had specifically to be addressed in unitisation schemes for fields straddling the UK–Norway boundary in the North Sea, where no JDZ was involved.
10 Some fiscal implications of this provision were the subject of arbitration proceedings involving private contractors and one of the governments, still not determined by the end of 2015.
11 Many treaties use the term "joint development area" or similar, whereas the usual generic term is "joint development zone"; this chapter uses each where relevant.
12 http://www.ctlo.com/mediacenter/Publications/2011–03–29-ThailandPetroleum Concessions-03March2011325679.pdf
13 http://www.eia.gov/countries/cab.cfm?fips = TH
14 Balance of 65 out of 100 of after-tax profits multiplied by 23.08% equals 20% remittance tax on the original 100.
15 Given the materiality of SRB, the assumption of meters drilled for the project example is critical. Very deep wells significantly reduce the SRB payment.
16 http://www.eia.gov/countries/cab.cfm?fips = NI
17 As stipulated in the Petroleum Decree No. 51 of 1969, as amended, Petroleum (Drilling and Production) Regulations of 1969, as amended, and Petroleum Profits Tax Act of 2004, as amended by subsequent Finance Decrees.
18 Earlier PSCs used cumulative production as the scale for determining profit shares.
19 The contractor, however, takes 100% of profit oil when IRR < 16%, so the cost recovery limit would have little impact early in the life of the field
20 Batista, Unitization, and JDZ.
21 http://www.macauhub.com.mo/en/2011/12/01/sao-tome-government-confirms-existence-of-oil-in-area-of-joint-oil-exploration-with-nigeria/
22 Using the Fiscal Analysis of Resource Industries (FARI) modeling system and database developed in the Fiscal Affairs Department of the IMF. For a detailed exposition of the FARI modeling framework and evaluation criteria for fiscal regimes, see Daniel, P. and others (2010). Luca and Mesa Puyo (2016) http://www.imf.org/external/np/fad/fari/. Excel based, FARI enables detailed design, modeling, and comparison of fiscal regimes across the entire life cycle of petroleum or mining projects. It is now widely employed

by staff in country and TA work and is increasingly used as a forecasting tool linked to the macro-economic framework for resource-rich countries.

23 The average effective tax rate (AETR) only becomes a meaningful in cases above marginal levels of profitability, since a case yielding zero NPV at the chosen discount rate has no surplus to divide.

24 We note that the outcome in the national Nigeria and STP case could be weighted 60/40 to reflect the attribution percentages in the JDZ.

25 For discussion of the relationship between JDZs and unitisation, see Cameron in this volume and Duval et al. (2009); for the case of Timor-Leste and Australia the literature is substantial; see, for example, Khamsi (2005) or Pereira Coutinho and Briosa e Gala (2015).

26 The Timor Gap Treaty also created zone B to the north and zone C to the south; in ZOCB the split was 90/10 in favor of Indonesia, in ZOCC 90/10 in favor of Australia. No petroleum activities took place in areas B or C, and they did not feature in the Timor Sea Treaty.

27 Procedures for technical redetermination of the reserve attributions were incorporated in the IUA for Greater Sunrise.

28 See press reports such as http://www.theguardian.com/world/2016/mar/22/australia-illegally-occupying-maritime-territory-of-timor-leste-protesters-say.

29 CMATS became the subject of a legal challenge by Timor-Leste at the International Court of Justice contested by Australia and unresolved by early 2016.

30 The Petroleum Mining Code for the JPDA, taken together with provisions of the TST, is equivalent to a petroleum law concerning the grant of rights and regulation of activities in a single jurisdiction.

31 Annex G in Schedule 1 of the TST (under Article 13(b)) is the Taxation Code for the Avoidance of Double Taxation and the Prevention of Fiscal Evasion in respect of Activities Connected with the JPDA.

32 It also applies to PSC 06–105, in which previous exploration identified the small Jahal and Kuda Tasi oil discoveries. Exploration expenditure and investment credits under a previous PSC were brought forward as an opening balance under the new PSC but excluded from further uplift under the new scheme.

33 The new PMC is not applied to Bayu-Undan and Sunrise either. These PSCs are subject to the Interim PMC (adapted from the PMC under the Timor Gap Treaty), since their PSCs were made under that version of the PMC.

34 The TST ascribes rights to the DA on behalf of the two governments; the Timor-Leste Petroleum Authority (ANP) now exercises the powers of the DA. We refer to the DA when describing powers under the TST and associated PSCs.

35 The PSCs in Timor-Leste's exclusive jurisdiction allow the government, on the announcement of a commercial discovery, to elect state participation up to 20% through a state-owned contractor. The government pays no compensation for past costs but would pay its proportionate share of future costs.

36 The Bayu-Undan additional profits tax and the general SPT are identical in design and rates. The net rate of 22.5% is achieved by charging a grossed-up rate of $22.5/(1-t)$, where t is the corporate income tax rate (30%), and allowing the resulting grossed-up rate of 32.143 percent as a deduction for income tax.

37 The ANP has published detailed information; see www.anp-tl.org. See also http://www.laohamutuk.org/Oil/Project/Kitan/10EniKitan.htm. Woodside estimates http://www.woodside.com.au/Our-Business/Developing/Pages/Sunrise.aspx#.Vm_82fmLSUk

38 Condensate is defined as crude oil in the PSC applying to Bayu-Undan.

39 The percentage ownership interests in the Sunrise JV were Woodside 33, ConocoPhillips 30, Shell 27, and Osaka Gas 10.

40 The reverse of the extra-territorial jurisdiction secured by Norway over pipelines from its continental shelf exporting gas to other European countries.

References

Becker-Weinberg, Vasco. (2014), *Joint Development of Hydrocarbon Deposits in the Law of the Sea* (Hamburg: Springer).

Crawford, James. (2012), *Brownlie's Principles of Public International Law*, 8th edition (Oxford: Oxford University Press).

Daniel, Philip and others. (2010). "Evaluating Fiscal Regimes for Resource Projects: An Example from Oil Development 2010," in Philip Daniel, Michael Keen and Charles McPherson (eds).

Daniel, Philip, Michael Keen and Charles McPherson, eds. (2010), *The Taxation of Petroleum and Minerals: Principles, Problems and Practice* (London and New York: Routledge).

Duval, Claude, Honoré Le Leuch, André Pertuzio and Jacqueline Lang Weaver. (2009), *International Petroleum Agreements: Legal, Economic and Policy Aspects*, 2nd edition (New York: Barrows).

Hestermeyer, H.P., D. König, N. Matz-Lück, V. Röben, A. Seibert-Fohr, P.-T. Stoll and S. Vöneky, eds. (2012), *Coexistence, Cooperation, and Solidarity, Liber Amicorum Rüdiger Wolfrum, Volume 1* (Leiden: Martinus Nijhoff).

Khamsi, Kathryn. (2005), "A Settlement to the Timor Sea Dispute?" *Harvard Asia Quarterly*, IX(4), Available at http://www.asiaquarterly.com/content/view/33/1.

Luca, Oana and Diego Mesa Puyo. (2016), *Fiscal Analysis of Resource Industries (FARI) Methodology, Technical Notes and Manuals* (Washington DC: International Monetary Fund).

Nordquist, Myron H. and John Norton Moore, eds. (2012), *Maritime Border Diplomacy*, Center for Oceans Law and Policy (Brill Online), Available at http://booksandjournals.brillonline.com/content/books/9789004230941.

Pawlak, Stanislaw. (2012), "Some Reflections on Factors Exerting Influence on Negotiations on Maritime Boundary Delimitation," in H.P. Hestermeyer, D. König, N. Matz-Lück, V. Röben, A. Seibert-Fohr, P.-T. Stoll and S. Vöneky (eds), *Coexistence, Cooperation, and Solidarity, Volume 1*, Leiden: Martinus Nijhoff, pp. 223–244.

Pereira Coutinho, F. and F. Briosa e Gala. (2015), "David and Goliath Revisited: A Tale about the Timor-Leste/Australia Timor Sea Agreements," *Texas Journal of Oil, Gas and Energy Law*, 10(2), 429–462.

12 Taxes, royalties and cross-border resource investments

*Jack M. Mintz**

1 Introduction

Developing economies that are dependent on non-renewable resources face two major objectives: attracting capital for major projects and deriving revenue to fund public services. These objectives need not be antagonistic since resource producers know that the government, typically owner of the resource, is entitled to benefits from resource extraction similar to landowners when resources are owned privately.

The relationship between the government as owner of the resource and the private company that plays a role in the exploration, development and extraction of resources is little different than a principal–agent relationship. The principal, the government, seeks revenue and other economic benefits from large extractive projects. The agent, the private producer, is invited to participate in projects and obtain a sufficient rate of return on projects to cover investment costs and risks, competitive with returns elsewhere. A government seeking the most able producer would need to give up some of the rents accruing from the project.[1] A stable regime reduces uncertainty not only for the private producer but also for a government reliant on volatile revenues.

Many resource-rich developing economies rely on foreign companies to provide the management, technology and capital needed for large extractive projects. Thus, many projects involve cross-border investments made by private producers, many of which are global companies operating at a large scale in countries.

This chapter is focused on company tax and resource royalty issues related to cross-border investments. The company income tax is a significant generator of revenues for developing economies not only in the resource sector but also in other sectors. The company income tax also serves as a backstop to the personal income tax in a country to ensure that income earned by owners left in the corporations is taxed. Other company taxes levied by developing countries that directly affect capital decisions include taxes on assets, financial transaction taxes and sales taxes on capital purchases, but the company income tax is the most significant and complex tax for analysis.[2]

Royalties are defined in this chapter as any type of payment made by private producers to governments for the use of resources.[3] They are usually thought of as charges assessed on volume or value of production, although it is becoming more common for government to impose "profit-based royalties", with project costs being deducted from revenues. These payments are intended to collect economic rents for governments from resource exploitation including levies related to "net profits", production sharing (that is similar to a net profit approach), revenues or cash flows. The net profit-based royalties have some similarity to company income taxes, although important differences arise, especially with the treatment of interest and their application to a specific project (so-called ring-fencing).

The main purpose of this chapter is to provide a characterization of several cross-border fiscal issues that impact the incentive to invest and the resource revenues derived by governments. A definition of economic rent is first provided as well as a characterization of the decisions made by non-renewable resource producers taking into account both company taxes and royalties using a "time-to-build" model.[4] A key point to emerge is that company income tax and royalty interact with each other such that even a well-designed rent-based royalty will be generally non-neutral when a company income tax is also imposed.

Section 3 then provides some cross-country comparisons of marginal effective and royalty tax rates (METRRs) for Australia, Brazil, Canada, Norway, United Kingdom and United States on oil exploration, development and extraction, which will be explained in more detail in what follows. Several cross-border issues are highlighted that impact taxes and royalties levied on resource investments. These relate to the use of tax structures such as transfer pricing and conduit financing that affect payment of tax in the host country. Cross-border financial structures also affect the discount rate for carrying forward unused deductions under rent-based royalties and a corporate tax.

The central conclusions from this analysis are that, generally, rent-based approaches to royalty design are appropriate so long as a creditable minimum revenue or output-based royalty is used to ensure governments obtain a certain level of revenues (see Chen and Mintz, 2012, for further details). A company income tax should follow the principle of neutrality with similar tax burdens on business activities with tax rates conditioned on international circumstances.

2 The meaning of economic rent

Economic rent arises from non-reproducible (or fixed) factors of production such as entrepreneurship, land and natural resources. It can also arise from the presence of natural or artificial barriers to entry that generate market power and special advantages that firms may possess (such as location, patents, etc.). More generally, rent is the surplus value of revenues net of all economic costs, including opportunity costs, which are subtracted from revenues arising from the sale of goods and services. Rent is thus measured as output multiplied by the difference between the price at which a resource can be sold and its unit cost of discovery, extraction and production, including a rate of return on capital that can be obtained by investing in projects with similar risk and scale.

In recent years, governments have resorted increasingly to rent-based systems by which costs are deductible in determining the royalty base rather than a conventional royalty based on a percentage of production revenues or a levy on output. A resource royalty based on "rents" is typically measured as revenue net of current and capital expenditures (an investment allowance is provided to carry forward unused deductions by a rate of interest to preserve the time value of money). In the non-renewable resource sector, the obvious example is the "cash flow tax", which is a form of rent tax on *ex post* returns.[5] Alternatively, the government will tax rents as return in excess of a minimum rate of return on capital (the R-base approach), which in principle is the same as the cash-flow approach on a present value basis, differing only in the timing of revenue streams (in the discussion that follows, the cash flow approach will be the main focus). Governments also use bonus bids for land tracts to raise revenue, which taxes rents on an *ex ante* basis.

Any tax or levy applied to pure economic rent will not distort the use of capital or other production factors. At the margin, firms employ capital, labour and other factors until the marginal return on the last unit employed is equal to its economic costs. In economic terms, rents are zero at the margin, negative if too much production takes place and positive if too little rent-earning production is undertaken by the producer. Hence, for marginal decisions – investment or otherwise – the rent earned is zero, as returns equal costs in using production factors. A pure rent-base tax will neither discourage nor encourage the investment or production decision since the levy is *neutral* in not affecting investment and technology decisions.

3 Impact of company taxes and royalty levies on incentive to invest

Taxes and resource royalties affect the decisions of resource firms with respect to their investments in exploration and development to develop reserves and extraction of output requiring capital and other inputs. Royalties and taxes of various types can distort firm decisions, thereby leading to suboptimal or inefficient production and fewer rents. Often much analysis is focused on the overall levy imposed on present value of investment without looking at distortionary effects. This section and theoretical appendix lay out a model to analyze the impact of company income taxes, capital taxes and sales taxes on capital purchases affecting the exploration, development and investment decisions of non-renewable resource companies. Before doing so, however, a heuristic explanation is provided of the "marginal effective tax and royalty rate" (METRR), which is the focus for our analysis on investment impacts.

3.1 Marginal effective tax and royalty rates

Conceptually, a business invests in capital until the rate of return on incremental dollars is equal to the cost of capital (at this point no further rents are earned). To measure the effect of taxes and royalties on investment decisions, the METRR is calculated as the amount of taxes and royalties paid as a percentage of the pre-tax-and-royalty net-of-risk return on capital that would be required to cover taxes, royalties and the financing of capital with debt and equity. Risk is incorporated in the analysis by measuring the certainty-equivalent rate of return on capital (this is the expected rate of return net-of-risk costs). To the extent that the tax or royalty system shares risks with the producers by allowing for the full refundability of losses, the government provides an implicit deduction for the cost of risk, thereby treating risk costs no different than costs like labour.[6] I shall assume this is the case for the analysis for the theoretical model.

In the analysis that follows, I focus on METRRs to determine how the investment decision is affected by tax and royalty systems.[7] As a simple illustration of the METRR, consider the following. If a business invests in capital at the margin that yields a pre-tax and royalty net-of- risk rate of return equal to 15% and, after taxes and royalties, a net-of-risk rate of return equal to 5%, then the METRR is 15% minus 5% divided by 15%, giving a result of 67%.[8]

The advantage of the marginal approach is that the variation in METRR across assets and industries provides a basis for analyzing capital distortions in fiscal systems. The higher the METRR, the lower will be investment since the tax adjusted cost of capital is higher, squeezing out marginal projects in an industry. Similarly, if one type of asset is favoured over others, companies will have an incentive to change the mix of assets including shifting expenditures from one stage of production to another, thereby impacting the technical choices made by firms in developing extractive projects. For example, fiscal systems typically provide incentives for exploration and development – it is not inconceivable that firms will push capital expenditure into the exploration or development phase that could have taken place post-production to reduce the present value of tax payments even though it adds cost to the project by investing too early.

With marginal analysis, there is no need to specify project revenues and costs since companies will invest in capital until the rate of return on capital is equal to the cost of capital (the weighted cost of debt and equity finance). This is in contrast to measuring the average tax rate which is equal to the present value of all levies paid divided by the present value of the project's cash flow (or the annualized amount of tax paid divided by the average or internal rate of return on capital). To estimate the average tax rate, one needs information on the certainty-equivalent value of revenues and costs, which are specific to each project (the cash flows and payments to governments will therefore depend on how much rents are earned).

Some analysts prefer average tax rate and cash flow analysis since resource projects are lumpy. However, firms do have the ability to change the scale and size of projects to some extent. Further, despite the size of large resource projects, each firm can be a small part of the industry, resulting in output being determined at the point at which marginal revenue is equal to marginal cost of production. Much of this debate goes back to Alfred Marshall's characterization of competitive markets in which the minimum efficient scale of a firm may still be relatively small compared to the market. Nonetheless, the average tax rate calculation to analyze a specific industry can be instructive for markets with one or two large projects.

Nonetheless, given the difficulty measuring rates of return or cash flows on a certainty-equivalent basis, theory would predict firms will invest if the rate of return on capital is at least as high as the marginal return. Since this enables the analyst to avoid measuring revenues and costs, the marginal analysis is also useful in this sense.

Studies[9] that focus on average cash flows earned by the industry require a specification of revenues and costs that are best representative of the industry even though they widely vary by project. Average effective tax and royalty rates are calculated as a share of the internal rate of return earned on projects, which is typically above the cost of capital used for marginal analysis due to the existence of rents (recall at the margin, rents are zero). The average effective tax and royalty rate is therefore sensitive to the internal rate of return. For example, with a high internal rate of return, a fiscal regime with a high statutory rate and accelerated cost deductions and tax credits could have an average effective tax and royalty rate that would be greater than the case of a regime with low rates and broad bases. The amount of tax paid on rents is equal to the statutory tax multiplied by the difference between revenues and costs, thereby leading to a higher share of tax paid compared to a project that earns a return close to the marginal return, assuming costs are the same. On the other hand, with a low internal rate of return, the opposite would hold. Thus, in comparison with the marginal analysis (that focuses on low internal rates of return equal to the observed cost of capital earned at the margin), the average effective tax rate analysis could lead to a conclusion that a high-rate narrow-base regime provides less incentive for investment than a low–rate broad-base regime, assuming a high internal rate of return on a projects. This conclusion might be appropriate if projects are lumpy and large relative to markets. On the other hand, marginal analysis may provide a more suitable answer if capital can shift by downsizing one project in favour of another.

The METRR does not provide an estimate of the overall taxes and royalties governments collect since those amounts depend on both the marginal and infra-marginal returns (rents) earned on an investment. It is not unusual, for example, for the METRR to be negative even though the government could be collecting revenues. The implication is that any losses on the marginal investment are being used to offset levies on rents or carried forward to shelter income from royalties in the future. The METRR is a benchmark with which to determine the effects of taxes and royalties on investment decisions.

As mentioned, the model provided in the appendix accounts for the time taken to develop non-renewable resource projects before they are available for extraction. There are several stages of production: exploration and development phase to discover reserves and make them available for extraction and a subsequent production phase that leads to output sold to the market. With these two stages, the analysis is based on a flow of inputs to develop a reserve available for production of oil and gas – a "time-to-build" analysis.[10] The following stage of production, extraction, depletes the discovered reserves until exhaustion.[11]

The METRR for resource companies is calculated for each type of asset expenditure: exploration, development, depreciable capital, land and inventories. The METRR on capital is equal to the annualized value of tax and royalty paid divided by the gross-of-tax-and royalty rate of return on capital. The analysis includes federal and provincial/state corporate income, capital and sales taxes, as well as provincial royalties. Various features of taxes are modelled including inventory valuation, capital cost allowances, statutory tax rates and the investment tax credit.

3.2 Comparative analysis

In this section, comparison of METRRs across different countries is provided based on three critical assumptions that shall be relaxed in what follows. First, transfer prices for outputs, inputs and financing costs are equal to market prices. Second, the cost of financing is based on the equity and debt financing costs from third parties (thereby abstracting from any multinational tax planning, which will be further discussed later). Third, losses are fully refundable (the discount rate used to carry forward any unused deductions is equal to the government bond rate since governments fully share risks).

METRRs are calculated for Australia, Brazil, Canada (five provinces), Norway, UK and U.S. (four states). The specific regimes are described in detail in Mintz and Chen (2012), which also provides detailed equations used for each jurisdiction. Here a brief review is provided of the various 2012 tax and royalty systems, with some further details provided in an appendix to this chapter.

- Australia's has effectively two levies, the corporate income tax and the Petroleum Resource Rent Tax (PRTT), as state royalties are credited against the federal rent tax. The corporate income tax is applied at a rate of 30% on profits with a deduction for depreciation, inventory, reclamation costs and the PRTT as well as expensing for exploration and development. The PRRT tax rate for offshore projects is 40%, under which exploration and rehabilitation expenditures are expensed and may be carried forward at an uplift rate of 15% points above the government long-term bond rate (LTBR). Other capital expenditure may be carried forward at a rate of 5% points above LTBR.
- Brazil has both a company tax and resource royalties applied to oil production. The combined company tax is applied at a 34% rate on profits, with deductions provided for exploration (expensed) while development and capital is depreciated. Other costs including royalties are deductible from profits under the company tax. The revenue-based royalty is 10% on the value of products sold, net of any indirect taxes and transportation costs using common carriers. A 1% landowner fee, applicable to onshore activities only, shares the same base as royalties. Rental fees are based on

the area of fields and location; the signature bonus is a lump-sum payment due upon signing the contract. A special participation (SP) fee is levied on substantial profits (net of all the other oil and gas levies) that surpass the threshold on a field-by-field basis, which threshold volume varies by location (onshore or offshore; the latter is further differentiated by water depth) and declines with the production years. The SP rate is progressive from 10% to 40%, depending on the aforementioned varying thresholds.

- Canada has federal and provincial corporate income taxes applied to oil as well as provincial royalties (the provinces are owners of resources in their own jurisdictions). The federal-provincial corporate income tax varies from 25% in Alberta to 29% in Newfoundland & Labrador. Under the corporate income tax, exploration, reclamation costs and provincial royalties are expensed, development expenditures written off at a 30% declining balance rate and depreciation of other assets written off at a 25% declining balance rate. Provincial royalties for conventional oil are assessed on revenues with rates varying by price and volume of each well. "Net profit" royalties apply to Alberta oil sands, British Columbia shale gas and Canada Atlantic offshore oil and gas projects. The Alberta royalty is fashioned after a cash-flow approach with a carry-forward of unused deductions at the LTBR. The royalty rates on payouts (net of recovered costs) are price sensitive, varying from a minimum of 25% to a maximum of 40%. A revenue-based minimum tax is also imposed on all provinces that are credited against the net profit royalty. The Atlantic offshore and BC shale gas royalties do not allow unsuccessful exploration costs to be deducted from the royalty base (unlike the corporate income tax).
- Norway assesses two taxes on offshore oil production: the regular corporate income tax at a rate of 28% and a non-deductible supplementary tax at a 50% rate based on a cash-flow approach. The corporate income rate is 28%. Exploration costs are expensed. A cash refund is provided for tax losses resulting from exploration. Oil production facilities and pipelines may be depreciated within 6 years with a straight-line rate up to 16.66%. The cash-flow tax base is the corporate tax base grossed up by financing cost and net of an uplift factor (7.5% of the cost price of depreciable operating assets including development expenditures for the first 4 consecutive years) and unused uplift carried forward from previous years.
- The United Kingdom offshore royalty for petroleum has many features similar to the Norwegian system. The 2012 UK corporate income tax rate is 28%, except a ring-fence corporation tax of 30% is applied to petroleum with allowances provided for exploration costs, development and depreciation costs. A supplementary tax (the "royalty" for purposes here) is 32% and non-deductible from the ring-fence company tax. Both the corporate income and supplementary taxes provide deductions for the following: (1) 100% of the cost of exploration, appraisal, development and installation of production, (2) a 100% first-year allowance for development expenditure is provided except for the costs of acquiring mineral assets, which attracts a

10% annual relief (some development expenditures may only be depreciated under the corporate income tax and (3) a 10% ring-fence expenditure supplement (uplift factor) for up to 6 years. Post-production capital is depreciated under the corporate income tax while expensed under the supplementary tax. Inventories are treated on a first-in-first-out basis for the corporate income tax.

- The United States assesses both a corporate income tax at the federal and state levels as well as severance taxes (similar to revenue-based royalties) at the state level (except Pennsylvania, which has no severance tax). Oil and gas companies benefit from the reduced federal corporate income tax rate on resource profits (32.9% instead of 35%). Exploration and development are expensed or depleted after commencement of production as elected by the company. State corporate income tax rates vary – these taxes are deductible from the federal rate. Texas also levies a 1% franchise tax on margins (revenues net of cost of goods sold) in lieu of a corporate income tax. Severance tax rates are 5% of revenues in Arkansas and Colorado, with lower rates applying to first years of production. Texas imposes a royalty based on sales at a rate of 16.67 to 25% as well as a severance tax (the royalty is deductible from the severance tax).

The effects of these various regimes are shown in Table 12.1 for each type of capital and jurisdiction. Figure 12.1 provides both the aggregate METRR and decomposed rates when excluding certain levies.

- The highest METRRs in Table 12.1 and Figure 12.1 tend to be those jurisdictions that apply revenue-based royalties: U.S. states, Alberta and Saskatchewan (for conventional oil) and Brazil. This is not surprising; revenue-based royalties provide no deduction for costs and therefore increase the cost of capital for all types of capital expenditures including exploration and development. On the other hand, rent-based royalties in the Alberta oil sands, Canadian Atlantic offshore, Australia and the UK tend to have much lower METRRs since costs are deductible from the revenue base.
- The cases of Australia, Newfoundland & Labrador and Nova Scotia are particularly notable since exploration is provided a large incentive as shown by a negative METRR. In large part, this arises from an excessively high uplift factor for carrying forward unused exploration expenditure written against future payouts (a similar situation arises for Canadian Atlantic Offshore). The carry-forward rate is an issue that will be further discussed in what follows.
- It is also worthwhile to note that Alberta oil sand royalty on its own imposes no tax at the margin.[12] However, in the presence of the company income tax, an otherwise neutral royalty increases the METRR even though, in principle, a cash flow tax is a pure rent tax (unused deductions are carried forward at the government bond rate for oil sands investments, which is far less generous than in Australia or Canada Atlantic offshore). For example,

Table 12.1 METRRs by jurisdiction (in percent), 2012

	Exploration	*Development*	*Depreciable*	*Inventory*	*Aggregate*
Canada					
B.C.*	28.5	32.5	29.5	23.2	30.2
Alberta:					
Conventional	48.4	51.8	21.9	23.2	40.3
Oil sands	−2.9	5.6	33.3	33.1	27.7
Saskatchewan	37.4	41.2	33.7	26.4	37.4
Newfoundland	4.9	−26.8	−26.8	NA	−6.8
Nova Scotia	−7.4	−49.1	−73.2	32.1	−26.0
The U.S.					
Arkansas	24.0	26.6	35.2	26.3	28.8
Colorado	28.6	31.0	33.3	25.2	31.0
Pennsylvania	4.2	7.7	38.4	28.2	17.5
Texas	31.7	33.8	32.1	23.2	32.5
Australia	−132.2	13.2	29.4	38.3	−19.6
Brazil	48.3	49.7	74.1	45.6	57.7
Norway	−3.3	14.9	64.1	83.0	28.5
The UK	−4.0	−0.8	4.1	70.8	4.6

Source: Mintz and Chen (2012)

* Assumes that the retail sales tax in BC is reinstated and the Atlantic Investment Tax Credit for oil and gas activities is fully phased out as proposed in the 2012 Federal Budget in Canada.

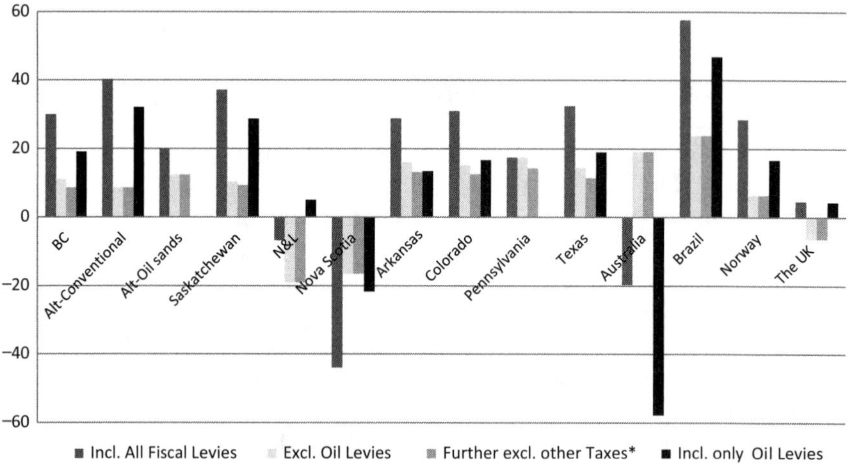

Figure 12.1 Decomposing the effective tax and royalty rate 2012

* Other taxes included sales taxes on capital purchases and asset-based taxes.

Several observations are made here with respect to these estimates.

in the case of royalty deductibility under the company tax, neutrality can be reestablished for the cash flow tax by making two corrections to the company tax (Mintz, 2010). First, annual capital cost allowances under the company income tax should be calculated on the cost basis of assets net of the value of the deduction provided under the royalty base. Second, an investment tax credit should be provided to offset the impact of a reduced value for the deduction of expenses from the rent-based royalty base. The investment tax credit rate should be equal to the royalty rate multiplied by the company income tax rate.

- The rent base for assessing supplementary taxes on petroleum in the UK and Norway are not pure cash-flow taxes as in the case of Alberta oil sands. Norway limits carry-forwards for unused deductions to 4 years even though it does provide up-front refunds for unused exploration deductions. The UK does not provide expensing for inventories.
- Other taxes on capital impact the incentive to invest in a jurisdiction. For example, the retail sales taxes in Saskatchewan, British Columbia and the U.S.[13] increase the cost of capital in those jurisdictions since many capital goods are subject to tax.
- Inflation also affects the cost of capital since depreciation and inventory cost deductions are based on the original cost of assets, which is offset by the deduction of nominal debt interest charges under the company tax. Brazil has a relatively high inflation rate compared to other jurisdictions.

This analysis provides a benchmark for examining the impact of multinational cross-border planning for company taxes and rent-based royalty systems, which is discussed in the next section.

4 Multinational cross-border fiscal issues

Governments, as owners of the resource, want to ensure that they derive a reasonable and fair amount of revenue from extractive industry projects. Multinational companies have a fiduciary duty to their shareholders to reduce tax and royalty payments by adopting various tax planning techniques that are in accordance with the law. Such tax planning can result in the shifting of profits from high- to low-tax jurisdictions including tax havens, leading to a loss of revenues paid to government. Given a recent focus on aggressive tax avoidance, multinationals face the need to balance the benefits of tax minimization with reputation effects arising from little or no payment of taxes and royalties in a country.[14]

As mentioned, the specific tax planning issues addressed here are with respect to transfer pricing, financing structures and discount rates for carrying forward unused deductions. Each of these issues would impact the analysis provided in the previous section.

4.1 Transfer pricing

The analysis assumes that taxes and royalties are based on market-determined prices for outputs and inputs. However, in many situations, multinationals operating in a developing country are selling their products to related parties abroad. Under the OECD transfer pricing guidelines (OECD 2010), transfer prices for transactions between related parties should follow the arm's length standard. If comparable uncontrolled prices are observed between unrelated parties (after adjustments such as transportation costs, quality and volumes), the arm's length standard could be implemented by the use of market prices. Such is the case of many extractive industry products, as observed by Bernard and Weiner (1990) in the case of U.S. petroleum.

Nonetheless, transfer-pricing issues still abound in the extractive industry since the point of production is often distant from the market where traded prices are observed. This requires a determination of the output and input prices on an arm's length basis between related parties with regard to distribution of products, overhead costs, intangibles, intellectual property and risks. As for the determination of transfer prices for intangibles, intellectual property and risks, a country would likely follow international practices for determining fees, royalties and financing costs between related prices. These practices are little different than for other industries and therefore shall not be discussed in this section.

Both the revenue-based and rent-based royalties as well as the corporate income tax require a determination of the "net-selling price" of sales of extracted products at the wellhead. Given that the observed prices are away from the point of extraction, the net-selling price received by the producer is assessed as the market price net of transport and other distribution costs (such as gas compression equipment). This issue is therefore similar to a transfer-pricing problem when measuring profitability for distribution companies (selling price less a margin for distribution costs). The net selling price should reflect comparable distribution cost margins. The allowance could be based on actual costs, which could result in low or negligible revenues during downturns, or a presumptive margin could be provided instead as a portion of the gross selling prices. If the company can incur costs lower than the presumptive margin through efficiencies in distribution, the company will have an incentive to keep costs low.

Another issue particularly with the rent-based royalty and corporate income tax that allows costs to be deductible is the treatment of overhead costs such as general administrative and financing costs that are not easily observable to be attributed to a specific extractive project. These overhead costs of multinationals are difficult for a developing country to measure or audit. Therefore, as seen in Australia, Canada and the UK, rent-based royalties, a presumptive allowance, is often provided for overhead costs (either as a share of revenues or uplift factor for costs).

Assuming that allowances approximate accurately net-selling prices and overhead costs attributed to an extractive industry project, then the METRR calculations are appropriate.

As a further point, net-profit royalty systems typically include ring-fencing whereby revenues and costs are measured with respect to a specific project rather than taxing all the projects held by a company together (under the company income tax, all sources of income and costs incurred by projects in a jurisdiction are combined to assess the income base). While costs can be attributed to the specific project, overheads (general and administrative expenses) become that much more significant to measure when joint factors of production are involved in the company's operations. If transfer prices for overhead costs are understated for profits or rents in the host country, both company tax and rent-based royalty revenue will be understated.

4.2 Tax-efficient financing structures

Even if transfer prices reflect arm's length pricing, it is not difficult for multinationals to shift profits by structuring financing in favourable terms. The use of offshore entities holding assets in low-tax jurisdictions provide financial opportunities to reduce taxes on income and capital gains earned in a host country. Two particular structures are discussed here: direct financing and indirect financing following Mintz and Weichenrieder (2010) and Chen and Mintz (2008).

Direct financing structures involve financial transactions between a parent and an affiliate to reduce taxes paid in a high-tax-rate jurisdiction resulting in higher taxes paid in a low-tax-rate jurisdiction. Assume the multinational is taxed on its parent profits at the rate u and abroad at the rate u^0 on affiliate profits. Also, assume that dividends and capital gains on equity income earned by the parent on its equity investment in the affiliate are tax exempt and inter-affiliate interests are fully taxed. Let N be the equity transfer from the shareholder to parent and N^0 is the equity transfer from parent to the subsidiary. B is debt borrowed by the parent from third parties, X^0 is the inter-affiliate loan from the parent to subsidiary and B^0 is debt borrowed by the subsidiary. For simplicity, assume interest rates are the same across the two countries (so that exchange rates are constant over time). No withholding taxes are imposed on interest or dividends by the capital-importing country.

To understand the incentive effects of company taxes on financing, the marginal decision to finance one incremental unit of capital in the host country by an affiliate is considered, restricted to three methods by which a multinational parent funds capital investments by an affiliate in the host country:

(i) The parent borrows (B) in the home country, transfers equity (N^0) to the affiliate and the subsidiary remits dividends or the parent repurchases shares to earn capital gains in the foreign affiliate.

(ii) The parent borrows in the home country (B) and transfers funds via internal financing (X^0) to the affiliate in the host country. Interest at the rate i on the internal debt is remitted back to the parent.

(iii) The affiliate borrows funds from third parties (including offshore institutions) and invests the funds in the host country. The after-tax income covers the interest cost of borrowed money from third parties, leaving no excess marginal income to be paid to the parent.

If the parent borrows, the cost of borrowing is $i(1 - u)$. The funds are transferred as equity, N^0, to the affiliate who invests the funds in the resource-producing jurisdiction. The marginal after-tax income generated by investment in the host country is $Y(1 - u^0)$, and dividend and capital gain income earned by the parent on its investment in the affiliate is exempt from the parent's country tax. The simple cost of capital for the investment when the parent provides debt financing is:

$$(1) \quad Y = i(1 - u)/(1 - u^0)$$

Instead, suppose the affiliate borrows funds from the parent instead of receiving a transfer of equity. The cost of debt finance for the parent is $i(1 - u)$ that is reinvested as an internal loan, F, to the affiliate, whereby the parent receives net interest income equal to $i(1 - u)$. Given that the home country fully taxes interest received from abroad, after-tax income earned on internal debt fully offsets the parent's cost of debt finance (therefore a wash). The affiliate is able to deduct interest expense, implying the cost of debt financing is $i(1 - u^0)$ with the project generating marginal after-tax income of $Y(1 - u^0)$. The cost of capital for internal loan financing is therefore equal to:

$$(2) \quad Y = i$$

The third case is for the affiliate to borrow from third parties and deduct interest costs at $i(1 - u^0)$ to generate marginal income $Y(1 - u^0)$. This is identical to the case of internal loan financing so the cost of capital remains the same as equation (2).

It can be easily shown that the affiliate should borrow B^0 from the market or the parent if the company tax rate in the home country is less than that of the affiliate ($u < u^0$). If the host country has the higher tax rate, profits will be maximized by the affiliate borrowing from the market or the parent since the tax saving is equal to iu^0 in the host country (any equity income transferred to the parent is exempt from tax by the home country).

However, the result is different if the parent borrows money and injects equity into the affiliate. The interest deduction is taken in the parent's country tax rate with a tax savings at iu at a lower tax saving. In particular, the cost of finance for home country borrowing is higher at $i(1 - u)$ than for host country borrowing at $i(1 - u^0)$.

Obviously, the contrary holds if $u > u^0$. If the home country tax rate were higher than that of the host country, the parent would borrow funds and transfer equity to the affiliate. Income earned in the host country is taxed at the rate u^0, while an interest deduction taken in the home country saves taxes at the rate u. Overall, the cost of capital is lower in equation (1) than in equation (2) due to tax arbitrage by borrowing in a country with a high corporate income tax rate to earn income taxed at a lower rate.

If inflation rates differ across jurisdictions, the location of debt finance will be affected. If the host country has a higher inflation rate (π^0) than the home country (π), its currency would be expected to depreciate in accordance with purchasing power parity. As a result, the nominal interest rate in the host country would be higher than the interest rate in the home country: $i^0 > i$. With an expected depreciation of the host country exchange rate, a capital loss is accrued to the lender and capital gain to the borrowing parent for its investment in the host country equal to the difference between the host and home country inflation rates: $-\pi + \pi^0$. In this case, countries with weak currencies have a lower cost of debt finance given the deductibility of nominal interest from the corporate tax. Overall, the cost of debt finance in the home country is only lower in the host country if $i(1 - u) < i^0(1 - u^0) - \pi + \pi^0$.

So what happens to the METRR? If the cost of finance in the host country (taking into account corporate tax deductibility and exchange rate depreciation) is less than the home country ($i^0(1 - u^0) - \pi^0 + \pi < i(1 - u)$), then the analysis provided is unaffected. However, if the cost of finance in the home country is less than in the host country, $i(1 - u) < i^0(1 - u^0) - \pi^0 + \pi$), the parent will borrow in the home country to finance investments in the host country. The cost of finance in equation (3) becomes[15]

$$(3') \quad R = B(i^0(1 - u^0) - \pi^0 + \pi) + (1 - B)\rho - \pi.$$

The impact of 3' is to lower the METRR in a host country when a parent has the incentive to borrow funds in their jurisdiction to fund investments.[16] Thus, if the capital export country has a higher corporate income tax rate than that prevailing in the host country, the METRR will be lower to the extent that debt is borrowed in the home country (each case of cross-border investments by country would need to be evaluated separately[17]).

Multinational companies also use tax indirect financing structures with one or multiple conduits to reduce the cost of finance. The key is that a break occurs between the inclusion and deduction of income, thereby enabling multiple deductions for financing costs (see Mintz, 2004; Mintz and Weichenrieder, 2010 for detailed analysis). A simple case is an intermediate operating in a tax haven by which the intermediate pays no tax on its income, no withholding taxes are imposed on cross-border flows of interest or dividends and the home country does not treat such income as subject to home country tax.[18]

The effect of these conduit structures is to enable double- (or multiple-) dip deductions for financing costs. A conduit is an intermediate placed between the parent and affiliate operating in separate, low-tax jurisdictions.

A parent borrows in the home country and deducts interest expense to reduce home country tax. Transferring equity to the conduit, the conduit lends the funds to an affiliate in another jurisdiction – the loan interest is deductible in the host country. The conduit pays little or no tax on income received from the affiliate, while the interest is a deductible charge against the affiliate's company income, with little or no withholding tax pay on the interest paid to the conduit. The conduit in turn pays tax-exempt income to the parent (typically dividends), with little or no withholding tax deducted by the conduit jurisdiction. Overall, the multinational is able to achieve two interest deductions for a single investment placed in the host country where the affiliate operates.

Tax havens such as those in the Caribbean Islands have often been used to effect double-dip financing deductions. So have special entities in developed countries such as Belgium, Luxembourg and the Netherlands been used to achieve similar tax benefits under indirect financing structures. With U.S. check-the-box rules,[19] hybrid or reverse hybrid (tower) structures have been used to achieve double-dip interest deductions without routing funds through a third country. For example, this has been widely used for cross-border investment flows between Canada and the United States: an intermediate is established that is recognized as a corporation by the Canadian government and a partner by the U.S. government.

Under indirect financing involving one conduit and a double-dip interest deduction, the cost of finance is the following:

$$(3'')\ R = B(i^0(1 - u + x - u^0) - \pi^0 + \pi) + (1 - B)\rho - \pi.$$

With x being the withholding tax imposed by the host country on the loan to the affiliate or the tax rate imposed by the home country on income received by the conduit entity from next-tier affiliates.

The effect of both direct and indirect financing on the METRR is illustrated in Table 3.2 for a Canadian parent. The domestic investment case is for company financing capital with 40% debt. The base case is a Canadian parent that borrows 40% of domestic financing at home and 25% in the host country (the lower effective tax rates reflect a higher overall debt–asset ratio of 55%). The third column reports the effective tax rates assuming that 5 percentage points of debt is shifted to the jurisdiction with the lowest cost of financing due to lower corporate tax rate and weak currencies (maintaining a 55% overall debt to asset ratio). The final case is for conduit financing with double-dip interest deductions.

Obviously, indirect financing through conduits enables companies to reduce the METRR the most compared to the direct financing structure, although not that severely in the case of Brazil (with a relatively high withholding tax rate on interest) and Texas, where the royalty and severance tax are assessed on revenues only.

Table 12.2 METRRs by jurisdiction for a canadian parent 2012

	Domestic			
	Investment	*Base Case*	*Debt Shifting*	*Conduit financing*
Australia	−19.6	−35.4	−39.8	−46.6
Brazil	57.7	50.1	46.9	46.0
Norway	28.5	24.3	23.3	17.2
The UK	4.6	3.2	1.3	−2.1
The U.S. – Texas	32.5	31.4	30.0	27.7

4.3 Discount rates

Discount rates play a critical role in determining royalties assessed on rent or "net profits". In the case of the cash flow approach, the discount rate is used to carry forward unused deductions, which is particularly important at the beginning of projects when exploration and development expenditures are incurred before the realization of income. With the R-base royalty, the return on investments reflecting the opportunity cost of investing in other similar activities is exempt (this exempt return is the "normal" rate of return with rents being the excess amount).

Some jurisdictions, such as Australia and Nova Scotia, have permitted quite high discount rates, which are expressed as the government bond rate plus a factor to incorporate risk (such as 15 points in the case of exploration costs in Australia). Others have measured the exempt rate of return as the current long-term bond rate as in the case of Alberta oil sand investments.

Many analysts[20] would argue that the riskless (government) bond rate is an appropriate proxy for the multinational's discount rate since the government already implicitly deducts the cost of risk through loss offsetting provisions under the net profit royalty (see, for example, Australia, 2010). However, risk sharing by governments is often not perfect – the government through refunds may not share losses at time of bankruptcy and losses at the end of the project in the case of ring-fencing. Moreover, unlike rent-based royalties that typically allow companies to carry forward losses, company income tax losses are carried forward to limited periods at no rate of interest. Nonetheless, including risk in the discount rate as measured for stockowners in stock markets is not appropriate since governments share a significant share of losses under rent-based royalty systems.

If the discount rate used to carry forward losses is incorrect, it will affect the cost of capital as specified in measuring the METRR. For example, if the discount rate is too low relative to the firm's financing costs, the METRR will be higher. If the allowable discount rate is too high relative, the METRR will be lower.[21]

In principle, the use of the long-term government bond rate, as suggested by the Mirrlees Review, is not correct for multinational discount rates to determine

Table 12.3 Financing cost by type of investors, 2012

	10-year govt bond rate	*10-year corporate bond rate*	*Base case*	*Debt shifting*	*Conduit financing*
Australia	3.4	6.9	5.7	5.5	5.3
Brazil	na	8.9	7.4	6.9	6.8
Norway	2.1	5.9	4.8	4.8	4.4
UK	1.9	6.7	5.5	5.4	5.1
Texas	1.8	6.2	5.0	4.9	4.6

Note: The 10-year corporate bond rate is estimated by taking U.S. corporate bond rates, adjusting for differences in inflation rates across countries (purchasing power parity). Long-term government bond rates are taken from the OECD (http://stats.oecd.org/index.aspx?querytype=view&queryname=86) and thus not strictly comparable.

carry-forward of losses. Not only do governments not fully share risks with the private sector, such discount rates ignore tax effects, which vary for risk-free equity and debt costs of finance. Once accounting for international tax planning, the multinational's nominal cost of finance could well be above or below the government bond rate (the nominal cost being in equations 3, 3' and 3" except for the inflation rate being added back).

Table 12.3 illustrates the nominal cost of finance (including equity) for different jurisdictions compared to the corporate bond rate taken as a surrogate for non-refundable bankruptcy risk. If the 10-year government bond rate is used to proxy the discount rate, it will be too low when governments do not fully share risks such as in the case of corporate bankruptcy. It will be too high if tax planning reduces the financing cost, once accounting for the tax savings from interest deductibility.

Overall, government bond rates, which have been abnormally low since 2008, could underestimate the appropriate discount rate. On the other hand, the use of a corporate bond rate may be too high since tax-planning effects reduce corporate bond financing costs.

5 Conclusions

This chapter focuses on the company tax and resource royalty issues related to cross-border investments. The company income tax is a significant generator of revenues for governments not only in the resource sector but also in other sectors. Royalties are aimed at deriving economic rents from resource exploitation including levies related to "rents" including "net profits", production sharing (that is similar to a net profit approach), revenues or cash flows. The company tax and rent-based royalties interact with each other in important ways, resulting in a cash-flow tax, for example, not being neutral in the presence of a company tax.

This analysis characterizes several cross-border fiscal issues that impact the incentive to invest and the resource revenues derived by governments.

Cross-country comparisons of marginal effective tax and royalty rates (METRRs) for Australia, Brazil, Canada, Norway, United Kingdom and United States on oil exploration, development and extraction are contrasted, demonstrating the revenue-based royalty systems such as those used in the United States and Brazil, tend to result in relative high taxes on marginal investments that are expected to earn little rent. This is further complicated by several general cross-border issues such as transfer pricing, conduit financing and the discount rate for carrying forward unused deductions under rent-based royalties.

Notes

* I wish to thank Duanjie Chen, who assisted with the empirical analysis in this chapter, and participants at the International Monetary Fund conference on "Resources without Borders", May 2013. I am very grateful for the astute comments provided by Michael Keen and Artur Świstak.

1 See Laffont and Martimort (2002). As the authors demonstrate, the principal, knowing the most cost-efficient producers, designs a contract to attract the best agent to produce the resource. This requires the government to share some of the rents with the agent.

2 Some of the analysis in this chapter follows Mintz and Chen (2012).

3 In this chapter, I shall use the term "royalty" to apply to any type of levy, including profit- or rent-based ones. The alternative approach is to define royalties specifically as a percentage of revenues or a levy on output from the sale of extracted product and resource taxation to refer to both regular taxes and rent-based or profit-based payments to governments for extraction. (See Daniel, Keen and McPherson (2010.)

4 MacKie-Mason and Mintz (1991).

5 The Henry report (Australia, 2010) recommended a mining tax on rents based on the cash flow approach. Companies expense costs are deducted from revenues, and any unused deductions are carried forward at the government bond rate. The Henry report recommended that any unused deductions left at the end of the project would be refunded at the cash flow royalty rate to ensure that the government fully shares risks (this is equivalent to giving a full deduction for the cost of risk). See further discussion in Mintz (2010).

6 This proposition is well known in the literature, which implies that the risk premium from capital asset pricing models is reduced by the factor one minus the tax rate (see Gordon and Wilson, 1989, and Mintz, 1995).

7 An alternative approach is to model an expected average tax rate based on the assumption that investments are indivisible (such as large-scale projects or ownership of intellectual property). Companies can therefore earn a rate of return on capital that is more than the cost of capital ("economic rent"). Taxing rents across jurisdictions could also impact the decision to invest in large-scale investments (Devereux and Griffith, 2003). To calculate the average tax rate, it requires knowing the pre-tax rate of return on capital net of risk. Empirically, this is virtually unknown, but we do know that firms, even with fixed costs, will intensively invest in assets at the margin when the risk-adjusted rate of return on capital is equal to the cost of capital. Thus, the METRR captures the minimum rate of return or hurdle rate needed by investors to compensate for the cost of capital and taxes.

8 The 5% rate of return is the after-tax required return for the project to attract financing from shareholders. To be clear, the empirical analysis that follows does not assume

that 5% is the after-tax rate of return for a project. Instead, the after-tax required rate of return is based on a modelling of capital market equilibrium for observable interest rates.

9 Smith (2012) provides a detailed survey on various models used to analyze fiscal impact on investments in extractive industries.

10 The "time-to-build" analysis results in a higher cost of capital for a company since its income is only earned at a later time. Tax payments are affected since tax deductions for exploration and development spending are taken prior to income being earned when the resource is exploited. The delay in creating income raises the cost of capital, but the mismatch of income and expenses under the tax system provides a tax benefit that reduces the cost of capital.

11 In this time-to-build model, it is assumed for simplicity that the debt to asset ratio is fixed over time. A more complex treatment of financing is discussed in Mackie-Mason and Mintz (1991).

12 In these calculations for Alberta oil sands, it is assumed that the price of oil is fixed over time rather than varying. While this simplifies the analysis, varying royalty rates impose greater tax cost on companies since the government-expected revenues increase progressively with profits. On the other hand, companies can take advantage of tax planning opportunities such as investing when royalty rates are high to maximize the value of deductions and holding back investment when royalty rates are low.

13 Due to lack of data, our analysis does not include unfunded VAT on capital purchases in Brazil, which could have a significant impact on the cost of capital and overall METRRs.

14 It is an issue that is currently being studied by the G20, with analysis provided by the OECD base erosion study (OECD 2013).

15 See also Mintz and Tsiopoulos (1994) for a detailed discussion of the cost of finance in the presence of inflation and corporate taxation in the presence of exemption and tax crediting.

16 Note that this analysis is further complicated with respect to foreign investments undertaken by U.S. companies given that the U.S. is the only major capital-exporting country to tax foreign-source dividends received by U.S. parents. See Chen and Mintz (2009) for further details.

17 Given the complexity of evaluating different cases, the reader is referred to Chen and Mintz (2009) to see the impact for non-resource companies.

18 Multiple examples exist. Taking one example, a Canadian parent invests equity in a Barbados international business company that pays tax at a rate varying from 0.25 to 2.5% (the schedule is actually regressive, with high rates associated with lower income). In turn, the Barbados entity loans the funds to a foreign affiliate, where the investment takes place (such as Germany). The Barbados entity receives interest, deductible from German tax, with little Barbados tax paid. Under the Canada-Barbados treaty, dividends are paid to the Canadian company exempt from withholding tax and Canadian tax. If the Canadian parent also borrows to fund the equity transfer to the Barbados affiliate, two interest deductions are possible for one investment in Germany. Many countries, including the United States, which taxes foreign remitted income (with a tax credit for foreign taxes), provide similar opportunities for multiple interest deductions. These tax-efficient structures are limited by thin-capitalization or earnings-stripping rules imposed by capital-importing countries, foreign income taxation by the capital exporter and denial of treaty benefits, resulting in high withholding tax rates.

19 K. Mullis (2011) provides some description of hybrids and check-the-box rules.

20 See for example Institute of Fiscal Studies (the Mirrlees Review), *Tax by Design*, Oxford University Press, United Kingdom, 2011.

21 In Mintz and Chen (2012), the high discount rates afforded to investments in Australia, Newfoundland & Labrador and Nova Scotia lowered the METRR.

References

Australia. (2010), *Australia's Future Tax System Review* (Chaired by Dr. Ken Henry), (Australia: Canberra).

Bernard, Jean-Thomas and Robert Weiner. (1990), "Multinational Corporations, Transfer Prices and Taxes: Evidence from the U.S. Petroleum Industry," in Assaf Razin and Joel Slemrod (eds), *Taxation in the Global Economy* (Chicago: University of Chicago Press), pp. 123–160.

Boadway, Robin, Neil Bruce, Kenneth McKenzie and Jack Mintz. (1987), "Marginal Effective Tax Rates for Capital in the Canadian Mining Industry," *Canadian Journal of Economics*, 30(1), 1–16.

Boadway, Robin, Neil Bruce and Jack Mintz. (1984), "Taxation, Inflation and the Effective Marginal Tax Rate on Capital in Canada," *Canadian Journal of Economics*, 17(1), 62–79.

Chen, Duanjie and Jack Mintz. (2008), "Taxation of Canadian Inbound and Outbound Investments," Advisory Panel on Canada's System of International Taxation, Finance Canada, Ottawa, Canada. Available at http://publications.gc.ca/collections/collection_2010/fin/F34-3-13-2009-eng.pdf.

Daniel, Phillip, Michael Keen and Charles McPherson. (2010), "Evaluating Fiscal Regimes for Resource Projects: An Example from Oil Development," in Philip Daniel, Michaekl Keen and Charles Mcpherson (eds), *The Taxation of Petroleum and Minerals: Principles, Problems and Practice* (Routledge Explorations in Environmental Economics) (New York: Routledge and Washington: International Monetary Fund), pp. 187–240.

Devereux, Michael P. and Rachael Griffith. (2003), "Evaluating Tax Policy for Location Decisions," *International Tax and Public Finance*, 10, 107–126.

Gordon, Roger and John D. Wilson. (1989), "Measuring the Efficiency Cost of Taxing Risky Capital Income," *American Economic Review*, 79(3), 427–439.

Laffont, Jean-Jacques and David Martimort. (2002), *The Theory of Incentives: The Principal-Agent Model* (Princeton: NJ: Princeton University Press).

MacKie-Mason, Jeffrey K. and Jack Mintz. (1991), "Taxation and Uncertainty When Capital Takes Time to Build," Draft, University of Toronto, December 1991.

McKenzie, Kenneth J., Mario Mansour and Ariane Brûlé. (1998), "The Calculation of Marginal Effective Tax Rates," Working Paper 1997–15 (Ottawa: Department of Finance).

Mintz, J. (1990), "Corporate Tax Holidays and Investment," *World Bank Economic Review*, 4(2), 81–102.

Mintz, Jack. (1995), "The Corporate Income Tax: A Survey," *Fiscal Studies*, 16(4), 23–68.

Mintz, Jack. (2004), "Conduit Entities: The Implications of Indirect Tax Efficient Financing Structures for Real Investment," *International Tax and Public Finance*, 11(4), 419–434.

Mintz, Jack. (2010), "Evaluation of the Business Tax Recommendations of the Henry Review and the Australian Government Response," in Chris Evans, Richard Krever and Peter Mellor (eds), *Australia's Future Tax System: The Prospects after Henry : Essays in Honour of John W Freebairn* (Pyrmont, NSW: Thomson Reuters), pp. 161–182.

Mintz, Jack and Duanjie Chen. (2012), "Capturing Economic Rents from Resources Through Royalties and Taxes," SPP Research Papers," *SPP Research Papers*, 12–30 (Calgary: The School of Public Policy, University of Calgary).

Mintz, Jack and Thomas A. Tsiopoulos. (1994), "The Effectiveness of Corporate Tax Incentives for Foreign Direct Investment in the Presence of Tax Crediting," *Journal of Public Economics*, 55(2), 233–255.

Mintz, Jack and Alfons Weichenrieder. (2010), *The Indirect Side of Direct Investment* (Cambridge MA: MIT Press).

Mullis, K. (2011), "Check-the-Box and Hybrids: A Second Look at Elective U.S. Tax Classification for Foreign Entities," *Tax Notes International*, November 4, 2011.

Organization of Economic Cooperation and Development. (2010), *OECD Transfer Pricing Guidelines for Multinational Enterprises and Tax Administrations 2010* (Paris: OECD).

Organization of Economic Cooperation and Development. (2013), *Action Plan on Base Erosion and Profit Shifting* (Paris: OECD).

Smith, James. (2012), "Issues in Extractive Resource Taxation: A Review of Research Methods and Models," IMF Working Paper WP/12/287 (Washington: International Monetary Fund).

Theoretical appendix

The theoretical model follows that found in Boadway, Bruce and Mintz (1984), Boadway et al. (1987) and McKenzie, Mansour and Brûlé (1998), with an adjustment to recognize that it takes time to build up reserves with exploration and development before extraction takes place. It is a time-to-build model in the sense capital (reserves) must be created first before being depleted by the firm by extracting the resource to be sold to the market (MacKie-Mason and Mintz, 1991; Mintz and Chen, 2012). The "time-to-build" analysis results in a higher cost of capital for a company since income is earned after spending on exploration and development has taken place with a financing cost. Tax payments are affected since tax deductions for exploration and development expenditures are often expensed prior to income being earned (unless governments restrict deductions to be taken when income is earned, which we have accounted for when relevant). This leads to a mismatching of income and costs for tax purposes. The delay in creating income raises the cost of capital but the deductions taken earlier than when income is earned reduced tax payments and the cost of capital as shown in what follows.

A resource firm maximizes the present value of cash flows from its project subject to the constraint that the extracted resources is equal to the amounts discovered over time. We abstract from uncertainty since its incorporation with full loss offsetting under the tax system would not affect the measure of the marginal effective tax and royalty rates. Let T be the period in which reserves are discovered and prepared for extraction that begins at that time.

(A.1) Max $V = \sum_0^\infty (1 + R)\text{–}^t CF_t\, dt$

(A.2) subject to $\sum_T^\infty Q_t[L_t, k_t] = X = \sum_0^T f[e_t]$ (accumulated reserves equals total extraction)

with $CF_t = P_t\, Q_t[L_t, k_t] - w_t L_t - (\delta K_t + k_t)(1 + \pi)^{t-} \mathrm{TAX}_{c[t]} - \mathrm{TAX}_{R[t]}$ for $t \geq T$

$CF_t = - e_t\, (1 + \pi)^{t-}\, T_{c[t]}$ for $t \leq T$

V is the present value of the firm's nominal cash flows CF, discounted by the nominal financing rate R over the lifetime of the firm's project. The nominal cost of finance is the weighted average of debt and equity finance (R = Bi

$(1 - u) + (1 - B)\rho$) used by the firm for all of its projects, adjusted for the deductibility of interest expense (B is the portion of assets financed by debt, i is the nominal cost of debt and ρ is nominal cost of equity, net of risk with all values expressed in certainty-equivalent terms[1]). These costs are determined by international markets and can depend on tax planning opportunities.

Note that P_t = nominal price of output normalized to one and rises at the same inflation rate as other prices ($P_t = P(1 + \pi)^t$) and $w_t L_t$ are current costs (which we will later denote as C and $w_t = w(1 + \pi)^t$). We note that these costs are equivalent to market prices, abstracting from any transfer pricing issues that is discussed in the text). The marginal productivity of outputs declines with the use of factors of production. Current costs, $C_t[Q_t, k_t]$, Q_K and Q_L, can therefore be treated as a strictly joint convex in output Q (denoted as $C_Q > 0$ and $C_{QQ} > 0$) and capital that reduces costs (denoted as $C_K < 0$ and $C_{KK} < 0$) with K_t = depreciable capital stock, k_t = new investment = $K_{t+1} - K_t$ and δ = economic depreciation. (Note that $C_Q = w/Q_L$ with profit maximization). Capital is treated as the numeraire with a real price equal to one.

Note that $f[e_t]$ are reserves found through spending on exploration in period t with the function being strictly concave in expenditure on exploration and development ($f' > 0$ and $f'' < 0$).

$\text{TAX}_{c[t]}$ = company tax payments (paid in each period and can be negative) and
$\text{TAX}_{R[t]}$ = royalty payments in each period t (only paid after extraction begins).

The company tax is imposed on the revenues earned from the sale of resources net of the costs of production, which include current extraction costs, capital cost allowances and exploration and development costs (exploration is expensed, but development is capitalized and written off at the declining balance rate σ). This implies the following:

(A.3) $\text{TAX}_{c[t]} = u\{P_t Q_t \text{–} wL_t(1 + \pi)^{t-} \alpha D_t - \sigma E_t(1 + \pi)^{t-} T_{R[t]}\}$
(A.4) $D_t = (\delta K_s + k_s)(1 + \pi)^{t-} \alpha D_{t-1}$
(A.5) $E_t = e_t(1 + \pi)^{t-} \sigma E_{t-1}$
(A.6) with α = capital cost allowance rate, D_s = the undepreciated capital cost base and E_s = the undepreciated "stock" of exploration and development spending at time s.

Manipulating the terms associated with capital cost allowances and investment, $(\delta K_t + k_t)(1 + \pi)^t$, in equation (A.1) with the insertion of terms in (A.3), (A.4) and (A.5), one can show that the investment costs are reduced by the present value of capital allowances which is denoted as adjusted cash flow CF_t:

$$CF_t = \{PQ_t \text{–} wL_t\}(1 - u)(1 + \pi)^{t-} (\delta K_t + k_t)(1 - uZ)(1 + \pi)^{t-}\text{TAX}_{R[t]}(1 - u)$$

for $t \geq T$
$CF_t = -e_t(1 - uZ')(1 + \pi)^{t-}\text{TAX}_{R[t]}(1 - u)$ for $t < T$
with $Z = \alpha(1 + R)/(\alpha + R)$ and $Z' = \sigma(1 + R)/(\sigma + R)$.[2]

Next, a typical royalty based on the value of production is analyzed. This is followed by a rent-based royalty following the cash flow approach. Note that "payments" in the exploration and development phase are "negative" if such costs are deductible from the rent base, which will be the case for the rent-based royalty.

Revenue-based royalty

Revenue-based royalties are a percentage of the value of extracted output, and the corporate income tax system allows companies to deduct exploration and development expenses against other income earned. Let τ be the ad valorem payment on sales, PQ, so that $T_R = \tau PQ$ (suppressing time scripts here on in unless needed). Maximizing equation (A.1), subject to (A.2) and (A.2'), choosing L, K, k and E, with appropriate substitutions, yield the following:

Output decision

The choice of Q yields the following result (λ is the Lagrange multiplier for the constraint in (A.2)):

(A.7) $\quad (1 + r)^{-t}(P(1 - \tau) - C_Q)(1 - u) = \lambda$
with $r = R - \pi = Bi(1 - u) + (1 - B)\rho - \pi$.

The implied Hotelling Rule by using two first-order conditions is the following: $\{(p_{t+1-}p_t)(1 - \tau) - (C_{Q,t+1} - C_{Q,t})\} / \{p_t(1 - \tau) - C_{Q,t}\}. = r$. The firm extracts output until the net of royalty gain from holding a unit of reserve is equal to financing costs that could be saved by selling one more unit of output.
The shadow price of extracted output λ is equal to marginal value of extracting a marginal unit of output. The royalty rate on ad valorem sales generally reduces quasi-rents and the incentive to extract since the royalty reduces revenues relative to costs of extraction. On the other hand, the deductibility of interest expense from taxable income lowers the cost of finance, r, and increases the present value of the marginal quasi-rent, $P(1 - \tau) - C_Q)$). The lower interest rate means that firms need a lower gain in quasi-rents and therefore causes extraction to take place in earlier.

Depreciable capital

The choice of capital stock and new investment, post-exploration and development yields the following cost of capital for depreciable capital:

(A.8) $\quad -C_K = (\delta + R - \pi)(1 - uZ)/(1 - u)$

This is the familiar cost of capital expression, noting that R is the weighted average of the cost of debt and equity finance and Z is the present value of depreciation.

Exploration and development

The choice of exploration and development, e, yields the following costs:

$$\text{(A.9)} \quad (P_T - C_T')f_t' = (1 - uZ)(1 + r)^{(T - t)}/[(1 - u)\{1 - \tau P/(P - C')\}]$$

The quasi-rent earned by investing in exploration $(P_T - C_T')f_t'$ is equal to the interest-adjusted cost of exploration (the price of exploration and development is set equal to unity) divided by the one minus the royalty imposed on the cost of capital. The term in the denominator $\tau P/(P - C')$ is the ad valorem tax paid as a share of the quasi-rents on incremental sales (this is expected to be less than one so long as the ad valorem tax rate is less than the margin $(P - C')/P$). The cost of exploration is reduced by interest deductions taken early at time t relative to the earning of income at time T. Given the deductibility of interest expense from income, the effect of corporate taxation is to reduce the real cost of finance (r) and the discount factor $(1 + r)^{(T - t)}$ resulting in a lower cost of capital (and lower effective tax rate on capital).

Rent-based royalty

The rent-based royalty is assumed to be a rate applied to revenues or payouts net of operating costs after the full recovery of exploration and development costs. This cash flow approach requires both current and capital costs to be expensed. Interest expense is not deductible, but unused deductions, fully written off in later years, are carried forward at the riskless bond rate (the uplift factor).

The royalty payment after payout is the following: $T_R = \tau[P_tQ_t - C(Q_t,K_t)(1 + \pi)^{t-}(\delta K_t + k_t)(1 + \pi)^{t-} e_t(1 + \pi)^t]$, which is substituted into equation (A.3).

Choice of output

The determination of output, Q, accords with the following Euler equation:

$$\text{(A.10)} \quad (1 + r)^{-t}(1 - \tau)(P - C')(1 - u) = \lambda$$

implying that only interest deductibility of debt financing costs under the corporate income tax (incorporated in r) affects the extraction decision: $\{(p_t + 1 - p_t) - (C_{Q,t+1} - C_{Q,t})\} / \{p_t - C_{Q,t}\}. = r$.

Depreciable capital

The user cost for depreciable capital is similar to equation (A.9), but royalties directly affect the cost of capital because current costs are deductible from the royalty base. That is, changes in the stock of capital reduce current costs, which are netted from royalty payments.

$$\text{(A.11)} \quad -C_K = (\delta + R - \pi)\{1 - \tau(1 - u) - uZ)\}/[(1 - u)(1 - \tau)]$$

Exploration and development

The user cost for exploration and development for the cash flow tax is the following:

$$\text{(A.12)} \quad (P - C')f_t' = (1 - uZ' - \tau(1 - u))(1 + r)^{(T-t)}/[(1 - u)(1 - \tau)].$$

If the company tax terms are zero ($u = 0$ and $Z = 1$), the royalty terms appearing in equations (A.12) to (A.14) disappear. Otherwise, the rent-based royalty is not neutral, as it increases the company tax burden on capital. Government might fully share returns, risk and the cost of investment but not the company tax on marginal investments.

12A.1 Data Appendix: non-tax parameters by country, 2012

CANADA:	*B.C.*	*Alberta*	*Saskatchewan*	*Nfld.*	*N.S.*
Fed-prov company tax rate	25%	25%	27%	29%	31%
Rent-based royalty: τ	Varying*	Varying**	None	Varying	2-tier

* For shale oil only. ** Long-term government bond rate.

U.S.:	*Arkansas*	*Colorado*	*Pennsylvania*	*Texas*
Company tax rates	36.3%	35.0%	38.6%	32.5%
Combined fed-state: $U_c = U_f(1 - U_s) + U_s$ with $U_f = 31.85\%$				
State CIT rate	6.5%	4.63%	9.9%	1.0%
Revenue-based royalty: g*	17%	21%	None	24%

* This is the combined rate for both severance tax and royalty taking into account deductibility.

Other Countries	*Australia*	*Brazil*	*Norway*	*UK*
Combined tax and royalty rates	30%	34%	78%	62%
Company tax rates	30%	34%	28%	30%
Revenue-based royalty: g	None	11%	None	None
Rent-based royalty rate:	40%	Varying	50%	32%

(*Continued*)

12A.1 Data Appendix: non-tax parameters by country, 2012 Continued

	Australia	*Brazil*	*Canada*	*Norway*	*UK*	*U.S.*
Inflation rate: π^*	3.3%	5.1%	2%	2.1%	2.9%	2.4%
			Commonly shared non-tax parameters			
Real cost of debt finance**			3.8%			
Debt–asset ratio			40.0%			
Nominal cost of equity finance			5.3%			
Nominal cost of finance			4.9%			
Net of tax real return			3.4%			
Time to build:						
Exploration			5-year			
Development			1-year			
Time from making investment to payout:						
Exploration			10-year			
Development			6-year			
Capital weights**						
Depreciable assets			33.3%			
Inventory			2.4%			
Exploration			26.7%			
Development			37.6%			
Aggregate-including E&D			100%			

* Our estimate based on CPI for 2005–11, published by the World Bank up to 2010 and *The Economist* for 2011.

** Adopted from our Canadian model and applied across-borders.

*** It is the sum of the country-specific inflation rate and the cross-border real interest rate.

Notes

1 Note that it is assumed that full refundability of losses is provided in this model.

2 For an explicit derivation, see J. Mintz (1990).

13 Tax competition and coordination in extractive industries

*Mario Mansour and Artur Świstak**

1 Introduction

Tax competition has been studied extensively in the economic literature, mainly out of concern that countries may collectively[1] lose revenues when they set their tax policies independently of each other – relative to setting them cooperatively. Little attention has been given, however, to the issue of tax competition and coordination specifically in the extractive industries (EIs), where appropriately designed taxation could be particularly efficient given a number of sector-specific characteristics.

First, locational rent associated with EIs is potentially very high. This is the excess return that investors may earn from bringing the resource to market, relative to the minimum return they require. It is location specific when investors have a chance to earn this rent (or a portion of it) only if they invest in the jurisdiction where the resource is located. The implication is that government can tax such rent with very little impact on investors' behavior – and since investors tend to be foreigners, especially in developing countries, their welfare should be of little concern to governments. It might seem that given such rent, the sector would not be subject (at least not to the same extent) to the forces that tax competition exerts on other (more mobile) factors and activities. But if, for some reason, downward tax competition in EI does happen,[2] the revenue loss, especially in developing countries, could be substantial. IMF (2012) reports that revenue from EIs can be very high, exceeding 10 percent of GDP in 22 countries; in Sub-Saharan Africa, increases in government revenue since the early 1990s have come largely from upstream EIs (Figure 13.1). The exhaustibility of natural resources means that governments have only one chance to get their tax policy right.

Second, EIs exhibit substantial up-front investments, especially in exploration – but also in development and capital outlays for extraction. Given the sunken nature of such investments, governments may be tempted to bid their taxes down to attract investment but later increase them to extract a higher share of revenue. The question arises as to how this "time-inconsistency" problem interacts with tax competition concerns and whether tax coordination can alleviate (or even worsen) it. The problem is compounded by the high uncertainty

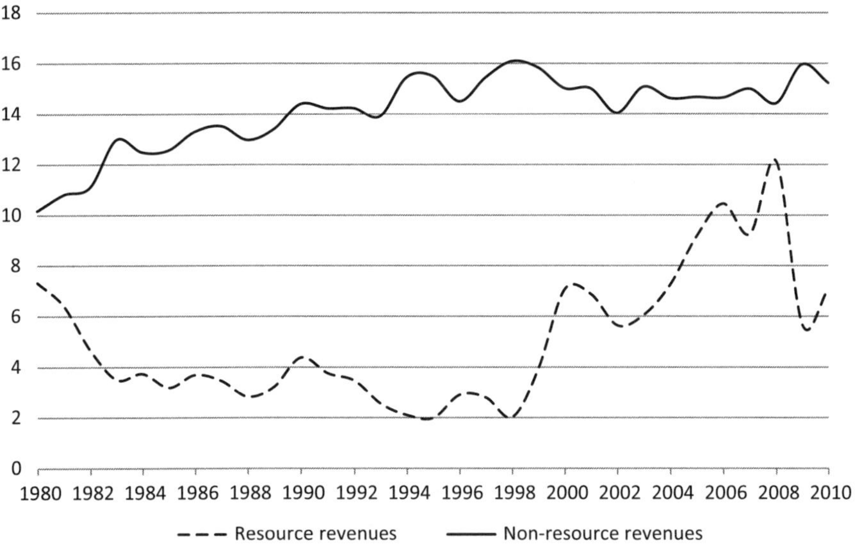

Figure 13.1 Composition of tax revenue in Sub-Saharan Africa: resource vs. non-resource; 1980–2010

Source: Mansour (2014)

regarding investment in EIs (i.e. the quantity and quality of the resource that can be developed and price uncertainty on inputs and output) and by the asymmetric information between investors and governments, with the latter generally suffering an informational disadvantage.

This chapter discusses issues of tax competition and coordination in upstream EIs. Is tax competition in EIs happening? And which taxes[3] does it affect? Should governments coordinate taxes affecting EIs? What form should this coordination take? These are difficult questions that the literature has not fully resolved. Our aim in discussing them here is modest; we seek to provide some guidance on whether these should be significant concerns for policy makers and, if so, possible ways to address them. We do not discuss certain forms of limited coordination in tax policy and administration, such as tax treaties (covered in Chapter 5, Daniel and Thuronyi, this volume), and, specifically for the EIs, common development zones (covered in Chapter 10, Cameron, this volume) and Chapter 11, Daniel, Veung and Watson, this volume).

The term "tax competition" encompasses many forms of competition among tax jurisdictions and within them: competition for cross-border shoppers (e.g. through consumption taxes); competition for mobile factors (e.g. real and financial capital through corporate taxes or labor through personal income taxes and payroll taxes); competition for voters (e.g. through lower or higher property taxes in states of a federation to attract people with a set of particular preferences for local public goods); and "vertical tax competition" between levels of governments in a federation for the same tax base (e.g. royalties and CIT could be imposed by both the central and state governments in a federation).

Tax competition could also have the objective of attracting a tax base, such as profits, without any impact on real activities.[4] To limit our discussion, we define tax competition as "non-cooperative tax setting among jurisdictions with the aim to attract mobile factors of production (capital and labor) or firms in EIs". We therefore exclude tax competition to attract profit shifting. Although these two categories of competition are difficult to disentangle, this exclusion should not be problematic for our purpose since resource-rich countries rarely set their tax rates so low that they are likely to attract paper profits. Resource-rich countries, especially developing, would probably lose from setting tax rates too low to compete for paper profits rather than setting them reasonably high to tax the resource rent.[5]

Under this definition, the major taxes that can be used by countries to compete include (1) CIT and other taxes on production, such as royalties and resource rent taxes (RRTs); (2) tariffs on imports of capital and intermediate inputs and tariffs on exports, which, although rare, are still important in some developing countries for EIs; (3) cascading sales taxes; (4) withholding taxes on payments to non-residents; and (5) labor taxes in general and additional taxes on expatriates in particular – which may take the form of fees for visas and work permits. These taxes have varying impacts on effective tax rates on capital and labor and hence may affect both the decision to locate and marginal decisions (e.g. to expand, or not, and exploration and production activities). To simplify the discussion, and also due to data constraints, we limit the analysis to the instruments in 1, 2, and 3.

The chapter is organized as follows. Section 2 tries to draw some lessons from the general literature on tax competition and coordination for the EI sector. Section 3 brings these to the specific context of the EI sector and attempts to answer some basic questions such as whether tax competition in EI is happening and what countries can or should do about it. Section 4 reviews experiences in tax coordination, drawing mainly from those in the European Union (EU) and the West African Economic and Monetary Union (WAEMU), and IMF technical assistance to developing and resource-rich countries, identifying along the way remaining challenges. Section 5 concludes.

2 Lessons from the literature on tax competition and coordination

The main issue that the tax competition literature addresses is the possibility that countries may be collectively worse off setting their tax policies alone rather than cooperatively because policy decision in one country have externalities (or spillovers) that affect the tax base of other countries. Hence, in the absence of tax coordination, tax rates may be set lower or higher than the optimal level dictated solely by national considerations. The prominent role of foreign direct investment in the resource sector, especially in developing countries, may dampen tax competition for lower rates since taxing foreigners should be less of a concern to governments than taxing their own citizens or companies. This may explain, at least in part, why we do not observe downward pressure on average effective tax rates in the resource sector (more on this later).

The literature has mushroomed in the past two decades as globalization (including the marked decline in tariff and non-tariff barriers to trade in goods and services, capital, and to a much lesser extent labor) exerted downward pressure on taxes on mobile factors and firms, which in turn raised concerns as to the viability of such taxes as sources of government revenue. The CIT has occupied center stage of the debate, but other taxes have attracted attention as well, such as those on labor, portfolio income, and consumption. At the same time, developing countries suffered significant loss of tariff revenues that some were not able to fully recover using domestic taxes.[6] This section provides a selective review of major lessons from this literature, both theoretical and empirical, with an eye to the questions posed earlier. We also seek to clarify some of the misconceptions about tax competition, which often come up in IMF technical assistance work in tax policy.

Keen and Konrad (2012) provide one of the most recent and comprehensive accounts of the theoretical literature on tax competition (mainly capital tax competition). One main lesson from their work is that the real world is still far more complex than current economic models can handle, especially in terms of differences across countries – in, for instance, size, economic structures, institutions, the complexity of tax systems, and the arbitrage opportunities they create. They also conclude that the literature has not yet reached any definitive conclusion on whether tax competition is "bad" or "good"[7] and not even how to identify the former type – since this is the part that policy makers would want to suppress through coordination. They do suggest, however, that enough progress has been made to provide some useful guidance on how countries may effectively coordinate their tax policies. For example, agreeing on minimum tax rates somewhat above the lowest set in a non-cooperative outcome is more likely to be effective than full harmonization of taxes – in simple models at least, it produces a better revenue outcome for all participating countries (including that obliged to raise its tax rate) and is less stringent than full harmonization.[8] But even if successful, such agreements may not be able to fully accommodate the dynamic nature of tax competition, the conditions and implications of which constantly change. In other words, what is good and feasible today for a group of countries may not be so a few years into the future.

One important issue discussed in Keen and Konrad (2012) is whether tax coordination across a subset of countries is feasible and worth undertaking. The question is relevant for the simple reason that it is virtually impossible for countries to coordinate in the absence of a supra-national entity that can enforce commitment (and, if need be, arrange compensating payments) – because some countries may gain more from opting out. And since such supra-national structures exist only regionally (e.g. in the EU), in practice the question of tax coordination is often one among a sub-set of countries rather than worldwide. The literature suggests, and the empirical literature seems to support,[9] that a sub-set of countries can benefit from coordinating, when its taxes exhibit "strategic complementarity" with the rest of the world – that is, when non-participating countries' best response is to move their tax rates in the same direction as the sub-set. The issue of regional coordination is particularly important for the EI sector, where production of certain minerals can be highly concentrated in a few countries, and the setting of minimum tax rates may help such countries extract more revenues from the resource rent – countries need not be located in the same geographical region, and given the concentration of the resource, agreement on minimum rates might be easier to reach.

Devereux and Loretz (2012) review the empirical literature on source-based corporate tax competition, one of the main forms of competition that we are concerned with in this chapter.[10] Countries can compete on many elements of the corporate tax: income shifting is usually sensitive to differences in statutory tax rates, while real investment is sensitive to effective tax rates.[11] The authors review 74 studies of tax competition, classified according to the complexity of the methodology (trends, domestic determinants, and strategic interactions[12]) and the studied variables (statutory indicators, tax revenues, other taxes, and expenditures). They conclude that downward corporate tax competition has taken place in the EU and that accession of new (smaller) member states has exerted further pressure on EU CIT rates.[13]

Genschel and Schwarz (2011) provide a non-technical account of the literature, covering issues related to competition and coordination in consumption, labor, and corporate taxation. Their survey of empirical studies concludes that international tax competition has been ongoing mostly in the area of corporate taxation and to a lesser extent in the area of excise taxation. The revenue loss attributed to this last form is insignificant given that it occurs primarily in populated areas located close to international borders, and its impact declines rapidly with distance from the borders. There is no evidence that countries compete in the areas of value-added and personal income taxes. These results are broadly consistent with the empirical literature on the sensitivity of investment, labor, and consumption to cross-country differences in tax rates. Interestingly, the authors predict that CIT competition will slow down, primarily because of the impact of the 2008 crisis on corporate profits and revenue, which has constrained government budgets, and because the international community is more willing to address certain forms of tax competition through tax coordination – the authors refer primarily to the BEPS initiative (OECD 2013a, 2013b) and its potential impact on profit shifting.

Another strand of the literature on tax competition concerns that between the various levels of government within a single country, such as federations and unitary nations with regional governments. The insights from this literature, reviewed by Boadway and Tremblay (2012),[14] may have implications for competition and coordination among countries. One element of interest is "vertical tax competition and coordination" and the related issue of "revenue assignment" between the central and regional governments. The implications of vertical tax competition for countries rich in natural resources are potentially important for two reasons. First, many of these countries, including those in the developing world, have regional governments that exert significant political influence and to which some fiscal powers have been devolved by their constitutions (e.g. Algeria, Mali, Niger, Democratic Republic of Congo, Indonesia). Regions often regard the resource as belonging to them (even when it is legally owned by a unitary state), proceeds from which are to be spent as they see fit. There are tensions between this view and the objectives of a central government that may be more concerned with issues that are beneficial to the country as a whole, such as equity, education to all citizens, health services for those who cannot afford it, and so forth, all of which need to be financed (partially at least) from the resource rent. The higher the share of resource revenue in total tax revenue, the higher are these tensions and the more complicated is coordination between the center and the regions.[15] In low-income countries, these issues are compounded by the fact that mobilization of non-resource tax revenue still faces many hurdles, especially those taxes considered best suited to serve equity objectives, such as personal income taxes and property taxes (IMF, 2011).

Second, absent a tax coordination framework at the national level, it will be difficult for a federated country to coordinate its tax policies effectively with other countries. This is because local tax setting can undermine (and render non-credible) the coordination efforts of a central government when both levels of governments share the same or similar tax bases. In federated developing countries, the standard coordination model that has so far prevailed is that of the central government raising most tax revenue and then transferring a portion to state governments. In principle, this model makes sense since it obviates the need to coordinate tax policies within a federated structure, but it has proven untenable, especially in federations rich in natural resources – for the political reasons noted already. A combination of both transfers and tax assignment is likely to be more sustainable over time, as experience has shown in Canada, Germany, and the United States.

Despite the fact that corporate tax competition has been ongoing, corporate tax revenue as a share of GDP has not declined and has even increased in some countries (Devereux and Sørensen, 2006; Norregaard and Khan, 2007; Stewart and Webb, 2006).[16] A number of explanations have been provided for the case of OECD countries, including base broadening (Devereux and Sørensen, 2006); increase in incorporation as a vehicle of earning business income in a sample of EU countries, or, put differently, a shift from personal income taxes to CIT (de Mooij and Nicodème, 2006), reflecting growing differences in top CIT and PIT rates; privatization, or a shift from dividend income paid by state-controlled companies to governments to CIT (Azmat, Manning and Van Reenen, 2007), and high profitability of certain sectors, particularly the financial sector (prior to the 2008 crisis). There is also the argument that reductions in CIT rates may have had Laffer-type effects, leading to large increases in investment and earnings; but Devereux, Griffith and Klemm (2002) report that marginal effective tax rates have generally not fallen greatly, casting doubt on the Laffer-effect hypothesis.[17]

Keen and Mansour (2010b) report similar results for the robustness of CIT revenue in Sub-Saharan Africa, despite (and unlike OECD countries) base narrowing.[18] They suggest that the increase in the profit-to-GDP ratio, due, among other things, to growth in new sectors such as mobile telephony, may have played a role in preserving CIT revenue. However, more recent evidence suggests that CIT rate competition in the WAEMU is associated with a decline in CIT revenue for some member states (Mansour and Rota-Graziosi, 2013).

In summary, tax competition is happening, mostly in the CIT area, but revenue from this source has so far been broadly resilient. Whether this will continue is not clear, especially given the 2008 crisis and its impact on corporate profits and CIT revenues, which is likely to cause shifts in the worldwide allocation of capital and may prompt governments to take policy measures that they would not have considered before.[19] It seems though that effective tax coordination at an international level is unlikely to occur in the foreseeable future, and so tax competition and its consequences will remain an issue on governments' policy agendas. Even regional tax coordination, which could yield some benefits, may be difficult to achieve – as the experience of the EU in promoting the CCCBT (discussed in Chapter 2, this volume), WAEMU, and the ongoing work on a code of conduct in the East African Community (EAC) suggest.

3 Tax competition in extractive industries

Is tax competition in EIs happening? What can countries do about it? And what are the difficulties that countries may face in considering some forms of coordination?

3.1 Do countries tax-compete in extractive industries?

The question of whether countries tax-compete in EIs is relatively easy to answer if we limit it to the CIT area, since as we just discussed this is happening in most OECD countries and many developing countries. But it is important to note that the decline in CIT rates has been different across countries and that there is evidence suggesting that those rich in natural resources have reduced their rates less than those that are not. In Sub-Saharan Africa, for example (Figure 13.2), the decline in the average CIT rate between 1990 and 2010 was less in resource countries (10.3 points)[20] than in non-resource countries (13.7 points) and much less in countries very rich in natural resources such as the Central African Economic and Monetary Community (CEMAC) region (3 points only).

Beyond CIT competition, the analysis is complicated because standard CIT provisions, especially those related to the tax base, do not always apply, and the EI sector is generally subject to other taxes (e.g. royalties) or non-tax contractual arrangements. This is particularly the case for oil and gas, where many countries, especially developing countries, use production sharing agreements to extract

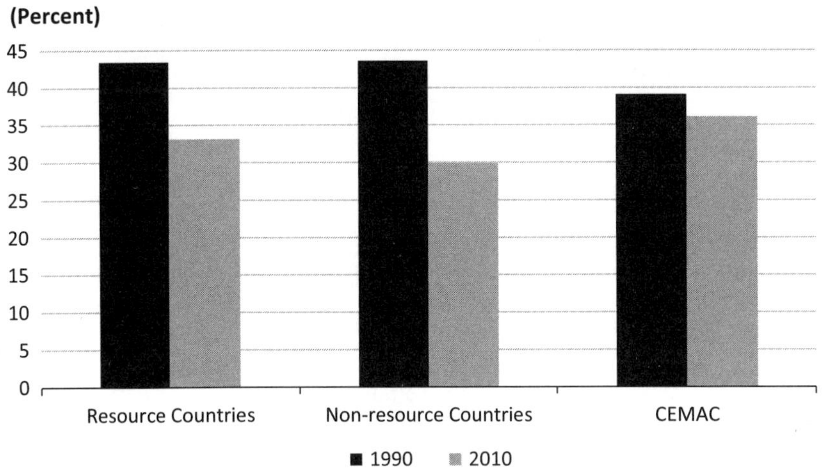

Figure 13.2 CIT rates in Sub-Saharan Africa

Source: Mansour (2014)

their share of the resource rent. The mining sector is also subject to special rules in many developing countries by which governments sign contractual agreements with foreign investors for specific (typically ring-fenced) mining projects. These special tax characteristics of mining taxation systems make tax-competitive behavior difficult to identify. Different state participation schemes, in fiscal terms that in substantive terms are no different from taxation, further blur the picture and complicate the assessment of tax competition phenomena in EIs.

There is anecdotal evidence that policy makers consider other countries' EI tax regimes when setting tax policy. For example, IMF technical assistance in resource taxation policy often benchmarks a country's tax system as it applies to EIs against other countries' at the request of countries' authorities, concerned with the competitiveness of their fiscal regimes. Note, however, that the emphasis of policy makers is often on CIT and royalty rates; the tax base is rarely a concern – or not as much as it should be. This type of anecdotal evidence says little about the form of tax competition or its direction; a country may be concerned with upward tax competition[21] and want to compare to other countries in order to gauge by how much it can increase its tax rates. There is some evidence from IMF technical assistance that this has occurred since the late 1990s as commodity prices soared to unexpected levels – although governments' concerns may have shifted since commodity prices started declining in 2014.

A more robust way to weigh whether countries tax-compete for locational decisions in EIs is to examine average effective tax rates (AETRs). As we noted earlier, the AETR is the best available measure to gauge the incentives to locate in one jurisdiction among a number that offer similar investment opportunities. We estimate these for a sample of copper producing countries and a sample of gas producing countries at two different times: early 2000s and early 2010s. During this decade, production and prices rose dramatically worldwide: copper prices almost quadrupled, while production increased by 25 percent only (Figure 13.3); gas production increased by 40 percent while price almost tripled (Figure 13.4), except in North America, where domestic natural gas is abundant (including shale gas).[22]

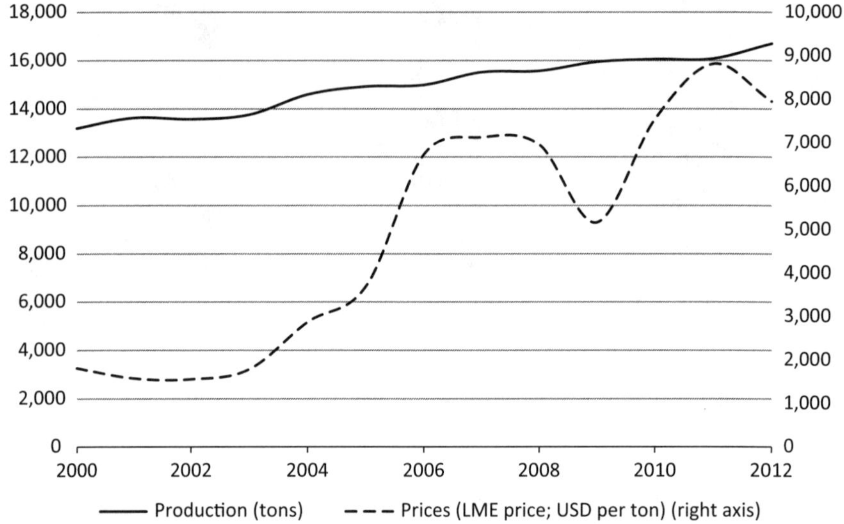

Figure 13.3 Worldwide mine production and prices of copper, 2000–2012

Source: International Copper Study Group (ICSG).

Note: Prices are annual averages (in USD) from the London Metal Exchange.

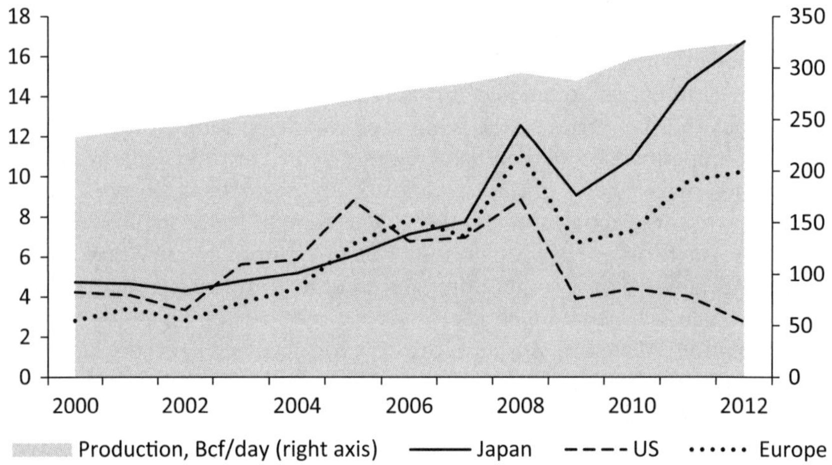

Figure 13.4 Worldwide production and prices of natural gas, 2000–2012

Source: BP Statistical Review of World Energy, June 2013.

Note: Bcf/day means billion cubic feet per day; prices are in USD per million British thermal units; for Europe unweighted average of UK and German prices is used.

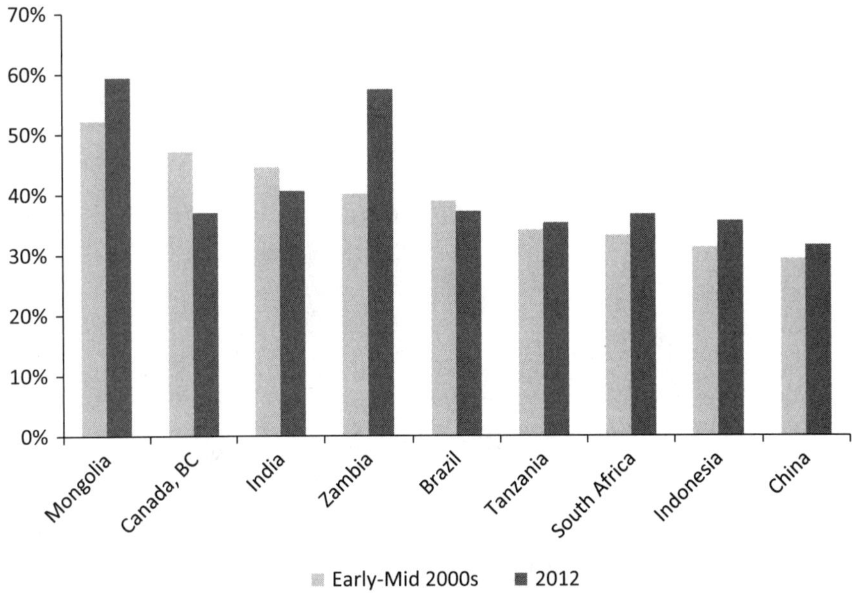

Figure 13.5 AETRs for copper mining in selected countries

Source: Authors' calculations.

BC: British Columbia.

Figure 13.5 shows the AETR[23] results for a hypothetical copper mining project.[24] The rates increased in six countries and decreased in Canada (British Columbia) and India, where they were relatively high in the early 2000s – the small decline in the Brazil AETR is due to a more favorable depreciation scheme. Moreover, there is some convergence of AETRs. These results are mainly driven by an increase in royalty rates[25] between the two periods in all countries in the sample. CIT rates remained constant in all countries for the past decade, with the exception of Canada, where the decline in the AETR is mainly due to a decline in the federal government CIT rate from 22.12 to 15 percent, and India, where the CIT surtax was reduced from 10 to 5 percent. Since all types of ferrous metals are generally subject to the same CIT and royalty regimes, an extension of the analysis to other minerals will likely yield similar results.

Figure 13.6 shows the AETR[26] for a stylized gas project.[27] Rates increased in most of the countries, except Malaysia, Norway, and Nigeria, where they remained broadly constant, and Canada (British Columbia) where they decreased. As in mining, convergence of AETRs is easy to observe. The case of Tanzania and Mozambique may be explained by massive offshore natural gas discoveries – hence, improved geological prospectivity. The same is true for Poland, where vast resources of shale gas were discovered, prompting the government to design a new regime. In neither of these can the increases be

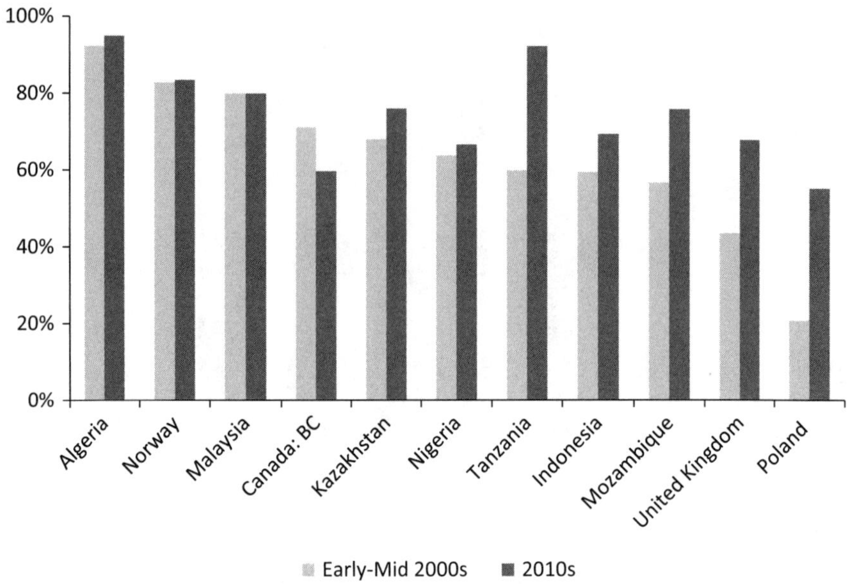

Figure 13.6 AETRs for natural gas production in selected countries

Source: Authors' calculations.

explained by the CIT. In Indonesia, Tanzania, and Mozambique, they stem mostly from changes to their production sharing formulae. In the United Kingdom and Poland, it is a result of an additional tax on cash flow.

The increase in the AETRs in many countries suggests that downward tax competition in the sector may not be a concern. Indeed, it is upward tax competition that seems to be a concern, which may be related to the issue of time inconsistency or, as noted earlier, the prominent role of foreign ownership of large resource projects, especially in developing countries. In this case, one form of coordination that countries may want to pursue is to impose maximum tax rates. Maximum rates would allow countries not to pass the point at which tax levels could hurt optimal production, hence revenues. They are also a form of signaling to investors that tax rates would not reach confiscatory levels. But at what level should a maximum tax rate be set? Figure 13.6, for example, suggests a maximum rate close to 100 percent, which may not be useful as a signaling mechanism. This is an issue to which no clear-cut answer can yet be given.

3.2 Is tax coordination in extractive industries needed?

This section considers whether tax coordination in EIs is (or is not) needed, taking into account the general discussion on theory and empirics and the AETRs presented in the previous section.

The main argument in favor of not coordinating tax policy for EIs relates to the presence of location-specific rent. Theory suggests that countries can tax at 100 percent the return that exceeds the investors' required rate of return (and other compensation for managerial and technical expertise) when the excess is due to such rent. The intuition is simple: investors make their decisions based on the risk-adjusted post-tax rate of return; when such a hurdle is reached, they are insensitive to the level of the tax rate because the resource is immobile. Provided that such a hurdle return can be observed or calculated, a country can impose tax at a rate of 100 percent once an investment project has realized its required rate of return – so long as there are no alternatives elsewhere yielding a higher net return. The choice of the tax structure is, however, key to the validity of the argument; it has to be perfectly neutral on investment decisions – as with, for instance, a cash-flow tax with remuneration (at an appropriate rate) or refund of negative cash flows or an allowance for corporate equity.

The theoretical argument has found some support in the empirical literature. For example, in his study on FDI in the EU, Stöwhase (2005) estimates the tax elasticity of outward FDI from three major EU countries by sector;[28] he finds that FDI in the primary sector is insensitive to differences in both forward-looking and backward-looking AETRs across countries. These results are important because empirical studies about the sensitivity of FDI to tax-rate differentials tend to find significant and relatively high elasticities on average, without differentiating the elasticity by sector.[29]

Boadway and Keen (2010) develop a number of other arguments why tax competition in EIs might occur and whether tax coordination is desirable. These arguments are not strictly related to the extraction of the resource itself but more to the market conditions of needed capital and labor inputs and strategic considerations by large firms. We review them here, and add a few of our own.

The first argument is that it is so hard to attract certain special skills (managerial and technical) or highly specialized equipment in EIs that are short in supply that governments must provide an overall attractive tax package. There are two difficulties with this argument. First, it is not clear why the tax incentive must be provided to the project rather than directly to the skill that is in short supply. From a cost-effectiveness point of view, it makes more sense to compete on the skills needed by, for example, providing wage-based incentives rather than on the project as a whole by, for example, providing time-bound CIT holidays. Second, basic supply-and-demand theory tells us that if something is in short supply, its value increases enough to encourage new entrants. The argument is therefore one of transition to a new equilibrium – although transition in EIs could take some time given the nature of the industry and commodity price volatility.

Another argument is that under certain market conditions, a large firm with influence on the international price of a product may deliberately choose to restrict its production to increase prices or keep them from falling. It is not clear what the tax competition and coordination implications of such market imperfection are. Might other countries provide tax incentives in order to compensate for the shortage? It is not clear what role tax coordination can play in order to discourage firms from constraining production. In fact, constraining countries from tax competing could play in favor of the firm constraining demand and make the situation worse for all countries – in terms of paying higher consumption prices, but the country where production is constrained presumably gains higher tax revenues given higher prices and hence has no incentive to coordinate.

The third argument is that countries may simply want to behave like others for marketing purposes. A country may perceive it to be beneficial when it can say that its tax regime is similar to neighboring countries or to the largest producers of a given resource commodity. For example, if a country has a much higher AETR than other countries, investors may shun it for profitability reasons; on the other hand, if the AETR is too low, investors may take it as an indication of poor governance or lack of credibility (i.e. that once the resource is discovered and reserves estimated, the country would increase its taxes). The AETR analysis in the previous section lends some support to this; rates for copper and natural gas converged over the past decade. But convergence to a positive and higher AETR argues in favor of a maximum tax rate, not a minimum – as the standard tax competition model suggests.

There are other reasons tax coordination may be desirable. One is that politicians generally discount the future at high rates and prefer to have revenue to spend today rather than when they are no longer in power. At constant prices, this simply means encouraging firms to produce more. It would generate more revenue to the government if the value of incentives provided (in terms of revenue loss) is lower than the increase in the government's share of revenue from additional production.

A country may also tax compete in a disputed area (with other countries) in order to make it attractive for companies to invest given the legal and, in some cases, high security risks regarding disputed areas – and, perhaps, the other non-tax factors that are typically weak in such areas, such as lack of investment in public infrastructure. Some investors are prepared to take such risks, but they also face the reputational risk – of accepting to operate in areas without clarity as to which country has a legitimate claim to the areas. Tax competition may signal in this case the inability of a government to resolve its dispute with neighboring countries – perhaps even risk of future conflict – and may discourage (rather than encourage) investors who value reputational risks.

Finally, it is possible that countries tax compete simply because they are weak in negotiating skills with major players in EIs. This is particularly the case in developing countries, where EI projects may be negotiated between investors and the government or a state enterprise, and a contract is agreed that contains the tax provisions. This situation can be aggravated by institutional fragmentation and weakness within the country and by corruption.

It is very difficult to empirically substantiate these arguments, both individually and when they interact. Some of them are driven by market imperfections, either for the resource itself or for capital and labor inputs needed to extract it; others are more closely related to the political economy of managing natural resources. In the first instance, addressing the imperfections at the country level may be a better policy response than seeking tax coordination with other countries. In all cases, however, there seems to be some support, in principle, for a minimum level of taxation, at least to protect weak countries that are new in EIs from making policy mistakes they will regret later. Note too that countries that can maintain a fairly high level of taxes should also benefit from such a strategy or at least have nothing to lose. Our analysis also suggests that a maximum level of taxation may be useful – countries may gain from signaling collectively their willingness to address the commitment problem. The question then is how this can be done. What taxes should governments coordinate? In the next section, we discuss the difficulties in coordinating taxes on EIs, which stems primarily from the variety of policy instruments used by governments to extract their share of the resource rent.

3.3 Difficulties in coordinating taxes on extractive industries

Tax coordination in EIs is made difficult by a number of factors that are specific to the sector or perhaps more common and important than in other sectors.

First, the number of taxes or levies deployed to tax EIs is typically higher than in non-EI sectors, and these taxes are more complex in their application than those in other sectors. This is particularly the case in developing countries, where in addition to profit taxes and royalties, governments may have a stake in EI projects (either free or carried), may require signature and production bonuses, and may create state enterprises that play a key role in research and development as well as extraction.[30]

The number of taxes is important because coordination of one tax could shift tax competition to other taxes, with non-trivial consequences for revenue and efficiency.[31] For example, if coordination imposes a minimum CIT rate and a common base, countries can cut their royalty or rent tax rates to compete. In this case, the objective of securing revenue by imposing a minimum rate is undermined by the loss of royalty revenue; moreover, the temporal profile of revenue changes. The reverse holds if coordination imposes a maximum CIT rate; a country constrained by the maximum and seeking to preserve revenue may increase export taxes, royalties, or other fees, which are more distortionary than profit taxes. Similar arguments apply to competition through tax bases rather than rates. Table 13.1 lists the main taxes that are applied to EIs around the world and provides a very brief indication of possible variations across countries in the calculation of the base. It is easy to see that for coordination to have a chance of succeeding, in terms of imposing a hard constraint on countries' EI tax policies, rationalization of the number of taxes is a prerequisite – coordination on all of these taxes would be impossible to achieve.

Second, production sharing agreements (PSAs) are widely used in developing countries for capturing resource rent. These are contractual arrangements

Table 13.1 Taxes generally applicable to extractive industries

Input taxes	*Output taxes*	*Profit and rent taxes*
External tariffs: Prevalent mostly in developing countries and applied to both intermediate and capital inputs.	*Export tariffs*: Rare in general but exist in some countries, especially on raw minerals. They function as royalties in some cases (more convenient to levy at the point of export).	
Excise taxes: Specific or ad-valorem. Can be very important, especially on energy products used in processing minerals, including electricity generation in remote areas.		
		Equity participation (free) and production sharing: Latter varies in the definition of the base, especially in terms of limitations on deductibility of certain expenses (much like the standard profit tax).
	Royalties: Can be specific or (more common) ad-valorem. Latter often calculated on a base that is somewhere between turnover and accounting profits (measured on accrual basis).	
		Rent taxes: Surtaxes, progressive profit tax, various types of cash-flow taxes.
Sales taxes: Can fall on inputs to the extent not refunded. Neutral if VAT-style with proper refund or suspension mechanism.		
		Standard profit taxes: Differences in base across countries are mainly in treatment of capital goods, loss carry-forward, and limitations on certain expenses (e.g. interest expense; HQ management fees, etc.)
Signature bonuses: Vary enormously across countries (some do not have them). Could also be classified as output taxes. *Surface fees*: Taxes on land as an input. Generally not very important in terms of revenue generation.	*Production bonuses:* Vary with the level of production and may act as imperfect rent taxes.	

Source: Prepared by the authors.

whose fiscal terms, often negotiated between investors and government, are locked for fairly long periods and often with guarantees of stability.[32] If stability is asymmetric, providing guarantees against increases in taxes but allowing for decreases, coordination that attempts to increase taxes or stem a decline in tax rates may be ineffective for existing investment.

Third, the abundance of resource revenue may weaken the incentives for good tax policy practice, including tax coordination. If the gains from coordination are marginal relative to existing natural resource wealth, a country may simply prefer to set policy freely rather than be constrained. There are exceptions, however, such as the case of joint development zones (e.g. the Saudi-Kuwaiti neutral zone), where two or more countries may be more amenable to agree on a common tax regime to allow a company to extract minerals from the zone and share the revenue, as discussed in Chapter 10 (Cameron, this volume) and Chapter 11 (Daniel, Veung and Watson, this volume). It is fair to say though that non-tax considerations such as those noted earlier play a more important role in these situations.

4 Experience in tax coordination in extractive industries

Experiences in tax coordination are generally not sector specific; the only exception we know of is the WAEMU Mining Code regulation of 2002. In this section, we review experiences in direct and indirect tax coordination, with an emphasis on the implications for EIs.

4.1 Direct tax coordination

Many of the regional economic blocs around the world have reached various levels of integration of their trade regimes, but only the EU and WAEMU have reached some modest degree of coordination in their direct taxes, primarily certain aspects of the corporate income tax and the taxation of portfolio income, and only WAEMU has attempted to coordinate the taxation of the mining sector.

There are two separate measures in the EU that aim to tackle tax competition: the Code of Conduct for business taxation and the State Aid Rules; both are general and not limited to direct taxes. A third initiative currently being debated, and strictly related to the corporate tax, is the common consolidated corporate tax base (CCCTB).[33] All the measures are of general application, and none of them focuses specifically on EIs.[34] We consider each in turn.

The Code of Conduct for business taxation was one of the first proposed explicit tax coordination measures.[35] It has never become a binding law – it is merely a political commitment of the member states, endorsed by a resolution of the European Council,[36] to respect principles of fair competition and to refrain from harmful tax competition. The code covers both tax laws or regulations and administrative practices (e.g. concessionary tax decisions and rulings) and refers to any tax measure that may provide for a significantly lower effective level of taxation than that generally applied in a given member country. Only tax measures used to support the economic development of particular regions within the EU received special attention. The Code does not consider them to be potentially harmful, as long as they are in proportion to "the aims sought", which is difficult to achieve in tax design, particularly for measures with no limits on benefits – such as tax holidays.

State Aid rules, contained in the EU treaty, may be considered another form of tax coordination as they contribute to the objective of unimpeded functioning of the internal market by tackling harmful tax competition. They do not refer explicitly to tax policy design. Any measure that distorts or threatens to distort competition by favoring certain undertakings or the production of certain goods and thus affecting trade between the member states may be considered a state aid. It is then straightforward that certain tax measures that may provide recipients an advantage by reducing or relieving them of taxes of general application (e.g. accelerated depreciation, provisions, etc.) are potentially liable to these rules.[37] In contrast to the Code of Conduct principles, the member states are legally obliged to comply with the State Aid rules and must seek a prior approval from the European Commission before granting tax subsidies. The European Court of Justice, with a power to revoke discriminatory tax features, plays an important role in enforcing these rules.

The proposed CCCTB goes much farther than the two preceding measures in relation to the taxation of corporate income. The proposal is to create common rules for calculating the corporate income tax base and allocating it to member states according to a formula. It is important to note, however, that tax rates would continue to be set at the national level. That would imply a significant degree of tax coordination with respect to the use of tax allowances, deductions, including depreciation schemes, loss carry-forward, and other tax measures affecting the calculation of the CIT base. In effect, corporate tax competition under a CCCTB would be driven primarily by the statutory rate – since base competition would be neutralized. However, the CCCTB, as proposed in 2011, is intended to remain voluntary;[38] it would exist as a separate tax code, in parallel to national ones. In that sense, its coordinative impact may therefore be limited.

The second experience with direct tax coordination is the WAEMU.[39] Unlike the EU, the WAEMU, since 2008, coordinates the CIT base and rate not through a Code of Conduct but through legally binding directives: one that defines the CIT base and one that limits the rate to a minimum of 25 percent and a maximum of 30.[40] Coordination of the base leaves some flexibility for countries to compete. For example, the rules for tax depreciation and limitations on interest expenses are left for national laws to set. But the most important source of tax competition among WAEMU countries is through the derogatory regimes provided for in non-tax legislation, such as Investment Codes, Free Zone Codes, and other sectoral codes, which are explicitly permitted under Article 8 of the CIT base directive.[41] These are the main reasons tax coordination among WAEMU states has not been effective. Indeed, Mansour and Rota-Graziosi (2013) argued that the CIT directives may have intensified tax competition by limiting member countries' abilities to act within their tax laws but giving them unfettered liberty to legislate tax provisions in non-tax laws.

Another peculiarity of the WAEMU, and the only example we know of, is a regulation[42] specifically coordinating taxation of the mining sector, introduced in 2003. It provides that firms are subject to the general tax laws of member states and to a royalty whose base and rates will be determined later by regulation – to our knowledge, these have not been issued. The regulation also provided for stability of the tax regime – presumably, both for taxes imposed at the national level and the royalty that was to be fixed regionally for all member states – during the life of the investment. The stability is asymmetric, insuring against increases in taxes but allowing taxpayers to benefit from reductions.[43] In terms of tax incentives, the regulation provided for the exemption of virtually all taxes and fees during the exploration phase. The main incentives provided during the production phase are accelerated depreciation and a three-year tax holiday from profit and payroll taxes; the modalities for the coverage and calculation of accelerated depreciation have not been issued.

Together with the CIT directives, the mining regulation would have harmonized substantially member states' tax regimes and limited their freedom to set tax policy for the sector. However, the absence of agreement on royalty rates in regulations and the fact that countries can tax-compete for CIT through sectoral legislation make coordination ineffective. All this is indicative of the political difficulties of tax coordination in general and in the EI sector more specifically.

4.2 Tariff and indirect tax coordination

In this sub-section, we examine briefly the implications of tariff and indirect tax coordination as it affects the EIs, drawing from IMF technical assistance experience in Sub-Saharan Africa. As with direct tax coordination discussed in the previous sub-section, measures of tariff and indirect tax coordination around the world are generally not sector specific. But because they deal with the taxation of goods and services rather than incomes, they can be designed to mimic, to a significant degree, turnover taxes. For example, an excise tax can be designed to mimic a royalty or an export tax in a country that produces gold primarily for export.

4.2.1 Tariffs

In principle, reducing import tariffs is desirable since it enhances production efficiency and reduces consumer prices. Provided that countries are not constrained by the choice of tax instruments and can substitute efficient taxes (e.g. VAT, rent tax) for distortionary tariffs (and this is a strong assumption, particularly for low-income countries), tariff competition should improve welfare without reducing government revenue.[44] Importantly, countries can achieve such results unilaterally, without any need for coordinating their actions. This is particularly important for resource-rich developing countries, where capital goods for EIs are generally imported; replacing tariffs on capital goods with more efficient domestic taxes (e.g. property taxes or consumption taxes) can enhance a country's attractiveness as a destination for EI investment.

This is broadly what happened in developed countries in the past 50 years: tariffs and cascading sales taxes have been replaced by the VAT, which has become a major revenue source. The story in developing countries is somewhat different. These countries seem to be constrained in the choice of policy instruments to raise revenue; some have not been able to fully replace the revenue loss from tariff reduction with other revenue sources, such as the VAT. Precisely why this is the case is not clear. There is no empirical evidence on why some countries have done better than others in replacing lost trade revenue.

After a marked decline in the 1990s, the share of tariff revenues in GDP in low- and lower-middle-income developing countries has stabilized during the past decade – at around 2.5 percent for the first group and 4.5 percent for the second. Tax systems have become increasingly reliant on the taxation of final consumption goods and less on that of inputs and capital goods. One important reason for this is that tariff coordination in a number of regions (e.g. WAEMU, EAC, Common Market for Eastern and Southern Africa [COMESA]) was used as an opportunity to reduce the level and number of tariffs on inputs and capital goods – EAC and COMESA have eliminated the latter. So even if not needed, tariff coordination through the formation of custom unions has given countries the policy momentum to reduce tariff rates on inputs.

Another important reason is the interaction of tariff and domestic tax policies. As noted earlier in this chapter, domestic tax policy is fraught with tax incentives legislated in non-tax laws. These laws, including EI-specific laws, typically provide time-bound exemptions or reduction in tariffs which result, *de facto*, in the application of effective tariff rates that are more numerous and generally lower than statutory rates. Tariff coordination through customs unions obviates the need to provide tariff exemptions and renders the tax system more transparent and visible to investors.

4.2.2 Value-added taxes

The VAT is an area where misconceptions about whether coordination is desirable abound. Being a consumption tax, the VAT should, if well designed, not be subject to the forces of tax competition – at least not those affecting investment location decisions, particularly in the EI sector – and, as noted earlier, empirical evidence tends to support this. One issue, though, that deserves attention in developing countries, is the implication of the limitation on refunds for the cost of capital and hence for tax competition and coordination. This is an area in which coordination could have a similar impact as that of VAT rate convergence in WAEMU.[45] For EIs, the issue arises primarily in relation to intermediate inputs, such as energy consumption and capital goods, though the latter are frequently exempted during the development phase of a project. The issue is not merely a policy issue; administrative practices frequently constitute a significant constraint for EI firms in receiving their VAT refunds within reasonable time (see Harrison and Krelove, 2005).

Delaying or disallowing refund payments can be seen as upward tax competition. This can be particularly important when governments are constrained by stability clauses not to impose new taxes on EIs or to increase existing ones. In such a case, VAT coordination, especially rules and regulations relating to the payment of refunds, can be seen as a mechanism to alleviate, collectively, the commitment problem and is beneficial from an efficiency point of view – since it reduces effective tax rates on inputs.

Difficulties in the payment of VAT refunds often give rise to exemptions and other types of reliefs. Rather than seeking a solution to the underlying problem with timely refunds (or suspension), countries often resort to granting concessions. Such a practice quickly proliferates. Investors, while lobbying for input VAT concessions, use examples of other countries to win similar favorable treatment. For governments, it can be easier (and more visible) to create a level playing field by granting exemptions in line with other countries rather than refunding.

There are a number of other specific challenges that VAT may pose to businesses operating in EIs. Ambiguous treatment of settlements between partners in unincorporated joint ventures (not uncommon in the petroleum industry), different approaches to the taxation of services supplied to offshore facilities, or impediments to zero-rating of exports[46] are just a few examples (see Świstak, 2016). They create uncertainty and add to compliance costs and hence may affect investment decisions. Pressures to alleviate unrecovered or inappropriate input taxes are best met with ensuring proper design and implementation, rather than by ad hoc exceptional treatments.

4.2.3 *Excises*

Excise taxes affect the production sector of the economy primarily when they are imposed on inputs. For EIs, energy products (e.g. diesel, electricity) tend to be a significant input. Therefore, countries may compete downward on excises in order to attract particular elements of the extraction process. For example, an EI firm may decide to extract a mineral (say copper or cobalt) in one country but do most of the work needed to bring it to a concentrate form in a neighboring country. This would call for coordination of excises on energy products among neighboring countries, such as agreeing on minimum rates and common rules to value the tax base.[47] But since many non-tax factors come into play in making such decisions, and since energy products are more widely consumed (and not just by EI firms), it is unlikely that the EI sector on its own could be the main motivator for coordination.

5 Concluding remarks

The theoretical literature on tax competition and coordination does not provide unambiguous answers to the questions on tax competition and coordination posed in this chapter. The argument that downward tax competition in EIs may be causing significant revenue loss does not seem to hold. New evidence presented here suggests that AETRs in key EIs have actually increased during the first decade of this century, a period characterized by significant increases in commodity prices, and there is some evidence that CIT rates in resource-rich countries have declined much less than in non–resource-rich countries.[48] This suggests that tax competition in EIs may be less of a concern to governments than it is in other sectors.

It can, of course, be dangerous to extrapolate from past trends, and the analysis suggests that there can be a case, for a set of countries producing a homogenous resource, to impose minimum and maximum tax rates on EIs – hedging against the time inconsistency issue and providing some assurances that tax rates will not be increased to confiscatory levels once substantial costs have been sunk. Given the complexity of tax systems in EIs, in particular the number of taxes deployed by governments in developing countries, it is by no means trivial how such coordination can be accomplished.

Our analysis does not consider situations in which the tax treatment of EIs is negotiated between government and investors and the terms are not publicly available – although this is implicit, we use only tax rates and base rules that are publicly available. In other words, tax competition may be taking place in ways that are difficult or impossible to observe and measure. This is quite possible given that transparency and political economy issues play significant roles in EIs. An interesting question then is whether tax coordination is realistically possible in such situations.

Tariff and indirect tax competition, when they affect production decisions, can improve incentives and efficiency and can be replaced by less distortionary taxes to preserve revenues. Customs unions may create an impetus to lower tariff rates and replace cascading sales taxes with VATs, but they are by no means necessary since countries could achieve the efficiency benefits of such policies without coordination and without loss of revenues. Getting national policies right in this area seems to be the overriding factor for improving the conditions for EI growth – especially in terms of reducing the cost of capital for exploration and development.

Notes

* We thank Michael Keen, Victor Thuronyi, and Philip Daniel for very helpful comments and Victor Kitange and Chandara Veung for collating comparative tax data and undertaking effective tax rates analysis.

1 The word "collectively" implies that, individually, some countries might lose and others might gain from tax competition. This also implies that for tax coordination to work, and hence for revenues to be higher relative to uncooperative tax setting in all jurisdictions,

countries that gain from tax competition must be compensated; the compensation provides the incentive to cooperate.

2 Downward tax competition occurs when countries bid down their tax rates in an effort to attract investment they believe would otherwise locate in other countries.

3 There is an ongoing and old debate in the literature regarding whether certain levies on EIs are "taxes" or "fees" for the use of property (e.g. royalties). In this chapter, we simply consider all levies on EIs to be taxes, to the extent that they are compulsory payments to government, and their revenue and behavioral implications can be analyzed like taxes.

4 The G20 has recently put this form of tax competition on the top of its agenda, in the form of the base erosion and profit shifting (BEPS) initiative, spearheaded by the OECD. The initiative, very broadly speaking, seeks to tighten the design of certain elements of the OECD bilateral tax treaty model and transfer pricing guidelines and widen the scope and depth of tax information sharing across countries; the outcomes are summarized in the appendix to Chapter 2, Keen and Mullins (this volume). The OECD has sought to broaden participation in this initiative to non-G20/OECD members.

5 There are exceptions, however, as in some countries of the Gulf Cooperation Council; but the history of these examples suggest that the origin of low or no taxation of corporate profits in the non-resource sector is not tax competition for paper profits. Generally, countries that can rely entirely on natural resources may become unintentionally attractive tax havens because they do not need taxes, and particularly the corporate tax.

6 See on this Baunsgaard and Keen (2010), Keen and Mansour (2010a) for Sub-Saharan Africa, and IMF (2005).

7 Tax competition can, in principle, be beneficial in preventing governments from setting taxes, and hence spending, too high (see for instance the discussion in Edwards and Keen (1996) – though fiscal rules seem likely to be a preferable way of achieving this, since they do not directly restrict instrument choice.

8 This is because raising the tax rate set by a low-tax country leads others to set higher rates than they otherwise would, conveying a benefit to the low-tax country that more than offsets the direct impact of a small increase in its own rate. But even a minimum tax is not easy to build consensus around (see Osterloh and Heinemann, 2013).

9 See the review by Devereux and Loretz (2012).

10 This refers to competition in the taxation of corporate profits sourced in a tax jurisdiction, as opposed to residence-based taxation, which seeks to attract residency of investors rather than their investment activities. Source-based tax competition is possible because taxation in the residence country is now largely absent or (primarily in the United States) allows indefinite deferral of taxation of profits sourced in foreign countries. The basic theoretical model of this type of competition predicts (under rather strict conditions) that source taxes on corporate profits should be set to zero. Although this is largely inconsistent with what we observe in practice, the extensive provision of CIT holidays in developing countries (often renewable and targeting FDI) lends some support to this basic model.

11 There are two forward-looking effective tax rates commonly used in tax policy analysis: the marginal effective tax rate (METR) and the average effective tax rate (AETR). The first is a theoretical construct of the gap between the pre- and post-tax return on a unit of investment that is marginally worth undertaking. The second, also a theoretical construct in a forward-looking sense, is the ratio (in present value) of tax on expected future profits to pre-tax expected net cash flows – typically measured over the life of an investment. The METR is a measure of the incentive or disincentive that the tax system provides to investors on marginal decisions (e.g. buying new machinery, increasing exploration expenses, holding higher levels of inventory). The AETR is a measure of whether an investment project, such as mining gold in a country, is worth undertaking; it is more relevant than the METR for location decisions such as deciding to invest in one country rather than another.

12 The standard econometric specification to test for strategic interactions between countries is a reaction function that takes the general form $t_i = a\sum_j W_{ij}t_j + bX_i + e_i$, where ***i*** and ***j*** are country indices, ***t*** is a tax rate, ***w*** is a weight matrix used to average the ***t***s across countries, ***X*** is a vector of socio-economic variables affecting the tax rate, and ***e*** is a normally distributed error. A positively sloped reaction function (***a*** > 0) indicates strategic complementarities in tax rate setting between countries.

13 The authors are critical of previous trend analyses of rates or revenues (particularly the latter) and econometric specifications that ignore, in the explanatory variables, the studied variables in other countries. Their conclusions are primarily based on recent studies using reaction functions.

14 This literature on *fiscal federalism* is broader than the tax competition literature; it covers revenue and expenditure policy and their assignment across levels of governments.

15 In principle, the complexity in coordinating taxes should be related to the number of entities that need to coordinate. But experience shows that the amount of revenue at stake is also important even when the number of players is small. For example, in the Democratic Republic of Congo, copper mining is essentially concentrated in the province of Katanga, yet tax coordination between the central government and the provinces in the taxation of natural resources has proven very difficult.

16 This increase predates the 2008 crisis and its impact on corporate profits, which may or may not be temporary.

17 This evidence is becoming outdated. New research is needed, especially in light of the impact of the 2008 crisis on corporate profits and CIT revenues.

18 Unlike most studies, the authors construct a database that excludes from CIT revenue the share of upstream activities in mining and oil and gas, which presumably are less affected by the forces of tax competition than other sectors.

19 This has already happened in certain areas, such as the taxation of the financial sector in Europe.

20 Resource countries are defined as those that reported revenues from the resource sector (CIT on profits from upstream activities, royalties, or production sharing), regardless of their relative share in total tax revenues (Mansour, 2014).

21 Upward tax competition occurs when countries increase their tax rates as a response to an increase in other countries. In the EI sector, it could occur when countries decide to capture a higher share of the resource rent due to a favorable change in commodity prices or geological prospectivity (e.g. massive discoveries of natural gas in Rovuma Basin in East Africa or shale gas in Eastern Europe).

22 Oil and mineral prices have been falling since mid-2014. Although the recent significant drop in prices does not affect our analysis (as its time span extends only to early 2010s), we do note it may create a pressure for governments to adjust fiscal terms downward if faced with a threat of, say, mine closure. Whether countries will compete to save their mine, especially when held by a multinational company with mining operations in several countries, is yet to be seen. It will be an interesting topic for future research in the field of tax competition in EIs.

23 Net present value discounted at 7 percent. Income tax, royalty, and state participation, where applicable, are taken into account. No indirect taxes, withholding taxes, and surface fees are included in the calculations.

24 The project economics are as follows: life of 21 years, of which 3 years for exploration/development; production of 12 million tons (0.66 million annually); capital expenditures are USD 7.9 billion; decommissioning costs are USD 0.2 billion; unit operating and processing costs is USD 1.16 per ton in 2012 prices; copper price is USD 6,000 per ton, increasing at 2 percent per annum over the project's life.

25 Not all royalty regimes' bases are similar, and some have elements of net income taxation; they remain, however, generally more distortionary to marginal investment than income or rent-type taxes.

26 Net present value discounted at 7 percent. Royalties, profit gas, bonuses, income taxes, and additional profit taxes are taken into account. No indirect, property, and withholding taxes are included in the calculations.

27 Project economics are as follows: life of 38 years, of which 6 years for exploration/development and 2 for decommissioning; no condensate or other liquids are produced; production is 6 Tcf (260 Bcf annually, with a plateau reached in the sixth year of production); capital expenditures are USD 4.8 billion; decommissioning costs are USD 1.4 billion; unit operating and liquefaction cost is USD 6.1 per Mcf in 2012 prices; gas prices are USD 14 per MMBtu, increasing at 2 percent per annum over the project's life.

28 The three countries are the UK, Germany, and the Netherlands. The sectors are primary (includes EIs), manufacturing, and services.

29 See, for example, the synthesis of empirical studies by de Mooij and Everdeen (2003).

30 We do not include here taxes that are levied by EI enterprises on behalf of their employees or shareholders, which include wage taxes and social security contributions, withholding taxes on dividends, interest, and various payments to non-residents. For these, the enterprise simply acts as the withholding agent for the government.

31 The experience of Poland may serve as an illustration of tax competition shifting to other taxes. The 2014 law on special hydrocarbon tax (Ustawa o specjalnym podatku weglowodorowym) does not provide for an extended period of loss carry-forward under the CIT (above the general limit of five years), as it could constitute a state aid (forbidden under the EU rules, see discussion in section 4.2 of this chapter). Instead, the amount of lost tax benefit resulting from non-deduction of losses due to the expiration of the five-year period may be offset against royalty payments.

32 For a description of and issues with fiscal stability, see Daniel and Sunley (2010) and Mansour and Nakhle (2016). The latter documents a trend toward more asymmetry in fiscal stability in the oil and gas sector since the late 1990s.

33 In June 2015, the European Commission presented a strategy to re-launch the common consolidated corporate tax base (CCCTB). For more details, see Communication from The Commission to the European Parliament and the Council (Brussels, COM (2015) 302 final), available at: https://ec.europa.eu/priorities/sites/beta-political/files/com_2015_302_en.pdf

34 Art. 100 of the EC's Directive Proposal foresees specific rules for oil and gas in ascertaining location of sales for purposes of apportionment of the consolidated tax base, that is, place of extraction/production and not destination of sales are taken into account (Brussels, COM (2011) 12/14).

35 *A package to tackle harmful tax competition in the European Union* (1997), COM (97)564 (Annex I).

36 Conclusions of the ECOFIN Council Meeting on December 1, 1997, concerning taxation policy (98/C 2/01).

37 See EC Notice on the application of State Aid rules to measures relating to direct business taxation (98/C 384/03).

38 The EC is considering a proposal to make the CCCTB mandatory for certain companies. The criteria determining which companies should use the CCCTB rules are not known yet. See supra note 35.

39 A detailed account of the WAEMU tax and tariff coordination framework is provided by Mansour and Rota-Graziosi (2014).

40 These are, respectively, directive 01/2008/CM/UEMOA and directive 08/2008/CM/UEMOA.

41 These regimes potentially violate the State Aid rule in article 88 of the WAEMU Treaty, which explicitly prohibits "public aid that could distort competition by favoring certain enterprises or production activities" (translation from French by the authors).

42 Unlike a directive, a regulation must be adopted as is by member states.

43 There are no good reasons for a country to provide asymmetric stability. Moreover, in the WAEMU tax coordination context, stability for the CIT is of limited use since tax rates are bound by both a minimum and a maximum.

44 The theoretical case for this is spelled out in Keen and Ligthart (2002 and 2005).

45 The issue is much less important in developed countries but not insignificant. See, for example, Lejeune (2011) on the lessons from VATs in the EU. Other jurisdictions, such as the Canadian province of Quebec, limit refunds of VATs on certain inputs, including energy products.

46 For example, in 2013, Zambia effectively suspended zero-rating of minerals for lack of adequate proofs of export. The rules in place did not cater sufficiently for all International Commercial Terms (Incoterms rules) or situations in which minerals were exported by trading companies rather than directly by mining companies.

47 Transportation costs play a significant role in how competition and coordination may play out. For example, rough uncut diamonds can be transported anywhere around the world at virtually no cost relative to their market value; the case of unprocessed copper or cobalt is very different.

48 Our sample of countries is, however, by no means comprehensive; an extension of the analysis to a broader sample and a longer period for the AETRs may shed more light on this issue.

References

Azmat, Ghazala, Alan Manning and John Van Reenen. (2007), "Privatization, Entry Regulation and the Decline of the Labor's Share of GDP: A Cross-Country Analysis of the Network Industries," Discussion Paper 806 (London: London School of Economics and Political Science, Centre for Economic Performance).

Baunsgaard, Thomas and Michael Keen. (2010), "Tax Revenue and (or?) Trade Liberalization," *Journal of Public Economics*, 94(9–10), 563–577.

Boadway, Robin and Michael Keen. (2010), "Theoretical Perspectives on Resource Tax Design," in Philip Daniel, Michael Keen and Charles McPherson (eds), *The Taxation of Petroleum and Minerals: Principles, Problems and Practice* (London, New York: Routledge), 13–74.

Boadway, Robin and Jean-François Tremblay. (2012), "Reassessment of the Tiebout Model," *Journal of Public Economics*, 96, 1063–1078.

Daniel, Philip and Emil M. Sunley. (2010), "Contractual Assurances of Fiscal Stability," in Philip Daniel, Michael Keen and Charles McPherson (eds), *The Taxation of Petroleum and Minerals: Principles, Problems and Practice* (London, New York: Routledge), 405–424.

Devereux, Michael, Rachel Griffith and Alexander Klemm. (2002), "Corporate Income Tax Reform and International Tax Competition," *Economic Policy*, 17(35), 451–495.

Devereux, Michael and Simon Loretz. (2012), "What do We Know about Corporate Tax Competition," WP 12/29, Center for Business Taxation, Oxford University.

Devereux, Michael and Peter Birch Sørensen. (2006), "The Corporate Income Tax: International Trends and Options for Fundamental Reforms," Economic Paper 264 (Brussels: European Commission).

de Mooij, Ruud and Sjef Everdeen. (2003), "Taxation and Foreign Direct Investment: A Synthesis of Empirical Research," *International Tax and Public Finance*, 10(6), 673–694.

de Mooij, Ruud and Gaëtan Nicodème. (2006), "Corporate Tax Policy, Entrepreneurship and Incorporation in the EU," Working Paper 1883, (Munich: CESifo).

Genschel, Philipp and Peter Schwarz. (2011), "Tax Competition: A Literature Review," *Socio-Economic Review*, 9, 339–370.

Harrison, Graham and Russell Krelove. (2005), "VAT Refunds: A Review of Country Experience," Working Paper 05/218 (Washington, DC: International Monetary Fund).

International Copper Study Group; 2010 and 2012 Annual Reports.

International Monetary Fund. (2005), *Dealing with the Revenue Consequences of Trade Reforms* (Washington, DC: International Monetary Fund).

International Monetary Fund. (2011), *Revenue Mobilization in Developing Countries* (Washington, DC: International Monetary Fund).

International Monetary Fund. (2012), *Fiscal Regimes for Extractive Industries: Design and Implementation* (Washington, DC: International Monetary Fund).

Keen, Michael and Kai A. Konrad. (2012), "International Tax Competition and Coordination," in Alan J. Auerbach, Raj Chetty, Martin Feldstein, and Emmanuel Saez (eds), *Handbook of Public Economics, vol. 5* (Amsterdam, Boston, Heidelberg, London, New York, Oxford, Paris, San Diego, San Francisco, Singapore, Sidney, Tokyo: North-Holland), pp. 257–328.

Keen, Michael and Jenny E. Ligthart. (2002), "Co-ordinating Tariff Reduction and Domestic Tax Reform," *Journal of International Economics*, 56, 490–507.

Keen, Michael and Jenny E. Ligthart. (2005), "Co-ordinating Tariff Reduction and Domestic Tax Reform under Imperfect Competition," *Review of International Economics*, 13, 385–390.

Keen, Michael and Mario Mansour. (2010a), "Revenue Mobilization in Sub-Saharan Africa: Challenges from Globalization I – Trade Reform," *Development Policy Review*, 28(5), 553–571.

Keen, Michael and Mario Mansour. (2010b), "Revenue Mobilization in Sub-Saharan Africa: Challenges from Globalization II – Corporate Taxation," *Development Policy Review*, 28(5).

Lejeune, Ine. (2011), "The EU VAT Experience: What are the Lessons?" *The VAT Reader: What a Federal Consumption Tax Would Mean for America* (Falls Church, VA: Tax Analysts).

Mansour, Mario. (2014), "A Tax Revenue Dataset for Sub-Saharan Africa: 1980–2010," *Revue d'Économie du Développement*, 22, 99–128.

Mansour, Mario and Carole Nakhle. (2016), "Fiscal Stabilization in Oil and Gas Contracts: Evidence and Implications," SP 37 (London: Oxford Institute for Energy Studies).

Mansour, Mario and Grégoire Rota-Graziosi. (2014), "Tax Coordination and Competition in the West African Economic and Monetary Union," *Tax Notes International*, 74(2), 183–204.

OECD. (2013a), *Addressing Base Erosion and Profit Shifting* (Paris: OECD).

OECD. (2013b), *Action Plan on Base Erosion and Profit Shifting* (Paris: OECD).

Osterloh, Steffen and Friedrich Heinemann. (2013), "The Political Economy of Corporate Harmonization – Why European Politicians (Dis)like Minimum Tax Rates?," *European Journal of Political Economy*, 29, 18–37.

Norregaard, John and Tehmina Khan. (2007), "Tax Policy: Recent Trends and Coming Challenges," Working Paper 07/274 (Washington, DC: International Monetary Fund).

Stewart, Kenneth and Michael Webb. (2006), "International Competition in Corporate Taxation: Evidence from the OECD Time Series," *Economic Policy*, 45, 153–201.

Stöwhase, Sven. (2005), "Tax-Rate Differentials and Sector-Specific Foreign Direct Investment: Empirical Evidence from the EU," *FinanzArchiv*, 61(4), 535–558.

Świstak, Artur. "Value Added Tax in Extractive Industries," Working Paper, IMF.

Index

Note: Page numbers in *italic* indicate a figure, while page numbers in **bold** indicate a table on the corresponding page.